Master the Conventions

GRAMMAR FOR WRITING

Grades 9–12

COMPO
USAGE OSITION
GRAM
MAR SCI
MECHAN ON

COMPOCOMPOCOM
USAGE∽USAGE∽USAG

welcome to
Grammar for Writing

Grammar for Writing is a new program for today's secondary school students. It offers a complete course in grammar, usage, and mechanics—with an emphasis on writing—intended to help build the communication skills needed in a rapidly changing world.

The program takes the "mystery" out of grammar and helps develop better and more confident writers.

Grammar for Writing illustrates how the rules of grammar, usage, and mechanics—the conventions of standard English—can help students develop writing that is not just "correct" but powerful and persuasive, too.

Grammar for Writing has been designed with today's students in mind. Grammar rules are presented and explained in a clear and simple manner so that students can grasp them quickly and apply them to their writing immediately.

"Research studies clearly and consistently show that the most effective way to help students use the conventions of writing is to teach grammar in the context of writing."

Beverly Ann Chin

AUTHORSHIP

A broad-based team of experienced curriculum specialists and professional writers, working under the direction of *Beverly Ann Chin*, professor of English at the University of Montana and past-president of the National Council of Teachers of English (NCTE), developed the new *Grammar for Writing* series to help prepare today's secondary students to be effective writers in school, on writing assessments, on standardized tests, for college admission and placement, and for the workplace.

COMPOCOMPOCO
USAGEOUSAGEOUS

COMPO
USAGE OSITION
GRAM
MAR
MECHAN

Sadlier-Oxford introduces *Grammar for Writing*, Grades 9–12: a course in grammar, usage, and mechanics with an emphasis on writing at each grade level.

Program Features

- Informal, student-friendly tone
- Practical, two-page lesson format
  Rules + Examples + Practice Exercises
- Strong emphasis on writing

new!

fourth course Gr. 9

fifth course Gr. 10

sixth course Gr. 11

complete course Gr. 12

- **Composition** unit (Chapters 1–3) at each grade level provides seven writing workshops teaching the types of writing often required of students.

- **Abundant exercises** include cooperative activities and practice with revising, editing, and proofreading.

- **Flexible lesson format** allows students to write exercises alone, with a partner, in small groups, or with the whole class.

- Emphasis on **persuasive writing** in *Write What You Think* exercises encourages critical thinking.

- Mid-chapter **reviews**, chapter reviews, and cumulative reviews reinforce lesson concepts.

- Four-page **tests** in standardized test format follow the grammar, usage, and mechanics sections in each student book.

- Chapter openers feature striking **photos** as writing prompts and real **student writing models**.

Punctuation: All the Other Marks

14

- **Teacher's Edition** includes answers to exercises and valuable teaching tips.

Begin with Writing

"Grammar for Writing helps students communicate effectively with a variety of audiences and for different purposes."

Beverly Ann Chin

Enriching Your Vocabulary

Just as word knowledge aids students' listening and reading comprehension, an effective speaking and writing vocabulary is critical to developing writing skills.

Authentic Writing

Models of published works set the expectation that students will learn to write clearly, coherently, and expressively.

Student Writing ▶

Authentic student models make writing relevant.

Fourth Course, page 52

COMPOSITION
Lesson 3.4

Enriching Your Vocabulary

Voracious comes from the Latin verb *vorare*, meaning "to swallow up, eat greedily, or devour." This versatile adjective may be used in both a literal [concrete] and a figurative [an abstract] sense. A person who has a *voracious* appetite is likely to eat huge quantities of food. Someone with a hunger for knowledge may be a *voracious* reader.

Reference to the poem "The Rime of the Ancient Mariner" by Coleridge

Thesis statement

Example

Writing About Literature: Analyzing Fiction

When you write about a story or novel, you usually create one of three kinds of essays. The three serve very different purposes.

1. In a **personal response** essay, you write about how you felt and what you thought as you read, about the passages that seemed particularly meaningful, and about the other works that the story reminded you of.

2. In an **evaluation**, you write about how good or bad the work is. Your evaluation is based on objective **criteria**, or standards, that are used to measure the excellence of a literary form. For example, here are two criteria for measuring a short story:
   • The characters are believable.
   • The plot engages the reader's interest.

3. In a **literary analysis**, you discuss one or more of the **elements of fiction**: characters, plot, setting, point of view, and theme.

The following excerpt is from a long literary analysis of Ernest Hemingway's novel *The Old Man and the Sea*. Here, Carlos Baker discusses the feelings that the main character, Santiago, has for birds and fish while he is battling a marlin.

Hemingway's Ancient Mariner
an excerpt from an essay by Carlos Baker

[1]According to the ancient mariner of Coleridge, "[h]e prayeth best who loveth best all things both great and small." [2]Along with humility, pride, and piety, Hemingway's ancient mariner [Santiago] is richly endowed with the quality of compassion. [3]Of course, he is not so foolish as to love all creatures equally. [4]He dislikes, for example, the Portuguese men-of-war, whose beautiful "purple, formalized, iridescent, gelatinous" bubbles serve to buoy up the "long deadly purple filaments" which trail a yard behind them in the water and contain a poison which will paralyze the unwary passersby. . . . [5]He has another set of enemies in the water of the tropic sea.

Internet
Visit us at
www.sadlier-oxford.com

52

Complete Course, page 168

STUDENT WRITING
Expository Essay

What I Learned About Life from Selling Shoes
by Katherine Ivers
high school student, Meriden, Connecticut

I know you're asking, "What could you possibly learn from selling shoes?" But the vast knowledge I have acquired from this minimum-wage job will last a lifetime.

Hired right before Christmas, I was about to receive a crash course in responsibility. Amid the decorations, elevator music, and hordes of customers, I learned my first lesson—patience. This virtue, unbeknownst to the six million crazed customers waving and shoving shoes in my face, is the only reason many of them were not bludgeoned to death by a high heel.

Another very important lesson is stress management. I faced the triple necessity of balancing honors courses at school, holding down a part-time job, and retaining a social life. . . .

I also learned to master quickly the art of budgeting time. I eat dinner, talk to my boss, and study for a trig quiz in fifteen minutes. Going to the bathroom can wait. In the shoe department, I learned something else that surprised me: Men and women are different! I never saw a man try on a pair of shoes and inquire whether they made his ankles look fat. On the other hand, I never saw a woman so anxious to get out of the mall that she purchased any shoe without trying it on. I learned to appreciate and adapt to these differences.

I learned, too, that physical fitness plays an important role. How many people get

---

Writing Workshops

In-depth lessons set the stage for students to see themselves as readers, writers, and communicators.

Writing About Literature:
Analyzing Fiction

Exercise 19 Organize and Draft Your Essay

Before you start writing, review your notes. Choose two or three of your most important points. Then sit down and start writing—anywhere in the essay. Do not worry about perfect sentences. Just get your ideas down in sentences and paragraphs so that you will have something to revise.

• **Introduction, body, conclusion** Make sure you have included everything that belongs in each of the three basic parts.

• **Title** Think of a possible title; try out several. Your title should suggest both the work and your essay's focus.

> **A Literary Analysis**
> **INTRODUCTION**
> • Author and title of work
> • Brief plot summary
> • Thesis statement
> **BODY**
> • Major point 1
>   Support, support
> • Major point 2
>   Support, support
> **CONCLUSION**

Step-by-Step Exercises

Lessons lead students through the writing process with exercises providing hands-on practice. Students develop and use strategies for assessing their final compositions before presenting their writing to different audiences.

Exercise 20 Revise and Edit Your Essay

Let the draft sit awhile. Then use the four revising strategies suggested in Lesson 1.3. Read for accurate content, clear organization, and appropriate style for your purpose and audience. As you and your peer editors revise, ask these questions:

• Is the essay coherent, or well-organized?

• Are the general statements clearly expressed but

• Have you elaborated enough to support or "pr

• Is everything unified, or directly related to, the

Exercise 21 Edit, Proofread, and Pub

Double-check each quotation for accuracy and al satisfied that you have corrected all errors in gra papers with a partner to check for any you may h

You might form two reading-and-discussion grou novels. Take turns reading aloud papers to the ap have read the work you have written about, see i they have comments or ideas to add. Your group novels that members might enjoy.

You might also compile a "lit crit" anthology of e Then share the anthology with other English clas

Writing Strategies

Detailed strategies point out critical writing suggestions, enabling students to communicate clearly in many different situations.

COMPOSITION
Lesson 2.3

Coherence

❧ Each of your paragraphs should be **coherent**; that is, its sentences should be sensibly organized so that your reader can follow your thoughts easily.

STRATEGIES FOR WRITING COHERENTLY

1. **Be Clear** Express your thoughts simply and directly.

2. **Guide the Reader** Use signposts that show the reader what lies ahead and how thoughts relate to one another. Some signposts are transitional expressions like those on page 27. Others are pronouns and synonyms (words that mean almost the same thing), which refer to terms you have already used. Repeating key words or terms also improves coherence.

3. **Put Your Thoughts in Order** Arrange information so that "first things come first."

   The following list includes four common ways of organizing paragraphs and essays. Unless you have a good reason not to do so, choose one of these orders as a framework.

   • **Chronological Order** Organizing your writing chronologically means telling about events in the order in which they occurred. Use chronological order for narrative paragraphs, which may tell a true story or a fictional one; for writing about a historical event; and for describing steps in a process.

   • **Spatial Order** Organize your paragraph spatially when you want to describe a person, an animal, a place, or an object. Include details in an orderly way; moving from left to right, top to bottom, near to far, or inside to outside.

   • **Order of Importance** Organize your paragraph by degree of importance when trying to persuade your audience. State the least important reasons and other details first, and end with the most important ones—or the reverse.

Strengthen Grammar and Usage Skills

"Grammar for Writing helps students use writing strategies and the writing process to communicate with different audiences for a variety of purposes."

Beverly Ann Chin

Writing Hints

Students learn practical advice for applying the skills of grammar, usage, and mechanics to their own paragraphs and essays.

Combining Sentences: Inserting Phrases

● Combine related sentences by inserting a phrase from one sentence into another sentence.

Sometimes, you must alter the words from one sentence to create a phrase for another sentence. Sometimes, you can simply pick up a phrase from one sentence and move it to another sentence.

ORIGINAL   Benny was traveling through Europe. He visited several circuses.
COMBINED   **Traveling through Europe**, Benny visited several circuses. [participial phrase]

ORIGINAL   Lisa plays in a band. The band is in New York. Janet and Rebecca are the other members of her band.
COMBINED   Lisa plays **in a band in New York with Janet and Rebecca**. [prepositional phrases]

ORIGINAL   We have time. We will buy the tickets at the ticket window. The ticket window is by the third-base line.
COMBINED   We have time **to buy the tickets at the ticket window by the third-base line**. [infinitive phrase containing two prepositional phrases]

ORIGINAL   My uncle enjoys something. He enjoys walking briskly.
COMBINED   **Walking briskly** is something my uncle enjoys. [gerund phrase]

Often there is more than one way to combine sentences. Here are two other versions of the last sentence.

COMBINED   **To walk briskly** is something my uncle enjoys. [infinitive phrase]

COMBINED   My uncle enjoys **walking briskly**. [gerund phrase at end]

In addition to creating a verbal or a prepositional phrase to put in another sentence, you can convert a sentence to an appositive phrase (see Lesson 6.2) and transfer it to another sentence.

ORIGINAL   My uncle lives in St. Louis now. He is an immigrant from Russia.
COMBINED   My uncle, **a Russian immigrant**, lives in St. Louis now.

Enriching Your Vocabulary

The adjective *apt* comes from the Latin *aptus*, which means "suited, fitted, or appropriate." The class valedictorian offered *apt* advice to the new graduates. *Aptitude*, as used on page 162, is derived from *aptus* and the suffix *-tudo* (condition or quality). Do you have an *aptitude* for a particular sport?

Writing Hint

Too many prepositional phrases in sentences can make them confusing and singsongy. Avoid this problem by breaking apart and rewording sentences.

The cashmere sweaters are **on the rack next to the ties on display in front of the shirt counter**.

The cashmere sweaters are displayed **on a rack**. They're **next to the ties**. You'll find the ties displayed **in front of the shirt counter**.

Sentence Combining ▲

Frequent lessons teaching sentence combining give students the practice they need to master this valuable skill.

Complete Course, page 239

Skill Building

Thorough and clear presentation of grammar and usage concepts builds skills that students apply to their own writing.

▼

Using Object Pronouns

USAGE
Lesson 10.2

Object Pronouns	
SINGULAR	**PLURAL**
me, you, him, her, it	us, you, them

🖋 Use an **object pronoun** when the pronoun functions as the direct object (DO), indirect object (IO), or object complement (OC) of a sentence or a clause.

       IO   IO   DO
My father gave Dolores and **me** the keys to the car.

       DO
We thanked **him** for the keys.

        DO   DO OC
The family counselor made **you** and **me us**.

🖋 Use an object pronoun when the pronoun functions as the object of a preposition (OP) in a sentence or clause.

          OP   OP
Dad handed the keys to Dolores and **me**.

    OP   OP
For both of **us**, driving Dad's car was a big responsibility.

P.S. Don't become confused by the many terms that include the word *object*. Just get a general sense of how an object differs from a subject.

Exercise 4 **Choosing the Correct Pronoun**

Underline the pronoun in parentheses that correctly completes each sentence.

1. Every actor in his heart believes everything bad that's printed about (he, him). —Orson Welles

2. There is nothing which (we, us) receive with so much reluctance as advice. —Joseph Addison

3. Everything intercepts (we, us) from ourselves. —Ralph Waldo Emerson

4. A man in passion rides a horse that runs away with (he, him). —Thomas Fuller

5. We shape our buildings; thereafter, they shape (we, us). —Winston Churchill

■ See **Grammar,** Lesson 5.7, for more on direct and indirect objects and Lesson 5.9 for more on object complements.

Editing Tip

Avoid this common error: "between you and I." Always say or write, "between you and me."

Cross References

References help students find related material throughout the book.

P.S. Features

Students begin to recognize that some rules and definitions are more important than others.

Step by Step

Strategies familiarize students with an alternate presentation of the more complex concepts of grammar.

Step by Step

To decide whether to use a subject pronoun or an object pronoun:

1. Decide what function the pronoun performs in the sentence.

2. If th...
   pred...
   subj...

3. If th...
   an i...
   com...
   prep...

Working Together

Exercise 14 **Writing Paragraphs**

The information in the table is about mean, or average, verbal and math scores of college-bound seniors from 1988 to 1997. Use the information in the table to write one or more paragraphs about trends in the Scholastic Aptitude Test (SAT) scores over that ten-year period. Exchange papers with a partner, and make suggestions for improving each other's paragraphs. Try combining related sentences by inserting phrases.

■ Refer to **Composition,** Lessons 3.4 and 3.5, to find strategies for writing an expository paragraph and essay.

SAT Mean Verbal and Math Scores of College-Bound Seniors										
	1988	1989	1990	1991	1992	1993	1994	1995	1996	1997
VERBAL SCORES	505	504	500	499	500	500	499	504	505	505
Males	512	510	505	503	504	504	501	505	507	507
Females	499	498	496	495	496	497	497	502	503	503
MATH SCORES	501	502	501	500	501	503	504	506	508	511
Males	521	523	521	520	521	524	523	525	527	530
Females	483	482	483	482	484	484	487	490	492	494

Source: The College Board

Complete Course, page 162

Working Together

Frequent opportunities for students to work cooperatively help them realize that there are many ways to revise, edit, and proofread the same material.

Master the Mechanics of Writing

"Grammar for Writing helps students apply knowledge of writing conventions — punctuation, capitalization, and spelling — to their own writing and to the writing of others."

Beverly Ann Chin

Mechanics ▶

The conventions of mechanics include punctuation, capitalization, and spelling.

Thematic Practice Sets

Thematically related exercises encourage students to apply their new skills.

Semicolons

A **semicolon** can show that two or more ideas are closely related.

◖ Use a semicolon to join independent clauses in a compound sentence *without* a coordinating conjunction.

Claude McKay was a great poet and essayist of the Harlem Renaissance**;** McKay did not write much after 1930. [Semicolon alone joins two independent clauses.]

Claude McKay had few equals as a poet**; however**, his novels were not as well crafted. [Semicolon (before conjunctive adverb) joins two independent clauses.]

Claude McKay had few equals as a poet**; as a result**, his poems still appear in textbooks. [Semicolon (before transitional expression) joins two independent clauses.]

Claude McKay was a great poet and essayist of the Harlem Renaissance, **but** he did not write much after 1930. [With a coordinating conjunction, a comma joins two independent clauses.]

You may use a semicolon between independent clauses joined by coordinating conjunctions if either clause contains a comma. But you don't have to.

She was the last one to read**;** but when she recited her poems, we were glad we'd stayed.

◖ Use a semicolon to separate items in a series when one or more of the items contain a comma.

McKay was born in Upper Clarendon Parish, Jamaica**;** Langston Hughes was born in Joplin, Missouri, but grew up in Lawrence, Kansas**;** and Countee Cullen, born in Louisville, Kentucky, and adopted by a Methodist minister, grew up in New York City.

**MECHANICS
Lesson 14.2**

Common Conjunctive Adverbs

accordingly	meanwhile
also	moreover
besides	nevertheless
consequently	otherwise
furthermore	still
however	then
indeed	therefore

Common Transitional Expressions

as a result	in fact
for example	in other
for instance	words
from that	on the other
point on	hand
in addition	that is

Editing Tip

Do not use a semicolon between an independent clause and a dependent clause or phrase.

We read poems by Langston Hughes⁄who is probably the best known of the Harlem Renaissance poets.

Exercise 3

Some of the
colons. Re
proper pu

1. Khalil
poets

2. Jean T
his lat

Exercise 4 Combining Sentences into Compound Sentences

On a separate piece of paper, combine each set of independent clauses into a compound sentence. Do *not* use coordinating conjunctions. You may introduce conjunctive adverbs and transitional expressions. Check your combined sentences for proper punctuation.

1. Zora Neale Hurston believed that folklore was priceless. It constitutes the art of the people, who never recognized it as art.

2. Hurston was a self-styled literary anthropologist. She used literary techniques to shape oral narratives.

3. She created a new literary language. The language reflected the poetry in the oral culture of rural blacks in the South.

4. Hurston wrote four novels, a memoir, and more than fifty shorter works. She was more prolific than any black woman writer had been before.

5. Hurston grew up in Eatonville, Florida. Eatonville was the first incorporated black community in the United States.

6. Hurston's mother was a teacher in Eatonville. Hurston's father served three terms as mayor there.

7. Hurston worked while in high school and college. She worked as a maid, waitress, and manicurist.

8. As an English major at Howard University, Hurston began writing short stories and poems. She joined the literary club there.

316 *Chapter 14 • Punctuation: All the Other Marks*

Skills Instruction

Concrete instruction focusing on relevant mechanical skills helps improve students' understanding of writing conventions.

MECHANICS
Lesson 14.4

Quotation Marks

Lesson 14.3 shows italics (underlining) for certain works of art. This lesson tells when to use quotation marks for shorter works and for other purposes as well.

❦ Use **quotation marks** for titles of short works.

POEMS	"Ode to a Grecian Urn" "The Lake Isle of Innisfree"
SHORT STORIES	"Araby" "The Fall of the House of Usher"
ARTICLES	"Going Out of Our Gourds Over Pumpkins"
SONGS	"The Star-Spangled Banner" "Penny Lane"
SINGLE TV PROGRAMS	"Rescue at Sea" (an episode of *American Experience*)
PARTS OF BOOKS	Part I, "Essays and Memoirs"

❦ Use quotation marks at the beginning and end of a direct quotation, but not with an indirect quotation.

Introduce a short, one-sentence quotation with a comma or a colon; introduce a quotation that is a long sentence or more than one sentence with a colon.

> Of T. S. Eliot, critics wrote, "Eliot was better equipped than any other poet to bring free verse into the twentieth century."

When only a word or two is quoted, use a lowercase letter if the quoted words do not begin the sentence.

> T. S. Eliot referred to W. B. Yeats as "the greatest poet."
> [no capital letter in quotation]

❦ Use single quotation marks for titles or quotes within a quotation.

> Brenda asked, "Have you read T. S. Eliot's poem 'Gerontion'?"

❦ The following rules apply to quotation marks with other marks.

Commas and periods These marks g[...]

> "Dinner is ready," he announced.

Semicolons and colons These marks [...]
quotation mark.

> Here are three reasons I like "Araby": i[...]

Question marks and exclamation [...]
quotation marks if the quotation is a q[...]
go outside if the whole sentence is a q[...]

> "Did everyone read the poem?" she a[...]
> Was she surprised when you said, "No[...]

Editing Tip

Don't use two question marks with a single quotation mark.

Do you know the line after "Where have all the flowers gone?"?

Don't use quotation marks for nicknames or slang.

His nickname is "Spike"; he's a "yuppie."

Editing Tips

Features help students avoid the pitfalls of writing by alerting them to possible problem areas and common errors.

after death.

10. Eavan Boland dedicated her 1967 book of poems, "New Territory," to her mother.

Working Together

Exercise 8 **Write Your Own Exercise**

On a separate piece of paper, write one or more complete sentences for each item below. Mention actual titles wherever possible, but leave out all punctuation marks. Then exchange papers with a classmate. See if you agree on how to punctuate each sentence.

1. Your thoughts about an episode of a TV program you watched recently (Make up a name for the episode if you don't remember it.)

2. A song that you've heard recently

3. A direct quotation (actual or made up) at the beginning of a sentence

4. A quotation within a quotation

5. A short story or magazine article you've read and your thoughts about it

6. A poem you've read and your thoughts about it

7. A title of a chapter of a book you are reading and a summary of that chapter

Abundant Practice ▶

Thorough exercises reinforce lesson concepts.

320 *Chapter 14 • Punctuation: All the Other Marks*

visit us at **www.sadlier-oxford.com**   **T9**

Instructional Support

Teacher's Edition

- **Presents ideas and prompts for students' writing**
- **Includes strategies for effective grammar instruction**
- **Provides assessment rubrics for evaluating students' writing**
- **Supplies checklists for revising, editing, and proofreading**
- **Provides answers on the page and in the Answer Key**

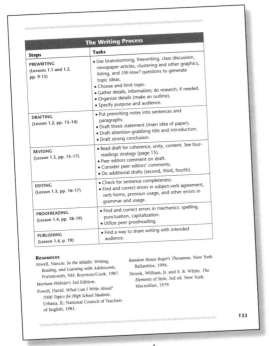

Writing Process Guidelines ▲

- List the steps of the writing process
- Provide strategies for teaching each of the steps
- Help customize instruction for varying ability levels

▼ **Annotated Teacher's Edition Pages**

Provide convenient on-page answers and annotations

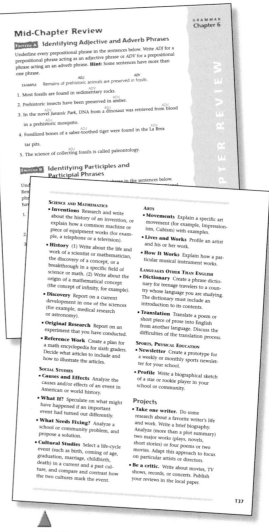

▲

Writing Across the Curriculum

- **Gives teachers a variety of writing ideas and projects**

Introduction and Conclusion

❑ Does the introduction make you want to read more? What suggestions can you make for improving it?

❑ Does it introduce the topic and the main idea?

❑ Does the conclusion end the essay strongly?

You may want to offer students variations on peer checklists from time to time. One option is to generate mode-specific checklists such as the ones below or even assignment-specific checklists. (See also the discussion of rubrics on pp. 52–55.)

Mode-Specific Checklists	
Checklist for Persuasive Writing	❑ Is the writer's opinion clearly stated?
	❑ Does the writer give at least two reasons to support that opinion?
	❑ Are the reasons themselves supported by convincing evidence (facts, statistics, examples, anecdotes, quotations, and so on)?
	❑ Do you understand what the writer wants the reader to do?
	❑ Has the writer persuaded you? Why or why not?
Checklist for Narrative Writing	❑ Does the beginning make you want to read more?
	❑ Does the writer *show* characters in action and let you hear what they say, or does the writer simply *tell* you about characters?
	❑ Does the writing include sensory details?
	❑ Are the writer's comparisons relevant and illuminating?
	❑ Has the writer used specific nouns and vivid verbs (especially, as alternatives for *said*)?
	❑ Is the ending satisfying?
Checklist for Descriptive Writing	❑ Can you picture the setting?
	❑ Does the writing include specific sensory details?
	❑ Are the comparisons fresh?
	❑ Does the organization of details (for example, proceeding from near to far, left to right, or top to bottom) make sense?
	❑ Does the description establish an overall mood? What is it?

Editing and Proofreading

As previously mentioned, this series separates the revising task (which focuses on content, style, and organization) from the editing task (which focuses on grammar and usage). Proofreading is the stage of the writing process when students look for mechanical errors in spelling, punctuation, and capitalization. These checklists provide references either for the teacher or the student.

Editing Checklist

❑ Is every sentence grammatically complete (not a fragment or a run-on)? *Lesson 5.1*

❑ Do subjects and verbs agree in number and gender? *Chapter 9*

❑ Are the correct forms of pronouns used? *Chapter 10*

❑ Does each pronoun clearly refer to an antecedent? *Lesson 10.5*

❑ Are verb tenses used consistently, unless there is good reason to vary them? *Chapter 8*

❑ Are the correct forms of irregular verbs used? *Chapter 8*

❑ Are the correct forms of plural nouns and the comparative forms of adjectives and adverbs used? *Chapter 4*

Proofreading Checklist

❑ Is every word spelled correctly? Check a dictionary if you're unsure. *Chapter 16*

❑ Have homonyms been confused (*their* instead of *there*, for example)? *Chapter 16*

❑ Do proper nouns and proper adjectives begin with capital letters? *Chapter 15*

❑ Does every sentence begin with a capital letter and end with an end punctuation mark? *Chapters 13 and 14*

❑ Are commas used correctly in all of their many uses? *Chapter 13*

❑ Is dialogue punctuated correctly? *Lesson 14.6*

Resources

In the classroom, students should have access to several copies of a good college dictionary and a dictionary-style thesaurus.

Grammar for Writing and ELL Problems		
Problem Area in English	Comment	Grammar for Writing Treatment, Fourth Course
ADJECTIVE CLAUSES	Forming and positioning adjective clauses cause problems for speakers of Asian languages, of Arabic and Hebrew, and even of Latin-based languages.	Lesson 7.2
ARTICLES	ELL students often leave out the article before a singular count noun.	Lesson 4.4
CAPITALIZATION	Arabic, Chinese, and Hebrew do not use capital letters; Dutch and German capitalize some forms of the second-person pronoun; German caps all nouns.	Chapter 15
EXPLETIVES	Spanish speakers sometimes omit subjects, saying "Is raining."	Chapter 5 covers the "It is raining" sentence structure.
HOMOPHONES	Speakers of Asian languages in particular may be confused by the concept of words sounding alike but having different meanings.	Chapter 12
NEGATION	Multiple negation is common in French and Russian, among other languages.	Lesson 11.3
PLURALS	Some Asian languages have no plural forms for nouns.	Lesson 4.1, Chapter 9, Lesson 16.4
PREFIXES AND SUFFIXES	These word parts are absent in Asian languages.	Lesson 16.3
PREPOSITIONS	English distinguishes between in and on; Spanish uses en for both.	Lessons 4.7 and 6.1
SILENT LETTERS	There are no silent letters in Spanish.	Chapter 16
SUBJECTS, DOUBLE	Some languages add personal pronouns as suffixes or prefixes, leading ELL speakers to say, "Maria she is pretty."	Lessons 5.2, 5.5, 10.1
TENSES	• Certain English verbs don't work in the present progressive, but ESL students may say or write, "I am knowing the answer." • In some languages, time is not signaled by word endings but rather by words that native English speakers would call adverbs.	Lessons 4.3 and 8.5
WORD ORDER	• In some languages, word order determines the part of speech. For example, the verb is the last word in sentences in Turkish, Korean, and Japanese. • In Russian, subject and object may switch places without affecting meaning.	Lessons 5.1, 5.2, 5.8, 5.9, and 13.1

▲ Practical Teacher Checklists

- Checklists for evaluating types of writing
- Checklists for monitoring the writing process

◀ Support for English Language Learners

- Shows how specific content in English might pose difficulties in another language and where to find help within *Grammar for Writing*

Assessment

Ongoing Assessment ▶ in the Student Edition

- Mid-Chapter and Chapter Review Exercises
- Cumulative Review of Units
- Grammar, Usage, and Mechanics Tests

Fourth Course, page 187

Fourth Course, page 165

Fourth Course, page 167

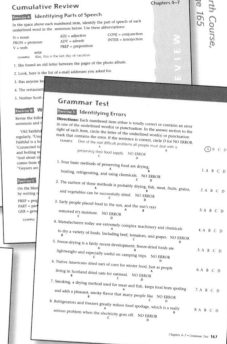

...in the ▶ Teacher's Edition

- Rubrics for Evaluating Students' Writing

Fourth Course, page T54

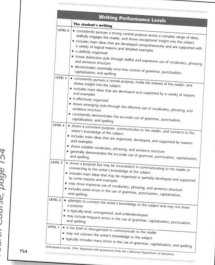

Fourth Course Test Booklet, page

...and in the Student Test Booklet ▶

Also available is a student Test Booklet for each grade level. The Test Booklets extend testing and assessment opportunities and include comprehensive standardized chapter tests that review and reinforce new concepts. A Diagnostic Test and a Mastery Test help teachers identify problem areas and place students within the program.

to order call toll free **1-800-221-5175**

Technology

Complete Course, page 124

Portfolio Projects

At the beginning of each chapter of *Grammar for Writing*, an Internet prompt directs students to the Sadlier-Oxford website, where they will find a portfolio project suggestion incorporating the concepts from the chapter. Teacher suggestions support each project with assessment suggestions and teaching guidelines.

STUDENT WRITING
Narrative Essay

Working Pride
by Lacey Waldron
high school student, El Cajon, California

As I drove to my job interview on a sunny Saturday afternoon, my palms began to sweat. This was my first job interview, and I wanted to make sure I did everything perfectly. I thought to myself, "What should I say? How should I act?" As I came up to a white duplex that read "DR. McDONALD'S OFFICE," I started to panic. Looking at the clock, I realized I had ten minutes until I had to be in the office. I kept reminding myself that everything would be okay, but that was very hard to believe as my stomach began to turn in circles. After parking my car and fixing myself up, I slowly walked up to the office. Turning the knob of the large, oak door, it was time—time to suck up my fear and put my best foot forward. The first person that I met as I walked through the door was a lady named Mary. Mary seemed like she was a very kind hearted woman. She made me feel at home instantly. Before I knew it, a man who was skinny and had gray hair came walking out; it was Dr. McDonald.

I walked over and met him halfway, and he said, "You must be Lacey." I shook his hand firmly and remembered to make eye contact. I also remembered what my mom had advised me minutes earlier and told myself to relax. After a short interview, Dr. McDonald finished by saying, "I will call you and tell you when I want you to start working." I thanked him, shook his hand again, and walked out to my car.

"I GOT IT!" I said, "I GOT THE JOB!!" I couldn't wait to tell my mom the good news!

Getting my first job has really affected my life; it teaches me responsibility and gives me something to do rather than to get into trouble. My parents also seem to look at me as more responsible, and that's enough of a reward for me. Having money of my own has its ups and downs at times. But having the job that I am proud of is a valuable achievement that can never be forgotten.

Lacey Waldron organizes her personal narrative chronologically—in the order the events happened. She uses transition words and expressions such as *after*, *first*, and *before*. She also includes dialogue to make the reader feel close to the action. In the last paragraph, Lacey explains the significance of the event—what the incident meant to her.

Reread Lacey's essay and notice that each sentence is a little different from the one before. As you work on sentences in this chapter, think about how you can manipulate them communicate your ideas in an interesting way.

124 *Chapter 5 • Parts of a Sentence*

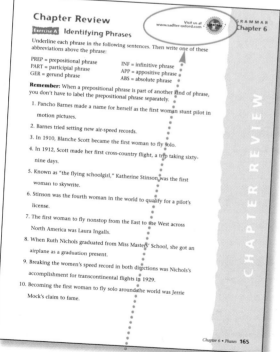

Complete Course, page 165

Chapter Review

Exercise A Identifying Phrases

Underline each phrase in the following sentences. Then write one of these abbreviations above the phrase:

PREP = prepositional phrase
PART = participial phrase
GER = gerund phrase

INF = infinitive phrase
APP = appositive phrase
ABS = absolute phrase

Remember: When a prepositional phrase is part of another kind of phrase, you don't have to label the prepositional phrase separately.

1. Pancho Barnes made a name for herself as the first woman stunt pilot in motion pictures.

2. Barnes tried setting new air-speed records.

3. In 1910, Blanche Scott became the first woman to fly solo.

4. In 1912, Scott made her first cross-country flight, a trip taking sixty-nine days.

5. Known as "the flying schoolgirl," Katherine Stinson was the first woman to skywrite.

6. Stinson was the fourth woman in the world to qualify for a pilot's license.

7. The first woman to fly nonstop from the East to the West across North America was Laura Ingalls.

8. When Ruth Nichols graduated from Miss Masters' School, she got an airplane as a graduation present.

9. Breaking the women's speed record in both directions was Nichols's accomplishment for transcontinental flights in 1929.

10. Becoming the first woman to fly solo around the world was Jerrie Mock's claim to fame.

GRAMMAR
Chapter 6

CHAPTER REVIEW

Chapter 6 • Phrases **165**

Publishing Hyperlinks

In each Chapter Review, an Internet prompt directs students to discover hyperlinks to student writing and publishing websites, as well as a list of creative ways for students to publish their writing, both on-line and in print publications.

ALTERNATE ASSESSMENT OPPORTUNITIES

ON THE INTERNET

- Chapter-specific portfolio project assignments
- Opportunities for long-term projects

TEACHER SUPPORT

- Suggestions for providing support for projects

Content Overview

	UNIT I: COMPOSITION	UNIT II: GRAMMAR
	Writing Workshops	Parts of Speech / Phrases / Clauses

Columns (Unit I — Writing Workshops): The Writing Process, Writing Paragraphs, Writing Essays, Narrative Writing, Persuasive Writing, Expository Writing, Writing About Literature, Research Paper, Special Writing Tasks

Columns (Unit II — Parts of Speech): Combining Sentences, Parts of a Sentence, Subjects and Predicates, Sentence Fragments, Run-on Sentences, Direct and Indirect Objects, Predicate Nominatives and Adjectives, Object Complements

Columns (Unit II — Phrases): Prepositional Phrases, Participial Phrases, Gerund Phrases, Infinitive Phrases, Appositive Phrases

Columns (Unit II — Clauses): Adjective Clauses, Adverb Clauses, Noun Clauses, Sentence Structures, Parallel Struct...

Course	Coverage
Fourth Course — Grade 9	■ across columns
Fifth Course — Grade 10	■ across columns
Sixth Course — Grade 11	■ across columns
Complete Course — Grade 12	■ across columns

UNIT III: USAGE   UNIT IV: MECHANICS

Using Verbs	...ular Verbs; Verb Tenses; Active Voice; Mood
Agreement	Person and Number, Compound Subjects; Indefinite Pronouns
Using Pronouns	Subject and Object Pronouns; Who or Whom?; Agreement with Antecedents
Using Modifiers	Degrees of Comparison; Double Negatives; Misplaced and Dangling Modifiers; Usage Handbook
Punctuation	End Marks and Abbreviations; Commas in a Series; Compound Sentences and Phrases; Colons and Semicolons; Italics; Quotation Marks; Dashes, Parentheses, Brackets, Ellipses; Titles
Capitalization	Organizations, Religions, School Subjects; Historical Events, Documents, Periods; Calendar Items, Brand Names; Business Writing
Spelling	Spelling Rules; Prefixes and Suffixes; Noun Plurals; Commonly Misspelled Words

The chart contains four rows marked with ■ indicating lessons dedicated to each listed topic across the columns above.

KEY

■ = Lesson(s) dedicated to listed topic

Master the Conventions

GRAMMAR FOR WRITING

Grades 9–12

COMPOSITION

USAGE

MECHANICS

GRAMMAR

Sadlier-Oxford
A Division of William H. Sadlier, Inc.
New York, NY 10005-1002
www.sadlier-oxford.com

to order call toll free **1-800-221-5175**

complete course

SADLIER-OXFORD

GRAMMAR
FOR WRITING

Teacher's Edition

Sadlier-Oxford
A Division of William H. Sadlier, Inc.
New York, New York 10005-1002

Teacher's Edition: ISBN: 0-8215-0322-7
Student Edition: ISBN: 0-8215-0312-X

Printed in the United States of America

123456789/05 04 03 02 01 00 99

CONTENTS

Introduction to Complete Course

Grammar for Writing Complete Course is one part of a new grammar and composition program for high school students, grades 9–12. This book provides a full year's work—all the grammar and writing that students need to know plus assignments and exercises to fill the school year. Used together with a literature program and literature-based writing assignments, this book gives you a powerful component to a complete language arts program for students.

This series emphasizes grammar as it applies to writing. It has a user-friendly tone. Its minilessons zoom right to the essentials. Its teaching is prescriptive—with easy-to-follow rules, definitions, instructions, and examples. Students are encouraged to view good grammar not as a list of rules that must be memorized for their own sake but as a valuable tool that can help them improve their writing.

Grammar for Writing prepares students for standardized testing.

The grammar, usage, and mechanics sections address the conventions of standard English that students need to know for state assessment tests and national tests, such as the PSAT and SAT. The three Grammar, Usage, and Mechanics Tests in standardized test format (error recognition and error correction) prepare students for the writing exam in the PSAT test. Two-page Mid-Chapter, Chapter, and Cumulative Reviews reinforce and test students' understanding of writing and grammar concepts. In addition, there is a separate forty-eight page Test Booklet.

Grammar for Writing helps students meet the standards for writing.

In the writing sections and throughout the text, students learn to express and develop their ideas coherently and concisely. In Chapter 3, "Writing Workshops," students proceed step-by-step through the writing process as they write for a variety of audiences and for different purposes. They conduct research on issues that interest them, using libraries and electronic databases. The text gives students repeated practice in revising and editing samples of poor writing. Students correct errors in grammar, usage, and mechanics; they use sentence-combining strategies to improve the flow of their writing.

Use *Grammar for Writing* with students of varying ability levels.

Exercises can be done individually by students needing to learn, review, and practice a particular grammar, usage, or mechanics concept. Frequently, exercises are done cooperatively with a partner or small group. You might pair LEP (Limited English Proficiency) students with more proficient students to create an informal tutoring-buddy system. Give mainstreamed ELL (English Language Learner) students many opportunities to *hear* standard English used correctly. You might have them read aloud corrected exercise sentences and paragraphs, for example, and use small-group activities to give ELL students speaking and listening practice. Advanced students might go over lessons and exercises with less advanced students. Challenge these students to do more writing, to create new exercises, and to turn their "Write What You Think" exercises into longer papers.

Use *Grammar for Writing* with a variety of schedules.

At the beginning or end of a class period, students can work on minilessons (the teaching text and exercises). You might go over the teaching text in class and assign the exercises to be started in class and finished as homework. Students can also meet in writing groups or with partners to work on both cooperative-learning exercises marked by the "Working Together"

label and ongoing writing projects, such as the exercises in Chapter 3. Students can meet regularly in writing groups and in peer editing sessions.

If the whole class shows repeated weakness in one grammar concept (say subject-verb agreement), set aside a block of time to go over the appropriate lesson(s) carefully. Assign the exercises as group, partner, or individual work; and meet as a class or in small groups to compare exercise answers. Comparing finished writing is especially useful when students do a Revising and Editing Worksheet exercise (see page 120). Since there are no single right answers to these worksheets, students will learn even more by seeing and discussing how other groups or teams have revised the flawed writing samples.

Grammar for Writing improves students' critical thinking skills.

The "Write What You Think" exercises throughout the book give students practice in developing, supporting, and evaluating arguments on real-life issues. Students develop and strengthen their persuasive skills by giving logical reasons and evidence to support their opinions.

In most of the lessons in Chapter 3, a series of questions, marked by a "Critical Thinking" label, leads students to analyze professional models of writing. These questions might be used as an assignment or as a prompt for class discussion.

Features and Benefits of Grammar for Writing

Throughout the book, *Grammar for Writing* honors its commitment to teach the fundamentals of grammar through the context of writing. The following charts itemize how both the unit called "Composition" and the units called "Grammar," "Usage," and "Mechanics" incorporate features that help today's students express their thoughts clearly and succinctly.

Unit: Composition	
Feature	**Benefit**
LESSONS	Students spend more time working on writing assignments than reading about writing.
EASY-TO-SCAN LISTS OF ADVICE	Students can locate strategies, directions, and other help faster than is possible with extensive, run-on instruction.
WRITING HINTS	Students learn that writers consider not only important, general principles—such as coherence—but also practical, specific problems—such as "How can I figure out if this topic is too broad?" and "How should I publish this piece?"
"WRITING WORKSHOPS" SETUP	Students realize that regardless of what they write, they can *always* apply the multistage writing process.
COOPERATIVE-LEARNING EXERCISES *Working Together*	Students learn that *every* writer needs an editor; students learn that a writing prompt may stimulate many different responses.
Modes of Writing	**Benefit**
NARRATIVE	Students tell a story—a fictional or true narrative. They use steps, critical events, or chronological order.
PERSUASIVE	Students learn to convince a reader. They use well-reasoned arguments, persuasive language, and emotional appeals in order of importance.
EXPOSITORY	Students explain or inform; they state the main idea. They use facts, examples, quotations, statistics, and definitions presented in a logical order.

Units: Grammar, Usage, Mechanics

Feature	Benefit
SUCCINCT INSTRUCTION	Students quickly move on to exercises.
COOPERATIVE-LEARNING EXERCISES *Working Together*	Students realize that a particular sentence-level problem may yield a variety of solutions.
"WRITE WHAT YOU THINK" EXERCISES	Students doing these persuasive-writing activities get ongoing practice in supporting an opinion with reasons and examples.
WRITING HINTS	Students learn that the end purpose of grammar, usage, and mechanics is applying those skills to paragraphs and essays.
EDITING TIPS	Students, forewarned of common errors, have a head start in working through exercises instead of feeling trapped or tricked by them.
STEP-BY-STEPS	Students exposed to an alternative presentation of the more complex concepts have a greater chance of understanding them.
P.S. NOTES	Students begin to recognize that some rules and definitions are more important than others.
REVISING AND EDITING WORKSHEETS	Students get opportunities to see that all drafts need revising and editing—and that multiple solutions exist.
REVIEWS, REVIEWS, REVIEWS	Students learn, through mid-chapter, chapter, and cumulative reviews, that in reviewing any written material, they must be on the lookout for several potential sentence-level problems—that real writing doesn't neatly present only one problem at a time.
TESTS IN STANDARDIZED FORMATS	Students lose some fear of test taking by developing competence in error-recognition and error-correction question formats.
ENRICHING YOUR VOCABULARY	Students develop vocabulary skills by being exposed to words used in context and by immediately reading their meanings in a sidebar.

The Role of Grammar in Improving Students' Writing

by Beverly Ann Chin

Grammar is the sound, structure, and meaning system of language. All languages have grammar, and each language has its own grammar. People who speak the same language are able to communicate because they intuitively know the grammar system of that language—that is, the rules of making meaning. Students who are native speakers of English already know English grammar. They recognize the sounds of English words, the meanings of those words, and the different ways of putting words together to make meaningful sentences.

However, while students may be effective speakers of English, they need guidance to become effective writers. They need to learn how to apply their knowledge of grammatical concepts from oral language to written language.

Effective grammar instruction shows students what they already know about grammar, and it helps them use this knowledge as they write. By connecting their knowledge of oral language to written language, teachers can demystify abstract grammatical terminology so that students can write—and read—with greater competence and confidence.

What Does Research Say About Grammar and the Teaching of Writing?

Strong research evidence suggests that the most beneficial way of helping students improve their command of grammar in writing is to use students' writing as the basis for discussing grammatical concepts. Researchers agree that it is more effective to teach punctuation, sentence variety, and usage in the context of writing than to approach the topic by teaching isolated skills (Calkins, 1980; DiStefano and Killion, 1984; Harris, 1962).

As students revise and edit their writing, teachers can provide grammar instruction that guides students in their attempts to identify and correct problems in sentence structure and usage. For example, if a teacher sees that many students are writing sentences containing misplaced modifiers, the teacher can present a minilesson on this concept using examples from student writing. The teacher can have students edit their own and each other's drafts for this problem.

Integrating grammar instruction into the revising and editing process helps students make immediate applications, thus allowing them to see the relevance of grammar in their own writing.

To What Specific Aspects of Writing Does Grammar Contribute?

Because writing is a complex activity for many students, teachers should focus on the grammatical concepts that are essential for the clear communication of meaning.

Research on the teaching of grammar since the early 1900s shows that grammar instruction that is separate from writing instruction does not improve students' writing competence (Braddock and others, 1963; Hillocks, 1986). In addition, research indicates that the transfer of formal grammar instruction to writing is not applicable to larger elements of composition. Through detailed studies of students' writing, Shaughnessy (1977) concludes that the best grammar instruction is one that gives the greatest return for the least investment of time. Shaughnessy advocates four important grammatical concepts: the sentence, inflection, tense, and agreement. She recommends that teachers encourage students to examine grammatical errors in their own writing. She also cautions teachers not to overemphasize grammatical terminology to the detriment of students' ability to understand and apply the concepts.

Weaver (1998) proposes a similar approach to teaching grammar in the context of writing. She writes, "What all students need . . . is guidance in understanding and applying those aspects of grammar that are most relevant to writing." In a chart as reproduced here, Weaver proposes five grammatical concepts that enable writers to show improvement in sentence revision, style, and editing.

A minimum of grammar for maximum benefits

1. Teaching concepts of subject, verb, sentence, clause, phrase, and related concepts for editing
2. Teaching style through sentence combining and sentence generating
3. Teaching sentence sense through the manipulation of syntactic elements
4. Teaching both the power of dialects and the dialects of power
5. Teaching punctuation and mechanics for convention, clarity, and style

(Weaver, 1998, pp. 21–23)

Rather than striving to teach all grammatical concepts to all students, teachers should prioritize and provide instruction on the grammatical elements that most affect their students' ability to write effectively. Teachers should also be sensitive to individual students' readiness to learn and apply grammatical concepts.

How Does Sentence Combining Improve Writing?

Sentence combining is the strategy of joining short sentences into longer, more complex sentences. As students engage in sentence-combining activities, they learn how to vary sentence structure in order to change meaning and style. Numerous studies (Mellon, 1969; O'Hare, 1973; Cooper, 1975; Shaughnessy, 1977; Hillocks, 1986; Strong, 1986) show that the use of sentence combining is an effective method for improving students' writing. The value of sentence combining is most evident as students recognize the effect of sentence variety (beginnings, lengths, complexities) in their own writing.

Hillocks (1986) stated that "sentence-combining practice provides writers with systematic knowledge of syntactic possibilities, the access to which allows them to sort through alternatives in their heads as well as on paper and to choose those which are most apt" (150). Research also shows that sentence combining is more effective than freewriting in enhancing the quality of student writing (Hillocks, 1986).

Hillocks and Smith (1991) show that systematic practice in sentence combining can increase students' knowledge of syntactic structures as well as improve the quality of their sentences, particularly when stylistic effects are discussed as well. Sentence-combining exercises can be either written or oral, structured or unstructured. Structured sentence-combining exercises give students more guidance in the ways to create the new sentences; unstructured sentence-combining exercises allow for more variation, but they still require students to create logical, meaningful sentences. Hillocks (1986) reports that, in many studies, sentence-combining exercises

produce significant increases in students' sentence-writing maturity.

Given Noguchi's (1991) analysis that grammar choices affect writing style, sentence combining is an effective method that helps students develop fluency and variety in their own writing style. Students can discover sentence variety, length, parallelism, and other syntactic devices by comparing their sentences with sentences from other writers. They also discover the decisions writers make when they revise sentences for their effect on readers.

Teachers can design their own sentence-combining activities by using short sentences from student writing or other appropriate sources. For example, teachers who notice many choppy sentences in students' writing can place these sentences on an overhead for all their students to read. Teachers can then ask different students to combine orally the short sentences in a variety of ways. As students share their different sentence combinations, their teacher can show students how they are naturally applying grammatical concepts such as clauses, phrases, modification, conjunctions, appositives, antecedents, and verb forms.

By participating in oral and written sentence-combining activities, students discover the relationships among meaning, sentence structure, usage, and punctuation. When presented as a revising strategy, sentence-combining activities help students identify short, choppy sentences in their own writing, leading them to combine their ideas in more fluid and sophisticated ways. As students generate more complex sentences from shorter sentences, they discover how the arrangement of phrases and clauses affects meaning and their readers.

What Strategies Can Teachers Use to Teach *Grammar for Writing*?
Grammar instruction is most naturally integrated during the revising, editing, and proofreading phases of the writing process. After students have written their first drafts and feel comfortable with the ideas and organization of their writing, teachers may wish to employ various strategies to help students see grammatical concepts as language choices that can enhance their writing purpose.

For example, teachers can help students revise for effective word choices in a writing conference. As the teacher and student discuss the real audience(s) for the writing, the teacher can ask the student to consider how formal or informal the writing should be. The teacher can remind the student that all people vary their level of language (formal to informal) in oral conversations, depending on their listeners and the speaking context. The teacher can then help the student identify words that change the level of formality in their writing.

Teachers can help students revise boring, monotonous sentences by having a partner read aloud the writing to the student writer. As the partner reads the writing aloud to the writer, both the partner and the writer can recognize when too many sentences begin with "It is" or "There are." Both the partner and the writer can discuss ways to vary the sentence beginnings. After the writer revises the sentences, the partner can read the sentences aloud, and both can discuss the effectiveness of the revision.

Teachers can help students edit from passive voice to active voice by presenting a minilesson. In editing groups, students can exchange papers and look for verbs that often signal the passive voice, such as "was" and "been." When students find these verbs, they can read the sentence aloud to their partners and discuss whether the voice is passive and, if so, if the sentence might be strengthened with an active-voice verb. The student writer can decide which voice is most effective and appropriate for the writing purpose and audience.

Teachers can help students become better proofreaders through peer editing groups. Based on the writing abilities of students, teachers can assign different proofreading tasks to specific individuals in each group. For example, one person in the group can proofread for spelling errors, another person for agreement errors, another person for fragments and run-ons, and another person for punctuation errors. As students develop increasing skill in proofreading, they can become responsible for more proofreading areas. Collaborating with classmates in peer editing groups helps students improve their own grammar skills as well as understand the importance of grammar as a tool for effective communication.

As teachers integrate grammar instruction into writing instruction, they should use the grammar terms that make sense to the students. By incorporating grammar terms naturally into the processes of revising, editing, and proofreading, teachers help students understand and apply grammar purposefully to their own (student) writing. Strategies such as writing conferences, partnership writing, grammar minilessons, and peer response groups are all valuable methods for integrating grammar into writing instruction.

How Does the Teaching of Grammar Relate to the National Content Standards for Students?

The National Council of Teachers of English and the International Reading Association (1996) published *Standards for the English Language Arts*, which defines "what students should know and be able to do with language" (p. 1). While the twelve content standards are presented as a list, they are closely intertwined and emphasize the complex interactions among language skills. Standards 4, 5, and 6 most directly address students' ability to write.

Standard 4: "Students adjust their use of spoken, written, and visual language (e.g., conventions, style, vocabulary) to communicate effectively with a variety of audiences and for different purposes" (p. 3).

Standard 5: "Students employ a wide range of strategies as they write and use different writing process elements appropriately to communicate with different audiences for a variety of purposes" (p. 3).

Standard 6: "Students apply knowledge of language structure, language conventions (e.g., spelling and punctuation), media techniques, figurative language, and genre to create, critique, and discuss print and nonprint texts" (p. 3).

According to the standards:

By closely observing students' writing processes and carefully reading their work, teachers can see which aspects of language structure are giving students trouble and help them learn these concepts through direct instruction and practice. It is also important for students to discover that grammar, spelling, and punctuation are useful not only in the context of fixing problems or mistakes; they can be studied effectively in a workshop context in which students work together to expand their repertoire of syntactic and verbal styles. When students connect the study of grammar and language patterns to the wider purposes of communication and artistic development, they are considerably more likely to incorporate such study into their working knowledge (p. 37).

The national content standards for English language arts are based on professional research and the best classroom practices. While the standards acknowledge the importance of grammar concepts, they clearly recommend that students learn and apply their knowledge of grammar for the purpose of effective communication. By embedding grammar instruction into writing instruction, teachers can positively affect students' actual writing skills.

References

Braddock, R., Lloyd-Jones, R., & Schoer, L. *Research in Written Composition.* Urbana, IL: National Council of Teachers of English, 1963.

Calkins, L. M. "When Children Want to Punctuate: Basic Skills Belong in Context." *Language Arts* 57 (1980): 567–73.

Cooper, C. "Research Roundup: Oral and Written Composition." *English Journal* 64 (1975): 72.

DiStefano, P., and Killion, J. "Assessing Writing Skills Through a Process Approach." *English Education* 16,4 (1984): 203–7.

Harris, R. J. "An Experimental Inquiry into the Functions and Value of Formal Grammar in the Teaching of Written English to Children Aged Twelve to Fourteen." Ph.D. Diss., University of London, 1962.

Hillocks, G., Jr. *Research on Written Composition: New Directions for Teaching.* Urbana, IL: ERIC Clearinghouse on Reading and Communication Skills and the National Conference on Research in English, 1986.

Hillocks, G., Jr., and Smith, M. "Grammar and Usage." In *Handbook of Research on Teaching the English Language Arts,* edited by J. Flood, J. M. Jensen, D. Lapp, and J. R. Squire. New York: Macmillan, 1991. 591–603.

Mellon, J. C. *Transformational Sentence-Combining: A Method for Enhancing the Development of Syntactic Fluency in English Composition.* NCTE Research Report No. 10. Urbana, IL: National Council of Teachers of English, 1969.

National Council of Teachers of English and the International Reading Association. *Standards for the English Language Arts.* Urbana, IL: National Council of Teachers of English, 1996.

Noguchi, R. R. *Grammar and the Teaching of Writing: Limits and Possibilities.* Urbana, IL: National Council of Teachers of English, 1991.

O'Hare, F. *Sentence-Combining: Improving Student Writing Without Formal Grammar Instruction.* Urbana, IL: National Council of Teachers of English, 1973.

Shaughnessy, M. P. *Errors and Expectations: A Guide for the Teacher of Basic Writing.* New York: Oxford University Press, 1977.

Strong, W. *Creative Approaches to Sentence Combining.* Urbana, IL: ERIC and the National Council of Teachers of English, 1986.

Weaver, C. *Lessons to Share on Teaching Grammar in Context.* Portsmouth, NH: Heinemann, 1998.

Why Grammar?

The definitions of grammar vary. In this series, the term *grammar* means not only the description of parts of speech and parts of a sentence but also the topics often labeled usage and mechanics.

The question of whether to teach grammar—and, if so, how—has confronted secondary-school English teachers for years. From the 1960s through the 1980s, university-level scholarship argued against formal grammar instruction. But teachers at middle school and high school levels have had to face several unsettling realities that have surfaced in the wake of this argument.

- Some students—even native English speakers—haven't mastered the conventions of standard written English.

- Some students are not scoring well on standardized tests that require recognizing and correcting sentence-level errors.

- Some parents have demanded that schools teach their children writing skills that will get them into college, land them better entry-level jobs, and advance them in a chosen career.

In this age of raising standards, it is the philosophy of this series that all students need to know and use the conventions of standard English. To accomplish this goal, students need thorough and coherent teaching and practice. The random coverage of grammar in integrated literature anthologies is not sufficient to help students meet the standards.

How to Engage Students in the Study of Grammar

The following suggestions will help improve the study of grammar in secondary-school classrooms.

Tell Students Why They Are Using *Grammar for Writing*

To succeed in high school, on tests, and in college, students must be able to use conventions of standard English. They are learning skills and habits to last a lifetime. In jobs that require them to deal with the public (such as customer service representatives, sales personnel, and professional jobs), employees need to be able to use standard English. Companies require their white-collar employees to write and speak correctly because they represent the company. In business letters, memos, and e-mail, employees must express themselves according to the conventions of standard English.

Acknowledge That Students Already Know Grammar

Native speakers of English start speaking at a very early age. They learn where to place which words. *Grammar for Writing* helps students get around the spots that give most of us writers trouble. Students will be more open to embarking on a study of grammar if they realize there really is a limited number of concepts to deal with in order to improve their writing.

"P.S." Feature

The little P.S. feature at the end of many lessons reassures students that they don't need to memorize or remember all of the terms in the lesson. It tells them which terms are important—and why.

Grammar Concepts

1. subject-verb agreement
2. verb forms and tenses
3. pronoun-antecedent agreement
4. pronoun reference and case
5. degree of modifiers
6. positioning of modifiers
7. run-on sentences and fragments
8. spelling
9. punctuation
10. commonly confused words

The Writing Process

The writing process movement dates back to the early 1970s, when Donald Murray published his article, "Teaching Writing as a Process, Not a Product." Faculty members at the University of New Hampshire (including Donald Murray, Donald Graves, Lucy Calkins, Nancie Atwell, and Thomas Newkirk) gave the writing process movement a home, training teachers and reporting on writing process theory in action. "Children want to write," Donald Graves wrote in 1983 (*Writing: Teachers and Children at Work*, Heinemann). "They want to write the first day they attend school." Today, the writing process movement dominates English classrooms from kindergarten through college.

Writing Workshops

At the core of the writing process are minilessons, peer response groups, and writing workshops (see Chapter 3). In a writing workshop, students complete a sustained writing activity in stages that involve planning, drafting, and revising. Prewriting (the planning stage) and revising (the improving stage) are most heavily emphasized.

You will find a writing workshop in each of the lessons in Chapter 3 of the Complete Course book. All of these workshops deal with the following common types of writing that students are asked to do throughout their school career:

Writing Workshops

- Narrative Writing: Autobiographical Incident (pp. 37–41)
- Narrative Writing: Eyewitness Report (pp. 42–46)
- Persuasive Writing (pp. 47–52)
- Expository Writing: Compare and Contrast Essay (pp. 53–59)
- Expository Writing: Cause-Effect Essay (pp. 60–65)
- Expository Writing: Problem-Solution Essay (pp. 66–70)
- Writing About Literature: Analyzing a Work (pp. 71–76)
- Expository Writing: Research Paper (pp. 77–92)
- Special Writing Tasks: Résumé and Cover Letter (pp. 93–98)

How to Use Them These writing workshops are flexible and can be used in different ways to meet your classroom needs. With the whole class, you might read and discuss the professional model and go over the Writing Strategies that appear in each workshop. Notice that in each workshop the exercises take students step-by-step through the writing process. By the time they complete all of the exercises, students will have completed a finished piece of writing of the type specified in the workshop. Students may work in small groups or with partners to talk about the critical thinking questions following the model and to give each other feedback on the exercises. If you prefer, students can work through the exercises individually—in class or as homework.

Writing Groups Try to make the writing groups heterogeneous, with a mixture of students of different ability levels. You might even try to have a mix of different learning styles in each group. A comfortable number for a writing group is four to six students. ELL students who are mainstreamed into regular English classes will benefit from speaking/listening interactions with members of their small writing groups.

Using the Writing Process

Emphasize to students that the writing process isn't the same for everyone. Some students like to outline carefully; others just plunge ahead from rough notes and start writing. Some begin writing with a title and introduction; others find it easier to start with the body and do an introduction and conclusion later.

Explain also that the process is recursive; that is, students can return to an earlier stage to gather more information. Or they may try out a topic and find that it just doesn't work, so they discard that topic and start over again in the topic selection process. Some teachers require students to do several drafts, revising each one. Others focus on just one draft. Many teachers don't separate revising and editing; they consider all the tasks to be revising.

Steps in the writing process may have different names, but basically it goes like this:

The Writing Process	
Steps	**Tasks**
PREWRITING (Lessons 1.1 and 1.2, pp. 9–14)	▪ Use brainstorming, freewriting, class discussion, newspaper articles, clustering and other graphics, listing, and *5W-How?* questions to generate topic ideas. ▪ Choose and limit topic. ▪ Gather details, information; do research, if needed. ▪ Organize details (make an outline). ▪ Specify purpose and audience.
DRAFTING (Lesson 1.2, pp. 14–15)	▪ Put prewriting notes into sentences and paragraphs. ▪ Draft thesis statement (main idea of paper). ▪ Draft attention-grabbing title and introduction. ▪ Draft strong conclusion.
REVISING (Lesson 1.3, p. 16)	▪ Read draft for coherence, unity, content. See four-readings strategy (page 16). ▪ Peer editors comment on draft. ▪ Consider peer editors' comments. ▪ Do additional drafts (second, third, fourth).
EDITING (Lesson 1.3, p. 17)	▪ Check for sentence completeness. ▪ Find and correct errors in subject-verb agreement, verb forms, pronoun usage, and other errors in grammar and usage.
PROOFREADING (Lesson 1.4, pp. 19–20)	▪ Find and correct errors in mechanics: spelling, punctuation, capitalization. ▪ Utilize peer proofreading.
PUBLISHING (Lesson 1.4, p. 20)	▪ Find a way to share writing with intended audience.

Resources

Atwell, Nancie. *In the Middle: Writing, Reading, and Learning with Adolescents.* Portsmouth, NH: Boynton/Cook, 1987.

Merriam-Webster's 3rd Edition.

Powell, David. *What Can I Write About? 7000 Topics for High School Students.* Urbana, IL: National Council of Teachers of English, 1981.

Random House Roget's Thesaurus. New York: Ballantine, 1996.

Strunk, William, Jr., and E. B. White. *The Elements of Style,* 3rd ed. New York: Macmillan, 1979.

Purposes of Writing

Help students see that there are many reasons for writing—now and in the future. Basically, these can be broken down into three categories: personal writing (self-expression), real-life writing, and writing for school.

Personal Writing

Writing as self-expression began to be emphasized in the mid-1960s, when progressive teachers introduced journals, freewriting, and other kinds of personal writing into the classrooms. James Moffett (1973) sees self-expressive modes of writing as a way of engaging student writers, even those with limited English proficiency. Everyone has stories to tell, ideas and feelings to communicate.

Journals/Diaries Encourage students to start a special notebook in which they record ideas and experiences. They might also include a list or description of "things I like"; or they can tape into their notebook excerpts from articles, poems, songs, cartoons/comic strips, photos, and ads that they find appealing. Over the course of months, such a journal becomes a rich source of topic ideas and details. Remind students to include in these journals or diaries only those things they're willing to share with their classmates.

- **Writing Logs** Prewriting notes, ideas for writing topics, proofreading logs, reflections on their writing experiences

- **Reading Logs** A record of books they've read and their comments, questions, and responses; responses to particular stories and poems, novels, essays they've read

- **Learning Logs** A record of important ideas and concepts they've learned

Sketchbooks Some students may want to create a sketchbook. They might sketch people, places, objects, and events from memory or direct observation. Encourage them to express what they've sketched in words, too. They might write on the back of a sketch or, if they're using a looseleaf notebook, interleave sketches and written descriptions.

Creative Writing Encourage students to write original poems and stories in conjunction with their study and discussion of literature genres. These may be individual, partner, or group efforts. Share finished works in class—on bulletin boards, in oral readings, or in a class newsletter or literary magazine. Tell students who are interested in creative writing to look for student writing contests and magazines (print and electronic) that publish student writing.

Real-life Writing

Experienced teachers know that students are motivated when they write for a real-life purpose and a specific audience. Here are just a few of the real-life writing situations students may engage in.

Forms, Applications, Résumés Students must follow directions and develop the ability to summarize and express ideas clearly and concisely.

All Kinds of Letters Some letters are social (thank-you notes, friendly letters, and pen-pal letters) and chatty. Others are business letters (order letters, complaint letters, letters to the editor) and formal. Students need to write in the appropriate form and language.

Research As part of their research projects, students may write letters requesting information or interviews. They may need to write letters of acknowledgment and thanks.

E-mail Students may write formal e-mail messages (requesting information, asking questions of an expert) and informal messages to friends and family. They need to learn the "netiquette"—the accepted conventions for writing e-mail messages.

Persuasion Students express and support their opinions when they write letters to the editor (see the writing workshop, p. 47), proposals for solving a school or community problem, and letters to elected representatives. The Write What You Think exercises throughout the Pupil's Edition (see, for example, p. 104) give them repeated practice in writing for persuasive purposes.

Work At work, students may write letters, memos, and reports. Their writing must communicate ideas clearly and concisely.

Writing for School

Students know how important writing skills are in all their classes. Here are just a few of the reasons to write in school.

Reports In history, science, math, and other classes, students are asked to research, organize, and communicate ideas in written and oral reports. (See "Writing Across the Curriculum," pp. T36–T37.)

Paragraphs Paragraph practice helps students gain skill in expressing and developing their ideas. (See Chapter 2, pp. 22–35, for lessons devoted to developing paragraph-writing skills.) In the minicontext of writing a single paragraph, students develop all of the following:

- a natural voice
- flow (sentences that read smoothly in a sequence)
- coherence (ideas that are easy to follow)
- unity (ideas and supporting details that stick to a topic).

Essays By the end of the Complete Course, students should be applying their paragraph-writing skills to longer papers. (See Chapter 3, "Writing Workshops," pp. 37–98.) Encourage students to write as much as they need to in order to express what they want to say.

Writing for Tests Increasingly, an essay question or two will appear as part of standardized tests. This is part of the performance assessment movement—students are graded on how well they accomplish a writing task in the given time frame. They must formulate, develop, organize, and express their ideas in a limited time. The skills they learn in practicing paragraph development (Chapter 2) and in the writing workshops (Chapter 3) will stand them in good stead on essay tests.

Writing for a Wider Audience Within the context of school, students have many opportunities to use their writing for a real purpose and audience.

- school paper (articles, letters to the editor, critical reviews)
- literary magazine or classroom newsletter of students' creative writing
- speeches for school-wide campaigns (elections, assemblies, rallies)
- scripts (school radio broadcasts and theater productions)
- press releases and publicity (school events and productions)

Writing Across the Curriculum in *Grammar for Writing*

Writing-across-the-curriculum programs began in the late 1960s with several researchers at the University of London Institute of Education. They proposed that writing should be an essential part of students' learning in all classes, not just in English, from kindergarten through university level. In some American schools, this policy manifests itself by encouraging teachers in all subject areas to give writing assignments, which they then help their students carry out according to the writing-process paradigm with, at times, advice from English-teacher colleagues. In other American schools, writing across the curriculum remains the purview of the language arts department in hopes that students' interest will be sparked with a variety of writing opportunities.

The following are some cross-curricular writing assignments—in addition to those that can be found throughout *Grammar for Writing*—that students can explore either under your guidance in English classes or under the guidance of subject-area teachers.

Writing Ideas

All of the following suggestions can be done as individual projects, or students can work with partners or small groups. Students should be willing to publish—that is, share—what they've written, making sure it's the best writing they can produce.

SCIENCE AND MATHEMATICS

- **Inventions** Research and write about the history of an invention, or explain how a common machine or piece of equipment works (for example, a telephone or a television).

- **History** (1) Write about the life and work of a scientist or mathematician, the discovery of a concept, or a breakthrough in a specific field of science or math. (2) Write about the origin of a mathematical concept (the concept of infinity, for example).

- **Discovery** Report on a current development in one of the sciences (for example, medical research or astronomy).

- **Original Research** Report on an experiment that you have conducted.

- **Reference Work** Create a plan for a math encyclopedia for sixth graders. Decide what articles to include and how to illustrate the articles.

SOCIAL STUDIES

- **Causes and Effects** Analyze the causes and/or effects of an event in American or world history.

- **What If?** Speculate on what might have happened if an important event had turned out differently.

- **What Needs Fixing?** Analyze a school or community problem, and propose a solution.

- **Cultural Studies** Select a life-cycle event (such as birth, coming of age, graduation, marriage, childbirth, death) in a current and a past culture, and compare and contrast how the two cultures mark the event.

ARTS

- **Movements** Explain a specific art movement (for example, Impressionism, Cubism) with examples.

- **Lives and Works** Profile an artist and his or her work.

- **How It Works** Explain how a particular musical instrument works.

LANGUAGES OTHER THAN ENGLISH

- **Dictionary** Create a phrase dictionary for teenage travelers to a country whose language you are studying. The dictionary must include an introduction to its contents.

- **Translation** Translate a poem or short piece of prose into English from another language. Discuss the difficulties of the translation process.

SPORTS, PHYSICAL EDUCATION

- **Newsletter** Create a prototype for a weekly or monthly sports newsletter for your school.

- **Profile** Write a biographical sketch of a star or rookie player in your school or community.

Projects

- **Take one writer.** Do some research about a favorite writer's life and work. Write a brief biography. Analyze (more than a plot summary) two major works (plays, novels, short stories) or four poems or two movies. Adapt this approach to focus on particular artists or directors.

- **Be a critic.** Write about movies, TV shows, records, or concerts. Publish your reviews in the local paper.

- **Write your memoirs.** Write not just about one autobiographical incident—but several (see pp. 37–41). Give the book of memoirs to family members, or put it in a drawer and take it out in the year 2025.

- **Write about your heritage.** What holidays do you celebrate, and how do you celebrate them? What customs and traditions do you follow? What sayings did you hear as you were growing up? Work with other students to write a multicultural memoir about holidays.

- **Interview relatives or neighbors who are senior citizens.** Ask what they remember about their early days, what life was like where and when they grew up. Summarize your interview into discrete articles and send them to the local paper of the senior citizen's hometown.

- **Do a Foxfire project.** Interview students, teachers, family members, and neighbors. Find out what they know how to do well. Get step-by-step directions to do a particular project; add photographs, diagrams, and drawings. Publish a how-to flyer or booklet.

- **Make life better.** Work to solve an actual school or community problem. Do some research. Consider possible solutions. Write a proposal to someone in charge, and lobby whoever is in power. Write editorials and letters to the editor in support of your issue.

- **Write creatively.** Set some parameters on content and language.

Encourage interested students to write original short stories, poems, or essays. Have an open mike (microphone) night or day in class with students reading what they've written. Invite other classes, parents, and families. Have students research places that publish student writing, and have them send in their work. Counsel them in advance about rejection slips.

- **Make up writing prompts on topics that will interest students.** Have students clip newspaper articles, summarize local news, and so on. Post these in the classroom, and discuss them with students. This activity is a great way to get students interested in community events, government, and voting. Make up brief prompts you're sure students can respond to in writing without further research. For example:

  You've been asked by the principal to come up with a proposal that will improve the school. Write your proposal and defend it.

Resources

Fulweiler, Toby, and Art Young, eds. *Programs That Work: Models and Methods for Writing Across the Curriculum.* Portsmouth, NH: Boynton/Cook, 1990.

"Ideas for Teachers" column in *English Journal.* Urbana, IL: National Council of Teachers of English, 1996.

Moffett, James. *Student-Centered Language Arts and Reading, K–12: A Handbook for Teachers.* Boston: Houghton Mifflin, 1973.

Step-by-Step Revising, Editing, and Proofreading

Many of your students would probably be happy turning in their first draft as a final paper. Help them to understand that the revising, editing, and proofreading stages in the writing process raise the standards for their own writing. What they learn from repeated practice in revising and peer editing sticks: Over the course of a year, students produce better organized, better written first drafts based on what they've learned through revising and editing.

Note that this series distinguishes between revising and editing—two steps that many teachers lump together as revising. We've separated these steps because it's hard for students to look critically at a piece of writing and see everything at once:

- **Revising** is concerned with content, organization, style, and word choice (see p. 16 in the Pupil's Edition and the four-step strategy for revising).

- **Editing** involves grammar and usage concerns.

- **Proofreading** refers to checking for errors in spelling, capitalization, and punctuation.

Self-Editing

Encourage students to let their first draft sit awhile so they can approach it with "fresh eyes." Before they share their drafts with one or more peer editors, encourage them to do a round of self-editing. They can use the Revising and Editing checklists (see pp. T41–T43) that you gave them as handouts at the beginning of the year. They can also refer to the four-step revision strategy on p. 16 of the Pupil's Edition.

Peer Editing

In the days before peer editing, teachers spent a lot of their evenings marking up student papers with red pen or pencil, filling margins with abbreviations such as *Awk* (Awkward), *Frag* (Fragment), and *Sp* (Spelling). Peer editing has not only helped lighten your paper load; it is also one of the most powerful tools of the writing process. Whether students comment on each other's papers in **writing groups** or one on one as a single writer and **peer editor**, they develop skills and strategies that transfer to their own writing:

- They learn what to look for in evaluating a draft.
- They learn to ask questions about organization and content.
- They learn from others' approaches to the same assignment.
- They even learn to be tactful in expressing their comments.

It's important to get the peer editing process underway as soon as students have completed their first draft and have had a chance to do some self-evaluation of it—so writers don't lose momentum. If margins are at least an inch on either side, peer editors may write comments directly on their own copy (printed or photocopied) of the draft. In some high-tech classrooms, drafts are posted on a computer. Students might write their comments directly under the draft or even e-mail their comments to the writer.

Forming Writing Groups

Writing process expert Nancie Atwell reports that in her classes she lets students choose the classmate or classmates they think can help them on the part of a paper they are struggling with at the time. "In the writing workshop," she says, "small groups form and disband in the minutes it takes for a writer to call on one or more other writers, move to a conference corner, share a piece or discuss a problem, and go back to work with a new perspective on the writing" (*In the Middle: Writing, Reading, and Learning with Adolescents*, p. 41).

You may want to organize students into groups that stay together for several weeks or throughout the time devoted to one writing workshop. Such stable groups work well with block scheduling and with ongoing projects. Students get to know and trust each other as they try out topic ideas,

discuss specific writing problems, and share their drafts and revisions.

The members of the same group might work together on a writing project—for example, a compare and contrast paper or any of the project ideas mentioned on pages T37–T38. Think of having a writing group do speaking/listening and media projects, too: perhaps a panel discussion with a question-and-answer period on a problem or issue that the group researches, or maybe a multimedia project.

Peer Editing Abbreviated

Depending on your class, you might use a brief peer editing checklist like the following; or the longer, more detailed checklists that follow:

Brief Peer Editing Checklist

What Are the Strong Points?
- What are the best parts of the paper?
- What has the writer done especially well?

What Are the Weak Points?
- What parts of the paper need more work?
- Do you have any questions about the paper?
- Can you make any specific suggestions for improving the writing?

Revising in Greater Depth

Here is a much more detailed Revising Checklist, one that students may refer to in revising their own work and when commenting on each other's papers. You might want to produce another version of this checklist (and the editing and proofreading ones as well) for students to refer to throughout the year. This checklist applies to expository writing, the kind of writing that students are most often asked to do in school (a comparison and contrast essay, for example, or a critical review). In addition, see the boxed revising questions on page T42, which refer specifically to persuasive, narrative, and descriptive writing.

Revising Checklist

Purpose and Audience
❑ How well does the writing accomplish its intended purpose?

❑ Are the language and details appropriate for the intended audience?

Main Idea
❑ What is the main idea? Is it clearly and directly stated?

Supporting Details
❑ How well does the writer develop the main idea and major points? Are there enough interesting supporting details?

❑ Would the writing be improved by dropping or by adding information? Where? What's missing?

❑ Do you have unanswered questions? What are they?

❑ Would adding details make the writing more interesting? Where? What kind of details would you suggest?

Organization
❑ How well can you follow the writer's ideas?

❑ Would a different organization help?

❑ Do any parts of the draft stray from the main idea?

Sentence Style
❑ Do transitions help the reader follow ideas?

❑ Can unnecessary words, details, and sentences be dropped?

❑ Do sentences read smoothly? Can some be combined?

❑ Do sentence lengths, beginnings, and structures vary?

Voice
❑ Does the writing sound natural? Are word choices and sentence structures awkward and difficult?

❑ Is the writing appropriate for the intended audience?

Word by Word
❑ Are words used precisely? Can you find vague, overused words that should be replaced? Would vivid verbs and specific nouns improve the writing? Where?

❑ Are the sentences overloaded with too many modifiers or too many prepositional phrases?

❑ Can you spot any clichés?

Title
❑ Does the title capture the reader's interest? Does it accurately reflect the paper's content?

Introduction and Conclusion

❏ Does the introduction make you want to read more? What suggestions can you make for improving it?

❏ Does it introduce the topic and the main idea?

❏ Does the conclusion end the essay strongly?

You may want to offer students variations on peer checklists from time to time. One option is to generate mode-specific checklists such as the ones below or even assignment-specific checklists. (See also the discussion of rubrics on pp. T53–T54.)

Mode-Specific Checklists	
Checklist for Persuasive Writing	❏ Is the writer's opinion clearly stated? ❏ Does the writer give at least two reasons to support that opinion? ❏ Are the reasons themselves supported by convincing evidence (facts, statistics, examples, anecdotes, quotations, and so on)? ❏ Do you understand what the writer wants the reader to do? ❏ Has the writer persuaded you? Why or why not?
Checklist for Narrative Writing	❏ Does the beginning make you want to read more? ❏ Does the writer *show* characters in action and let you hear what they say, or does the writer simply *tell* you about characters? ❏ Does the writing include sensory details? ❏ Are the writer's comparisons relevant and illuminating? ❏ Has the writer used specific nouns and vivid verbs (especially, as alternatives for *said*)? ❏ Is the ending satisfying?
Checklist for Descriptive Writing	❏ Can you picture the setting? ❏ Does the writing include specific sensory details? ❏ Are the comparisons fresh? ❏ Does the organization of details (for example, proceeding from near to far, left to right, or top to bottom) make sense? ❏ Does the description establish an overall mood? What is it?

Editing and Proofreading

As previously mentioned, this series separates the revising task (which focuses on content, style, and organization) from the editing task (which focuses on grammar and usage). Proofreading is the stage of the writing process when students look for mechanical errors in spelling, punctuation, and capitalization. These checklists provide references for either the teacher or the student.

Editing Checklist

❑ Is every sentence grammatically complete (not a fragment or a run-on)? *Lesson 5.1*

❑ Do subjects and verbs agree in number and gender? *Chapter 9*

❑ Are the correct forms of pronouns used? *Chapter 10*

❑ Does each pronoun clearly refer to an antecedent? *Lesson 10.5*

❑ Are verb tenses used consistently, unless there is a good reason to vary them? *Lesson 8.4*

❑ Are the correct forms of irregular verbs used? *Lessons 8.2–8.3*

❑ Are the correct forms of plural nouns and the comparative forms of adjectives and adverbs used? *Lessons 11.1, 11.2, and 16.4*

Proofreading Checklist

❑ Is every word spelled correctly? Check a dictionary if you're unsure. *Lesson 16.1*

❑ Have homophones been confused (*their* instead of *there*, for example)? *Chapter 12*

❑ Do proper nouns and proper adjectives begin with capital letters? *Chapter 15*

❑ Does every sentence begin with a capital letter and end with an end punctuation mark? *Chapters 13 and 14*

❑ Are commas used correctly in all of their many uses? *Chapter 13*

❑ Is dialogue punctuated correctly? *Lesson 14.5*

Resources

In the classroom, students should have access to several copies of a good college dictionary and a dictionary-style thesaurus.

Vocabulary

In many lessons, you'll find an extra feature: Enriching Your Vocabulary. One word from an example or exercise sentence is explored in depth. These vocabulary side features give the word's origin, meanings, related forms, and some information about how and when the word is used. Some of them also offer an example sentence that uses the vocabulary word. In the Complete Course, words highlighted in the vocabulary side features have been drawn from Sadlier's *Vocabulary Workshop* program.

How to Use These Vocabulary Features

Make sure students digest these features by taking a few minutes to go over each one—whenever you can fit these features in—with the whole class. Here are some suggested activities for using these side features and for helping students to acquire new vocabulary words:

- **Create your own exercise.** This type of exercise appears occasionally in the Grammar, Usage, and Mechanics chapters. Ask students to think of other example sentences using the word in the Enriching Your Vocabulary feature. Have them do this as an individual writing assignment or, better yet, ask volunteers to write example sentences on the board. Discuss with the class as a whole or in small groups whether the example sentences use the words precisely.

- **Check a dictionary.** Try to have several good dictionaries in class (an unabridged dictionary and two or three different college dictionaries). Ask students to compare the etymologies and meanings given in several dictionaries: Do they agree with the vocabulary note in the text and with each other? This kind of activity gives students practice in dictionary skills, which will help them work independently to discover the meanings, origins, and usage of unfamiliar words they find in their reading.

- **Create new vocabulary features.** Once you've covered several of the vocabulary features, ask students to imitate the approach. Have each student write an original Enriching Your Vocabulary feature for one unfamiliar word they come across in a literature selection, newspaper, or magazine—even one that they hear on television or radio. Have students share their features with the class or a small group. You might do this on a weekly basis.

- **Keep a vocabulary notebook.** Have students keep a notebook (or part of a notebook) devoted to new words they encounter in their reading. Encourage them to include words from other subjects, too. For each entry, they might list brief definitions and example sentences. On a regular basis, you might have students get together in small groups to teach each other the words they've recorded in their notebooks.

- **Compile a dictionary.** As an ongoing cooperative activity, you might have students work in small groups to create their own minidictionaries for a field that interests them: computer jargon, sports terms, music terminology, and so on. Give students a choice of which group to join, but limit group size to four or five.

- **Introduce word puzzles and games.** Enrich your classroom with word puzzles and games (crossword puzzles from the newspaper, anagrams, and so on) that students can use when they've completed their classwork. Encourage students to work together in teams to make up other puzzles, word games, and puns.

Other Approaches to Vocabulary Study

Here are some other tried-and-true ways to enlarge students' vocabulary:

Reading and More Reading Many studies show that the most effective way for students to enlarge their vocabulary is through the sustained silent reading of books that they choose. Assemble a classroom library that includes a wide range of materials for students with varying abilities. You might work with a school or public librarian (media specialist) to create a minilibrary containing books

designed to appeal to your students. Emphasize multicultural content and authors, popular young adult (YA) fiction, and interesting nonfiction. Add the classics that you think will appeal to your students. Students might meet in reading groups to discuss what they're reading and to recommend books to each other. You might have them write critical reviews or present oral reports. They can write in reading logs—noting their informal responses and questions about what they have read.

Context clues Teach or review the skills needed to use **context clues**, the words and sentences surrounding an unfamiliar word that help students guess the word's meaning. Give students example sentences showing the following kinds of context clues: definitions, appositives, synonyms, comparison/contrast, and other kinds of clues embedded in surrounding sentences.

Internet Explain to students that another tool for improving vocabulary might be using recommended Internet sites:

http://www.m-w.com/netdict.htm The thesaurus link gives related words, contrasted words, and antonyms. Recommended for all four grade levels.

http://www.thesaurus.com/ This is Roget online. It offers extensive lists. No antonyms are given. It is a fairly sophisticated site and best for the higher grades.

Connecting Technology to Grammar for Writing

Computers make both writing and researching so much easier. Students love working—as well as playing—on computers, but if your students and classrooms do not have access to computers, that fact won't affect the quality of their writing. Assure them that excellent writing still arrives in longhand on ruled paper (or however you require that it be turned in).

Word Processing: Writing on the Computer

The positive side of word processing is that both revising and editing is a snap and printed papers are clean and legible. The negative side of word processing is that it's easy for students to copy others' papers and turn in the work as their own. You can avoid plagiarism by requiring students to hand in various stages of their work, such as prewriting notes, outlines, and lists of sources.

Here are the basic skills students must know in order to produce papers on a word processing program:

- how to create and save documents
- how to set margins and line spacing
- how to select fonts (encourage them not to get too fancy)
- how to print documents

Writing Process

Word processing can be used for every stage in the writing process. Here are some specific suggestions:

Prewriting

- To gather ideas for topics, students can use the computer for freewriting, brainstorming, and listing. For freewriting, tell students to turn down the brightness on the monitor so they're not distracted by what they've already written.

- Students can take notes on the computer instead of on note cards. Encourage them to set up separate documents for each source. When they organize their notes, they'll work from printouts of their notes and can highlight the information they find most useful. Tell students that just as they should write a heading on their note cards and include the page number of the source, so, too, should they put in headings and note page numbers whenever they take notes.

- Working with printouts of their notes, students can easily draft and rework an outline on a computer, using tabs for indenting.

Drafting

- Remind students how important it is to save their work regularly and to back up their documents in case of a power failure or computer crash.

- Assure students that there is no "right" way to write on a computer. Some students (those who say they "think better" writing in longhand and those who are new to keyboarding) may prefer writing and revising in longhand. That's acceptable, too. Remind them to leave wide margins and extra space around their handwritten drafts so that there's room to revise. As preparation for revising, double spacing is a good idea so that there is room to revise on computer printouts.

Revising

The best part of word processing is revising. It's easy to replace, insert, move, and delete words, sentences, and paragraphs.

- Encourage students to try out changes and various different versions and to read aloud to themselves what they've written. If they don't want to "lose" a version of their writing, they can keep the original, make a copy, and revise on the copy.

- Some students find it easier to print out a draft, revise in longhand in pencil or pen, and then keyboard their changes. Others prefer revising directly on-screen. Any way that works is fine.

Proofreading

Most word processing programs have built-in grammar and spell checkers. Make sure students realize that these aren't foolproof. Students still must proofread their own papers carefully; exchanging papers with a peer proofreader is an extra safeguard. Students should proofread first drafts, revised drafts, and the final paper.

- Advise students to proofread by reading the whole paper slowly. Reading aloud to themselves might help.

- Warn students that a spell checker won't detect extra words, missing words, and words used incorrectly. As long as a word is spelled correctly, the spell checker approves. For instance, it lets the two errors in this sentence pass unnoticed:

  Mickey order too pizzas with peppers, mushrooms, and olives.

- Grammar checkers will alert students to errors in capitalization, commonly confused words, hyphenation errors, misused words, double negatives, passive construction, punctuation, sentence structure, subject-verb agreement, wordiness, and so on. However, no grammar checker is foolproof. A grammar checker may indicate an error when there is no error, and it may make suggestions that are incorrect. Tell students that the responsibility for correct grammar in their writing is theirs alone.

- Encourage proofreading skills in your class by insisting that students who use word processors turn in a clean final paper—without ink corrections or whiteout.

Harnessing Software for *Grammar for Writing*

Invite students to list and discuss the features of software that make writing easier for them. Raise their consciousness about the connections between technology and their writing assignments. Make sure that at least the following dozen features are at the top of your students' lists:

1. networking and e-mail For helping one another generate ideas during prewriting and for sharing responses to one another's drafts; for distribution—that is, publishing—of finished documents across the aisle or around the world

2. outlining software For help in organizing main ideas and details during prewriting and later

3. cut-and-paste function of a word processor For moving words, sentences, paragraphs, and sections during revising and editing

4. find-and-replace function of a word processor For global replacement of one term or spelling for another at any stage

5. save and save-as functions of a word processor For easily comparing and contrasting drafts

6. thesaurus tool on a word processor For quickly finding alternative vocabulary during any stage

7. spelling tool on a word processor For superficial proofreading (Students must do their own proofreading if they want to catch problems with homophones, typographical errors, and so on.)

8. grammar tool on a word processor For sentence-level analysis (Students must decide whether to accept the tool's suggested revision.)

9. drawing programs, page-design programs, and other features of desktop-publishing software For professional formatting and the inclusion of nontext material (e.g., photographs, drawings) in reports

10. online searches to locate pertinent documents For getting information and facts for research projects

11. discussion groups Whether synchronous or not, to provide access to people seriously interested in and often well informed about topics students are researching

12. hypertext links For direct access to online sources that a student has used in putting together a research report and that readers may want to review for themselves

Evaluating Internet Information

Emphasize to students that they should not believe everything they read, see, or hear on the Web. Information gleaned from a Web site could be coming from a twelve-year-old, a university library, or a business. Students must learn to evaluate information they find on the Web for bias, accuracy, and current information. They should get in the habit of double-checking what they find on the Web in additional sources.

To evaluate information, students need to know where it is coming from—literally. They must notice and make deductions based on the top-level domain, the three letters at or toward the end of a Web site's address. The letters have meaning.

- **.gov** A local, state, or national government [Information from such a source is generally reliable.]

- **.edu** An educational institution [The source may be a research department at an eminent university or a fourth-grade class.]

- **.org** An organization [Any organization may have an agenda—that is, a bias—which students must take into consideration.]

- **.com** A commercial—that is, business—source [Students must consider whether the site's information is biased to encourage purchases or other commercial interaction.]

- **.net** A network [Anyone can create a home page and post it here.]

Reliable Sites for Teachers and Students

You and your students may enjoy identifying Web sites helpful to class work by searching with key terms such as *standard English*, *grammar*, and *OWL* (for "online writing lab"). Here are sites that have been checked for reliability and suitability. Remember that Web sites are in constant flux and that sites change overnight. Do your own screening before recommending them to your students.

English as a Second Language
http://www.comenius.com This site includes "Fluency Through Fables" and "The Weekly Idiom." There are interactive features. There are links for many languages.

Grammar, Usage, Mechanics
http://andromeda.rutgers.edu/~jlynch /Writing/ The site is very clear and helpful on relevant grammatical issues.

http://webster.commnet.edu/HP/pages /darling/original.htm This takes the student to a site called "Guide to Grammatical Writing." There are features on sentences, paragraphs, essays, forms of communication (e.g., business letters), and grammar.

Research on the Web
http://www.marlboro.edu/~jsheehy/ writing/ This site is called the Clear Writing Program. It is full of useful information and includes links for *writing* as well as research.

http://ipl.org/teen/aplus/aplus.htm Here, students can access the writing process pages, the Web research pages, and a variety of links. This site is geared to teens.

Writing Process
http://owl.english.purdue.edu This site is geared more toward teachers than toward students, though students will find the writing links useful. These include over 130 handouts on the writing process, grammar, punctuation, job searches, business letters, ESL, and so on. There are extensive lists of Web research links and links to the Purdue libraries.

Using *Grammar for Writing* with English Language Learners

Variously called ESL (English as a Second Language) students, EFL (English as a Foreign Language) students, nonnative speakers, English-language learners (ELL), and multilingual writers, students for whom English is not a first language give you a chance to raise everyone's consciousness about the respect that all languages and dialects deserve. Here are some strategies for giving ELL students a chance to talk about languages and demonstrate what languages other than English sound and look like:

- Conduct an informal survey at the beginning of the term, asking students these questions:

  - What other languages do you speak, read, and write besides English?

  - What language(s) do you speak at home?

  - What language(s) besides English have you studied in school? How well do you speak it? Write it? Read it? Understand it when it is spoken to you?

  - How did you learn the rules for forming sentences in your first language? In the other language(s)?

- Give native English speakers a chance to hear the sounds of other languages by asking ELL students to translate into their native language and orally deliver conversational sentences based on the following English ones:

  - Hi. My name is _____.

  - I am _____ years old.

  - My hobbies are _____.

  - The kind of music I like best is _____, and _____ is one of my favorite songs.

  - Good-bye for now.

- Ask ELL students to identify ways in which their first language differs from English. Encourage them to talk about what is giving them the most trouble in learning to speak and write English.

Recognizing Problem Areas for ELL Students

The following table identifies some of the problems ELL students have with English. It lists chapters and lessons from the *Grammar for Writing* series to which you can direct students with those problems.

Grammar for Writing and ELL Problems

Problem Area in English	Comment	Grammar for Writing Treatment, Complete Course
ADJECTIVE CLAUSES	Forming and positioning adjective clauses cause problems for speakers of Asian languages, of Arabic and Hebrew, and even of Latin-based languages.	Lesson 7.2
ARTICLES	ELL students often leave out the article before a singular count noun.	Lesson 4.4
CAPITALIZATION	Arabic, Chinese, and Hebrew do not use capital letters; Dutch and German capitalize some forms of the second-person pronoun; German caps all nouns.	Chapter 15
EXPLETIVES	Spanish speakers sometimes omit subjects, saying "Is raining."	Chapter 5 covers the "It is raining" sentence structure.
HOMONYMS	Speakers of Asian languages in particular may be confused by the concept of words sounding alike but having different meanings.	Chapter 12
NEGATION	Multiple negation is common in French and Russian, among other languages.	Lesson 11.3
PLURALS	Some Asian languages have no plural forms for nouns.	Chapter 9, Lesson 16.4
PREFIXES AND SUFFIXES	These word parts are absent in Asian languages.	Lesson 16.3
PREPOSITIONS	English distinguishes between *in* and *on*; Spanish uses *en* for both.	Lessons 4.7 and 6.1
SILENT LETTERS	There are no silent letters in Spanish.	Chapter 16
SUBJECTS, DOUBLE	Some languages add personal pronouns as suffixes or prefixes, leading ELL speakers to say, "Maria she is pretty."	Lessons 5.2, 5.5, 10.1
TENSES	■ Certain English verbs don't work in the present progressive, but ESL students may say or write, "I am knowing the answer." ■ In some languages, time is not signaled by word endings but rather by words that native English speakers would call adverbs.	Lesson 8.4
WORD ORDER	■ In some languages, word order determines the part of speech. For example, the verb is the last word in sentences in Turkish, Korean, and Japanese. ■ In Russian, subject and object may switch places without affecting meaning.	Lessons 5.1, 5.2, 5.8, 5.9, and 13.1

Assessment in *Grammar for Writing*

The *Grammar for Writing* series has assessment built right in. In this age of assessment and accountability, you'll want some ongoing measures of how well students are doing in the course of the term. The series offers the following different types of assessment in each Pupil's Edition and Test Booklet:

Objective Evaluation

- **Mid-Chapter and Chapter Reviews** In each book, Mid-Chapter Reviews and Chapter Reviews help students review the grammar, usage, and mechanics concepts learned in the preceding lessons. Each review is broken down into exercises that focus on one lesson or one particular grammar, usage, or mechanics problem.

- **Cumulative Reviews** At the end of Chapters 7, 12, and 16, a two-page Cumulative Review covers the preceding chapters in that section. Use these Cumulative Reviews as mastery tests or diagnostic tests depending on your classroom needs.

- **Grammar, Usage, and Mechanics Tests** These objective tests differ from the Cumulative Reviews; the tests incorporate the standardized test format of the PSAT writing exam. Test items include both error recognition and error correction. Again, you may use these materials

either as mastery tests or diagnostic tests. Note that the optional assessment component of *Grammar for Writing*, the *Grammar for Writing Test Booklet*, contains test items in standardized-test formats, as well as other kinds of items.

Lightening the Paper Load

Consider letting students help you in scoring objective tests. Have students exchange papers and score them as you go over answers in class; ask for volunteers to give the answers. A whole-class discussion of test items gives students a chance to ask questions. This will reinforce understanding and help students who may still be confused.

Evaluating Responses to Writing Exercises

Grammar for Writing includes many writing exercises that can't be scored objectively, such as the exercises in the Composition Unit (Chapters 1–3), as well as the exercises based on notes, exercises with paragraphs needing revision, and the Revising and Editing Worksheets or Editing and Proofreading Worksheets in the grammar, usage, and mechanics sections (Chapters 4–16). It's up to you to decide whether—and how—to grade these writing exercises or to simply check that students have completed them.

Revising and Editing Worksheets

These one-page themed exercises are examples of poor writing. Students are directed to work individually or with a partner or group to improve the writing. Typically, instructions ask students to correct errors covered in the preceding lessons and to combine sentences and eliminate fragments and run-ons. *There is no single correct answer to any of the revision exercises in the Student Edition.*

What students will learn from these exercises—especially by comparing their revisions and edits with those of their classmates—is that there are many workable solutions to writing problems and many different ways to communicate the same idea. This empowering insight should make students more confident as they revise and edit their own writing. To get the most benefit from the Revising and Editing Worksheets, direct students to compare revisions (sentence-by-sentence or paragraph-by-paragraph) in a whole-class session.

It is impossible to give students' work a percentage score on the Revising and Editing Worksheets; they contain many errors and invite many ways to revise and edit. Also, remember that students may be working with partners or a group, so the final result is a shared effort. If you feel you must record a number score, try judging the revisions on a 1–4 scale (with four being "excellent"). Give students points for each of the following criteria, and then find the average score.

The revised and edited version:

- communicates ideas and information clearly.
- is made up of complete sentences (no fragments or run-ons) that read smoothly and naturally.
- has no errors related to the chapter's content.
- has no (or very few) errors in grammar and usage.
- uses punctuation correctly.
- spells words correctly.

Rubrics for Evaluating Students' Paragraphs and Essays

You can measure students' original writing using the rubrics on page T54, which help to identify students' performance levels. Note that the rubrics are generic (they apply to all types of essays) and are based on a six-point scale. (You may find that in your classroom a four-point scale, beginning at Level 4, is more suitable.)

At the beginning of the term, share these (or your own) rubrics with students as a handout that they can keep in their notebooks. Let students know exactly what your standards are, so that they know what to aim for. You might also give students copies of essays from unidentified writers as an example of each level of performance. Reading and discussing these sample essays will clarify for students what you expect of them.

Writing Performance Levels

	The student's writing
LEVEL 6	<ul><li>consistently pursues a strong central purpose across a complex range of ideas, skillfully engages the reader, and shows exceptional insight into the subject</li><li>includes main ideas that are developed comprehensively and are supported with a variety of logical reasons and detailed examples</li><li>is skillfully organized</li><li>shows distinctive style through skillful and expressive use of vocabulary, phrasing, and sentence structure</li><li>demonstrates essentially error-free control of grammar, punctuation, capitalization, and spelling</li></ul>
LEVEL 5	<ul><li>consistently pursues a central purpose, holds the interest of the reader, and shows insight into the subject</li><li>includes main ideas that are developed and supported by a variety of reasons and examples</li><li>is effectively organized</li><li>shows emerging style through the effective use of vocabulary, phrasing, and sentence structure</li><li>consistently demonstrates the accurate use of grammar, punctuation, capitalization, and spelling</li></ul>
LEVEL 4	<ul><li>shows a consistent purpose, communicates to the reader, and connects to the writer's knowledge of the subject</li><li>includes main ideas that are organized, developed, and supported by reasons and examples</li><li>shows suitable vocabulary, phrasing, and sentence structure</li><li>generally demonstrates the accurate use of grammar, punctuation, capitalization, and spelling</li></ul>
LEVEL 3	<ul><li>shows a purpose but may be inconsistent in communicating to the reader or connecting to the writer's knowledge of the subject</li><li>includes main ideas that may be organized or partially developed and supported by some reasons and examples</li><li>may show imprecise use of vocabulary, phrasing, and sentence structure</li><li>includes some errors in the use of grammar, punctuation, capitalization, and spelling</li></ul>
LEVEL 2	<ul><li>attempts to connect the writer's knowledge to the subject and may not show a purpose</li><li>is typically brief, unorganized, and underdeveloped</li><li>may include frequent errors in the use of grammar, capitalization, punctuation, and spelling</li></ul>
LEVEL 1	<ul><li>is too brief or disorganized to communicate to the reader</li><li>may not connect the writer's knowledge to the subject</li><li>typically includes many errors in the use of grammar, capitalization, and spelling</li></ul>

Performance Levels, 1994. Reprinted with permission from the California Department of Education.

Writing Portfolios

The movement for performance assessment has gained strength over many years. Today, writing portfolios, an essential part of performance assessment, are part of most English classrooms. Writing portfolios give students tangible evidence that their efforts pay off. The portfolios can be made available for review by students' new teachers in subsequent terms.

Many teachers have students create two different kinds of writing portfolios:

- **A works-in-progress portfolio** For every finished piece of writing, students include prewriting notes, outlines, early drafts, revised drafts, and even a brief reflection on their writing experience. Students may also include journals, sketches, logs, and notes about their reading.

- **A best-efforts portfolio** This portfolio shows only the *finished pieces of writing*, examples of what students think are their best writing efforts.

Teacher-Student Conferences

An integral part of performance assessment is teacher-student conferences. One-on-one conferencing helps you assess performance and motivates students to raise their own standards.

Test Booklet

For every course of *Grammar for Writing*, a separate Test Booklet is available for purchase. The Test Booklet contains a separate test for every chapter as well as a Diagnostic Test and a Mastery Test. Items take standardized test formats: error recognition and error correction.

Here is an example of an error recognition question from the Complete Course Mastery Test.

Directions: Fill in the circle of the letter for each sentence that contains an error.

1. Ⓐ Ⓑ Ⓒ Ⓓ
   A. He and I are on the school paper together.
   B. Of the two of them, she is the best skater.
   C. Just between you and me, our band needs work.
   D. Michel or Suki are representing our grade at the conference.

Note that there are two incorrect sentences; the circles for both B and D should be filled in.

Here's why:

B is incorrect. The sentence should use the word *better*, not *best*, because only two people are being compared, so the comparative form is needed.

D is incorrect. The verb should be *is*, not *are*. Two singular subjects connected by *or* take a singular verb.

Diagnostic Test

A four-page Diagnostic Test appears at the beginning of each Test Booklet. You may use this test at the beginning of the school term to determine students' strengths and weaknesses. Each question on the Diagnostic Test is devoted to a single problem area.

Tallying class results will also reveal the grammar, usage, and mechanics skills that the class as a whole needs to learn and review. Use the Diagnostic Test scores and the errors on students' first batch of papers to decide on which textbook lessons to use with the whole class and on which lessons should be reserved for individuals or small groups.

Mastery Test

Use the four-page Mastery Test to assess the progress students have made during the term. You might plan to hold brief individual conferences with each student to discuss the student's work as a whole and to identify those skills that still need work.

Students whose Mastery Test scores indicate that they are still having trouble (with subject-verb agreement, for example) might work together in small groups to review appropriate lessons and to go over the exercises together.

You might ask these students to create their own exercise items in the style of exercise items in the Pupil's Edition. For example, a pair of students working together might write ten sentences that test knowledge of clear pronoun references (similar to Exercise 13 on page 250 of the Complete Course, for example). Exercise writers can then exchange exercises with another team and work together to answer the exercise ques-

tions. Finally, both teams (writers and exercise takers) can get together to see if their answers agree.

Chapter Tests

Most Chapter Tests are four pages; a few are two pages long. Each Chapter Test focuses entirely on concepts taught in the chapter lessons. In addition to error recognition and error correction items in a standardized test format, many Chapter Tests end with a writing prompt. Four-page tests may also contain a paragraph to be revised.

Writing Prompts

These are a variety of writing exercises that are similar to the Write What You Think exercises in the Student Edition. Students are asked to express an opinion on a topic or issue related to the content of a preceding exercise. They don't need any additional information to express and support an opinion.

Paragraph Revision

Some of the four-page Chapter Tests contain paragraphs that students are to revise. These are similar to the revision exercises found in the Student Edition.

Test Book Answer Key

A separate Answer Key is provided with each package of student Test Booklets.

Answer Key

Chapter 4

Exercise 13 Combining Sentences

1. William, known as William the Conqueror, achieved an important victory in the invasion.
2. Ruthless William II was William's son.
3. William's grandson was named Stephen, also a triumphant soldier.
4. In the twelfth century, King Henry II quarreled loudly and angrily with the Archbishop of Canterbury.
5. Gallant King Richard I, who reigned in the last decade of the twelfth century, went on religious crusades.

Chapter 5

Exercise 7 Correcting Sentence Fragments

Answers will vary. Sample answers are given.

1. Nubia was an African empire that was rich in gold and emeralds.
2. In the Bible, its name is Kush, one of the many different names by which it was known.
3. The ancient Greeks called it Ethiopia, which was what the Romans called it.
4. Nubia was located along the Nile, stretching from Khartoum in Sudan north to present-day Aswan in Egypt.
5. Its land was extraordinarily hot and dry and was an unlikely location for an empire.
6. Nubia had much less fertile land than Egypt.
7. Archeologists have identified at least six different Nubian cultures that existed from 3800 B.C. through A.D. 600.
8. A rival to its northern neighbor, Egypt, Nubia conquered that nation in about 730 B.C.
9. Nubian kings ruled Egypt for about sixty years.
10. The Nubian civilization reached the height of its political and economic power in about 200 B.C. and lasted longer than the civilizations of ancient Greece and Rome.

Exercise 9 Compound Subjects, Compound Verbs

Answers will vary. Sample answers are given.

1. Juan's first choice for college and Tom's last choice are local schools. [*or* . . . is a local school.]
2. Rita's mother thinks highly of a college nearby but would understand another choice by Rita.
3. Both Carmen and Dolores dream about Europe after graduation.
4. Pat spoke with the college adviser and conducted research on the Internet about community colleges.
5. Jack, Suki, and Elijah will go to a state college. [*or* . . . to state colleges.]

Exercise 10 Compound Sentences

Answers will vary. Sample sentences are given.

1. The school soccer team has played poorly all season; therefore, it probably won't contend for the state championship.
2. The school basketball team has played well, so the coach expects an invitation to a tournament.
3. The center on the basketball team has had a great season; his performance has attracted the attention of college and professional coaches.
4. The softball team has had a disappointing season, and the lead pitcher attributes the losses to her knee injury.

5. The team's top swimmer has broken school records; moreover, her teammates are urging her to try out for the Olympics.

MID-CHAPTER REVIEW

Exercise B Combining Sentences
Answers will vary. Sample answers are given.

1. *It Happened One Night* won the Academy Award for best picture in 1934; its stars won the year's acting awards.

2. In 1935, both actor Victor McLaglen and director John Ford won for their work in *The Informer*.

3. The best picture of 1942 was *Mrs. Miniver*, and William Wyler won an award for directing it.

4. Frank Capra's *It Happened One Night*, *Mr. Deeds Goes to Town*, and *You Can't Take It with You* won as best-directed pictures in 1934, 1936, and 1938, respectively.

5. The Best Picture award in 1943 went to *Casablanca*; however, its famous stars did not win awards that year.

Exercise 12 Editing Run-on Sentences
Answers will vary. Sample answers are given.

1. A fragile layer of tissue coats coral reefs; this tissue is susceptible to diseases.

2. These diseases are old; however, in recent years they have intensified.

3. One ailment, which affects brain and star corals, is called black-band disease.

4. There are two types of white-band disease. Both threaten coral in the Caribbean.

5. Yellow-band disease, which is also known as yellow-blotch disease, attacks coral in the Caribbean too.

6. White pox gives some coral a white rash; it was first identified in 1996 in the Florida Keys.

7. White plague was first noted in 1977; then, in 1995, an even deadlier strain appeared.

8. Both natural events, such as El Niño, and increased tourism have played a role in the destruction of coral reefs.

9. Even though the coral in the Caribbean beckons me, I may stay on land and watch underwater movies instead.

10. If people stay away, maybe scientists can control the diseases.

Chapter 6

Exercise 5 Combining Sentences with Appositives
Answers will vary. Sample answers are given.

1. I watched my favorite television program, *Nerds on the Run*, tonight.

2. Greg studied hard for Tuesday's test, a science midterm.

3. I'm glad Ollie's, the closest Chinese restaurant, is open again.

4. I received an e-mail from my friend Suki in Thailand.

5. My sister's bird, Shakespeare, can laugh.

Exercise 13 Combining Sentences by Inserting Phrases

1. The College Board and the Educational Testing Service, the producers of the SAT I, produce other tests, too.

2. They also produce the SAT II tests, achievement tests in individual subjects.

3. In 1995, the College Board recalculated test takers' mean SAT I score, the average score.

4. Running from 200 to 800, the scores are also given as percentiles.

5. In 1941, the mean score, reflecting the results of only ten thousand students, was about 500.

6. Then more and more students took the test, resulting in lower individual scores.

7. To score well, students must prepare carefully for the test.
8. Preparing better now means higher scores.
9. Students take practice tests to gain confidence for the real test.

CHAPTER REVIEW

Exercise B Combining Sentences
Answers will vary. Sample sentences are given.

1. The 1941 film *Sergeant York*, starring Gary Cooper as York, is about the life of the pacifist soldier Alvin York.
2. Director Oliver Stone's film *JFK*, with its controversial interpretation, is about the assassination of President Kennedy in 1963.
3. The film *The Lion in Winter*, which portrayed a conflict between Henry II and Eleanor of Aquitaine, won many Oscars when it was released in 1968.
4. *Gandhi*, a movie about the life and times of Mohandas K. Gandhi, was the 1982 Best Picture of the Year.
5. In 1992, Spike Lee made a film biography of Malcolm X, an African American leader.
6. Kirk Douglas starred in *Lust for Life*, a 1956 film adapted from Irving Stone's biography of Vincent van Gogh.
7. Starring Meryl Streep and Robert Redford, *Out of Africa* is a film about the writer Karen Blixen.
8. From seeing Gordon Parks's 1976 film about the folk singer called Leadbelly, I learned that the folk singer's name was Huddie Ledbetter.
9. Steven Spielberg made a film about the courageous Oskar Schindler, showing one person making a great difference.
10. The television miniseries *Shogun* aired in 1980, introducing American audiences to the ways of imperial Japan.

Chapter 7

Exercise 9 Combining Sentences Using Adjective Clauses
Ask students to defend their decision about what information to subordinate. Sample answers are given.

1. Cisneros attended the Writers Workshop at the University of Iowa, where she learned to become a writer.
2. At the Writers Workshop, which has a terrific reputation, Cisneros improved her writing skills dramatically.
3. Her Mexican American heritage, which provided her with a source of ideas for her fiction, made her stand out among other young writers.
4. Cisneros, who wrote a group of stories about her childhood, put them in her first book, entitled *The House on Mango Street*.
5. Her next book, which won critical acclaim and earned her popular recognition, was entitled *Woman Hollering Creek*.

Exercise 10 Combining Sentences Using Adverb Clauses
Answers will vary. Sample answers are given.

1. After *Bless Me, Ultima* by Anaya won as the best novel written by a Chicano in 1972, Anaya wrote many other books.
2. Before Anaya became a full professor at the University of New Mexico, he taught in junior and senior high schools.
3. Anaya had already taught creative writing at the university for nineteen years when he retired in 1993.
4. Although Anaya has been described by *Newsweek* as "the most widely read Mexican American," until recently, his work was not known by many readers on the East Coast.

5. Even though his fame has given him a feeling of great satisfaction, Anaya remains by nature a quiet person.

Exercise 13 Revising Sentences to Create Parallel Structure
Answers will vary. Sample revisions are given.
1. The Middle East has witnessed decades of turmoil and a constant state of crisis.
2. Before the Gulf War, the United States and its allies tried persuasion and diplomacy.
3. Jordan borders Saudi Arabia, Iraq, and Syria.
4. In Egypt, you can see pyramids, ride along the Nile, and explore the streets of Cairo.
5. On Israel's Mediterranean beaches, you can try snorkeling and swimming.
6. In Iran, you can visit the ancient city of Isfahan, which is centrally located, and the city of Tehran, which is on the coast.
7. In Israel, people live in modern cities, in small towns, and on farms.
8. In Saudi Arabia, you can find schools for the children of American workers and for other students, too.
9. Some Americans like to work for oil companies in the Middle East for the high salaries and the lifestyle.
10. Visitors to Middle Eastern countries can visit never-changing communities and ever-changing ones.

CHAPTER REVIEW

Exercise D Editing to Create Parallel Structure
Answers will vary. Sample answers are given.
1. The historical period between the ninth and thirteenth centuries is called the Middle Ages, the Dark Ages, or the Medieval Period.
2. Some scholars describe the period as scientifically undeveloped, artistically backward, and Black Plague infested.
3. Other scholars describe the Middle Ages as teeming with ideas, exploding with energy, and flowering with economic growth.
4. Gothic cathedrals, originating in the Middle Ages, are both astonishingly tall and brilliantly lit.
5. Students at the universities in Paris that began during the Middle Ages learned what the great philosophers wrote, what the Church taught, and how to argue for their ideas.

GRAMMAR TEST: CHAPTERS 4–7

Exercise 3 Combining Sentences
Answers will vary. Sample sentences are given.
1. Whitman was a journalist, an essayist, and a poet.
2. Whitman held a variety of jobs, including teacher, printer, and newspaper writer.
3. He spent a great deal of time observing and walking, and he frequently went to the theater and the opera.
4. When Whitman's brother was wounded in the Civil War battle of Fredericksburg, Whitman went there to care for him, and the experience awakened him to the horrors of war.
5. "When Lilacs Last in the Dooryard Bloom'd," written in 1865, was Whitman's famous elegy on Lincoln.

Chapter 8

Exercise 8 Using the Active Voice
Answers will vary. Sample answers are given.
1. Keep the passive voice. The performer is not important. *Also accept,* In 1861, Kansas declared statehood.
2. Charles Dickens wrote *Great Expectations* in 1861.
3. Charles Garnier designed the Opera House in Paris.
4. Daily weather forecasts started in Great Britain.
5. In 1862, Union forces under Grant captured Forts Henry and Donelson.

6. In that same year, Victor Hugo penned *Les Misérables*.
7. In London, Gilbert Scott designed the Albert Memorial.
8. In 1863, the French captured Mexico City.
9. New Zealand's first railroad opened.
10. Louis Pasteur invented pasteurization in 1864.

Exercise 11 Revising and Editing a Paragraph

¹Whether she's dreaming or not, my friend claims that she has been granted two wishes that will come true. ²First of all, she wishes that each individual stop bickering with others. ³Then her goal is that each person pick a nonprofit organization to help. ⁴She thinks it is necessary that each of us take an active role in making our own piece of the world better. ⁵If she were able to improve the whole world with her two wishes, she would.

Chapter 11

CHAPTER REVIEW

Exercise B Editing Sentences
Answers may vary. Sample answers are given.

1. The pitcher took his cap, which was hanging from a hook in his locker.
2. The player's shoes, which were too small, hurt his feet.
3. The slumping batter learned a new trick, one which would help him, from an instructor.
4. While she was practicing in the batting cage, it began to rain.
5. The coach says our team needs to shape up because we are overweight and slow.
6. As manager, Reilly worked at a desk that was always piled with scouting reports.
7. With a big smile, the rookie got on the bus.

8. To keep the field in good condition, groundskeepers must give the grass lots of attention.
9. Management has arranged for the players to leave on a plane at 7 P.M.
10. The team was bought only by Mrs. Leary.
11. While he was running after a fly ball, he noticed some commotion in the stands.
12. The sports magazine's editorial applauded the team for trading players.
13. Because we are young but talented and aggressive, all sportswriters like our team's chances of winning.
14. People think that because we are young and inexperienced, we will make crucial mistakes.
15. C

Chapter 13

Exercise 5 Revising Sentences
Answers may vary. Sample answers are given.

1. At a world mathematics competition in Hong Kong, six American high school students astonished the judges.
2. For the first time in the history of the competition, all the students on the team achieved perfect scores on the exam.
3. In bringing home a win from the International Mathematical Olympics, the American team claimed victory over sixty-eight other countries.
4. Remarkably, every member of the American team answered all six questions correctly.
5. Because of its difficulty, the mathematics exam took a grueling nine hours to complete.
6. Consisting of only six questions, the test was brief.
7. However, by testing algebra, geometry, or numbers theory, each question was a complicated problem.

8. Since 1986, when Americans tied with Russian students, no American team has won the competition.

9. In training for the test, some teams, such as the one from China, live together and study year-round.

10. Hailing from New York, Massachusetts, Maryland, and Illinois, the Americans were coached by Walter Mientka, a professor of mathematics at the University of Nebraska.

Chapter 14

Exercise 9 Punctuating Dialogue
Answers may vary. Accept alternatives to dialogue breaks if they make sense.

[1]It's Friday, and Zoe and Joseph are having lunch in the school cafeteria. [2]"The new British group Ear Plugs is going to give a concert at the Imperial Theater next week," Zoe tells Joseph. [3]"When do tickets go on sale?" [4]Joseph asks. [5]"They're on sale starting tomorrow," Zoe replies. [6]"Well, why don't you go over there and get us a pair?" [7]"I can't," Zoe answers, "because tomorrow's a busy day for me. [8]My cousins are in town, and I have to show them around all day. [9]Why don't you go?" [10]"I can't do it either," says Joseph. [11]The two stare at each other across their food trays for what seems like hours. [12]"Are you talking to Nell again, Zoe?" [13]Joseph asks. [14]"Sort of," she replies. [15]"Well, can you 'sort of' sit through a concert with her?" he wonders aloud. [16]"I guess," Zoe answers. [17]"Are you thinking what I think you're thinking?" [18]He nods. [19]"OK," she says. [20]"I'll invite Nell to join us, and I'll ask her to go and pick up the tickets." [21]Joseph beams. [22]"Good thinking," he says.

Editing and Proofreading Worksheet 1
Answers will vary. A sample revision is given.

[1]What do writers John Updike and Robert Penn Warren have in common? [2]Well, among other things, [*accept no comma here*] each has written a poem about baseball. [3]John Updike, who has written other sports-related literature, wrote the poem "Tao in the Yankee Stadium Bleachers," and Robert Penn Warren wrote the poem "He Was Formidable." [4]Both of these poems appear in the book *Hummers, Knucklers, and Slow Curves: Contemporary Baseball Poems* (Urbana and Chicago: University of Illinois Press, 1991), an anthology. [5]The book's editor is Don Johnson.

[6]For people who thought that baseball and poetry were mutually exclusive, this is the book [7]to change their minds. [8]Baseball poetry, they'll see, goes beyond the ballad "Casey at the Bat"; this volume [*or . . . "Casey at the Bat." This volume. . . .*] includes eighty-four poems written by fifty-seven poets in the 1950s through the 1980s. [*or . . . the 1950's through the 1980's.*] [9]Some of them first appeared in the baseball literary magazine, *Spitfire*. [10]The poems Johnson has included here are as "varied, evocative, and enigmatic as the game itself," he claims. [11]They are odes, not to famous or legendary players, but to the game— [12]from the major leagues to the minor leagues, high school games, Little League contests, and pickup games in neighborhood fields or on the streets. [*or . . . but to the game, from the major leagues to. . . .*]

[13]The collection of poems in this book gets at the essence of the game of baseball. [14]For example, one poem, "The Base Stealer," begins by describing the potential base thief as follows: "taut like a tightrope walker." [15]Another, entitled "Pitcher," starts with the sentence "His art is eccentricity."

[16]In his forward to the poems in the book, Johnson writes the following: "Baseball is poetry. [17]Baseball is ballet. [18]Baseball is chess. [19]Baseball is mystery."

Editing and Proofreading Worksheet 2
Answers will vary. A sample revision is given.

[1]The new department store that had opened in the mall was hiring. [2]Reggie and several of his classmates lined up to fill out job applications in the hopes of getting an interview. [3]"I certainly need this job," Reggie said. [*Accept new paragraph before Reggie's statement.*]

[4]"Not as much as I need it," Irene replied.

[5]"But I need it more than either of you since I'm only $500 short on the car I have my eye on," said Ben.

[6]Irene laughed and said, [7]"Ben, you'll never save $500. [8]Not by the time you're twenty-one. [9]Not by the time you're ninety-nine! [10]You'll spend everything they pay you."

[11]Now Reggie laughed and said, "Hey, none of us even has the job yet, and there are fifty kids in line here for ten jobs."

[12]"What skills and qualities do you think they'll be looking for?" asked Ben. "Will they be impressed that I worked as a sales clerk?"

[13]"Did you say 'a sales clerk'?" Irene asked. [14]"You mean the time you worked at your uncle's bowling alley and handed out shoes?" she continued.

[15]"Oh, I pointed out where the balls were, too, and answered all the questions I was asked," he replied.

[16]Just as Ben was beginning to embellish his explanation, they came to the head of the line. [17]Reggie was the first to be spoken to.

[18]"Do you speak French fluently? [19]How about Russian? [20]Are you familiar with *blinis*, *fois gras*, and caviar? [21]We are looking for experienced sales help in the gourmet department." [Note italics for foreign words not in English dictionary; no italics for foreign words in English dictionary.]

[22]"Oh," said Reggie.

[23]"Oh," said Irene.

[24]"*Bon jour*," answered Ben.

CHAPTER REVIEW

Exercise C Adding Punctuation to Dialogue

Student's continuations will vary; look for variety in dialogue tags.

[1]Their senior year has just ended, and Maya and Dan are talking about their summers. [2]"The college I got into has asked me to read several books during the next two months," Maya complained, "but I'll be traveling and then so busy working that I don't know where I'll find the time." [Accept new paragraph before Maya's statement.]

[3]"How many books are we talking about?" Dan asked.

[4]"Eight!"

[5]"Really? [6]Eight?" [7]Dan responded. [8]"My school wants me to read four novels, but I've already read two of them."

[9]"Which ones?" Maya asked.

[10]"Oh, I read *Ragtime* by E. L. Doctorow and also Doris Lessing's *The Golden Notebook*," Dan replied.

[11]"*Ragtime* is on my list, too, Dan. [12]Maybe I'll just see the play or rent the video."

[13]"Don't do that," Dan answered. [14]"The book is far better than either one; you'll really like it."

[15]"Well," Maya wondered aloud, "what about the other seven on my list?"

Chapter 16

CHAPTER REVIEW

Exercise A Spelling with Prefixes and Suffixes

Sample answers are given. Students may think of others.

announced	copied
announcing	copying
announcement	miscopied
unannounced	miscopy
readable	miscopying
reading	recopy
unreadable	recopied
reread	recopying
rereading	imagined

misread	imagining
misreading	imaginable
reappoint	unimaginable
reappointed	tasted
reappointing	tasteful
reappointment	tasting
preappoint	retaste
appointed	retasted
appointing	retasting
appointment	tastefully
disappoint	untasted
disappointed	distaste
disappointing	distasteful
disappointment	distastefully

**CUMULATIVE REVIEW:
CHAPTERS 13–16**

Exercise D Proofreading a Passage

Doriot Anthony Dwyer, the great-grandniece of Susan B. Anthony, achieved a distinction of her own: She was the first woman to be appointed to a first chair in a major symphony orchestra. Dwyer, who began playing the flute at the age of eight, was trained at the Eastman School of Music in Rochester, New York. After getting her B.S. in music in 1943, she joined the Washington National Symphony. Two years later, she joined the Los Angeles Philharmonic as the second flutist. Then, in 1952, she joined the Boston Symphony as the first-chair flutist. In 1974, Dwyer was named to the Women's Hall of Fame of the Seneca Falls Historical Society in Seneca Falls, New York.

complete course

SADLIER-OXFORD

GRAMMAR FOR WRITING

Phyllis Goldenberg   Carol Domblewski

Elaine Epstein   Martin Lee

Senior Series Consultant

Beverly Ann Chin
Professor of English
University of Montana

Sadlier-Oxford
A Division of William H. Sadlier, Inc.
New York, New York 10005-1002

Reviewers

Dr. Muriel Harris
Writing Lab Director
English Dept.
Purdue University
West Lafayette, IN

Keith Yost
Program Director,
Humanities and
Language Arts
Tomball, TX

Ellen Young Swain
English Teacher
Cimarron High School
Cimarron, NM

Mel Farberman
Asst. Principal
of English
Cardozo High School
Bayside, NY

Galen Rosenberg
English Dept.
Coordinator
Los Altos High School
Los Altos, CA

Patricia Stack
English Teacher
South Park School
District
Library, PA

Donald L. Stephan
Retired English
Dept. Chair
Sidney High School
Sidney, OH

Rose F. Schmitt
English Teacher
Florida Air Academy
Melbourne, FL

Cary Fuller
English Teacher
Rye Country
Day School
Rye, NY

Roxanne Hoblitt
English Teacher
Belgrade High School
Belgrade, MT

Brad Rinn
English Teacher
Roseville High School
Roseville, CA

Barbara A. Mylite
UFT Teacher Center
Specialist
New York City Board
of Education

Patrick O'Reilly
English Teacher
Freeport High School
Freeport, NY

Peter J. Accardi
English Teacher
Chaminade High
School
Mineola, NY

John Manear
English Dept. Chair
Seton-La Salle
High School
Pittsburgh, PA

Carolyn Phipps
English Teacher
Wooddale High
School
Memphis, TN

Wanda Porter
English Dept. Head
Kamehameha
Secondary School
Honolulu, HI

Student Writers

Adam Andress
Clearwater, FL

Katherine Boone
Dallas, TX

Mark Boucher
Pennington, NJ

Jason Farago
Scarsdale, NY

Molly Gondek
Rocky Hill, CA

Pat Healy
Grosse Pointe
Farms, MI

Katherine Ivers
Meriden, CT

Rachel Kamins
Middletown, CT

Gene Liu
San Francisco, CA

Uthara Srinivasan
Flossmoor, IL

Anh Van Vu
Houston, TX

Lacey Waldron
El Cajon, CA

Andrew Young
Yonkers, NY

Acknowledgments

Every good faith effort has been made to locate the owners of copyrighted material to arrange permission to reprint selections. In several cases this has proved impossible.

Thanks to the following for permission to reprint copyrighted materials.

Excerpt from "A Personal Account of the Fall of the Berlin Wall" by Andreas Ramos. Copyright ©1994 by Andreas Ramos. Reprinted by permission of the author.

Excerpt from "Baseball's Negro Leagues" by Matthew Eisenberg. Copyright © 1994 by *The Concord Review*, www.tcr.org

"The Lincoln–Douglas Debates," an excerpt reprinted with the permission of Simon & Schuster, Inc. from *Lincoln* by David Herbert Donald. Copyright © 1995 by David Herbert Donald

"On Hardy's *The Mayor of Casterbridge*" by Dennis Potter. Copyright © 1978 by Dennis Potter.

"Silk Parachute" by John McPhee. Reprinted by permission; © 1997 John McPhee. Originally in *The New Yorker*. All rights reserved.

"Ten Reasons Why I Vote" by Ellen Goodman. Reprinted with permission of *The Miami Herald*.

"The Ticks Are Back" by Frederic Golden. © 1998 Time Inc. Reprinted with permission.

"Understanding Human Behavior," an excerpt from *Understanding Human Behavior: an Introduction to Psychology*, Second Edition by James V. McConnell, copyright © 1977 by Holt, Rhinehart and Winston, reprinted by permission of the publisher.

Photo Credits

Graphistock/ David Sokosh: Ch. 6.
International Stock/Ryan Williams: Ch. 10.

Hulton Getty-Liaison Agency: Ch. 12.
Photonica/Dean Hollowood: Ch. 7; Sharon Smith: Ch. 11;

Ray Dean: Ch. 15; Simon Larbatestier: Ch. 16.
Tony Stone Images/James Martin: Ch. 1; Ray Massey: Ch. 2; Lucien Clergue: Ch. 3;

Laurence Dutton: Chs. 4 & 5; P. Crowthers & S. Carter: Ch. 8; Myron Ch. 9; Paul Edmondson: Ch. 13; Jon Ortner: Ch. 14.

Dear Student:

This book is designed to take the mystery out of grammar and to help you become a better, more confident writer. *Grammar for Writing* does just what its title suggests: it shows how the rules of grammar, usage, and mechanics—the conventions of standard English—can make your writing not just correct but more powerful and persuasive, too.

As a student, you are being challenged to write correctly and effectively not only in your English classes but also in social studies, science, and history classes as well. High schools all over America have raised their expectations for graduates. If you have taken a standardized test recently or are preparing to take one soon, you know this only too well. The writing sections of these tests have grown more rigorous and more demanding than ever.

However, there are reasons to speak and write well other than to score well on standardized tests. People judge you by the way you write and speak. Your use of English is evaluated in the writing you do in school, on job and college applications, and in many different kinds of careers. That doesn't mean that you have to say, "To whom am I speaking?" when a friend calls, but you should be able to speak and write correctly when the situation calls for it—in a formal speaking or writing assignment, on a test, and in an interview. The more you practice using standard English, the more comfortable and confident you will become when you write and speak.

As you become a more confident writer, you will find new excitement in recording your thoughts, ideas, opinions, and experiences. You will also see that communicating effectively is the most important way to influence others. As you write about the topics you care about, you will find that people in every part of your life—your teachers, your peers, your bosses, your parents, and your community—gain respect for you and are influenced by the things you write and say.

No textbook can make writing easy. Good writers work hard and revise their work often to find just the right words to move their audience. Consequently, in *Grammar for Writing* you will find a lot of exercises called "Write What You Think." These exercises are designed to help you develop clear, logical arguments to persuade people that your opinion is right. These exercises will sharpen your thinking as well as your writing skills.

Of course, you already know how to write. You've been doing it for years. No one has to prove to you that writing is important—it just *is*. But your writing can always be improved, and the best way to improve it is to learn and practice the skills and strategies in this book. In *Grammar for Writing*, we have tried to present the rules of grammar as simply as possible; whether you are merely refreshing your memory or are learning the concepts for the first time, you'll be able to understand the rules and apply them to your writing.

All of the skills you learn and practice in this book—grammar, writing, thinking—will last you a lifetime.

Good luck, and study well!

CONTENTS

COMPOSITION

GRAMMAR

USAGE

MECHANICS

The Writing Process

Prewriting

◖ **Prewriting** is all the thinking, planning, and organizing you do
before you actually start writing.

Sometimes, you have a burning desire to write, and you know exactly what
you want to say. More often, though, you and other writers can't start
writing so quickly. Here are five of the many strategies that writers find
helpful during the prewriting stage, when they face a blank page or screen.

PREWRITING STRATEGIES

1. *What if?* **questions** One way to demonstrate creativity is to imagine
   what hasn't happened or what might happen in the future.

You might ask yourself far-out questions about anything. For example,
"What if I had been born in a different age?" and "What if I didn't live in
this country?" Or ask *What if?* questions about a broad assigned topic that
you need to narrow down. For example, if a teacher assigns you the general
topic "The Way West," you might make a list such as the following *What
if?* questions; they can help you focus on a challenging but narrower topic.

> What if gold had not been discovered in 1848 in California?
>
> What if there had been railroads all the way to California in 1848—
> or airplanes?
>
> What if the Rocky Mountains had been impassable?

2. **Brainstorming** Brainstorming is related to *What if?* questions
   because when you brainstorm, you let your mind roam freely to create
   an open-ended list of words and phrases.

Begin by selecting a single word or topic, and write down everything that
comes to mind regarding that word or topic. Don't evaluate what you
write down; just keep those ideas coming. If you brainstorm with a group
or a partner, make sure one person keeps the record of everything that is
said, and do not criticize one another's contributions to the list. When
you run out of thoughts, go through the list item by item, and circle the
entries that most appeal to you as topics to write about.

Enriching Your Vocabulary

A *strategy* is a plan
for achieving a
particular goal.
The related word,
stratagem, is a trick
meant to achieve a
goal through some
deception. The
stratagem of the
Greeks in the war
against Troy was
to pretend to
withdraw, leaving
behind them the
Trojan Horse, a
giant wooden horse
that concealed a
powerful raiding
army.

ASSIGNMENT: *Select an aspect of law in the old West, and write three hundred words about it.*

BRAINSTORMING LIST:

Cowboys	*Ranchers*	*Tombstone & other towns*
Famous gunfighters	*Wyatt Earp*	*Saloons and card games*
Stagecoach holdups	*Nonviolence?*	*Stereotypes of lawmen in movies and TV*

3. Freewriting This strategy for finding a topic to write about is similar to brainstorming but involves *nonstop* writing.

When you freewrite, let your writing wander. Don't worry about writing complete sentences or about grammar or spelling. If you get stuck, just write the same word over until you get a new thought. Keep moving forward; don't back up to make corrections. Write without stopping for five minutes.

TOPIC: *Cattle drives*

When did cattle drives happen? For how long? Where did they start from? Texas? Where did they end? Why? How many cowboys needed for how many animals? What were the trails like? Life on the trails, life on the trails, what can I say about that? How about the dangers and pleasures of life on the trail? Or how about famous cowboys? Cow towns? Why did cattle drives happen? Huh? That's a pretty basic question. Basic is good. OK. That's what I want to focus on. What the purpose of the cattle drives was in the first place.

4. Clustering, Mapping, or Webbing If you already know a topic well, this strategy is helpful for gathering and organizing details or for breaking a large topic into smaller parts.

First, write your topic (or any word or phrase) in the middle of a piece of paper, and then circle it. Around the circled topic, write subtopics—related words and phrases. Circle each new word or phrase, and connect it to your original topic. Each new word or phrase may have subtopics, too. Keep going until you run out of thoughts. Refer to the example on the following page.

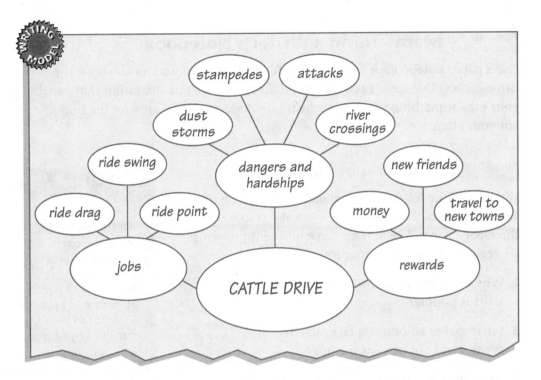

5. Writer's Notebook This prewriting strategy involves keeping a separate notebook or folder (paper or electronic) in which you jot down experiences and thoughts about anything that interests you.

Try to keep the writer's notebook going at all times. Then, when your teacher gives you an assignment to "write about something that you care about," you can convert your writer's notebook notes into effective paragraphs, essays, and short stories. Include in your notebook any quotations or thoughts you get from films, interviews, artworks, or even cartoons. Explain in your notebook why these ideas affected you.

Mon. 5/2.

Home sick; watched hours of TV. Saw movie about lonely, hard, but rewarding life of homesteader in the old West. Got new appreciation of value of hard work and perseverance. Life was tough then! Simple pleasures were important—still are, I think. What must life have been like for my great-grandparents when they first came to this country and struggled to get a foothold? I wonder. Ought to find out sometime.

Exercise 1 Maintaining a Writer's Notebook

Use a paper notebook or an electronic file to keep a quotation notebook for three consecutive days. Each day, write down at least one quotation that caught your ear—something you read or heard. Include a note about why the quotation got your attention. Students' quotations will vary.

Exercise 2 Thinking of Topic Ideas

For each of the following numbered items, come up with two topics that you could write about in a one- to three-page paper. Use at least three different prewriting strategies to generate writing topics. Students' topics will vary. Ask them to describe the different prewriting strategies they used to generate their writing topics.

1. Why a particular celebrity, politician, or artist is popular

2. What makes an object, place, activity, or event stand out in your memory

3. Something unusual that happened to you and that you're willing to share with readers

4. A school, local, or national issue you care about

Exercise 3 Narrowing a Topic

Choose two of the broad, general topics below. For each one you select, suggest three narrower topics that you can cover in a three-page essay.

TOO BROAD Television

LIMITED The fall's new sitcoms; Monday night's lineup; the best soap opera

1. Flowers
2. Sea Travel
3. Settling North America
4. College

Writing Hint

All five prewriting strategies covered here deal with *narrowing a topic*. Narrowing is a key to successful writing. How can you tell if a topic is too broad, too narrow, or just right?

- If you can break your topic down into more than five subtopics, it may be too broad. Consider one of the narrower subtopics to write about.

- If you cannot break your topic down into more than two subtopics, it may be too narrow already. Think more broadly.

Students' topics will vary, but each one should be limited enough to explore fully within three pages.

Exercise 4 Gathering Supporting Details

Choose one of the narrower topics you identified in Exercise 3. Generate ideas and details about that topic by brainstorming, clustering, or asking *What if?* questions. Students' topics will vary. Ask them to describe the different prewriting strategies they used to generate their supporting details. These notes will be used in Exercise 7, page 15, when students have learned to outline and draft a paragraph or essay.

Prewriting and Drafting

🖊 Use your prewriting notes to create an **outline**. An outline forces you to make two important decisions about your prewriting notes: (1) which main ideas and supporting details to use in your draft and (2) in what order to present them.

The outline at right is rough. You may wish to add details or to write your outline in full sentences. Either way, your outline should help guide you as you draft your paragraph or essay.

🖊 One of the most important questions to ask yourself before you write is "What should my style be?" Writing style is determined by two things: your audience and your purpose.

Your **audience** is the person or persons who will read what you write. Your **purpose** may be to describe, to explain, to tell what happened, to persuade, or to entertain. Or you may have a combination of purposes. Together, the audience and the purpose will determine your **style**—the manner in which you express your thoughts.

It may seem obvious, but you would be surprised at the differences between a persuasive letter to your congressional representative and an informative news article for your school paper—even if the information is the same in both cases. Consider the different styles of the following paragraphs.

WRITING MODEL

Rough Outline
1998 Home Run Race

Background on Roger Maris controversy

    Babe Ruth's record

    Maris breaks record

    Fan reaction

Mark McGwire sets pace in '98

    Steroid controversy

    Sammy Sosa keeps up

    Others also in race

McGwire and Sosa break Maris's record

    Dates and stats

Home run race great for baseball

    Attendance way up

    Every at-bat covered by TV

    Sportsmanship of two competitors hailed

    Baseball back as national pastime

WRITING MODEL

Dear Citizens!

The Acme Contractors are at it again! Enormous bulldozers have arrived on watershed lands near Route 567 and are destroying the habitat of some of New Jersey's last indigenous species. Within sight of three hotels, a sports complex, and a shopping mall lies the only remaining scrap of the swampy marshlands that once covered northern New Jersey. Write to your town councilors and demand that they rescind the permit to build, and that they protect this fragile ecosystem!

> *Dear Acme Contractors:*
>
> *As a resident of a neighboring town, I am concerned about the environmental impact of your construction project on Route 567 in Fayettesville, New Jersey. The watershed lands have already been tremendously damaged by the three hotels, sports complex, and shopping mall built nearby. Please send me documentation of any environmental impact studies you have done that show how you intend to preserve or minimize your impact on the habitat of the area's wildlife and on the fragile marshland ecosystem.*

The purpose of the letter to the Acme Contractors is to request information. The purpose of the letter to citizens is to persuade community members to act against the construction project. While the information in the letters is very similar, the different purposes and audiences yield letters with different styles. Consider your own purpose and audience before you begin writing.

● **Drafting** is the step in the writing process in which you put your thoughts into sentences and paragraphs.

When you have narrowed your topic, generated prewriting notes, laid out an outline, and considered your audience and purpose, it's time to apply the following strategies for writing your first draft.

DRAFTING STRATEGIES

1. Focus. Find a quiet place, and concentrate on the task.

Try to write your first draft in a single sitting. If you can't, take a break, and then put in another drafting session.

2. Start early. Allow enough time to let your draft sit awhile (overnight is ideal) before you go on to revise, edit, and proofread it.

Don't be a procrastinator. Write your first draft early so that you have enough time to revise it before handing it in.

3. Think in sentences. Write complete sentences, and vary their structures and lengths.

As you write, try to develop an awareness of each sentence. Listen to the way the sentences sound together in paragraphs. Say the sentences to yourself, or read them aloud.

4. **Stay flexible.** Follow the general direction of your outline, but feel free to add or drop details.

You may come up with brilliant new ideas as you write. Use them!

Exercise 5 Making an Outline

For this assignment, your audience is your language arts class. Your purpose is to inform. Choose a topic you know something about—a hobby, an interest, something you've recently studied. Generate prewriting notes. Then write an outline to plan a two- or three-page paper. Students' outlines will vary but should fit their topic and reflect supporting details. Check that outlines are suitable for a two- or three-page paper.

Exercise 6 Drafting Part of a Report

Using your outline for Exercise 5, draft two or three pages. Remember who your audience is and what your purpose is—to give information. Students' drafts will vary. This report will be revised and edited in Lesson 1.3, Exercise 10, page 18.

Exercise 7 Outlining and Drafting Another Paper *Working Together*

Use the prewriting notes you made for a limited topic in Exercise 4, page 12. First, choose and describe your audience and purpose in writing. Then prepare an outline. Before you begin drafting, meet with a partner or small group to discuss what you're planning to write. See if you can clearly summarize your topic, main idea(s), and supporting details. Use the Drafting Strategies above as you prepare your paper. Students' outlines and papers will vary but should pay attention to audience and purpose, and they should reflect any insights gathered in the small-group discussion.

Revising and Editing

◖ When you **revise** and **edit**, you shape your draft into its almost-final form.

At these stages in the writing process, you try to make your draft clearer. Now is the time to add new information, to cut words or sentences, to change the order in which information appears, and to replace weak words with more effective ones. At this point, you also can fix sentences that have grammar or usage problems such as misplaced modifiers or incorrect subject-verb agreement. Use the revising strategies below to help you improve your first draft.

REVISING STRATEGIES

1. **Content** Can you summarize your main idea(s) or the main event of your paper? Do you have enough supporting details? Do you have too many? Will adding or cutting details improve your paper? Do you need more background information? Is everything you've written relevant?

2. **Organization** Does your introduction grab the reader's attention? Can you improve your draft by rearranging paragraphs or by moving sentences? Do you present your information in an order that makes sense for your purpose and audience? Do you need to add any transitions? Do you have an effective concluding paragraph?

3. **Style** Do your sentences read smoothly? Have you varied their structures, beginnings, and lengths? Would some sentences work better combined? Is your writing too formal or informal? Have you deleted unnecessary words or phrases? Have you used parallel constructions wherever possible? In short, are you satifisfied with *how* you say *what* you say?

4. **Word Choice** Look for vague nouns, verbs, and modifiers that you can replace with more precise words. Look for clichés or overused words that you can replace with fresh ones to enliven your descriptions. Is your choice of vocabulary geared to your intended audience? Should you replace any difficult words with simpler ones? Do you need to define any technical terms you've used?

After revising for content, organization, style, and word choice, you must think about editing. When you edit, you look for grammar and usage errors. Keep the following editing issues in mind as you look over your paper.

EDITING STRATEGIES

1. **Complete Sentences** Are there any sentence fragments or run-on sentences? Does each sentence begin with a capital letter and end with an appropriate punctuation mark?

2. **Verbs** Do all present-tense verbs, present-perfect verbs, and present-progressive verbs agree with their subjects in tense and in number? Are verb tenses consistent and correct?

3. **Pronouns** Do all your pronouns agree with their antecedents? Are the pronoun references clear?

4. **Adjectives and Adverbs** Are your modifiers used correctly, with adjectives modifying nouns and pronouns and with adverbs modifying verbs, adjectives, and other adverbs? Are your comparisons complete? Have you used *-er/more* and *-est/most* forms correctly?

5. **Parallel Structure** Are similar grammatical forms used to express similar ideas? (See Grammar, Lesson 7.7, for more on parallel structure.)

◖ **Peer editing** involves giving feedback to your classmates and getting help from them on your writing. Peer editing can involve two partners or a small group.

Peer editors can make specific suggestions for improving your paper. They can ask questions about any unclear writing or help with word choice and with organization. They can also give positive feedback, telling you what they like best about your writing.

Some Questions for Peer Editors

1. Which parts of the paper do I like best and least? Where is the writing most interesting?

2. What are the main ideas, or themes?

3. Has the writer provided enough supporting details?

4. Are any sections of the paper unclear or incomplete?

5. Does the introduction grab me? Is the conclusion effective?

6. Does the word choice "sound like" the writer? Or do the words sound unnatural?

7. What advice can I give about grammar and usage?

Exercise 8 Revising and Editing a Letter to a Government Official

Focusing on the four issues of content, organization, style, and word choice, revise the following letter to a state representative. Your purpose is to persuade. There is no single correct way to revise this letter. Feel free to add additional details and to cut sentences that stray from the main idea. Consider adding transitions, combining or breaking apart sentences, and offering examples. Students' revisions will vary.

Dear Representative:

¹I'm writing to you. ²Because I wish to bring to your attention the icky state of our local park, James Park. ³The park, once beautiful and long a cherished neighborhood gathering place, has become a pain and even a hazard. ⁴It is no longer a place families can enjoy. ⁵Us, the concerned citizens of your district, urge you to look into ways to bring their park back.

⁶In the past, the park was the scene of picnics, concerts, fairs. ⁷And many positive community activities took place there. ⁸Sadly, these events don't happen now because our park has become a dangerous, run-down eyesore. ⁹The lighting is crummy, the benches are broke, the bicycle paths are overgrown, all the landscaping and ball fields are bad news, and all the rowboats leaking. ¹⁰There aren't enough workers to give our beloved park the care and attention it asks for. ¹¹In short, James Park is a disaster. ¹²You need to act. ¹³Show you care. ¹⁴Bring our park back to life, and you'll quickly discover how supportive your constituency was, you gotta care about stuff like this. ¹⁵Show us the dough!

Exercise 9 Revising and Editing a Paper

Use the guidelines in this lesson to revise any paper you've written for this or another class. In addition, edit the paper sentence by sentence by asking yourself the questions from Editing Strategies listed on page 17. Students' edits should reflect the information in Revising Strategies as well as the Editing Strategies.

Exercise 10 Peer Editing *Working Together*

1. Revise and edit the paper you drafted in Lesson 1.2, Exercise 6. Use the revising and editing strategies to improve your draft.

2. Work with a partner to peer edit your paper. Allow your partner to read your paper without your input. Your partner should respond to your writing using the peer editing questions on page 17 as a guide. Encourage your peer editor to make comments directly on your pages.

3. Review the peer editing comments on your paper and incorporate those that you feel will improve your writing. Don't be discouraged if you have to rewrite some passages. Students' revisions will vary.

Proofreading and Publishing

🔹 When you **proofread**, you search for mistakes in spelling, punctuation, and capitalization.

Readers will judge your writing, to a greater or lesser extent, by your use of the conventions of standard written English. Don't let errors in spelling, punctuation, and capitalization slip by. Even the most careful writers need to proofread their work!

PROOFREADING QUESTIONS

1. **Spelling** Are all words spelled correctly? Use a college dictionary or the spell checker on your computer to make necessary corrections. Watch out for words that you've spelled correctly but that don't fit the sentence (*their* instead of *there* or *they're*, for example). Your spell checker won't catch these homonyms.

2. **Capitalization** Do all proper nouns and proper adjectives begin with capital letters? Have you capitalized a word that's supposed to start with a lowercase letter? Do all your sentences or direct quotations begin with capital letters?

3. **Punctuation** Have you used commas and other punctuation marks correctly? Is dialogue correctly punctuated?

4. **Apostrophes** Do contractions and possessive nouns have apostrophes in the right place? Do possessive pronouns such as *its* have no apostrophe?

🔹 A **proofreading log** is a record of corrections you've made. It lists your mistakes in spelling, punctuation, and capitalization—and your corrections.

Keep a proofreading log in a separate notebook or folder. Review the information in your log occasionally so that you don't keep repeating the same mistakes. Use the marks on the chart on the following page to correct your errors.

🔹 **Publishing** means sharing or presenting what you've written.

Although some of your writing is meant for your eyes only, you may wish to share much of what you write with a wider audience. You can share it by reading aloud, e-mailing, or videotaping. You might also leave an anthology of writing models for future twelfth-graders.

Enriching Your Vocabulary

The verb *transpose*, used in proofreading (see page 20), comes from the Latin *transponere*, which means "to change the position of." *Transpose* can also be used in the sense of "to change in nature or form." The director *transposed* the setting of *Romeo and Juliet* from Verona to Civil War America.

■ See **Mechanics, Lesson 14.5,** for more on punctuating dialogue.

Writing Hint

To find out more about how to reach a wider audience, check out *Market Guide for Young Writers*, by Kathy Henderson. This book will help you submit your writing to national magazines and to writing contests.

Proofreading Symbols

CORRECTION	SYMBOL	EXAMPLE
Delete (remove).	ℓ	She ate a ~~a~~ peach.
Insert.	∧	He star^red in the movie.
Transpose (switch).	⌐⌐	I only ate one.
Capitalize.	≡	did Mayor Jones show up?
Make lowercase.	/	Were other Mayors there?
Start a new paragraph.	¶	¶"Yes," they cried.
Add space.	#	We visited New#York.
Close up space.	◡	She loves foot ball.

Exercise 11 **Proofreading a Paragraph**

Find and correct every error in the following paragraph. Write the corrected paragraph on a separate piece of paper. Answers will vary. A sample answer is given.

¹*A Portrait of the artist as a Young Man:* by James joyce is a novel in five sections. ²It is considered by many ~~two~~ to be the best example of a book that shows the psychological and ~~morale~~ moral development of its ~~mane~~ main character? ³It includes the rich symbolic and stream-of-consciousness language that characterized Joyce's later works. ⁴The novel is autobiographical, portraying the early years of Stephen Dedalus, a character who reappears in Joyce's masterpiece, *Ulysses* (1922). ⁵Joyce wrote each of the Five sections of *A Portrait of the Artist as a Young Man* ~~with a narrator who~~ in a third-person voice that reflects stephen's age and emotional State. ⁶For example, his earliest childhood memories are written in simple, childlike language.

You may wish to have students create an editing/proofreading practice for classmates. Have them write one or two paragraphs that have at least ten mistakes in grammar, usage, spelling, punctuation, and capitalization. Have them exchange paragraphs, and have each student correct the paragraph they receive.

Publishing Suggestions

WRITTEN WORDS
Magazine of student writing
School or local paper
Local or national poetry, story, or essay contest
Class anthology
Writing portfolio
Letters/e-mail

SPOKEN WORDS
Speech
Audiocassette
Oral interpretation
Radio broadcast
Reader's theater
Interview
Debate

MULTIMEDIA
Book with illustrations
Videotape
Performance with music
Bulletin board or library display
Community literature festival

Writing Effective Paragraphs and Essays

Unity

◗ A paragraph has **unity** (it is unified) when all of its sentences focus on a single main idea.

As you draft a paragraph, focus on one main idea. Your single focus will help your audience stay with you. Then, when you revise and edit, you'll have another chance to improve unity by dropping any irrelevant sentences or details.

◗ A **topic sentence** states the paragraph's main idea.

Although a topic sentence is most often the first or second sentence, announcing what's coming in the rest of the paragraph, you can place a topic sentence in the middle or at the end of a paragraph. When a topic sentence appears at the end of a paragraph, it serves as a summary statement.

Some paragraphs—especially, narrative and descriptive paragraphs—have no topic sentences. But even a paragraph without a directly stated topic sentence usually suggests, or implies, a main idea.

◗ A paragraph may have not only an opening topic sentence but also a **clincher sentence**, which ends the paragraph.

Use clincher sentences for the following purposes: to restate a topic, to summarize, to add persuasive power, and to create a transition to the main idea of the next paragraph.

Read the following two paragraphs about vintage baseball. Each is an example of a paragraph with unity.

Topic sentence stating boom in vintage baseball

Statistics that support main idea

Topic sentence about the Old Bethpage league

[1]To most people, the idea of playing baseball without a glove probably sounds like canoeing without a paddle. [2]At the Old Bethpage Village Restoration in Old Bethpage, New York, however, it's the only sporting way to play. [3]Vintage baseball is booming around the United States. [4]At least 70 programs are fielding teams that play by rules of past eras, which range from 1845 to 1924; many such clubs have appeared just in the past five years. [5]The biggest and most competitive of all is the Old Time Base Ball Program at Old Bethpage.

[6]"Ours is the only program with full-blown leagues," says Ken Balcom, the museum village's assistant site director. [7]Old-time baseball

games have been played here since 1980 as one of the village's living-history demonstrations, like quilt-making and black-

Incident that supports main idea — smithing. [8]The program got a boost four years ago when hundreds of baseball-hungry Long Islanders, disgusted that the major leagues' millionaires were out on strike, converged on Old Bethpage to watch or to play an older, purer game. [9]Today, the program

Clincher sentence involves 130 players, all volunteers, on ten teams in two leagues, over a 60-game season.

—Doug Stewart, "The Old Ball Game"

SKILLS FOR MAINTAINING UNITY

1. **Topic Sentence** As with any sentence, a topic sentence can be long or short, simple or complex. Stewart may have chosen any number of ways to state the main idea of his first paragraph. For example, he may have written the following topic sentence.

> The cry "Play ball" is changing to "Play *old* ball" as vintage baseball catches on around the country.

2. **One Main Idea** Each of the model paragraphs sticks to its main idea. Notice how Stewart grabs the reader with the first sentence of the first paragraph but avoids cluttering either paragraph with unnecessary sentences.

3. **Clincher Sentence** Stewart uses a clincher sentence at the end of the second paragraph to restate—with more specifics—the idea expressed in the topic sentence of the first paragraph.

Exercise 1 Revising a Paragraph

1. Which of the following sentences would work in place of the topic sentence in the first paragraph by Stewart? Give reasons for your choice.

    a. Playing vintage baseball is the only way to go.

    b. Old-time baseball programs are a new sensation. Expresses the same idea as the topic sentence: Vintage baseball is booming . . . .

2. Which of the following sentences could serve as a clincher sentence for the first paragraph by Stewart? Explain your choice.

    a. People are streaming to old-time baseball games in Old Bethpage and all over the country. This is a restatement of the paragraph's topic sentence.

    b. In vintage baseball games, like the real old-time baseball contests, the scores are very high.

Elaborating with Supporting Details

◗ **Elaboration**, or **development**, is the process of adding details to support a main idea.

You must make your paragraphs interesting, specific, and complete. To do so, develop or support each paragraph's main idea by using the following kinds of details: **facts**, **statistics**, **quotations**, **definitions**, **anecdotes** or **incidents**, **examples**, **reasons**, and **comparisons**.

Don't hesitate to use more than one kind of supporting detail in a paragraph. Just make certain that each sentence adds something to the paragraph that helps readers to better understand your subject or to appreciate your view.

The writer of the following paragraph realized that the first draft did not contain enough specific details to support her topic sentence. Notice the details she added during revision to elaborate on her main idea and to interest her readers.

Writing Hint

Wandering from one idea to a completely different idea is fine in freewriting but not in the paragraphs you're writing for an audience. Delete or revise sentences that do not support your main idea, or you may confuse readers.

WRITING MODEL

, from 776 B.C. to A.D. 394,
¹In ancient Greece athletic games took place every four years at
sacred site
of Olympia   Warring city-states always observed
the ~~same place~~. ²A truce ~~was always observed~~ as the games
dangerous chariot race in which drivers drove
teams of horses over a treacherous course
approached; it lasted for the duration of the contests. ³A ~~horse race~~

opened each series of Olympic games. ⁴But the greatest event was the
, which included a foot race, wrestling, jumping,
and throwing both the discus and the javelin
pentathlon. ⁵In 1896, a French baron revived the games in Athens.
^Pierre de Coubertin,

Exercise 2 Improving Unity and Adding Details

Revise the paragraph on the following page. Cross out any words or sentences that destroy the paragraph's unity by getting away from the main idea. Then, from the list below the paragraph, select the details that you think would improve it. Write the letter of the detail where you think

it belongs in the paragraph. You may want to insert some of the details as phrases
or clauses. Then write the fully revised paragraph on a separate piece of paper.

Answers may vary. A sample revision is given. For additional practice in adding details to a paragraph, assign

Exercise 2 in
Lesson 4.1,
page 102.

¹In addition to athletics, the ancient Greeks excelled in architecture. ²The
elegant but simple buildings they designed reflected their love of balance and
their appreciation of beauty. ³No buildings meant more to them than their
temples. ⁴^D~~Greek artisans produced fine pottery~~. ⁵The Parthenon, which is still
standing, is a good example of the Greek belief in harmony and proportion. ⁶Its
carefully carved columns create the impression of height and lightness. ⁷^C~~Greek
sculptors also believed in perfect harmony~~.

Details

A. Most Greeks were farmers who used ox-drawn plows.
B. Pericles rebuilt Athens.
C. Many public buildings of our time use graceful stone columns
   modeled on those of the Greeks.
D. The Greek temples were built in honor of gods and goddesses.

Exercise 3 Improving Unity and Adding Details

Work with a partner or small group to revise the following paragraph. Cross out
any words or sentences that destroy the paragraph's unity by getting away from
the main idea. Then write the letter of the detail where you think it belongs in
the paragraph. You may want to insert some of the details as phrases or clauses.
Then write the fully revised paragraph on a separate piece of paper.

Answers will vary. A sample revision is given. For additional practice in adding details to a paragraph, assign

Exercise C
on page 122.

¹Any discussion of written history should begin with the work of the great
Greek historians Herodotus (485–424 B.C.) and Thucydides (460–395 B.C.).
²Herodotus was the first to attempt to gather and analyze information about the
past. ³^AHe traveled widely and learned firsthand about cultures and geography.
⁴In so doing, he presented a great deal of useful information about the ancient
world. ⁵~~Egyptian scribes of an earlier era wanted only to show the deeds of the
pharaohs~~. ⁶Thucydides, who wrote *History of the Peloponnesian Wars*, improved
on the methods of Herodotus. ⁷^BHe tried to present a balanced perspective on
events and to include only information he could substantiate. ⁸^D~~In the century~~

~~following the wars between Athens and Sparta, Alexander spread Greek~~

~~civilization across a huge empire~~. Inserted details may be written as clauses.

Details

A. Herodotus wrote *History of the Persian Wars*.
B. Herodotus did not always distinguish fact from legend in his writings.
C. Athens was defeated by Sparta in the Peloponnesian Wars.
D. Thucydides set an example of impartial reporting for later historians.

Exercise 4 Writing a Paragraph from Notes

On a separate piece of paper, write a unified, well-developed paragraph based on the information on the note card below. You do not need to use all of the information. Make sure your paragraph contains a clear topic sentence.

Socrates (469–399 B.C.)

One of the most influential figures in history and philosophy

Son of poor stonecutter

Championed the use of reason to challenge conventional ideas

Spent his days talking and listening to people

Left no writings of his beliefs; Plato would record his ideas later

Believed that through knowledge people could discover how to act

His question-answer technique that used reason to examine beliefs came to be known as the "Socratic method."

Seen as troublemaker and dangerous corrupter of Athens' youth

Accused of not honoring the gods

Condemned to death by Athenian jury; had to drink hemlock (deadly poison)

Plato, his most famous pupil, was an aristocrat.

Plato was 28 when his mentor died.

Students' paragraphs will vary but should include a clear topic sentence, supporting details, and pertinent background information. See teacher pages for assessment rubrics. For more practice on writing a paragraph from notes, assign Exercise 6 in Lesson 7.3, page 174.

Coherence

🖋 Each of your paragraphs should be **coherent**; that is, its sentences should be sensibly organized so that your reader can follow your thoughts easily.

Another term for coherence is flow. Here are three tips for writing coherent paragraphs—paragraphs that flow well.

STRATEGIES FOR WRITING COHERENTLY

1. **Be Clear** The primary goals of any paragraph are simplicity and directness. Eliminate wordiness and avoid overly long and complicated sentences.

2. **Guide the Reader** Use signposts that alert the reader to what lies ahead and the relationship among thoughts. Signposts include transitional expressions (like those on page 28) and pronouns and synonyms that refer to terms you've already used. Repeating key words and phrases emphasizes important points and also helps to connect your thoughts. Using parallel structures also improves coherence.

3. **Put Your Thoughts in Order** Arrange information so that "first things come first."

🖋 You can choose from at least five common ways for organizing paragraphs and essays.

- **Chronological Order** Organizing your writing chronologically means telling about events in the order in which they occurred. Use chronological order for narrative paragraphs, for writing about a historical event, and for describing the steps in a process.

- **Spatial Order** Organize your ideas spatially when you wish to describe a person, place, or object. Provide details in an orderly way—for example, moving from left to right, top to bottom, near to far, or inside to outside.

- **Order of Importance** Organize your thoughts by degree of importance when you are writing to persuade your readers. Present your reasons and other details in order of increasing or decreasing importance.

- **Logical Order** Organize your ideas logically to give readers information in the order they need to know it. Use logic to determine which details to group together or where to provide definitions or background information.

■ See **Grammar**, Lesson 7.7, for more on parallel structure.

- **General-Specific Order** Make a general statement first, and then include the specifics that support the generalization. Or reverse your information, giving specific details first and ending with the generalization that grows out of the details.

The revisions in the following model show how one writer improved coherence, or flow, in response to the peer editor's notes in the margin.

Put in chronological order.

Eliminate repetition.

Add transition.

Add transition.

Add transition.

Add transition.
Eliminate wordiness.

Use pronoun.
Eliminate repetition.

[WRITING MODEL]

[1]Dinosaur hunting continues today. [2]Dinosaurs inhabited North America from the Triassic time right through the rest of the Jurassic and Cretaceous periods ~~in North America~~. [3]American dinosaur discovery dates from 1818, when *Anchisaurus* bones were found in Connecticut. [4]*Next,* Birdlike tracks were discovered in Massachusetts. [5]*Then,* In 1856, a Philadelphia anatomist identified three dinosaurs from fossil teeth. [6]*Soon after that,* In 1858, Hadrosaurus was described from a partial skeleton. [7]*But* Dinosaur discovery really got going in the 1870s, ~~when there began~~ *with* a fierce competition to find and name the largest ~~dinosaurs~~ *ones*. [8]The fossil remains of many ~~Late Jurassic~~ giants were discovered in the Late Jurassic rocks in Colorado and Wyoming.

Some Common Transitional Words and Expressions

To show **time**		To show **examples**		To show **order of importance**		To **compare**	
after	first	for example	namely	above all	second	also	as
afterward	immediately	for instance	that is	finally	then	and	similarly
at last	later	in addition		first	last	like	too
before	soon	in other words		most important		likewise	
during	then						
finally	when	To **summarize**		To show **cause**		To **contrast**	
		all in all	finally	**and effect**		although	but
To show **place**		as a result	therefore	as a result	since	however	still
above	inside	in conclusion	thus	because	so	in contrast (to)	yet
across	into	in summary		consequently	so that	nevertheless	
among	off			if . . . then	therefore	on the other hand	
behind	outside	To **emphasize**		for that reason			
below	there	for this reason	again				
between	through	moreover	in fact				
in front of	under	most important					

Exercise 5 Revising a Paragraph for Coherence

On a separate piece of paper, improve the following paragraph by putting its details into a clear spatial order. Make up details as necessary, and add transitional expressions, reorder information, and combine sentences. Make any other changes you think will improve the paragraph. Students' revised paragraphs will vary.

¹You enter the natural history museum by walking up several tiers of steps to the main door. ²You pass bronze signs with names of famous naturalists. ³Then you find yourself in a large room. ⁴There is a dome. ⁵There is also an information booth. ⁶That is in the center of the room. ⁷From there, you can make out the Hall of North American Mammals. ⁸If you look to the right, there's the Hall of African Mammals. ⁹Then there's the Egyptian Wing and then the Hall of Fishes. ¹⁰The other way has the Hall of Invertebrates, and then there's a room with huge bugs, and then there's the museum's restaurant. ¹¹If you're hungry. ¹²The second floor has many other exhibit halls, so does the third floor, too. ¹³My favorite exhibit way up on the third floor is the Hall of Biodiversity. ¹⁴Which is a new exhibit.

Exercise 6 Writing a Paragraph from Notes

Write a unified, coherent, well-developed paragraph based on the information in the note card below. You do not need to use all of the information. Be sure to include a clear topic sentence.

> **Pericles (495–429 B.C.)**
>
> Great leader of city-state of Athens during its Golden Age (460–430 B.C.)
>
> A nobleman; wealthy; well liked
>
> Supported democracy
> – people making decisions for themselves
> – an assembly of thousands of Athenian men met many times a year and voted on the city's business
>
> Activities: 1) built up navy, trade by sea; 2) hired best artists to create new buildings; 3) encouraged scientists, philosophers
>
> Died in 429 B.C. during war that Sparta (another city-state) started with Athens

Students' paragraphs will vary but should include a clear topic sentence. Students should stick to that topic and support it with related details or ideas from the card, and they should have a logical organization for those ideas. See teacher pages for assessment rubrics.

Types of Paragraphs and Longer Writing

Your purpose in writing may be to describe, to tell a story, to explain or inform, or to persuade. In this lesson, you'll examine these different purposes for writing paragraphs and longer pieces.

DESCRIPTIVE WRITING

Use the following suggestions when your purpose for writing is to tell about a person, emotion, animal, place, or object.

- **Use sensory details** to appeal to the reader's five senses (sight, hearing, smell, touch, and taste) and to create a **main impression**, or **mood**.

- **Use spatial order** to present the sensory details from left to right, top to bottom, near to far, or inside to outside.

Spatial order—far to near

Sight detail

Taste detail

Smell detail

Sound detail

> WRITING MODEL
>
> [1]Just below the bare, rocky summit, we unexpectedly came upon a swimming-pool-sized pond. [2]It was gray-green and tucked in amongst the weathered and gently rounded gray and green-gray boulders and jagged slabs of stone. [3]We sat for a moment and rested. [4]Moist clouds had enveloped the mountain, and we could see no more than a few hundred yards distant in any direction. [5]The icy water had a clean, fresh, invigorating taste. [6]Our deep breaths were rewarded with the bracing, moist mountain air, which was sweetened by the faint fragrance of the last of the pines just a few feet below us. [7]And it was quiet up there above the timber line, completely quiet. [8]Only the occasional harsh sounds of the hawks circling overhead intruded on the eerie silence.

NARRATIVE WRITING

When your purpose is to tell how to do something or to recount a story, either a fictional one or a true narrative, use the following suggestions.

- Break the process or story into its most critical steps or events.

- **Use chronological order** to relate the events in which they occurred. Chronological order is also useful when you explain a step-by-step process.

Event A

Event B

Event C

Event D

Event E

[WRITING MODEL]

¹The parking area was 4.5 miles from the traffic light, just as the ranger had said. ²We parked by a sturdy fence and put on our packs. ³After checking that all gear was in order, <u>we started out.</u> ⁴Following a short walk along a gently climbing old timber road, we spotted the trailhead on the right. ⁵<u>Now the real hike began.</u> ⁶Within a hundred yards or so, the narrow, rocky trail began to climb. ⁷Then it dipped and began to climb again, even more steeply, along the shoulder of the mountain. ⁸The challenging uphill trail made for some heavy breathing and demanded that we stop for rest, food, and water often. ⁹The views were breathtaking and becoming more so with each gain in elevation. ¹⁰Finally, after four hours of rigorous effort, <u>we sighted our destination.</u> ¹¹Within a few excited moments, we arrived at the top, thoroughly exhilarated. ¹²Our whoops and whistles could be heard for miles around.

EXPOSITORY WRITING

When your purpose is to explain or inform, you can write a comparison-contrast paragraph or essay, a cause-effect piece, a classification, or a definition—all forms of exposition. When writing any exposition, use the following suggestions.

• State your **main idea** as early and as clearly as possible.

• Use facts, examples, quotations, statistics, and definitions as supporting details to develop your main idea.

• Present details in a **logical order**—in a way that makes sense to the reader. Use transitions to help your reader follow your thinking (see page 28).

Main idea

Facts

Transition

Clincher
sentence

[WRITING MODEL]

¹<u>Using visual symbols rather than words to express information has become very popular.</u> ²One key use of visuals is in meteorology. ³Agreed-upon international weather symbols provide data that meteorologists the world over understand. ⁴<u>For example,</u> circles show sky coverage. ⁵An empty circle indicates a clear sky, whereas a totally shaded one means the sky is or will be overcast. ⁶A circle that is three-fourths shaded represents a very cloudy sky, and a circle that is one-fourth shaded means that the sky has only slight cloud cover. ⁷<u>Meteorologists around the globe use these and other effective symbols to indicate weather activity.</u>

PERSUASIVE WRITING

When your purpose is to convince someone that your opinion is correct or to move someone to action, use the following suggestions.

- Begin with a sentence that grabs the reader's attention.

- Include an **opinion statement** that clearly expresses your view.

- Supply **reasons and other evidence** (facts, examples, statistics, anecdotes, quotations) to support your opinion.

- Arrange supporting details in **order of importance**—from most to least important or the reverse.

- Include a **call to action** that tells what you want the reader to do.

Attention grabber and opinion statement

¹The hardest thing to do in all of professional sports is to successfully hit a pitched baseball. ²Whereas the best basketball players make about half their basket attempts, and the top football quarterbacks complete two-thirds of their pass attempts, the very best baseball hitters in all the world, on any professional level, get a hit only a third of the time. ³Yes, even the very best fail two-thirds of the time! ⁴That's because the ball that's thrown toward the batter, from a distance of about 66 feet, is traveling at speeds nearing 100 miles per hour. ⁵And while the batter is swinging a piece of wood that's less than three inches wide at its widest, the pitched ball is curving, rising, dropping, and spinning. ⁶If you don't agree, change out of your basketball uniform, remove your football helmet, take off your hockey gear, put down your pole or discus, and just step up to the plate.

Supporting evidence

Statistic

Call to action

Exercise 7 **Writing with Different Purposes**

Write a paragraph for two of the topics suggested below.

Students' two paragraphs will vary. Check that each contains a topic sentence, sticks to and supports its main idea, and is logically organized. See teacher pages for assessment rubrics.

1. A **persuasive paragraph** for or against grading students on report cards.

2. A **descriptive paragraph** about your favorite place, book, or music.

3. A **narrative paragraph** about an adventure, a contest, or a humorous event.

4. An **expository paragraph** explaining the rules of a game or giving information about a career you are considering.

Writing Essays

An **essay** is a multiparagraph piece of writing on a limited topic. An essay always has an introduction, a body, and a conclusion.

INTRODUCTION

The first paragraph of an essay accomplishes two things.

• It gets the reader interested in reading on.

• It presents the overall idea of the essay.

The essay's **overall idea** is presented in a sentence called a **claim**, a **controlling idea**, or a **thesis statement**.

A thesis statement is for an essay what a topic sentence is for a paragraph.

Each paragraph in the body of your essay should support your thesis statement. For instance, a paragraph about Clara Barton's nursing work during the Civil War could be part of an essay with the following thesis statement:

> In times of national crises, remarkable women stepped forward and made laudable contributions.

One effective way to begin an essay is to address the reader directly, as in the following example of a thesis statement.

> You may be generously contributing on an annual basis to the Help the Children Fund, but you may be surprised to learn that local governments are undercutting the fund's work on child labor.

An alternative for beginning an essay is to state your position directly.

> My recent interview with the executive director of the Help the Children Fund revealed troubling and disappointing developments in the organization's work on child labor.

A journalist writing a human-interest essay often builds a first paragraph around a specific example involving a particular person. Then, in the second paragraph of the essay, the journalist generalizes about a social phenomenon. The generalization is the thesis statement for the essay. Here's an example of the specifics-to-generalization essay introduction.

> It's the end of another long day at the factory for ten-year-old Ramon, and, just like yesterday, it is dark when he finally staggers home. His dinner is cold, but, as always, he is too tired and hungry to notice. Before long, he will be fast asleep.

Enriching Your Vocabulary

The Latin root of *laudable* is *laus*, meaning "glory" or "praise." As an adjective, *laudable* means "praiseworthy" or "commendable." The World Hunger Organization has made *laudable* efforts to bring food to families in hundreds of cities.

The Help the Children Fund, which last year announced a ten-nation campaign to move children like Ramon out of factories and back into classrooms, has reported ongoing resistance to its efforts. . . .

The side column lists other ways to begin an essay.

BODY

The body of an essay can include many paragraphs. This is where you write everything you have to say to support your thesis statement. Keep the following advice in mind about the body.

- **What Every Paragraph Needs** Think of the body as a series of main ideas: Each one expresses a topic sentence and is supported by details.

- **Clear Direction** Arrange your main ideas logically, in a way that makes them easy to follow. Begin with first things first—background information—and then move through your main ideas in the way readers need to know them. When you outline an essay prior to writing it, you are organizing the ideas for the body.

In a **formal outline**, you use letters, numbers, and Roman numerals to organize ideas and details.

- Place your title or a working title above the outline. Don't number it.

- Use Roman numerals to designate main ideas.

- Use capital letters to designate supporting details. (You must always have at least two or none at all.)

- Use numerals and then lowercase letters to designate further subdivisions.

A **topic outline** uses single words or short phrases.

Some teachers request a **sentence outline** in which each letter or numeral is followed by a complete sentence.

- **Importance of Coherence** Use transitional words that make your organization obvious to your readers. For instance, words such as *before*, *after*, *until*, and *suddenly* indicate a time order of events. Words such as *because*,

---

Some Ways to Begin an Essay

- anecdote • vivid image
- example • quotation
- question
- bit of dialogue
- startling statement or fact

Summer Camp Jobs

I. Counselor positions
   A. Waterfront
   B. Arts and crafts
      1. Pottery
      2. Weaving
      3. Sculpture
      4. Jewelry crafting
   C. Theater
      1. Acting and singing coach
      2. Costume designer
      3. Stage set designer

II. Other staff jobs
   A. Kitchen Staff
      1. Waiter
      2. Busperson
      3. Cook
   B. Bus driver
   C. Clinic work
   D. Landscaping and gardening

consequently, and *as a result* show a cause-effect relationship of ideas. You can also use other strategies to link your paragraphs so that your essay is coherent. For example, you can repeat key words and phrases to emphasize significant points or to connect related concepts.

- **Getting to the Point** Eliminate wordiness. Ask yourself, "What am I trying to say?" and then write it as clearly as you can, using precise nouns and vivid verbs and modifiers.

CONCLUSION

Don't go on and on. Know when to stop. Your conclusion can be as short as one or two sentences. Check the side column for ways to conclude an essay.

The most effective conclusions connect to the introduction. Avoid weak, unhelpful, or repetitious conclusions, such as "Well, that's all I know about."

Some Ways to End an Essay

- summary of main ideas
- comment on importance of topic
- thought-provoking question
- quotation
- prediction about the future
- call to action

Exercise 8 Drafting an Introduction

Assume that for an eyewitness essay, you choose to write about the time you watched a tightrope walker cross from the roof of one tall office building to the building across the street. Despite the high winds and distractions from the busy street below, the acrobat made the journey safely. Draft an introduction that will make the reader want to read your whole essay. Make up any details you need.
Students' introductions will vary.

Exercise 9 Drafting a Conclusion

Draft a concluding paragraph for a persuasive essay about proposed limits on the number of hours a teen can work during the school week. Make up any details that you need. Be sure to state your opinion and the key reasons for it.
Students' conclusions will vary.

Exercise 10 Revising an Essay

Choose an essay that you have written in the past. Revise the essay to strengthen the introduction, body, and conclusion. Eliminate sentences that destroy the unity of the essay. Reorganize the sentences within paragraphs, and move paragraphs, if necessary, so that information flows logically. Add details as appropriate. Revise or rewrite your conclusion to connect it to the essay's introduction.
Students' revisions will vary.

Writing
Workshops

Narrative Writing: Autobiographical Incident

Your life is a book in progress. When you write about an **autobiographical incident**, you tell a true story about something that happened to you, and you communicate the importance of the incident to your life. An autobiographical incident should focus on events both that took place in a brief period of time and that helped you understand yourself and your life a little better.

In his article "Silk Parachute," which appeared in the May 12, 1997 (Mother's Day), edition of *The New Yorker*, the writer John McPhee recalls several incidents from his childhood, each of which involves his mother. As you read, think about what each incident says about McPhee's mother and about what each experience meant to him.

Silk Parachute
by John McPhee

¹When your mother is ninety-nine years old, you have so many memories of her that they tend to overlap, intermingle, and blur. ²It is extremely difficult to single out one or two, impossible to remember any that exemplify the whole.

McPhee introduces his topic.

³It has been alleged that when I was in college she heard that I had stayed up all night playing poker and wrote me a letter that used the word "shame" forty-two times. ⁴I do not recall this.

⁵I do not recall being pulled out of my college room and into the church next door.

⁶It has been alleged that on December 24, 1936, when I was five years old, she sent me to my room at or close to 7 P.M. for using four-letter words while trimming the Christmas tree. ⁷I do not recall that.

Examples support topic.

⁸The assertion is absolutely false that when I came home from high school with an A-minus she demanded an explanation for the minus.

⁹It has been alleged that she spoiled me with protectionism, because I was the youngest child and therefore the most vulnerable to attack from overhead—an assertion that I cannot confirm or confute, except to say that facts don't lie.

¹⁰We lived only a few blocks from the elementary school and routinely ate lunch at home. ¹¹It is reported that the following dialogue and ensuing action occurred on January 22, 1941:

Uses the first-person point of view; presents the first incident

¹²"Eat your sandwich."

¹³"I don't want to eat my sandwich."

Quotes dialogue and lightheartedly introduces conflict

[14]"I made that sandwich, and you are going to eat it, Mister Man. [15]You filled yourself up on penny candy on the way home, and now you're not hungry."

[16]"I'm late. [17]I have to go. [18]I'll eat the sandwich on the way back to school."

[19]"Promise?"

[20]"Promise."

[21]Allegedly, I went up the street with the sandwich in my hand and buried it in a snowbank in front of Dr. Wright's house. [22]My mother, holding back the curtain in the window of the side door, was watching. [23]She came out in the bitter cold, wearing only a light dress, ran to the snowbank, dug out the sandwich, chased me up Nassau Street, and rammed the sandwich down my throat, snow and all. [24]I do not recall any detail of that story. [25]I believe it to be a total fabrication.

Presents second incident

[26]There was the case of the missing Cracker Jack at Lindel's corner store. [27]Flimsy evidence pointed to Mrs. McPhee's smallest child. [28]It has been averred that she laid the guilt on with the following words: " 'Like mother like son' is a saying so true, the world will judge largely of mother by you." [29]It has been asserted that she immediately repeated that proverb three times, and also recited it on other occasions too numerous to count. [30]I have absolutely no recollection of her saying that about the Cracker Jack or any other controlled substance.

Transiton paragraph

[31]We have now covered everything even faintly unsavory that has been reported about this person in ninety-nine years, and even those items are a collection of rumors, half-truths, prevarications, false allegations, inaccuracies, innuendos, and canards.

Presents third incident

[32]This is the mother who—when Alfred Knopf wrote her twenty-two-year-old son a letter saying, "The readers' reports in the case of your manuscript would not be very helpful, and I think might discourage you completely"—said, "Don't listen to Alfred Knopf. [33]Who does Alfred Knopf think he is, anyway? [34]Someone should go in there and k-nock his block off." [35]To the best of my recollection, that is what she said.

Alfred Knopf was a very influencial publisher.

Presents fourth incident

[36]I also recall her taking me, on or about March 8th, my birthday, to the theatre in New York every year, beginning in childhood. [37]I remember those journeys as if they were today. [38]I remember "A Connecticut Yankee," Wednesday, March 8, 1944. [39]Evidently, my father had written for the tickets because she and I sat in the last row of the second balcony. [40]Mother knew what to do about that. [41]She gave me for my birthday an elegant spyglass, sufficient in power to bring the Connecticut Yankee back from Vermont. [42]I sat there watching the play through my telescope, drawing as many guffaws from the surrounding audience as the comedy on the stage.

**Presents fifth
incident**

⁴³On one of those theatre days—when I was eleven or twelve—I asked her if we could start for the city early and go out to LaGuardia Field to see the comings and goings of airplanes. ⁴⁴The temperature was well below the freeze point and the March winds were so blustery that the wind-chill factor was forty below zero. ⁴⁵Or seemed to be. ⁴⁶My mother figured out how to take the subway to a stop in Jackson Heights and a bus from there—a feat I am unable to duplicate to this day. ⁴⁷At LaGuardia, she accompanied me to the observation deck and stood there in the icy wind for at least an hour, maybe two, while I, spellbound, watched the DC-3s coming in on final, their wings flapping in the gusts. ⁴⁸When we at last left the observation deck, we went downstairs into the terminal, where

**Provides vivid,
descriptive
details**

she bought me what appeared to be a black rubber ball but on closer inspection was a pair of hollow hemispheres hinged on one side and folded together. ⁴⁹They contained a silk parachute. ⁵⁰Opposite the hinge, each hemisphere had a small nib. ⁵¹A piece of string wrapped round and round the two nibs kept the ball closed. ⁵²If you threw it high into the air, the string unwound and the parachute blossomed. ⁵³If you sent it up with a tennis racquet, you could put it into the clouds. ⁵⁴Not until the development of the ten-megabyte hard disk would the world ever know such a fabulous toy. ⁵⁵Folded just so, the parachute never failed. ⁵⁶Always it floated back to you—silkily, beautifully—to start over and float back

**Makes suble
comparison
to mother**

again. ⁵⁷Even if you abused it, whacked it really hard—gracefully, lightly, it floated back to you.

Critical Thinking

After you read the autobiographical incident, answer the questions below. Use the following questions to lead a class discussion.

1. Choose one of the incidents McPhee narrates, and pay close attention to *how* he retells it. Analyze the order and the amount of space given to each of the following: background information, setting, dialogue, and report of what happened. Are there enough details to make the people, place, and event come to life? What details does McPhee omit?

2. Which of the incidents do you think best captures the kind of person McPhee's mother is? What do you think the silk parachute represents?

3. With a partner, read aloud one of the incidents. Then analyze the sentences for variety in length, structure, and beginnings.

Build Your Vocabulary. Which of these words from the article can you define: *intermingle* (sentence 1), *fabrication* (sentence 25), *canards* (sentence 31), *guffaws* (sentence 42), *nib* (sentence 50)? Look up the words you don't know in a dictionary. Add the ones you look up and their meanings to your vocabulary notebook.

Writing Strategies The purpose of writing an autobiographical incident is to narrate a series of events. The audience can be any that you choose. For example, you might write for children, for your peers, or for a faraway friend. Use the following strategies as you write.

1. **Select a meaningful incident.** An incident, which, in effect, is a mini-story, has a **plot**, **characters**, and a **setting**.

2. **Use the first person**. You—the storyteller—are the "I," the **narrator**, using the **first-person point of view**. Remember, as a first-person narrator, you do not know what other characters think, unless they tell you.

3. **Concentrate on time order**. An incident is often defined as an experience that happens all at once, in a few hours, or in a few days. An incident may consist of several individual events that occur in **chronological order**. But make sure your reader always knows how all the events fit together.

4. **Ask and answer questions**. Your readers will want to know *Who? What? Where? When? Why?* and *How?* (the *5W-How?* questions reporters answer at the beginning of a news story). If possible, introduce suspense into your narrative.

5. **Answer, "So what?"** You've selected an incident that's important to you. Your essay should tell how the incident changed you, what you discovered, or why you remember it. John McPhee's opening two sentences and final two sentences effectively link the incidents he describes.

6. **Include your thoughts and feelings**. This piece of advice relates to Strategy 5. Try to recall—or imagine—what you thought and felt at the time the incident took place—and what you feel and think about it now. Your thoughts and feelings will tell your readers the full significance of the incident.

7. **Sprinkle in sensory details**. A few details about sights, sounds, smells, tastes, and sensations of touch will help the reader imagine what you remember clearly. But don't get bogged down in sensory details at the expense of your plot.

8. **Generate some dialogue**. No one remembers exactly what was said long ago, but you probably have a general idea. Look back at how McPhee generates dialogue to enliven the first incident he describes. Try to do likewise.

Writing Hint

As you try to get across the importance of the event, keep in mind that it is more effective to *show* than *tell*. McPhee doesn't come out and say directly how much he appreciated his mother's acts of love but shows his appreciation through metaphor and tone.

Exercise 1 Get Started

You might, like McPhee, write about a remembrance of a person. Or you might write about a place, a time, or a feeling. Use one or two of the prewriting techniques mentioned in Lesson 1.1 to get ideas for incidents to write about. **Remember:** (1) The incident must be in some way important to you. (2) You must remember the incident vividly. (3) It must have taken place in a short time period.
Answers will vary. Refer to "Reasons to Write" in the teacher pages for prewriting suggestions.

Exercise 2 Plan Your Narrative

Use a **story map** to capture all the important elements in your narrative. You won't necessarily write your narrative in the order of the map's questions and answers, but the map will keep all the data in front of you. On a separate piece of paper, write the following questions and answer them with as much detail as possible. Answers will vary.

1. What is the **setting**?

2. Identify the main **characters**, and describe them briefly.

3. Identify the **conflict**, or problem, and briefly summarize the plot.

4. Why was the experience important to you?

Exercise 3 Draft the Autobiographical Incident

Use your prewriting notes to draft your incident. Be sure to summarize your feelings about the incident at least once in your essay.

Consider your classmates the audience for your narrative. You may also want to keep friends and relatives in mind as you write. Answers will vary. Suggest that students identify the audience and purpose in writing.

Exercise 4 Revise Your Autobiographical Incident *Working Together*

Read your essay aloud to yourself and then to a partner.

First, check that your order of events is clear. Use transition words to link your sentences. Then work on getting the sentences to read smoothly. See if you can replace vague, general nouns, verbs, and modifiers with more precise words. Go back over your essay to find and eliminate any padding.
Answers will vary. Students should refer to Lesson 1.3 for more revising strategies.

Exercise 5 Proofread and Publish

Carefully review your revised narrative for errors in spelling, punctuation, and capitalization. Think about sharing your narrative with friends and family, especially with anyone who was present when the incident happened.
Answers will vary. Mechanics, Chapters 13–16, address proofreading concerns.

Narrative Writing: Eyewitness Report

Like a report on an autobiographical incident, an **eyewitness report** is also a firsthand account of an incident but, in contrast, focuses more on the significance of the incident to the community or society than to the writer. In an eyewitness report, the narrator is an observer, not a participant.

An eyewitness report usually reads chronologically. It may have a first-person or third-person point of view. An effective eyewitness report includes anecdotes, sensory details, and dialogue.

from The Fall of the Berlin Wall
by Andreas Ramos

Ramos hooks readers by stating the magnitude of the incident.

Uses the first-person point of view

Proceeds chronologically

Gives vivid details. What's implied by the heavy media presence?

Builds suspense with these details

Describes setting

¹On Thursday, the 9th of November 1989, and Friday, the 10th, the TV and radio in Denmark was filled with news about the events in Berlin. ²The wall was about to fall. ³On Saturday morning, the 11th of November, I heard on the radio that East Germany was collapsing. ⁴[On] the spur of the moment, I suggested to Karen, my Danish wife, and two Danish friends that we should go to Berlin. . . .

⁵We arrived in [West] Berlin at 4:30 A.M., [the trip taking] five hours longer than usual. ⁶We drove first to Brandenburgerplatz, where the statue of Winged Victory stands atop a 50 meter column, which celebrates a military victory in the 1890s over Denmark. ⁷Cars were abandoned everywhere, wherever there was space. ⁸Over 5,000 people were there. . . . ⁹We left the car and began to walk through a village of television trucks, giant satellite dishes, emergency generators, and coils of cables and tents. ¹⁰Cameramen slept under satellite dishes. ¹¹At the wall, West German police and military [were] lined up to prevent chaos. ¹²West German military trucks were lined up against the wall to protect it from the West Germans. ¹³Hundreds of West German police stood in rows with their tall shields. ¹⁴On top of the wall, lined up at parade rest, stood East German soldiers with their rifles. ¹⁵Groups of West Germans stood around fires that they had built. ¹⁶No one knew what was going on.

¹⁷After a while, we walked to Potsdammer Platz. ¹⁸This used to be the center of Berlin. ¹⁹All traffic once passed through the Potsdammer Platz. ²⁰Now it was a large empty field, bisected by the wall. ²¹Nearby was the mound that was the remains of Hitler's bunker, from which he commanded Germany into total defeat. ²²We talked to Germans and many said that the next break in the wall would be here. ²³It was still very dark and cold at

Tells what people are doing and saying at time of breakthrough

6 A.M. [24]Perhaps 7,000 people were pressed together, shouting, cheering, clapping. [25]We pushed through the crowd. [26]From the East German side, we could hear the sound of heavy machines. [27]With a giant drill, they were punching holes in the wall. [28]Every time a drill poked through, everyone cheered. [29]The banks of klieg lights would come on. [30]People shot off fireworks and emergency flares and rescue rockets. [31]Many were using hammers to chip away at the wall. [32]There were countless holes. [33]At one place, a crowd of East German soldiers looked through a narrow hole. [34]We reached through and shook hands. [35]They couldn't see the crowd so they asked us what was going on and we described the scene for them. [36]Someone lent me a hammer and I knocked chunks of rubble from the wall, dropping several handfuls into my pocket. [37]The wall was made of cheap, brittle concrete: the Russians had used too much sand and water. . . .

Sight and sound details

[38]By 7 A.M., everything was out of control. [39]Police on horses watched. [40]There was nothing they could do. [41]The crowd had swollen. [42]People were blowing long alpine horns which made a huge noise. [43]There were fireworks, kites, flags and flags and flags, dogs, children. [44]The wall was finally breaking. [45]The cranes lifted slabs aside. [46]East and West German police had traded caps. [47]To get a better view, hundreds of people were climbing onto a shop on the West German side. [48]We scampered up a nine foot wall. [49]People helped each other; some lifted, others pulled. [50]All along the building, people poured up the wall. [51]At the Berlin Wall itself, which is 3 meters high, people had climbed up and were sitting astride. [52]The final slab was moved away. [53]A stream of East Germans began to pour through. [54]People applauded and slapped their backs. . . . [55]Near me, a knot of people cheered as the mayors of East Berlin and West Berlin met and shook hands. [56]I stood with several East German guards, their rifles slung over their shoulders. [57]I asked them if they had bullets in those things. [58]They grinned and said no. [59]From some houses, someone had set up loudspeakers and played [the portion of] Beethoven's ninth symphony [which contains the words] *"Alle Menschen werden Bruder"* ("All people become brothers"). [60]On top of every building were thousands of people. [61]Berlin was out of control. [62]There was no more government, neither in East nor in West. [63]The police and

Brings essay to close; announces meaning of the event

the army were helpless. [64]The soldiers themselves were overwhelmed by the event. [65]They were part of the crowd. [66]Their uniforms meant nothing. [67]The wall was down.

Critical Thinking

After you read the eyewitness report, answer the questions below.
Use the following questions to lead a class discussion.

1. Pay close attention to how Ramos describes what he witnesses. Is the order of events clear? Are there enough details to make the people, place, and event come to life? Too many?

2. Imagine the incident reported with dialogue. What, if anything, would the dialogue add?

3. Reread sentences 59–66. Are they facts or opinions? On what are the comments based?

4. With a partner, read aloud one of the lengthy passages in the report. Then analyze the sentences for variety in length, structure, and beginnings.

Build Your Vocabulary. Underline the unfamiliar words in the selection. Use a dictionary to look up their meaning and write brief definitions in the margin or in your notebook.

Writing Strategies

The purpose of writing an eyewitness report is to give an account of actual events. Your audience is made up of people who want to know about the event you describe. Use the following strategies to help.

1. **Brainstorm about incidents**. An eyewitness report is about a compelling incident, particularly one that is newsworthy. Incidents that lend themselves to eyewitness accounts include accidents, crimes, natural catastrophes, sporting events, political meetings, exciting performances, and other public gatherings. Select one to observe and report on. Although you may not have the opportunity to be present at an incident as monumental as the fall of the Berlin Wall, there's *always* something newsworthy happening.

2. **Find a beginning point**. Take notes as events develop, but when you write a narrative based on those notes, decide where to begin your retelling of the event. For example, after a brief introductory paragraph, Ramos picks up with his arrival *in* West Berlin, omitting details about his trip *to* Berlin.

3. **Use the first-person or third-person point of view**. Either way, make your readers feel as if they, too, are witnessing the event. Ramos puts readers in the midst of West Berlin with him as he roams around.

4. **Give sufficient details—in the right order!** While your overall report will proceed chronologically, some of it may benefit if you arrange details spatially. Focus on what the scene looks like, sounds like, or even smells like. Use vivid verbs, nouns, and modifiers to describe these sensory details and all

other details with precision. Include details that lend immediacy to your report. Ramos tells readers what he sees and hears from the time he arrives in Berlin to the actual fall of the wall.

5. **Make comparisons.** If possible, help readers understand what the incident is like and how it is similar to or different from other incidents you have witnessed or heard about. Ramos comments briefly in sentence 21 about another event that took place on this site.

6. **Find human interest**. Include quotations, if possible, from participants in the incident or from local authorities. Focus on specific participants, not just the general crowd. Ramos tells readers what the soldiers, politicians, and other participants are doing, such as playing a Beethoven symphony, climbing onto building tops, and hammering away at the wall.

> ## Writing Hint
>
> Think of an eyewitness reporter as similar to a cinematographer. Both present compelling visual images of unfolding events. Try to give readers a sense of seeing the events through the lens of a camera. Clue them in with transitional words and phrases that show time order or spatial order (see pages 27–28).

7. **Determine closure**. Let readers know where you are leaving them. Give them an idea of the significance of the event or of any long-term effects that may come from the event. Ramos lets readers know that the wall is down, the crowds are "out of control," and the authorities are helpless.

Exercise 6 Get Started

Brainstorm with classmates, or use one or two of the prewriting techniques in Lesson 1.1 to think of an incident that you remember or that you can cover and then write about. One source of ideas is the local newspaper or community calendar. Find events that are coming up in your area in the near future, such as a potentially heated political or civic meeting or a key ballgame.
Answers will vary. Students should use the prewriting suggestions in Lesson 1.1.

Exercise 7 Plan Your Eyewitness Report

You'll need to carefully observe what goes on around you in order to collect useful information during the incident. Jot your observations and impressions in a notebook while you're at the scene. If possible, tape-record interviews with participants, or photograph events as they unfold. Later, you may find it useful to draw a timeline or series-of-events chain to which you can transfer the notes you decide to use in your draft. If your report is about a past event, write down all the details you can remember. Then talk to others who witnessed the event with you. They may help you remember additional details. Answers will vary.

Exercise 8 Draft the Eyewitness Report

Draft your report in whatever way feels comfortable to you. Keep a specific
audience in mind throughout. Here are some pointers.
Answers will vary. Students should refer to Lesson 1.2 for drafting strategies.

• **Follow your organizational plan**. Make it chronological or spatial or both.

• **Grab the reader's attention.** Make readers want to find out what happens
and why it happens. Figure out how to draw them into the scene right from
the start.

• **Include details.** As you write, find a balance between too few and too
many details.

• **Give a solid conclusion.** Try to work in the drama or significance of
the event.

Exercise 9 Revise Your Eyewitness Report

Try reading your report aloud to yourself and then to a partner to get a sense of
its impact. When revising, keep these questions in mind:
Answers will vary. Students should refer to Lesson 1.3 for additional revising strategies.

• Does my introduction draw readers into my report?

• Is the order of events clear?

• Does my writing help readers visualize the event?

• Do my sentences read smoothly?

• Can I introduce more vivid or precise words?

• Have I eliminated any padding or unnecessary words?

• Do I convey the significance of the incident?

When you're satisfied with your report, share it with the members of your
writing group. Ask for their questions, comments, and suggestions.

Exercise 10 Proofread and Publish

Check your revised report for errors in spelling, punctuation, and capitalization.
Share your report with friends and family or with someone who took part in the
incident you've described. Consider submitting your account for publication in
the school or local paper.
Answers will vary. Students should refer to Lesson 1.4 for proofreading strategies and
publishing suggestions.

Persuasive Writing

When your goal is to **persuade**—that is, to win readers over to your point of view—you must build an argument based on logical appeals and on emotional appeals. As you read the following column by Ellen Goodman, see if you can identify the strategies she uses to try to persuade readers to vote.

Ten Reasons Why I Vote
by Ellen Goodman

[1]Let me confess that I have a record. [2]I am a political recidivist. [3]An incorrigible, repeat voter. [4]A career lever-pusher. [5]My electoral rap sheet is as long as your arm.

[6]Over the course of three decades, I have voted for presidents and schoolboard members. [7]I have voted in high hopes and high dudgeon. [8]I have voted in favor of candidates and merely against their opponents.

[9]I have voted for propositions written with such complexity that I needed Noam Chomsky [the well-known linguist] to deconstruct their meaning. [10]I have been a single-issue voter and a marginal voter. [11]I have even voted for people who ran unopposed.

[12]Hold an election and I'll be there. [13]I say this as a confession because I know that voting is no longer considered chic. [14]Voting is hopelessly dated—*circa* 1840, back when 80 percent of all eligible Americans voted in the presidential election. [15]It's also dated *circa* 45 years of age, the threshold above which two-thirds of us still go to the polls.

[16]Today is Nov. 5, 1996. [17]The Democrats say it's morning in America. [18]The Republicans say it's midnight. [19]And an entire cohort of Americans barely know what day it is. [20]Election Day.

[21]Absentee non-voters once were sheepish about their no-shows. [22]Today, they seem to believe they're on the disaffected high road. [23]It's cool to proclaim a pox on both sides, to swear that they're all alike and that it doesn't make any difference. [24]It's sophisticated to claim a profound—and not so profound—lack of interest.

[25]One unabashed 21-year-old named Dawn told a reporter at my newspaper, "I'm not into politics," as if voting were Thai food or runes. [26]Her companion Julie topped this indifference saying, "I think, like, what if I vote for him and help him get in and then he stinks? [27]It would be my fault."

Tongue-in-cheek comments grab attention.

Three paragraphs illustrate pro-voting position.

States that voting is unfashionable, according to many

Emotional appeals

Undercuts popular opinion by citing opponents' own words

²⁸As a working journalist, I have a union card that entitles me to cynicism. ²⁹I use it liberally. ³⁰But on Election Day, I also have a League of Women Voters, Norman Rockwell, John Philip Sousa, Frank Capra need to march down with Jane, Dick, and Spot to the local polling place.

³¹So allow me to offer Ten Reasons Why I Vote. ³²Get the handcuffs ready.

Logical appeals include anecdotes, statistics, facts, and emotions

1. ³³I vote because, when I was a kid, voting was grown-up. ³⁴Sue me; it's still a chit to adulthood.

2. ³⁵I vote because my dad ran for Congress in the 1950s. ³⁶And lost by 500 votes. ³⁷Enough said.

3. ³⁸I vote because even the lesser of two evils is the lesser of two evils.

4. ³⁹I vote because women spent over a century fighting for "the cause" so that I could vote. ⁴⁰Hear ye, Susan B.

5. ⁴¹I vote because I have never in my life been called by a pollster. ⁴²There's only one place to register my opinion: the booth in the school cafeteria.

6. ⁴³I vote because Election Day is for me a national day of stillness when the conflict and the attack ads suddenly halt, and the whole country waits to see what citizens will decide. ⁴⁴Sometimes what's corny is also true.

7. ⁴⁵I vote because my husband's college roommate is running for the state Senate up North, so I know for a fact that not all politicians today are rotten. ⁴⁶Go, Richard.

8. ⁴⁷I vote because I remember being a 13-year-old poll worker for my dad when a creep yelled in my face, "I wouldn't vote for him if he was the last man on Earth!" ⁴⁸I still vote to cancel his vote.

9. ⁴⁹I vote because, unlike a disaffected Julie and uninterested Dawn, I think, like, what if I don't vote for him and the other guy gets in and "he stinks?" ⁵⁰Yeah, "it would be my fault."

Acknowledges opponents' view but suggests she's not alone in her opinion

⁵¹All this is apolitically incorrect. ⁵²It's suspiciously hopeful in an era of hip political alienation. ⁵³It's as retro as civics class; it's unfit for any radio talk show. ⁵⁴But I suspect that Election Day has this effect on a bunch of unrepentant voters. ⁵⁵Consider this final reason:

Saves strongest reason for last

10. ⁵⁶Without blushing, I vote because it's what small-d democracy is about. ⁵⁷Because there are places where people fight for generations and stand for hours to cast a ballot, knowing what we ought to remember: that it makes a difference. ⁵⁸Not always a big difference. ⁵⁹Not always an immediate difference. ⁶⁰But a difference.

©1996 The Boston Globe

Critical Thinking

After you read the persuasive essay, answer the questions below.

Use the following questions to lead a class discussion.

1. What does Goodman admit in her opening few paragraphs? What tone do they set for the rest of the essay?

2. Summarize Goodman's reasons for voting. Which of her reasons do you find most persuasive?

3. What does Goodman mean when, in sentence 32, she tells readers to "get the handcuffs ready"?

4. What is Goodman's most effective emotional appeal? Which is the best logical appeal?

5. Who are all the people and groups that Goodman mentions? Why does she link Norman Rockwell, the League of Women Voters, Frank Capra, and others in one paragraph?

Build Your Vocabulary. Which of these words from the essay can you define: *incorrigible* (sentence 3), *dudgeon* (sentence 7), *cohort* (sentence 19), *unabashed* (sentence 25), *cynicism* (sentence 28)? Look up the words you don't know in a dictionary, and use the phonetic symbols to pronounce the words correctly. Add these words to your vocabulary notebook.

Writing Strategies

Usually, a **letter to the editor** is only a few paragraphs long. A **persuasive essay**, such as Goodman's, gives you more room to argue your point. For both types of persuasive writing, however, most of the following strategies apply.

1. **Clearly state your opinion**. Don't leave any doubt in your reader's mind about what you think. State your opinion as clearly as you can in a single sentence or two. The opinion statement (sometimes called a **thesis statement**) usually, but not always, belongs at the beginning.

2. **Give logical appeals in support of your opinion**. Logical appeals take the form of **reasons**. Usually, you'll need two or three strong and distinctly different reasons to support your opinion.

3. **Support each reason with strong evidence**. Use a variety of evidence.

   • Include **facts**, statements that can be proved true. Make sure that you get your facts from reliable reference sources. Check facts against other sources.

   • Quote or mention others, especially **experts**, who agree with you.

   • Provide **definitions** where appropriate. (In the model, Goodman provides a personalized definition of *Election Day*.)

- Employ **statistics**, facts expressed in numbers. Again, make sure all facts are accurate and clear.

- Use **examples** that illustrate your points clearly.

- Narrate an **anecdote**, a mini-story about an incident that actually happened, perhaps based on your personal experiences or observations.

4. **Use emotional appeals wisely**. Emotional appeals argue your case using the reader's fears, hopes, wishes, or sense of fairness. You can't rely on emotional appeals alone, but sometimes an emotional argument has more impact on your audience than a logical one. One tool for playing on emotions is **loaded words**—words carrying either positive or negative connotations, or slants.

5. **Present and, if possible, demolish counterarguments**. You should acknowledge the opposing view (counterargument), but then give reasons to prove the view wrong.

6. **Avoid false thinking**. Watch out for the following errors, each of which detracts from the power of your argument.

   - *Stereotyping*—overlooking individual differences among members of a group

   - *Using false analogies*—making weak or farfetched comparisons

   - *Overgeneralizing*—using data from a limited or unrepresentative sample

   - *Oversimplifying*—not considering the multiple causes for a particular situation

   - *Personalizing*—attacking the person when you should attack only the argument a person makes

7. **End with a call to action**. Sometimes, you need more from readers than agreement; you need them to *do* something—write a letter, donate money or time, vote for your candidate, or buy a product. At the end of your essay, invite or challenge your reader to take a particular course of action.

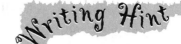

Writing Hint

Effective writers can demolish counter-arguments without resorting to hostility.

Building Your Argument

Opinion Statement

- Reason 1 supported by evidence

- Reason 2 supported by evidence

- Reason 3 supported by evidence

Restatement of opinion; Call to action (if appropriate)

Exercise 11 Choose a Topic

To come up with a topic for a letter to the editor or a persuasive essay, you can check the "Write What You Think" exercises throughout this book; pursue an issue or incident in the news; or survey classmates to learn what issues concern them and then select one issue. Whatever topic you choose, keep in mind that it must have the following two qualities:

Answers will vary. Students may refer to Lesson 1.1 for prewriting ideas.

• It must be arguable (something people disagree about).

• It must be important to you personally.

If you plan to write a letter to the editor in response to a news article or an editorial, be sure to record the title of the article or editorial with which you take issue, its author, and the date of publication. Keep it at hand when you write so that you can refer to it and quote from it as needed.

Exercise 12 State Your Position

Discuss with your writing group these possible position statements to be added to the first few paragraphs of Goodman's column. Which is the strongest? Why?

Answers will vary. Students should identify and discuss the strengths and weaknesses of each statement.

(a) I'd say that probably a citizen's biggest responsibilities include voting and paying taxes.

(b) Voting is good for the country.

(c) Voting in local, state, and national elections makes both logical and emotional sense to me.

Determine what you think about the topic you selected in Exercise 11, and try to state your position precisely and forcefully in one or two sentences. You might draft several versions of your position statement; then choose the best one.

Exercise 13 Support Your Opinion

While still in the prewriting stage, consider your audience. You need to keep your readers in mind in order to choose logical and emotional appeals that will have an impact on them. Determine how much background information they'll need before you launch into your argument. In preparing your notes, **be specific**: List specific examples, facts, and statistics from reliable sources. Avoid general expressions such as "most people" and "many states." Mention your sources; your audience will want to know that you've done careful research. Finally, **stay focused**. Keep your argument as tight as you can make it. Don't deal with unimportant details, particularly if you are writing to an editor.

Answers will vary. Drafts should reflect a coherent structure.

Exercise 14 Draft Your Letter or Essay

As you write your first draft, remember these four elements of effective writing:
Answers will vary.

- **Unity** The more support you give for your opinion, the more persuasive you'll be, as long as everything you say is **relevant**—to the point. For example, which of the following items would help to strengthen Goodman's argument?
See Lesson 2.1, Unity.

   a. Quotations from 21-year-olds who agree with her

   b. A table or graph showing the decline in the numbers of eligible voters who go to the polls

   c. A description of how easy it is to cast your ballot once you enter the voting booth

   d. A comparison of percentages of eligible voters who vote in other industrialized nations

Students' opinions will differ about the most effective addition. Have them justify their choice(s).

- **Coherence** As you follow a brief outline similar to the one in the box called "Building Your Argument," on page 50, let your readers know where your argument is headed. For example, mention the number of reasons you'll present, and, as you mention each one, alert readers with transitional words and phrases, such as *first, second, more importantly*, and *finally*.
See Lesson 2.3, Coherence.

- **Clarity** Concentrate on expressing every thought as clearly and succinctly as you can.

- **Tone** Try to establish a tone that shows that you know what you are talking about, that your information will be reliable, and that you firmly believe that your position is the right one—and that you are fair and open minded.

Exercise 15 Revise, Edit, Proofread, and Publish *Working Together*

First, look over your work for large-scale problems in content and organization. Check that you've accurately represented opposing arguments and have addressed those you've found unclear or incorrect. If you've appealed to your readers' emotions, check to make sure you've done so responsibly. Check that you've ended your essay by asking readers to change their minds or to take a particular course of action. Then go back over your essay to eliminate unnecessary or inappropriate words and to fix grammar, usage, and mechanics. Proofread to eliminate spelling errors. Share your work with the members of a writing group, and ask for their comments.

Answers will vary. Students might consider sending persuasive writing about a community issue to a local radio or TV station. They might also wish to present a persuasive essay as a speech.

Expository Writing: Compare and Contrast Essay

When you write a **compare and contrast essay**, you identify the ways two or more subjects are alike and the ways they are different. The following excerpt introduces the 1858 series of debates between Abraham Lincoln and Stephen A. Douglas, the challenger and the incumbent candidate for U.S. Senator representing Illinois. Both would run for President two years later. In the excerpt, David Herbert Donald **compares** and **contrasts** the two men.

The Lincoln–Douglas Debates
an excerpt from *Lincoln* by David Herbert Donald

[1]The seven formal debates between Lincoln and Douglas were. . . only a small part of the 1858 campaign, though they naturally attracted the greatest interest. [2]All of them followed the same format. [3]The speakers alternated in opening the debate. [4]The opening speaker was allowed an hour for his presentation; his opponent had an hour and a half for reply; and the initial speaker then had a final half hour for rebuttal. [5]Lincoln grumbled that the arrangement allowed Douglas to make four of the opening and closing statements, while he was allowed only three.

Background information

[6]As the Republican *New York Times* observed, Illinois in 1858 was "the most interesting political battle-ground in the Union," and newspapers throughout the country offered extensive coverage of the canvass. [7]Local papers, of course, gave it great attention. [8]For the first time reporters were assigned to cover candidates throughout the long campaign season. . . .

[9]Reporters noted how sharply the candidates contrasted in appearance. [10]Douglas, so short that he came up only to Lincoln's shoulder, was a ruddy, stout man, with regular features marred only by a curious horizontal ridge that stretched across the top of his nose, while Lincoln was exceptionally tall and painfully thin, with a melancholy physiognomy and sallow skin. [11]Douglas had a booming, authoritative voice, while Lincoln spoke in a piercing tenor, which at times became shrill and sharp. [12]Douglas used graceful gestures and bowed charmingly when applauded, in contrast to Lincoln, who moved his arms and hands awkwardly and looked like a jackknife folding up when he tried to bow.

Contrasts appearances; uses transition

Contrasts voices, speaking styles, gestures

[13]There was also a marked contrast in the way the candidates presented themselves to the public. [14]Douglas wished to appear a commanding figure, a statesman of national reputation. [15]Accompanied by his beautiful, regal second wife, Adèle Cutts, he usually traveled by special train, splendidly fitted out for comfort and for entertaining. [16]When he stood on the platform in his handsome new blue suit with silver buttons and in his immaculate linen, he was unquestionably a great United States senator reporting to

Contrasts public image each candidate sought

his loyal constituents. [17]Lincoln deliberately cultivated a different image. [18]When he went by train, he traveled in the regular passenger cars—a practice that afforded him endless opportunities for meeting the voters and talking about their concerns. [19]Except at the final debate in Alton, Mary Lincoln did not accompany him; it was not part of the persona he was projecting to display his elegantly dressed wife with her aristocratic bearing. [20]Lincoln took pains to wear his everyday clothes during the debates, appearing usually in what Carl Schurz, the German-American leader, who campaigned for the Republican ticket, described as "a rusty black frock-coat with sleeves that should have been longer" and black trousers that "permitted a very full view of his large feet."

Author builds on contrasts already established

[21]From time to time, Lincoln tried to capitalize on the differences between Douglas's appearance and his own. [22]The senator's followers, he said, anticipated that their leader at no distant day would become President and saw in his "round, jolly, fruitful face" promises of "postoffices, landoffices, marshalships, and cabinet appointments, chargeships and foreign missions, bursting and sprouting out in wonderful exuberance," while in Lincoln's "poor, lean, lank face" nobody ever saw "that any cabbages were sprouting out," because "nobody has ever expected me to be President." [23]There was nothing false about all this; Lincoln was in fact a homely man with simple tastes, indifferent to personal comfort. [24]It was important in this contest to present himself to the voters not as a man of considerable means and one of the most prominent lawyers in the state but as a countryman, shrewd and incorruptible.

Critical Thinking

After you read the compare and contrast essay, answer the questions below.
Use the following questions to lead a class discussion.

1. Overall, would you say that Donald emphasizes the similarities between the two statesmen or the differences? Explain.

2. The word *while* in sentence 10 is a **transition**; it indicates that a contrast will follow. List other transitional words and phrases Donald uses to help readers follow his thinking about Lincoln and Douglas. (See page 28 for a list of transitions.)

Build Your Vocabulary. Which of these words from the essay can you define from context clues or word roots: *ruddy* (sentence 10), *melancholy* (sentence 10), *physiognomy* (sentence 10), *sallow* (sentence 10), *persona* (sentence 19), *lank* (sentence 22)? Look up the words you don't know in a dictionary, and use the phonetic symbols to say them aloud. Add these terms to your vocabulary notebook.

Writing Strategies The purpose of writing a compare and contrast essay is to inform your readers about a subject or to explain a subject. It is critical, therefore, that you plan your essay carefully and that you organize your thoughts clearly. Use the following suggestions.

1. **Choose your subjects.** Pick two subjects (for example, two people, two places, two events, two objects, two points of view) that you know something about—and that you want to explore further.

2. **List their features.** Think of as many features, or categories, as possible to compare your subjects. For example, think about both in terms of their

appearances	histories, backgrounds
advantages or disadvantages	costs, benefits
actions, behaviors	effects on you or others
special qualities, traits	aspirations
points of view	public's expectations

Writing Hint

You may choose to write about similarities only, differences only, or both similarities and differences, perhaps emphasizing one or the other.

3. **Try a Venn diagram or a chart.** A Venn diagram is a useful prewriting graphic organizer for identifying your subjects' similarities and differences. The overlapping part of two circles contains the features that your subjects share. The outer parts of the circles contain your subjects' differences—what is unique to each. Examine the Venn diagram below, which shows the similarities and differences between Lincoln and Douglas.

DOUGLAS

1. Physical appearance: short, ruddy, stout; regular facial features, ridge

2. Public-speaking style: authoritative voice, graceful gestures, charming

3. Public image: commanding, well-dressed, regal; travels grandly; accompanied by wife

4. Expectations: to be President

Similarities (Implied)

1. Seek public office

2. Create public images

LINCOLN

1. Physical appearance: tall, thin; melancholy, sallow

2. Public-speaking style: shrill, piercing tenor; awkward movements

3. Public image: poorly dressed, homespun; travels like common people; not usually accompanied by wife

4. Expectations: not to be President

The comparison and contrast chart that follows is a different way to show the same information.

Comparison and Contrast Chart			
FEATURE	DOUGLAS	LINCOLN	SIMILAR (+) DIFFERENT (−)
Physical appearance	short, ruddy, stout; regular facial features, ridge	tall, thin; melancholy, sallow	−
Public-speaking style	booming, authoritative voice; graceful gestures, charming	shrill, piercing tenor; awkward movements	−
Public image	commanding, well-dressed, regal; travels grandly; accompanied by wife	poorly dressed, homespun; travels like common people; not usually accompanied by wife	−
Expectations	to be President	not to be President	−
Seeks public office?	yes	yes	+
Works on image	yes	yes	+

4. **Organize.** Use one of the two basic formats shown below and on the top of page 57 for a compare and contrast essay.

  • In the **block method**, shown below, you discuss all the features of one subject. Then you discuss the features as they relate to the second subject. You should discuss the features in the same order.

  • In the **point-by-point method**, shown on page 57, you first deal with one feature in both subject 1 and subject 2. You then present a second feature in both subject 1 and subject 2. Continue in this manner for the remaining features.

Block Method:
One subject at a time

All about Douglas

Feature 1: physical appearance
Feature 2: public-speaking style
Feature 3: public image
Feature 4: expectations

All about Lincoln

Feature 1: physical appearance
Feature 2: public-speaking style
Feature 3: public image
Feature 4: expectations

Point-by-Point Method:
One feature at a time

Feature 1: Physical appearance

Douglas: short, ruddy, stout; regular facial features, ridge

Lincoln: tall, thin; melancholy, sallow

Feature 2: Public-speaking style

Douglas: booming, authoritative voice; graceful gestures, charming

Lincoln: shrill, piercing tenor; awkward movements

Feature 3: Public image

Douglas: commanding, well-dressed, regal; travels grandly; accompanied by wife

Lincoln: poorly dressed, homespun; travels like common people; not usually accompanied by wife

Feature 4: Expectations

Douglas: to be President

Lincoln: not to be President

---

5. **Use clear transitions.** Transitional words and expressions help readers follow your thinking. *Like, similarly, just as, both, also,* and *in the same way* signal similarities. *Yet, on the other hand, in contrast, however, unlike, whereas, while,* and *nevertheless* signal differences. You can also use transitions such as *first, second, finally, more importantly,* and *most significantly* to highlight each new feature.

Exercise 16 Choose Subjects

Use one or all of the following questions to come up with two things to compare and contrast. Answers will vary. Students should refer to Lesson 1.1 for prewriting strategies.

- **What two things are somewhat similar but mostly different?** The subjects must have at least one feature in common. The easiest subjects to write about are specific, limited ones that you can observe directly. Try comparing and contrasting two of the following topics:

paintings	movies	singers	foods	places
TV shows	plays	actors	animals	buildings
poems	beaches	authors	talk-show hosts	articles of clothing

- **What has changed significantly with the passage of time?** You might compare a subject in the past with the same subject in the present. For example, what was Chicago like one hundred years ago, and how is it different today? How has television changed? How have women's lives changed?

Exercise 17 Gather Information

Which features of your two subjects will you examine as you compare and contrast? Brainstorm features by thinking about the categories listed in item 2 on page 55—and others. Then create a Venn diagram or a chart (see pages 55 and 56). As you work, use one or more of the following techniques. Answers will vary. Research may reveal weaknesses in students' topics. Encourage students to adjust their topics based on new information.

- **Inspect your subjects**. If your subjects are available for close inspection, take notes as you actually examine them. Consider using a camera or a tape recorder.

- **Do research.** Use encyclopedias and other reference sources to find information about subjects you don't know much about. Gather facts, examples, and specific details to back up your statements. Be sure to refer to more than one source so that you get a fuller view of your subjects. Consider doing other kinds of research, such as conducting interviews, on-line research, or watching relevant videos.

- **Don't confuse fact and opinion.** A fact is a statement everyone agrees is true or that you can prove. An opinion, on the other hand, is a person's idea or belief; it's not necessarily true or provable. Opinions backed up with reasons and other evidence are stronger than unsupported opinions.

Exercise 18 Organize Your Essay

Try these strategies for planning your comparison and contrast essay.
Answers will vary.

- **Don't overload the essay.** From the notes you've made about features of your subjects, choose only two or three features to focus on.

- **Pick a plan.** Some writers think that block organization works better for shorter papers but point-by-point organization for longer ones.

- **Make a rough outline.** Jot down your subjects and features in an order that makes the most sense to you. Your rough outline can look like one of the two sets of notes on pages 56 and 57.

Exercise 19 Drafting Your Essay

Consider these three hints as you write.
Answers will vary.

- **Tell the reader.** In your introduction, (1) identify your subjects, (2) let your readers know whether you'll discuss the subjects' similarities or differences or both, and (3) grab your readers' attention. Draft a **thesis statement** that summarizes your essay's main idea. Which of the thesis statements on the following page is strongest? Why?

Ask students to explain the weaknesses of choices *a* and *b*.
a. Lincoln and Douglas wanted the same thing but were different.

b. Although Lincoln and Douglas were politicians, they were different.

c. Lincoln and Douglas sought the same political office but differed in their appearance, in their oratory style, and in their public image. This statement identifies the subjects of the essay and alerts readers to the three points of comparison.

• **Begin writing.** Stick to your rough outline to explain the differences and similarities between your subjects.

• **Wrap it up.** In your **conclusion**, summarize your findings without simply repeating the similarities and differences you've fleshed out. Are your subjects more alike or more different? Is one feature more significant than the others? Share any new insights you have gained.

Exercise 20 **Revising and Editing**

Read your essay aloud to help you listen for what content is missing and for how to improve your writing style. When revising, keep these questions in mind:
Answers will vary. Students should refer to Lesson 1.3 for more revising strategies.

• Does my introduction draw readers into the essay?

• Does the order of features make sense?

• Have I explored the most important or the most interesting differences and similarities between my subjects? Have I given enough (or too many) examples?

• Have I used transitional words and phrases to clarify similarities and contrasts and to help readers follow my thoughts?

• Have I eliminated any unnecessary words?

When you're satisfied with your essay, share it with the members of your writing group. Ask for their questions, comments, and suggestions.

Exercise 21 **Proofread and Publish**

Give your paper a thorough going-over, and enlist a partner to check it, too. Once you've corrected errors in grammar, usage, mechanics, and spelling, find a way to share your paper with an audience. Your class might compile separate anthologies of comparison and contrast essays about history, ecology, literature, popular culture, and so forth. Contribute these anthologies to teachers in other departments or to the school library for future classes to use.
Answers will vary. Students should refer to Lesson 1.4 for proofreading strategies and publishing suggestions.

Expository Writing: Cause-Effect Essay

A **cause** is the condition, situation, or event that makes something occur. The result of that cause is called its **effect**. A **cause-effect essay** explores the link between one or more causes and the effect(s).

The following passage is from a case history reported in a psychology textbook. The author describes the treatments that a severely burned infant receives and the ways she responds.

from **Understanding Human Behavior**
by James V. McConnell

Background provides information to draw reader in.

[1]Their patient was a 17-month-old girl who suffered severe burns that covered 37 percent of her body. . . . [2]Medical care for the burns consisted chiefly of applying a stinging drug called silver nitrate, which was squirted over the little girl's bandages at frequent intervals by the nurses. [3]The doctors also began a series of skin grafts, but discontinued them when the infant's physical condition grew markedly worse. [4]After a month of treatment the little girl refused to eat; more than this, she became markedly upset whenever she was approached by any of the nursing staff.

[5]At this point social workers Shorkey and Taylor were called in to help. [6]They observed that the nurses, who were extremely disturbed at the child's condition, would frequently interrupt the painful treatment procedure and would attempt to soothe the little girl by talking to her, singing, and playing with her toys. [7]The more the nurses attempted to give the child love, the more violent the little girl became in her rejection of their attention and affection. [8]Indeed, it almost appeared that the staff members were making the child worse, not better.

Explains cause for girl's behavior

[9]Shorkey and Taylor reasoned that, in the infant's depressive state, <u>she simply could not discriminate between love and pain</u>. [10]To her, a nurse coming into the room had become a stimulus that too often was followed by unpleasant consequences (the silver nitrate). . . . [11]The infant had become conditioned to expect hurt rather than love whenever a nurse appeared on the scene. [12]Psychotherapy, then, should consist of helping the infant associate one set of stimuli with pain, another set with love and affection.

Description of treatment designed to establish new cause-effect relationships

[13]Shorkey and Taylor instituted the following changes: Whenever the nurses were to bathe the girl's bandages with silver nitrate, bright white lights were turned on. [14]The nursing staff wore green medical garments but were instructed not to talk or handle the infant unnecessarily, not to play with her, and not to spend one moment longer in the room than they had to. [15]Then, at other times, a set of red lights was turned on, the nursing staff

wore distinctive red garments, and they spent as much time as possible playing with the girl, rubbing the unburned parts of her body, talking to her, and giving her food. [16]Medication was never given during the "red light" or social-stimulation condition.

Two new treatments (causes) bring two new behaviors (effects)

[17]By the end of the second day the infant began responding differently to the two treatment situations. [18]That is, she continued to cry—but briefly—when the white lights were on and she was doused with the painful silver nitrate. [19]But when the red lights were on, her crying ceased and for the first time in several weeks she lost her fear of the staff members. [20]By the fourth day the infant began entering into little games with the staff; by the end of two weeks she was playing happily during the "red light" condition. [21]At this point the doctors

Conclusion: further causes and effects

resumed the skin grafts. [22]By the end of 6 weeks the little girl was well enough to be discharged from the hospital.

Critical Thinking

After you read the cause-effect essay, answer the following questions.

Use the following questions to lead a class discussion.

1. What cause-effect relationships does McConnell identify?

2. Explain how the effect stated in sentence 4 can be considered the cause for the action noted in sentence 5.

3. In your own words, explain what the social workers were trying to do in sentences 13–16. How would you rate their success?

Build Your Vocabulary. Look at the following words in context. What do you think each means: *discriminate* (sentence 9), *stimulus* (sentence 10), *stimuli* (sentence 12), *social-stimulation condition* (sentence 16)?

Writing Strategies

The purpose of a cause-effect essay is to explain an event, the result of an event, and often the reason the event came about. Use the following suggestions.

1. **Choose your topic.** Choose an issue that you genuinely wish to explore— perhaps an issue from history (for example, Why did the United States bomb Iraq in the 1990s?); one of the *How come?* questions small children ask (for example, Why is the sky blue?); an issue you've heard on TV and radio talk shows; or a behavioral change going on around you.

2. **Be open minded about causes and effects.** No matter what your topic is, you'll need to be careful not to make certain assumptions when you gather your information. **Don't oversimplify.** Here's why.

- **The first cause you spot is not necessarily the only one or the most important one.** For example, a low score on a test might be the result of insufficient studying, or it might be traced to lack of sleep or illness. Furthermore, the test might have been too hard or poorly constructed, or you might not have had enough time to complete it.

- **A cause may have effects other than the one you've linked it with.** For example, switching schools in the middle of the year is not the only effect of moving to a new town.

- **Distinguish among different kinds of causes. Immediate** causes come right before an effect; **underlying** causes may be far removed from an effect and, therefore, may not be readily apparent; some causes are part of a **cause-effect chain**, which is a series of events in which each cause creates an effect that, in turn, becomes the cause for another effect. An example of a cause-effect chain for McConnell's article is below.

CAUSE-EFFECT CHAIN

Cause A
Burned infant did not respond to medical treatment.

Effect A and Cause B
Social workers were called in.

Effect B and Cause C
Hospital implemented a new plan for treating infant.

Final Effect
Infant responded to treatment.

3. **Gather evidence.** Your writing will be more impressive and convincing if you offer credible evidence. Give your readers facts, statistical data, examples, incidents, and expert opinions. McConnell, for example, provides background information, gives descriptions of the infant's condition and her specific behaviors, and presents the expert views of social workers Shorkey and Taylor.

4. Determine an organization for your material. You might begin with a single cause and then explore the effects that it has. Or you might state an effect and trace its cause(s). You can present your information chronologically—particularly if you are reporting on a cause-event chain. Or, when there are several causes and effects to explore, you might order information in the order of importance. The three organizers below show plans for three different cause-effect essays. You may wish to use them as models when you write your own essay.

Writing Hint

Just because one event precedes another does not mean the first event necessarily causes the second one. For example, if you were to come down with a cold after standing in line for a movie on a freezing, blustery day, the weather may not be the only cause of your illness.

CAUSE-EFFECT ORGANIZERS

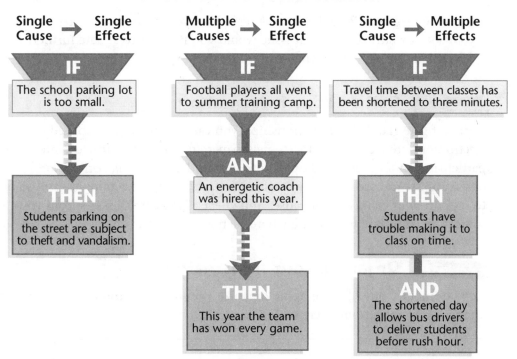

Single Cause → Single Effect

IF The school parking lot is too small.

THEN Students parking on the street are subject to theft and vandalism.

Multiple Causes → Single Effect

IF Football players all went to summer training camp.

AND An energetic coach was hired this year.

THEN This year the team has won every game.

Single Cause → Multiple Effects

IF Travel time between classes has been shortened to three minutes.

THEN Students have trouble making it to class on time.

AND The shortened day allows bus drivers to deliver students before rush hour.

5. Connect ideas. Transitional words and expressions help readers follow your thinking. Transitions such as *yet, therefore, as a result, so that, consequently,* and *because* are particularly helpful for writers and readers of cause-effect essays. *Next, after that, tomorrow, just before,* and *finally* are examples that show time order. *More important, of greater value, less important,* and *most significant* signal order of importance.

Exercise 22 Choose Your Topic

Use one or more of the following strategies to come up with a topic for a
cause-effect essay. Answers will vary. Prewriting strategies suggested in Lesson 1.1
may be useful.

- **Out of the Past** Think of a key historical event that interests you, and
  determine its underlying and immediate causes. Or ask yourself a *What if?*
  question that guides you to imagine what might have occurred had the event
  turned out differently. For example, what if the Russians had not launched the
  satellite that started the space race in the 1950s?

- **In the News** Form a stimulating question based on what you come across in
  periodicals, on TV, and on the radio. For example, why are people avoiding a
  particular food? Why do people want particular changes made in the law?

- **Right Under Your Nose** Look all around yourself. Why do people act as they
  do? What are the causes and effects of the simple events you witness every day?

- **Outside English Class** Refer to observations you've made in other classes. In
  your social studies class, what issue would you like to investigate further? In
  your science class, what went wrong with that experiment?

Exercise 23 Gather Your Information

To investigate cause-effect relationships, you can do research in printed or
electronic reference sources, locate newspaper and magazine articles, interview
participants in an event, and open your eyes and ears to make original
observations. You are looking for evidence (facts, statistics, examples, and so on)
to support your claims about causes and effects. Take careful notes from your
sources, making sure to indicate where each idea comes from.
Answers will vary.

Exercise 24 Organize Your Information

Copy or modify one of the graphic organizers on pages 62 and 63, and use it to
arrange your notes from Exercise 23.   Answers will vary.

Exercise 25 **Draft Your Essay**

Consider these hints for writing about the cause-effect relationship that you've identified and outlined graphically. Answers will vary. Chapter 2, Lessons 1–3, will help students develop a unified, coherent draft with ample support.

- **Present your thesis statement.** In your introduction, provide one or two sentences that express your main point.

- **Keep your audience in mind.** Think about how much your readers already know about your topic and what you'll need to tell them. Find a tone that will make readers receptive to your ideas and conclusions.

- **Follow your plan.** Be guided by but do not feel locked in to the graphic organizer. You may discover a sound reason to modify the picture.

- **Wrap it up.** In your conclusion, summarize your main point, and share any new insights you have gained.

Exercise 26 **Revise and Edit**

Read your essay aloud to yourself to get a sense of whether you have succeeded at what you set out to do. If you can, set it aside overnight before revising. When you revise, keep these questions in mind:

- Does my introduction draw readers into the essay?

- Have I provided enough evidence for each cause-effect relationship I suggest?

- Have I kept my writing as straightforward as possible?

- Have I used transitions to make my writing flow and to make relationships clear?

- Have I eliminated any unnecessary words?

When you're satisfied with your essay, share it with your writing group. Ask for their questions, comments, and suggestions.
Answers will vary.

Exercise 27 **Proofread and Publish** Working together

Give your paper a thorough going-over, and enlist a partner to check it, too. Once you've corrected errors in grammar, usage, mechanics, and spelling, find a way to share your paper with an audience. Consider distributing it to a club you belong to or to an interest group on the Internet.
Answers will vary. Students should refer to Lesson 1.4 for proofreading strategies and publishing suggestions.

Expository Writing: Problem-Solution Essay

In a **problem-solution essay**, you identify a significant problem, analyze it, and then propose one or more workable solutions.

The following article is from the Medicine column of the June 8, 1998, issue of *Time* magazine. In it, the authors identify and describe a problem. They then review possible solutions, pointing out both benefits and current drawbacks.

The Ticks Are Back
by Frederick Golden and Alice Park

Introduces problem in a way that hooks readers

[1]Those lush grasses and eruptions of colorful spring wildflowers around the country this week may seem like a benign by-product of El Niño's drenching rains. [2]But they could be a booby trap for outdoors-loving Americans. [3]Ready to pounce out of the dense vegetation on any passing body will be another effect of the moist, warmer-than-usual weather: battalions of speck-size ticks carrying the summertime scourge called Lyme disease.

Uses statistics to describe scope of problem in more detail

[4]Although the number of new cases of Lyme seemed to have peaked in the U.S. at 16,000 in 1996, public health officials are warning that this year's total could soar. [5]Since the first mysterious outbreak of arthritis-like pain and fever among residents near the Connecticut community of Lyme in 1975, at least 100,000 Americans have been infected with the disease. [6]Now endemic throughout the Northeast as well as parts of the Midwest and the West Coast, Lyme disease is caused by a corkscrew-shaped bacterium called *Borrelia burgdorferi*. [7]It is spread by the bite of ticks that usually live on mice and deer but also attach themselves to other warm-blooded creatures, including people. [8]Typically, within a month of a bite, a large, bull's-eye rash shows up at the site, accompanied by chills, fever, headache and painful joints. [9]Untreated, the infection may eventually lead to severe arthritis, facial palsy and irregular heartbeat. [10]Deaths, however, are rare.

Points out one kind of solution

Identifies a new, better solution

[11]Until now, only antibiotics have worked against Lyme disease. [12]But a new weapon may be at hand. [13]After a nationwide clinical trial involving some 11,000 people, an advisory panel last week urged the U.S. Food and Drug Administration to approve a novel vaccine developed by SmithKline Beecham under the name Lymerix. [14]The vaccine works when the tick is sucking the victim's blood, launching antibodies against the bacteria even before they've left the tick's gut. [15]Although it took three shots over 12 months to achieve it, the vaccine gave immunity to 90% of the test subjects ages 15 to 65 (it is somewhat less effective in the very old). [16]The only side effect reported was some soreness from the shots themselves.

[17]The vaccine is not a panacea, however. [18]"Right now the [immunization] schedule is not really user-friendly," admits Dr. Vijay Sikand of Tufts University School of Medicine, one of the participating

Provides data about downside of solution — physicians. [19]"You have to remember to come back 11 months after the second shot." [20]Nor did the panel recommend, pending further testing, use by pregnant women, people with chronic arthritis or youngsters under 18—a group with one of the highest risks of exposure. [21]So even if the FDA gives Lymerix a quick O.K., it won't be of much help against this summer's tick onslaught.

[22]Instead, if you're outdoor-bound in a tick-infested area this season, you would be well advised to take special precautions: dose yourself with a tick repellent, wear long sleeves and pants (with cuffs tucked

Concludes with cause-effect statement — stylishly under your socks) and avoid high grass. [23]If a close examination of personal nooks and crannies afterward reveals any suspect pinhead-size specks, remove them gently with tweezers.

Critical Thinking

After you read the problem-solution essay, answer the questions below.
Use the following questions to lead a class discussion.

1. How does the writer grab your attention in the opening paragraph? Notice that this problem-solution essay begins with a cause-effect relationship as discussed in Lesson 3.5. State the relationship in your own words.

2. Which paragraphs introduce and analyze the problem? Which paragraphs discuss solutions?

3. What's the problem with the new solution Golden and Park introduce?

Build Your Vocabulary. Look at the following words in context. What do you think each means: *benign* (sentence 1), *battalions* (sentence 3), *arthritis* (sentence 5), *antibiotics* (sentence 11), *panacea* (sentence 17)? Look up the meanings of the words you don't know. Add these words to your vocabulary notebook.

Enriching Your Vocabulary

A clue to the meaning of *panacea*, a cure-all, is its prefix *pan-* which means "all." Pan-American games involve athletes from North and South America. The plague was a *pandemic* disease because it spread over a large region.

Writing Strategies

The purpose of a problem-solution essay is to identify and explain a problem and to explain or report on a solution. Your audience, most likely, will be people who are interested in or concerned about the problem you are discussing. Use the following suggestions.

1. **Identify a problem.** The number of problems in need of solution is endless. We face large problems and small problems every day. To identify a problem to write about, review what you've already written in your notebooks or journals; brainstorm with friends and classmates; turn to TV,

radio, newspapers, and magazines for issues; or interview people active in local organizations. Try to pinpoint a problem for which possible solutions may exist. Steer clear of complicated problems that don't lend themselves to a brief essay.

2. **Explore the problem.** Think and read about the problem you chose. Pose a variety of questions such as the following: Who experiences this problem? How serious is the problem (a minor inconvenience or a major tribulation)? What proof, or evidence, supports your statement that the problem is indeed a problem? What tone should you take in discussing it? Can you break the problem down into parts, each of which might have a solution?

3. **Brainstorm solutions.** Think about the whole problem or parts of the problem. What have others said about handling the problem? What new thoughts can you add?

4. **Rank the possible solutions.** Determine which are ineffective solutions—and why. Then identify the best solution. Is it the best because it has the fewest negatives? Because it is the most practical? The cheapest? The most morally appropriate? List the evidence that proves the validity of your ranking.

5. **Address resistance.** Acknowledge arguments that some readers may raise against your proposed solution. Counter their resistance by providing additional information.

6. **Note how to implement the solution.** What step-by-step instructions can you give your readers about putting the solution into place?

7. **Organize your presentation.** Go back over your notes, and determine how much of your essay you will devote to the problem and how much to the solution. Distribute your notes from all the preceding strategies onto the frame at right or a variation of it.

Writing Hint

You don't have to work on a monumental problem. Consider choosing one that is somewhat lighter or one that you can treat with humor. For example, what's wrong with your school's colors or basketball uniforms? How can you get support for a new fight song?

A Problem-Solution Frame

Statement of Problem
- Proof

Possible Solutions
- Deficiencies

Best Solution
- Justification
- Steps for Implementation

Objections to Solution
- Defense of Solution

Conclusion

Exercise 28 Choose Your Topic

Use one or more of the prewriting strategies in Lesson 1.1 to come up with a topic for your problem-solution essay. Answers will vary.

Exercise 29 Gather Your Information

After you identify your problem, generate notes about the extent of the problem. List facts, statistics, and examples. Then start considering solutions for part or all of the problem. List as much information as possible for each solution—facts, statistics, examples, experts' opinions and quotations, and anecdotes. Which solutions pose their own problems? Note which solution you prefer and which ones you will emphasize in your essay. Answers will vary.

Exercise 30 Draft Your Essay

Consider these hints for writing about the problem you have identified and the solution you will put forth. These hints supplement the problem-solution frame on page 68. Answers will vary.

- **Introduce the problem, and elaborate on it.** In a few sentences, present and explain the problem. Think about how much your readers already know about the problem and what additional information you'll need to tell them. Use interesting statistics, quotations, or observations to grab and hold your readers' attention. Find a tone that will make readers receptive to your thinking.

- **Decide whether you will mention defective solutions or only your preferred solution.** Present the preferred solution in detail. Decide on an order for presenting the facts, statistics, experts' opinions and quotations, anecdotes, and examples that you have gathered.

- **Address your critics.** Consider drafting one or more paragraphs that answer the objections to your solution.

- **Itemize steps.** In a paragraph or list, tell readers how to carry out the solution.

- **Restate your case.** Your **conclusion** should include a compelling statement that supports your solution. It can be a thoughtful quotation or a question or statement that invites readers to think more about your ideas and to take them seriously.

Exercise 31 Revise and Edit

Read your essay aloud to yourself to get a sense of whether you have succeeded at what you set out to do. If you can, set it aside overnight before revising. When you revise, keep these questions in mind:

Answers will vary. Students should refer to Lesson 1.3 for more revising strategies.

• Does my introduction draw readers into the essay?

• Have I stated the problem clearly and fully?

• Have I presented a solution readers can understand? Have I provided a strong case for the solution, one backed by ample evidence?

• Does my conclusion give readers something to think about?

• Have I used transitional words and phrases to make my writing flow smoothly and to make relationships clear?

• Have I eliminated any unnecessary words?

• Does my conclusion summarize my solution effectively?

When you're satisfied with your essay, share it with the members of your writing group. Ask for their questions, comments, and suggestions.

Exercise 32 Proofread and Publish

Give your paper a thorough going-over, and enlist a partner to check it, too. Once you've corrected errors in grammar, usage, mechanics, and spelling, find a way to share your paper with an audience.

• If other students tackle the same problem but offer different solutions, consider participating with them in a debate or panel discussion. Debaters can use the essays to prepare their oral arguments.

• Submit to the school or local newspaper any essays that deal with issues of concern to your peers or to the community.

Answers will vary.

Writing About Literature: Analyzing a Work

When you set out to write about a work of literature, you generally choose among three common types of essays: (1) the **personal response essay**, in which you share the thoughts and emotions that strike you as you read particular passages in the work; (2) the **evaluation essay**, in which you rate a work of literature according to established criteria, such as believability of characters or plot; and (3) the **literary analysis**, in which you comment about the work as a whole from one perspective—for example, from the perspective of history, from the perspective of a certain philosophy of life, or from the perspective of one or more of the elements of literature (characterization, plotting, imagery, setting, and so on).

The following excerpt is part of an analysis of Thomas Hardy's novel *The Mayor of Casterbridge*. The author, Dennis Potter, explains how the characters in the novel inevitably fall to the twists of fate that Thomas Hardy has in store for them.

On Hardy's *The Mayor of Casterbridge*
by Dennis Potter

¹The story of Michael Henchard, who rose from itinerant haytrusser plodding the country roads with his young wife and child to be the richest corn merchant and chief citizen of Casterbridge and then fell back again into embittered poverty and loneliness, is the tragedy of a proud man buffeted by what Thomas Hardy calls 'the persistence of the unforeseen.' ²This ominous phrase comes in the last, sad sentence of the novel when the entranced reader can at last look back at the great surge of narrative and measure the inexorable tide of fate as it swamps the central character and all that he has worked for, all that he has loved.

³Henchard is not idly swept aside. ⁴He is tough and headstrong and passionate, a man with a tremendous will and a tenacious spirit—one of the greatest characters, indeed, in modern literature. ⁵We are pulled in to the turmoil of his life almost before he opens his mouth, for there is nothing but 'the voice of a weak bird singing a trite old evening song' to temper the taciturnity of the stern young man with the springless walk who takes his family and his basket of tools in the search for work. ⁶The novel begins its long journey with the same slow tread along the dusty road, but we soon sense in its steady rhythm the unfolding of a vast purpose and a noble struggle for self-fulfillment. ⁷And it is a journey that the reader makes, too —one which will illuminate the shape of his or her own life and thus press

Enriching Your Vocabulary

The noun *taciturnity* comes from the Latin verb *tacere*, which means "to be silent." Most often, the adjective form of the word, *taciturn*, is used. A person who thought deeply, yet seldom spoke, my grandfather was known all through the county for his *taciturnity*.

Thesis statement

Analysis of main character; relates to thesis

Quotation helps describe character

upon fundamental emotions which are scarcely half engaged by so many of the impoverishments of modern fiction: I envy anyone who is reading *The Mayor of Casterbridge* for the first time.

Short plot summary

[8]Within a few pages of the opening of the story, the young Henchard, through his own foolishness, has lost his wife and child. [9]It is this event which will forever haunt him, no matter how far he rises or how real his remorse. [10]The past cannot be disowned. [11]It rises up again and strikes him down, but not before Michael Henchard seems to have repaired the hole that has been torn out of his being by his own feckless behavior.

[12]The loops and coils of the plot, where accident, coincidence, even rain and sunshine bear down on the characters at the most crucial moments, give one not only the uncomfortable dislocations of 'the persistence of the unforeseen' but also a broad and vivid picture of rural England as its agriculture began to change. [13]The novel brings a whole community alive, and the things that count in it are money and work and the harvest, rumour and gossip and reputation, a complete mesh of life and circumstance in which the characters are also their own audience, their own remorseless judges. [14]Even the comical old yokels nodding their bald pates together in the pub are turned into witnesses who suddenly astound us with a long perspective of the ups and downs which bind these lives together in the streets of 'Casterbridge' (Dorchester) and the barns and fields beyond.

[15]Yet no matter how pinioned by the grip of their own destinies, the people in these pages are not paper boats on the tide or, more appropriately, mere stalks to be cut down by the scythe. [16]They defend themselves. [17]They scheme and plan and pit their energies against whatever persistence it is that sharpens or drains their passions, and we are unable to remain aloof from the pathos, the expectations, the loves or the rivalries which make this such a great novel. [18]The ironies and vagaries of fortune which afflict the characters spring out at the reader, too. [19]No-one who starts the book will altogether escape the tense pleasure or anxiety about '*What is going to happen?*' that pulses through the narrative. . . .

Refers back to thesis statement

[20]The book reminds us just as much of the continued certainties of our lives as of 'the persistence of the unforeseen' which haunts the man in the brown corduroy jacket pacing along the country road on a summer evening long ago. [21]He is making a path into our own imaginations.

Critical Thinking

After you have read the literary analysis, answer the questions below.
Use the following questions to lead a class discussion.

1. In your own words, summarize this excerpt of a literary analysis.

2. How does Potter interpret the phrase "the persistence of the unforseen" (sentence 1)?

3. From what you've read of Potter's essay, would you be interested in reading the novel? Why or why not?

4. Find examples of how Potter shows his respect for Hardy's writing.

Build Your Vocabulary. Which of these words from the essay can you define: *taciturnity* (sentence 5), *feckless* (sentence 11), *pates* (sentence 14), *pinioned* (sentence 15), *vagaries* (sentence 18)? Use context clues to help you. Then look up the words you don't know in a dictionary, and use the phonetic symbols to pronounce them correctly. Add these terms to your vocabulary notebook.

Writing Strategies

You will be asked to write many book reports in your academic career. The purpose of this type of writing is to examine a work carefully and to explain your interpretation of it. Your audience will usually be a teacher or peer who is familiar with the subject of your essay. Use the following suggestions.

1. **Present a thesis statement.** Somewhere in your introductory paragraph, make clear what your essay is going to do—what piece of literature you are going to analyze, from what perspective, and to what end (that is, what are you going to prove?).

2. **Determine how much plot summary to give.** Potter does not assume that his readers know the story well. When you suspect that your intended reader is not familiar with the work you are analyzing, invest a few sentences or a paragraph in a summary. If the work you are analyzing is very well known, you can forgo most of the plot summary.

3. **Proceed by balancing general statements (your main points) with specifics in support of them.**

   • Quote from the text where appropriate.

   • Refer to details (incidents and characters) in the text without quoting.

   • Make comparisons: A comparison or contrast with another work or other characters may clarify a point you are making.

   • Quote or summarize what an expert has written, making sure to give full credit to the expert.

4. **Use present tense.** When you refer to characters or events in the work, cast their actions in the present tense. Here are examples from Potter's essay:

Hencherd **is** not idly swept aside.

. . . the people in these pages **are** not paper boats on the tide . . .

The book **reminds** us . . .

5. **Keep your tone consistent.** Adopt and stay with a formal and serious tone. Generally, contractions, sentence fragments, and slang do not belong in literary analysis. You can, however, use images of your own; notice, for example, Potter's comment about the book, "I envy anyone who is reading *The Mayor of Casterbridge* for the first time."

> **Writing Hint**
>
> To quote from literature:
>
> • Make sure that you copy word for word with exact punctuation.
>
> • Set off as a block any quotations longer than three lines; do not enclose the block in quotation marks.
>
> • Use ellipsis points (. . .) to indicate that you've made a deletion from a passage.
>
> See Chapter 14 for details about quotation marks and ellipsis points.

QUESTIONS FOR LITERARY ANALYSIS

Use the following questions to get ideas for writing.

QUESTIONS FOR ANY LITERARY WORK

Characters: What do the characters want or need at the beginning of the work of literature? How do the characters change? Are the characters complex or simple? What can you say about the characters' motivations? About their speech? What does the main character learn or discover? What is that character's relationships with other characters like? How does the author reveal what the main characters are like?

Plot: What is the central conflict? Is it internal or external? How is it revealed and resolved? What larger meaning does the resolution suggest? Does the writer use foreshadowing or suspense?

Setting: How does the setting influence the action, the characters, and the outcome?

Point of view: Who tells the story? Why has the author selected this point of view? How would the work change if the story were told from a different point of view?

Theme: What universal insight about life or people does the work offer? Which passages or elements most clearly convey that insight? If the theme is not expressed directly, can you infer a theme from the outcome or by how the characters change?

Imagery: What effect is created by metaphor, simile, personification, and symbolism?

ADDITIONAL QUESTIONS FOR POETRY

Speaker: What can you say about the speaker of the poem? Is the speaker standing in for the poet or for another character?

Sound: What effect is created by any of the following: meter, rhythm, repetition, onomatopoeia, alliteration, consonance, rhyme scheme?

ADDITIONAL QUESTIONS FOR PLAYS

Structure: How does the division into acts and scenes underscore the theme of the play?

Stage directions: How do the stage directions help to convey the setting? How do they affect the delivery of lines and the action?

Exercise 33 Prewriting: Choose and Limit a Topic

Choose a piece of literature—a short story, a novel, a play, or a poem—to which you already have a strong personal response. In this workshop, you will have the opportunity to look at the work more deeply, more critically, and perhaps figure out what caused your initial response. Use the questions above and on page 74 to help you choose one literary element from the work to focus on. After choosing a literary element, consider narrowing your focus even further— perhaps to one character, one setting, or one image.
Answers will vary. Students should refer to Lesson 1.1 for prewriting strategies.

Exercise 34 Prewriting: Major Points and Supporting Details

As you reread the literary work, take notes on anything of relevance to the literary element you're studying. Next, form clear statements that generalize about the details of that literary element. Then, based on those statements, draft a thesis statement—one or two sentences that express what you will cover in your essay. Answers will vary.

Exercise 35 Organize and Draft Your Essay

Now you have the opportunity to take the statements about major points (and their corresponding details) that you prepared for Exercise 34 and decide in what order to present them in your essay. Sit down and start writing at any point in the essay—beginning or middle. What's important at this stage is getting your ideas down in sentences and paragraphs. Later, you can polish them. The draft stage may also be where you want to come up with a possible title for your essay. The title, ideally, should mention both the work of literature and hint at your essay's controlling idea.

Answers will vary. Students should refer to Lesson 1.2 for drafting strategies.

Exercise 36 Revise Your Essay

After you've given yourself a break from your essay, take it out, and read it with the following questions in mind.

Answers will vary. Students should refer to Lesson 1.3 for additional revising strategies.

• Does the introduction identify the work?

• Is the thrust of your essay clearly presented in a thesis statement?

• Are the general statements—the major points—clear but not wordy?

• Have you provided enough details to support each major point?

• Are all the details relevant?

• Is the organization of your essay easy to follow?

• Does the conclusion clearly and effectively wrap up your essay?

Exercise 37 Edit, Proofread, and Publish Your Essay

When you're satisfied that you have corrected all problems in grammar, usage, mechanics, and spelling, exchange papers with a partner so that you can help each other find errors you may have missed. Then consider sharing it with others. On the Internet, you might locate a discussion group dedicated to the author of the work you wrote about. Consider joining the discussion and posting all or part of your essay to the group for response and criticism.

Answers will vary. Students should refer to Lesson 1.4 for proofreading strategies and publishing suggestions.

Expository Writing: Research Paper

Researching a topic and writing a paper based on your research gives you an opportunity to become an expert on the topic. Since you will spend a lot of time on your topic for the period of your research and writing, select a topic that intrigues you and one that you want to learn more about.

There are at least five kinds of research papers.

1. **Summarizing/synthesizing paper.** In the most common type of research paper, you **summarize** or explain information that you have gathered from several sources. You **synthesize** (put together to form a new whole out of) what other writers have reported.

2. **Evaluation paper.** This research paper is similar to the first kind but also includes evaluation, or opinion of what your research reveals. For example, your paper might present several observers' statements about the cause of a particular effect and conclude with *your* statement about which observer seems most on target and why.

3. **Original research paper.** In this type of paper, you present and summarize your original research. For a social studies paper, you might present findings based upon surveys, questionnaires, or interviews you have conducted, drawing conclusions and making predictions from your data. In a science research paper, you might report on the results of a series of your own experiments.

4. **I-search paper.** In this type of paper, you tell the story of how you wrote your research paper. An I-search paper not only presents information you discovered about a topic but also explains why you chose that topic, how you conducted your research, and what you experienced along the way.

5. **Combination paper.** In this type of research paper, you would draw on elements from the others. You could, for instance, provide your own evaluation of or opinion on the research others have done.

On the following pages, you will find excerpts from a high school student's research paper, which synthesizes what other writers have written about the history, impact, and demise of Negro league baseball. The paper includes parenthetical identifications of sources and a Works Cited list, both of which are discussed later in the workshop.

4-line heading:
Name/Teacher/
Class/Due Date

Matthew Eisenberg
Mrs. Elizabeth Devine
AP United States History
May 1, 1994

Title, centered

Baseball's Negro Leagues

From 1898 to 1947, America's national pastime, baseball, fell prey to the racism in the country and excluded black players from white teams and leagues. Despite their acknowledged equality as players, black players were forced to play in inferior ballparks, under inferior conditions, because of their skin color. In the early years of all-black baseball, teams struggled to make money, players struggled to earn a living, and leagues struggled to stay together. By the 1930s, however, two new leagues had formed: the Negro American League and the Negro National League. It was during this period that black baseball flourished, and despite the disappointment of being left out of the major leagues, Negro ballplayers and teams made the two organizations a success.

Introductory paragraph; ends with 2-sentence thesis statement

Baseball had become a popular game during the Civil War, as bored soldiers looked for ways to spend their time in between battles (Palmer and Thorn 7). By 1872, as military governments ruled the South, the first black player, John Fowler, joined a professional league (Peterson 18). Fowler wandered from minor league to minor league, and although he played all nine positions, he never distinguished himself as a ballplayer (Peterson 21). Soon after Fowler, another black man joined the professional baseball ranks. Moses Fleetwood Walker, a student at Oberlin College, left school early to join the minor leagues with the Toledo club of the American Association. When that league was declared an official major league in 1885, Walker became the first black major leaguer. Despite threats of lynching from the Richmond club, Walker played on. Eventually too much pressure mounted against him, and Toledo released him. Walker's precedent, however, led the way for many more blacks in the following years (Peterson 21–24). In 1885, there were four blacks in white baseball, and by 1887, there were twenty (White 82).

Background information—two paragraphs

At the same time, however, the first all-black baseball team was formed in Babylon, Long Island. This team, chosen from waiters at area hotels, began barnstorming the Northeast with the players making $12 to $18 per week. In 1886, the Cuban Giants, as they were called to make people think they were foreigners, recruited some of the finest black ballplayers from all over the country. After beating one white team after another, they won wide acclaim by beating the Eastern League (an upper-level minor-league) champion, Bridgeport (White 11–23). In 1887, they joined with other newly formed Negro teams to form the League of Colored Baseball. Although it folded after a week because it was a financial disaster, in Solomon White's

Running head,
½ inch from top
of paper

words, "The short time of its existence served to bring out the fact that colored baseball players of ability were numerous" (26). Later that year, the Cuban Giants once more distinguished themselves by nearly beating the World Champion Detroit club (White 59).

Introduces establishment of color barrier

Although blacks were having success in white baseball, in 1887, Jim Crow began to take blacks away from the white game. Many players competing against blacks complained, and in Syracuse, several players were suspended for refusing to play (Peterson 28). With venom and hate, baseball great Adrian "Cap" Anson led the drive to segregate the game. In his book, Solomon White charges Anson with nearly single-handedly creating the color barrier. After entire teams refused to play against blacks, the clubs which they were on slowly began to release the blacks (Peterson 31). . . .

By 1889, there were just two blacks in white baseball: Fleet Walker and Dick Johnson, who both had distinguished themselves with their off-the-field class. Walker was released after the 1890 season, however. . . . By 1898, the barrier was complete, and no black players or teams remained in white baseball (Peterson 49). . . .

Background on early history of black professional baseball

In 1900, there were five black professional teams: the Cuban Giants, the Cuban X Giants, the Red Stockings, the Chicago Unions, and the Columbia Giants. Each barnstormed in a separate region of the country, and each was mildly successful playing blacks, whites, or each other (Peterson 59). In 1906 a new league formed made up of these teams, one that lasted for almost an entire year. The final game was played in front of ten thousand mostly black fans at the Philadelphia Athletics' stadium (Peterson 62–63). Between 1900 and 1920, many Negro teams were formed, most barnstormed, and a few leagues were attempted. Players would travel at night, often encountering problems, because of their race, with lodging and restaurants. They would play every day, sometimes two or three times (Peterson 63–65). Most made from $40 to $100 a month plus expenses, far below the salaries of white ballplayers (Peterson 70). It was a hard life for the ballplayers, especially those who knew they could have been superstars in white baseball. The greatest player of the era was John Lloyd, nicknamed the Black Honus Wagner. Wagner, the Hall of Fame shortstop, proudly acknowledged, "I am honored to have John Lloyd called the Black Wagner. It is a privilege to have been compared with him" (Peterson 73).

Topic sentence introduces "golden age" of Negro league baseball; following paragraphs provide support.

The 1930s and 1940s—an era of racism, segregation, and hate in this country—surprisingly became the golden age of Negro league baseball. Through hardship, depression, and war, all-time great players like Satchell Paige, Josh Gibson, Buck Leonard, and Cool Papa Bell showcased their tremendous talents in the leagues that were gaining fast acceptance among whites and blacks alike. The Negro leagues of the era were a tremendous success for various reasons.

The quality of play and the players delighted fans and helped gain blacks acceptance, easing the eventual integration of blacks and whites. The attendance is a testament to the fact that blacks finally had a game of their own and role models to look up to, and many whites also found enjoyment by watching Negro baseball. Financially, the Negro leagues grew to a two-million-dollar a year enterprise, the biggest black-dominated business in the country (Peterson 93). Finally, Negro league baseball provided many blacks with the chance to do what they loved most: play the game. As Bill Wright, a Negro league player for twenty-one years said, "I think people know now that it was a mistake not to let us play in the major leagues, but we didn't ever hold a grudge. We had too much fun" (Smith 80).

Andrew "Rube" Foster, an excellent pitcher in the early twentieth century, is widely considered the father of Negro league baseball. In 1919, he proposed the first Negro National League, made up of eight teams (Peterson 80–84). The league began a new era for black baseball, as crowds of eight thousand to ten thousand were common in 1920. Attendance soon fell as Foster's death in 1923 left the league with no strong leadership, but the profit made by clubs during the four years was undeniably a source of inspiration for the next series of pioneer owners.

The year 1933 saw two strong men emerge to create the second Negro National League. Cum Posey, founder of the Homestead Grays, and Gus Greenlee, founder of the Pittsburgh Crawfords, worked together to help found the longest-lasting league in Negro baseball. Both owners had made considerable money off their talent-rich teams and saw an even greater potential in organized baseball. The Crawfords, Grays, Chicago American Giants, Indianapolis ABC's, the Detroit Stars, and Columbus Blue Birds—and later the Nashville Elite and the Baltimore Black Sox—filled out the roster in 1933. Greenlee's strong and sometimes dictatorial hand helped the Negro National League rule the East Coast (Peterson 91–103).

Soon thereafter, H. G. Hall founded the Negro American League. At first it was quite unstable, as teams rotated in and out of the league. By the late 1930s, however, both leagues were on strong financial ground (Peterson 93). There were many problems at first, though, as weak leadership hurt the play on the field. It was not unusual for a player to attack an umpire who made an unfavorable call because there was rarely punishment handed down from the league hierarchy. As players began to realize that the owners were out solely for money, many jumped from team to team, often in mid-season, and played for whoever would pay the larger salary (Peterson 94–95).

Eisenberg 4

Despite this, there was little doubt that the Negro leagues were becoming the proving ground for black baseball players in the 1930s. Each team played between thirty and forty games a year, and the winners from each league played each other in the World Series (Peterson 277). Similarly, black ballplayers were beginning to gain fame as they became household names in black families, and many sportswriters began to openly wonder how these men would fare in the white leagues. The Negro leagues were no longer laughed at by white baseball, and in the next two decades many black players proved that they were equal to if not better than any white counterpart. . . .

With the influx of talent and the new respect for the league came a boom in attendance. While the first Negro National League's World Series in 1926 drew only nine thousand fans, the famous East-West games in the 1930s and 1940s never drew fewer than twenty thousand. These games, the brainchild of Gus Greenlee, were tremendous showcases of Negro talent. At the peak of Negro league baseball success, 1943, the East-West game was played at Comiskey Park, home of the Chicago White Sox, and drew 51,723 fans. Mostly blacks attended these games, but it was not uncommon for whites to attend. Regular season games also drew well, although not nearly as well as the East-West games, and a marquee player like Paige or Gibson could always draw a large interracial crowd of spectators (Peterson 100).

The league was a financial success for the owners, and the players were compensated nicely as well. By World War II, an average Negro league player would make about $400–$500 a month plus expenses, and stars could make nearly $1,000 per month. While these numbers did not compare to the salaries of white major leaguers, they were far superior to the money made in white minor leagues or by most blacks in America (Peterson 98). . . .

The Negro leagues may not have received the respect that major league baseball earned, but they certainly enjoyed a success of their own. Constantly battling racism and doubts about their ability, the players went on the field to play their game and, in so doing, earned the admiration of blacks and many whites alike. Life was not easy for black ballplayers, but they overcame the disappointment of being left out of the white game and proved that they could do just as well. By the end of the 1940s, the Negro leagues had become so successful in showcasing black baseball talent that the white leagues were forced to question the wisdom of their decision to exclude them. They could no longer claim to have the greatest talent in the country when everyone knew that only half of baseball's superstars actually played on white teams.

Eisenberg 5

Introduces new
topic: the need
to integrate

By 1940, pressure was mounting in major league baseball to allow blacks to play. Managers and many ballplayers called for the end of the racial barrier (Peterson 177). Bill Veeck led the charge in 1943 with an idea to buy the last-place Philadelphia Phillies and fill the team completely with Negro league stars. "I had not the slightest doubt that in 1944 . . . the Phils would have leaped from seventh place to the pennant," Veeck claimed (Peterson 180). Although Veeck failed when baseball's owners learned of his idea and didn't approve the sale of the team, it was a large step in integrating baseball.

In the mid-1940s, several baseball teams held tryouts for black players. The Boston Red Sox, for example, invited several players, most notably Jackie Robinson, to a private workout. Each player showcased tremendous talent but never heard from the team again. This was a typical scenario for most of the tryouts as, for one reason or another, the players never made the team (Peterson 183–86). Branch Rickey, president of the Brooklyn Dodgers, set out to change this pattern (Dixon and Hannigan 302).

Under the pretense that he was planning to buy a Negro league team, Rickey sent out scouts to watch Negro league games. These scouts would report back to Rickey on the best players, and Rickey would personally see many of them. Realizing that it would take more than just a great ballplayer to become baseball's pioneer, Rickey had specific criteria. One name kept popping up from all his scouts: Jackie Robinson, the fleet-footed second baseman of the Kansas City Monarchs. Although Robinson was not the best player in black baseball, he was an excellent ballplayer known for his competitive fire on the field and his gentlemanly conduct off of it. Robinson was a non-drinking, non-smoking, former tri-sport star at UCLA, and an army veteran (Dixon and Hannigan 188--89). He was signed by Rickey to the Triple-A Montreal Royals of the International League (Dixon and Hannigan 190). Ordered never to fight back against any racism he encountered, Robinson held up under the media's magnifying glass and the constant taunts of spectators and quietly became the Royals' star player. The next year, on April 15, 1947, he broke the color barrier when he started at second base on opening day for the Dodgers. Rickey had carefully orchestrated his debut, and, shortly before the season started, he traded a bunch of players who had spoken out against Robinson playing on the team. Robinson went on to win the National League Rookie of the Year award (Peterson 198). . . .

It is likely that if it had not been for the success of the Negro National League and the Negro American League, black baseball players would have had to wait years longer before breaking the color barrier. Similarly, had Robinson failed to impress the Montreal crowds or the Brooklyn Dodgers' front office, or simply reacted to the prejudice he faced with any rage or hint of retribution, it would have set Rickey's effort back several years. The Negro

Eisenberg 6

leagues had been successful in opening the door to so many opportunities that black players had never before been confronted with, and, given the chance, they proved their equality and often superiority to white ballplayers. The Negro leagues and the courage of Robinson gave Willie Mays, Hank Aaron, and even the great black players of today the opportunity to play in the major leagues.

And so, with the beginning of a new era for major league baseball, the era of the Negro leagues reached the beginning of the end. In 1947, every Negro league team lost money, and attendance plummeted (Peterson 201). As one Negro league star after another went to the major leagues, the league withered. Barnstorming once more became common, but now each team needed a gimmick. Clowns, cannibals, midgets, and many other sideshows were used to draw fans to the games. Only players with personality played on black teams because they were called upon to make jokes or humorous plays to keep the fans excited. Negro league baseball ceased to be a breeding ground for the finest black talent in America, and instead fans went to the major league parks, where they could see their black heroes play with whites for the first time in nearly sixty years (Dixon and Hannigan 302). The Negro American League and Negro National League survived on a small scale until they finally collapsed in 1960.

The Negro leagues, even with their faults, proved to the world the equality of blacks on the baseball field. At the time, every small step in the overall struggle against racism had an impact, and the fact that white baseball was forced to admit that it needed blacks lifted the spirits of many who were fighting the civil rights battle. Baseball had slammed the door on black players in the 1890s, and the blacks became such a success without whites that fifty years later many baseball executives were virtually begging to get them back. . . .

The impact of the Negro leagues has in many ways been lost among today's baseball players and fans. In a recent *Sports Illustrated* survey, several players didn't even know who Jackie Robinson was, but there is no way to tell what the game would have been like without him or without the Negro leagues. Baseball's Negro leagues, despite the tragic circumstances through which they were created, had a tremendous impact on the game of baseball and all of society, even if they are not well known today. Denied their dream, black players took the field and made that dream possible for generations to come, while winning the hearts and minds of millions of baseball fans in the process.

Background information—two paragraphs—on demise of Negro league baseball

Concluding paragraph: writer's final observations

Eisenberg 7

Works Cited

Centered title, 1 inch from top

Book by one author

Chadwick, Bruce. *When the Game Was Black and White*. New York: Abbeville, 1992.

Craft, David. *The Negro Leagues*. New York: Crescent, 1993.

Original interviews conducted by writer of research paper

Craig, Thomas. (National Baseball Hall of Fame and Museum). Telephone interview. April 8, 1994.

Dalin, David. (University of Hartford). Telephone interview. April 1, 1994.

Book by two authors

Dixon, Phil, and Patrick J. Hannigan. *The Negro Baseball Leagues*. Mattituck: Amereon, 1992.

Holway, John B. *Blackball Stars: Negro League Pioneers*. New York: Carroll, 1992.

James, Bill. *The Bill James Historical Baseball Abstract*. New York: Villard, 1986.

Palmer, Pete, and John Thorn. *Total Baseball*. New York: Warner, 1989.

Peterson, Robert. *Only the Ball Was White*. New York: Oxford UP, 1992.

Rogosin, Donn. *Invisible Men: Life in Baseball's Negro Leagues*. New York: Atheneum, 1983.

Magazine article

Smith, Shelley. "Remembering Their Game." *Sports Illustrated* 6 July 1992: 80+.

White, Solomon. *Official Baseball Guide*. Library of Baseball Classics. Columbia: Camden, 1997.

Writing Strategies The purpose of a research paper is to provide in-depth information on a limited topic. Apply the following strategies.

1. **Select a general topic.** Choose a field that interests you. Within that field, you need to come up with a topic limited enough so that you can do it justice given the time, reference sources, and space you've got. While searching for a topic, try the following ideas:

   • Skim articles in magazines and newspapers, even old ones.

   • Review your own writer's journal.

   • Visit science, art, or history museums.

   • Go to the zoo, a play, a botanical garden, a concert, an ethnic fair, or a celebration.

- Jot down ideas as you read for pleasure.

- Browse through your textbooks and through encyclopedias, atlases, and other reference sources.

- Talk with someone who works in a field that interests you.

2. **Limit your topic further.** Be sure you pick a topic that you can cover sufficiently within the length assigned for the paper, and be sure you can find adequate information. Narrowing a topic to the right size may require adjustments as you go. For example, a student trying to write a paper called "Black Players in Baseball" in just a few pages would find the topic much too broad; on the other hand, "Black Players' Batting Stats in the 1920s" is probably too narrow.

   Check to determine if you will be able to find at least four or five useful sources on your library's shelves, in an electronic database, and in the *Readers' Guide to Periodical Literature*.

3. **Budget your time.** Don't wait until the last minute. The list below suggests a sensible way to budget time for each step in the research process, given an eight-week time frame. Notice that you'll probably spend much more time doing research and taking notes than you will spend on actually writing your first draft.

Steps in Research Process	Time
Choose and limit topic	3 days
Find and evaluate sources; make bibliography cards	3 days
Take notes	1 ½ weeks
Draft thesis statement and title	2 days
Draft outline	1 week
Write first draft	1 week
Document sources	2 days
Revise	1 ½ weeks
Proofread	2 days
Prepare final manuscript	3 days

4. **Find multiple printed sources.** Chances are that you will need to consult both primary and secondary sources. A **primary source** is an original text or document, such as a literary work, a diary, a letter, a speech, an interview, or a historical document. A **secondary source** presents a writer's comments on a primary source. Reference books, biographies, literary criticism, and history and science textbooks are examples of secondary sources.

In many libraries, electronic databases have replaced card catalogs, the *Readers' Guide to Periodical Literature*, and newspaper indexes. InfoTrac's General Reference Center, available in many libraries, and other electronic indexes give you access not only to the titles of relevant magazine articles but also to the texts of the articles.

5. **Find Internet sources.** A contemporary researcher needs to be comfortable using computers hooked up to the World Wide Web for current information. If necessary, ask a librarian to help you conduct an online search on your topic. You will need to work with various search engines, and you will need to word your searches carefully. You will have an opportunity to follow online links to related topics. As you proceed, you will have to consider whether to modify your research topic in light of productive Web sites that you find unexpectedly.

Writing Hint

Had Matthew Eisenberg done his research in the late 1990s on the Internet, he might have found the Web site *http://www.blackbaseball.com* with stories, photos, surveys, and links to other sites.

6. **Evaluate possible sources.** Your secondary sources must meet the following criteria.

   • **Are sources up-to-date?** Which is a better source for information about the impact of escalating salaries in major league baseball: a twenty-year-old book or last week's *Sports Illustrated*?

   • **Are sources accurate?** Don't believe everything you read. Reliable sources are both accurate and unbiased. You might trust a *New York Times* article more than a column in a sensationalistic tabloid. Be especially careful about Internet sources. A university-connected site or a government database is usually a more reliable source than a personal home page by someone who has not yet established credibility as a reference source.

   • **Are sources appropriate for you?** Figure out for what audience the printed or electronic source is intended. Materials written for experts might be too technical, while those intended for younger readers might simplify issues too much for your purposes.

   • **Are sources relevant?** Finally, the information you collect for your research paper must directly relate to your limited topic. If a source isn't pertinent, either skip that source for now, or modify your research topic in a way that justifies using the source.

7. **Keep track of your sources.** For every source you use, make a source card (sometimes called a **bibliography source card**) that contains all essential

publishing information. Give each source a number, and write that number in the upper right-hand corner of the card. Then, when you take notes, instead of rewriting all this information on each note card, you can simply place the source's number in the upper right-hand corner of your note card for identification.

SAMPLE SOURCE CARD

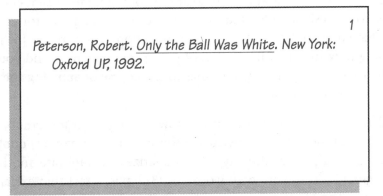

Peterson, Robert. *Only the Ball Was White*. New York: Oxford UP, 1992.

1

Number of source

8. **Take notes.** After you've read a source, you may quote it exactly if the writer's words perfectly express a point you want to make. Most often, though, put the information into your own words.

- You can **summarize** the information by giving only the most important ideas in your own words.

- Or you can **paraphrase** the information, restating every idea in the same order as in the original but in your own words.

At the top of each note card, write the main idea, and underline it.

SAMPLE NOTE CARD

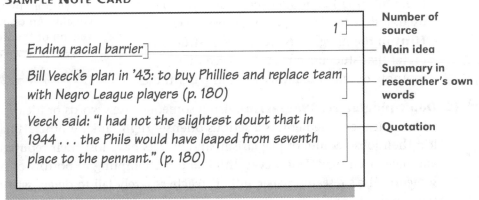

Ending racial barrier

Bill Veeck's plan in '43: to buy Phillies and replace team with Negro League players (p. 180)

Veeck said: "I had not the slightest doubt that in 1944 . . . the Phils would have leaped from seventh place to the pennant." (p. 180)

1

Number of source

Main idea

Summary in researcher's own words

Quotation

9. **Make an outline.** Sort your note cards into piles according to main ideas. You should wind up with at least three piles (usually, more), which you can then lay out as an outline for your paper.

10. **Draft a thesis statement.** Some researchers create the outline first; others draft a thesis statement first and then create the outline. Either sequence is acceptable. Your thesis statement announces the controlling idea for your paper; it often comes at the end of your introduction. It tells readers what you are going to write about in the rest of your paper. You may find yourself revising the thesis statement several times in the course of applying the writing process to a research project.

11. **Give credit.** Your research paper has to show where your information comes from. You'll need to acknowledge a source whenever you (1) quote a phrase, sentence, or passage directly; (2) summarize or paraphrase another person's original ideas in your own words; or (3) report a fact that exists in just one source. The Modern Language Association (MLA) has created a system for giving credit to sources.

   • You can use **parenthetical documentation** at the point of citing each quotation or borrowed idea. The information that you put in parentheses is brief: it consists of the author's last name and the page number(s) of the book from which you took the material; if there is no author for a source, then provide within the parentheses a shortened version of the title along with the page number; finally, if you use two sources by the same author, give the author's last name and a shortened title along with the page number(s).

   • You then must provide a **Works Cited list** at the end of your paper. On this list, which gives fuller information about each source you have used, follow the MLA guidelines (see **Writing Hint** in the margin). **Note:** Some instructors prefer that students cite each source in a footnote or endnote rather than in parentheses.

   Writing Hint

   For more information about MLA style, consult the *MLA Handbook for Writers of Research Papers*, 4th edition, by Joseph Gibaldi. An online version of the work is accessible at *www.mla.org*.

12. **Don't plagiarize. Plagiarism**, using someone else's words or ideas without acknowledgment, is a serious offense. High-ranking officials have lost their jobs because of plagiarism, and writers have lost their reputations and have been sued. Don't even think about attempting to borrow or buy someone else's research paper, either. Teachers rarely fail to detect writing that's not original.

Exercise 38 Prewriting: Consider and Limit your Topic

A teacher may give you a highly focused research assignment such as
the following: Answers will vary. Students should refer to Lesson 1.1 for prewriting strategies.

Explore the role of color imagery in Shakespeare's *Macbeth*, as commented on by at
least three critics.

Or a teacher may give you more freedom, as in the following assignment:

For your research paper, select an aspect of Shakespeare's *Macbeth* that we did not
discuss in class. Explain why this aspect should be part of next year's study of the
play. Cite critics who consider this aspect of the play important.

Or a teacher may leave the door wide open for you, inviting you to conduct a
research study on anything that interests you.

In any of these cases, you have to narrow, or focus, and personalize a topic so
that it reflects your own taste and thoughts. Depending on which of the
preceding scenarios your teacher presents you with, spend some time thinking
about and limiting a topic for a research paper that will run the length that
your teacher specifies. Write a paragraph telling what research question you
have chosen (and how you have chosen it). Include a sentence that identifies
your audience and purpose in exploring this research question.

Exercise 39 Prewriting: Gather Information

Use the following checklist as you think about collecting and evaluating sources.

• Will I need primary sources, secondary sources, or both in order to carry out
the assignment?

• What general sources can I check to get background information on my
limited topic?

• Now that I have background information, how do I proceed? Should I use
reference books, periodicals, the Internet, other media (movies, television,
radio, CD-ROMs), published interviews, or scientific studies?

• Do I need to conduct original research—through observation, interviews, or
surveys?

Write a paragraph giving and explaining your answers to the preceding
questions and others that you address during this stage.
Answers will vary.

Exercise 40 Prewriting: Getting to the Outline Stage

This exercise assumes that you have already proceeded through Writing Strategies 4–8 (pages 85–87). You may now be ready to arrange your notes and prepare an outline for your research paper. Begin by grouping related note cards together. Then move on to sequence the grouped cards in a way that makes sense to you: What will you deal with first? Second? Which notes do you probably not even need? Here are three common problems you may face while working with your note cards; here, too, are suggestions for dealing with the problems.

• **Too few main ideas** If all your notes basically deal with the same one or two main ideas, your research hasn't been broad enough, and you won't have enough to say in your research paper. You probably have to go back to your sources and find other related main ideas to include in your paper.

• **Not enough supporting information** It's not uncommon for researchers to discover that they have intriguing main ideas but not enough supporting details (examples, anecdotes, quotations, and so on) to convince readers of those main ideas. If you find that you have holes to fill, try to find additional sources that you can summarize, paraphrase, or quote.

• **Too much information** It's very difficult to discard information that you have worked hard to find. Still, it's better to eliminate unnecessary note cards now than bore your readers by repeating information or by using new information that may be interesting but not totally relevant. (Caution: Don't destroy material that you now think may be unnecessary; it just may turn out that you need that information after all.)

> **Plan for
> Research Paper**
>
> Title page or heading
>
> **Introduction**
> Attention grabber
>
> Thesis statement
>
> **Body**
> Main idea 1
>
>   Support A
>
>   Support B
>
> Main idea 2
>
>   Support A
>
>   Support B
>
> Main idea 3
>
>   Support A
>
>   Support B
>
> **Conclusion**
> Works Cited Page

When you've dealt with the preceding problems or others, move on to generating an outline for your paper. Use the boldfaced elements on the plan in the sidebar above as a guide for your outline. That is, substitute your specifics for the general categories in the plan. Use numerals and letters to designate elements on your outline and to keep the hierarchy, or relationship, of ideas clear in your own mind.
Answers will vary.

Exercise 41 Write a First Draft with Documentation

It usually makes sense for you to proceed from the beginning of the draft to the end, but if you get stuck at any point, try jumping ahead; come back to the difficult part later. One reason for generating an outline (Exercise 40) is to help you think about the research paper in distinct sections, and you may find some sections easier to write than others. Some writers prefer to write their introduction and conclusion—two critical points of the research paper—after they've written the body, but other writers write everything in sequence. Follow the approach that works for you. Answers will vary. Students should refer to Lesson 1.2 for drafting strategies.

As you draft, make sure you indicate in parentheses the source and page numbers from which you've taken information. You don't want to find yourself later with a draft that is missing its citations; such a draft is almost useless.

Watch your tone, your use of the pronoun *I*, and your use of quotations as you write.

- Tone refers to your attitude toward your topic. Generally, a research paper requires a serious tone. You shouldn't sound stiff and formal, but you shouldn't sound overly familiar and informal either.

- An I-search paper, as noted earlier, includes your commentary on your research process, but most other research papers generally avoid the first person.

- Don't let your draft turn into one long series of quotations. Use your own words as much as possible.

Exercise 42 Revise and Edit Your Draft

When you've finished your draft, set it aside for a while—ideally, overnight. Typically, getting some distance from your draft will help you edit with a fresh eye. Later, read through your draft several times, concentrating on a different issue each time—content, organization, style, diction. Ask yourself questions such as the following: Answers will vary. Students should refer to Lesson 1.3 for additional revising strategies.

- Do I have not enough or too many main ideas?

- Do I have not enough or too much support for my main ideas?

- Are my ideas in a logical, easy-to-follow order?

• Where would transitions make my sentences and paragraphs easier to follow?

• What can I do to improve my sentence structures and my word choice?

Then try to get a fair, sound reaction to your paper from classmates, friends, or relatives. You may find yourself revising your research paper more than once.

Exercise 43 **Proofread Your Paper**

Double-check each quotation for accuracy—and for correct capitalization and punctuation. Check each parenthetical reference and each item on your Works Cited list for correct form. When you are satisfied that you've fixed all errors in grammar, usage, mechanics, and spelling, ask someone else to review your work. Writers often can't see their own mistakes.

Answers will vary. Students should refer to Lesson 1.4 for proofreading strategies.

Exercise 44 **Prepare the Final Copy and Publish**

You will first publish your research paper by submitting it to your teacher or by otherwise following your teacher's directions. Be aware, though, that both print and electronic periodicals or other publications sometimes carry research papers by high school students. If, as suggested earlier, you have pursued a topic of genuine interest to yourself and are proud of your resulting research paper, you may want to share it with a larger community than your teacher and class.

Answers will vary.

Special Writing Tasks: Résumé and Cover Letter

Workplace writing includes memos, reports to supervisors, directions to colleagues, and business letters. Most people learn business-writing skills on the job. Two kinds of business communication you need to know about before you land a job—while you are looking for paid or volunteer work—are résumés and cover letters.

A **résumé** is an organized list of your educational background, extracurricular activities, and work experience. Usually, you send the same résumé out to several businesses or organizations. A **cover letter** (also called a **letter of application**) accompanies the résumé; it must not repeat what is on the résumé, but rather, it should explain how the general facts of your résumé match the needs of the specific organization or company you are sending it to. Together, the résumé and the cover letter often determine if you get a job interview.

Cover letters can be written in two different styles. In the **full-block style**, every line of the letter is aligned at the left-hand margin and paragraphs are not indented. In a **modified-block style**, the heading and the signature are indented about half-way into the page, and the first line of every paragraph is indented. The letter on page 95 is in the full-block style.

The following models illustrate appropriate content and acceptable format. You may modify the order and placement of elements on your own résumé, and you may use full- or modified-block style for your own letter. Your goal for both documents is clarity.

Writer's name, address, phone number, and e-mail address

Thomas L. Vandrosky
47 Beech Lane, Baltimore, MD 21204
(555) 567-8910 <thomvan@bpm.com>

Statement of objective

OBJECTIVE: Summer opportunity that builds on mentoring and leadership experiences

EDUCATION: Senior at Jackson High School, Baltimore, Maryland (graduation June 1999) G.P.A.: 3.2

Details about performance and programs outside of high school

National Honor Society, 1996 to present

U.S. Naval Academy Science & Engineering Seminar, Annapolis, June 1998
- Attended six-hour seminar for high school students interested in military career

Details about abilities; action verbs throughout; phrases rather than full sentences acceptable

ACTIVITIES AND SKILLS: President of Junior Class, Jackson High School
- Presided over weekly meetings
- Ran class recycling program

Student Council member during freshman and sophomore years

Debate Club member during junior and senior years (Maryland State Champions, 1998)

Swim Team member during sophomore, junior, and senior years
- Placed second in 100-yard breaststroke at State Championship, 1998
- Won 200-yard medley relay at State Championship, 1998

Current and prior work experience, including volunteer roles

WORK EXPERIENCE: Chemistry Lab Assistant, Harper College, Baltimore, Maryland, summer 1997
- Kept inventory of all lab equipment
- Set up lab stations before classes
- Substituted as lab partner for absent students

Mentor, Big Buddy Mentoring Program, Baltimore, Maryland, 1996 to present
- Meet weekly with fifth-grader to help with reading and writing
- Designed poster to recruit more volunteers

REFERENCES: Available upon request

Heading, including date

47 Beech Lane
Baltimore, MD 21204
March 1, 1999

Inside address: Get person's name and title or department name

Ms. Elena Rosen
Director
Forest Park Day Camp
Forest Park, MD 21205

Salutation (followed by colon)

Dear Ms. Rosen:

Body: concise, courteous; connects résumé to specific position

I am enclosing my résumé in response to your advertisement in the *Daily News*, February 27, for an assistant water counselor for the August session. As a member of my high school's State Championship team, I am a strong swimmer and can give introductory and intermediate swimming and diving lessons. Currently enrolled in a Red Cross class, I expect to receive certification in lifesaving and CPR on June 1.

My swim team membership and my other extracurricular and work experiences have prepared me for following rules, establishing procedures, and cooperating with colleagues. In addition, I have four younger brothers and sisters, who, along with the fifth-grader that I tutor, have made me familiar and comfortable with children.

I hope that I have an opportunity to meet with you in person as soon as possible.

Closing (followed by comma)

Sincerely,

Signature

Thomas Vandrosky

Typed name

Thomas Vandrosky

Critical
Thinking After you read the résumé and cover letter, answer the questions below.
Use the following questions to lead a class discussion.

1. What is the difference in form and in content between the model résumé and the model cover letter?

2. Into what parts is the résumé divided? The cover letter?

3. What do you think of Thomas's stated objective on his résumé? What role do you suppose the objective serves on a résumé?

4. If you were the director of the day camp, would you invite Thomas in for an interview to discuss his qualifications for the job? Why or why not?

SKILLS FOR WRITING A RÉSUMÉ

1. Include all vital information. Do not neglect to include phone numbers and addresses. If appropriate, tell when you are most easily available.

2. Limit the length. The person reviewing the résumé wants to spend only a matter of minutes with it, so it must be brief and easy to read. While you are still in high school, a résumé should not generally exceed one page.

3. Use specific action verbs. Do not force the person reviewing the résumé to guess what your responsibilities are or were.

4. Be honest and accurate. Integrity and attention to detail are among the most important qualities that an employer looks for in new employees. Careful proofreading of your résumé cannot be stressed enough.

SKILLS FOR WRITING A COVER LETTER

1. Make all parts of your letter conform to standard business-letter format. As noted earlier, you may opt for other positioning of the parts of a business letter. Actually, though, the full-block style shown here is the simplest to master. Pay particular attention to

• complete and accurate addresses (yours and theirs).

• polite salutation (ending with colon) and tone throughout.

• simple, straightforward language.

• information above and beyond what is in your résumé.

2. Make sure the purpose of your writing is clear. If there is indeed a job opening that you've heard about, explain how you acquired that information. Sometimes, there is no specific job opening as far as you know, but you hope that the recipient will keep you in mind for a future opening or lead you to people who are hiring. If you are writing under those conditions, tell the recipient (a) how you heard about him or her and (b) that you are requesting an **informational meeting** to learn more about the organization or industry; make it clear that you are not expecting a job offer at this time.

3. **Remember to date and sign the letter**.
   Omissions of date or signature can irritate recipients.

Exercise 45 Prewriting: State an Objective; Choose a Job

- Think of what you would like to do on a part-time, full-time, short-term, or permanent basis. Write a statement that indicates that you have skills, interests, and an immediate goal. You'll be able to use that statement on your résumé for the heading "Objective" or "Job Desired."

- Identify a job that would put you on the road to meeting your stated objective. To identify a job for this exercise, check newspaper classified ads, your school's placement or guidance office, bulletin boards in your community, and adult friends who may know about job openings.

- Write two lists—one with skills required by the job you've selected; one with skills and experiences that you have. If the two lists match closely, proceed with this workshop. Otherwise, keep looking for a job that better fits your experience.
Answers will vary.

Exercise 46 Prewriting: Gather Details for Your Résumé

For each category on the model résumé (beyond "Objective"), start generating notes about the facts of your life by answering the following questions:
Answers will vary.
Education
- Where do you go to school—including city and state?

- When do you expect to graduate?

- What is unusual or exceptional about your high school experience? Do you want to share any statistics? Tell about any special course of study?

> ### Writing Hint
>
> Appearance counts.
>
> - For résumé and cover letter, use white or ivory paper, 8½ x 11 inches.
>
> - Single space with double space between elements (see models).
>
> - If you are working on a computer, select a simple typeface and easy-to-read type size.
>
> - Leave ample margins (at least an inch) at the top, bottom, and both sides of the résumé and cover letter.

- What courses or training have you had outside high school? Do you want to give that information here, or would you rather save it for "Activities and Skills"?

Activities and Skills

Which clubs, teams, and other organizations do you belong to or have you belonged to?

Work Experience

What specific jobs have you had—paying or volunteer jobs? (Some high school students list volunteer jobs with "Activities and Skills.") Wherever possible, give an exact title, the name of the business or organization, and its city and state.

Exercise 47 Draft Your Résumé and Cover Letter

- Based on your preceding notes and the models that appeared earlier in this lesson, organize your experience into a multipart résumé. Use strong action verbs to describe your role in the jobs, organizations, clubs, and teams that you are putting on the résumé.

- Now study again the job you found out about in Exercise 45. In what way does your résumé fall short in telling the employer that you are suited for the job? Your answer to that question should form the basis for your cover letter. There, you should announce what opening you want to fill, how you heard about the opening, and why your general skills listed in the résumé make you appropriate for this specific job. Draft that cover letter now.
Answers will vary.

Exercise 48 Revise and Edit Your Résumé and Cover Letter

Working Together

Reread your résumé and cover letter carefully. Where do they fall short in persuading the employer to give you an interview? What does a classmate who has read your résumé and cover letter think about them? Fix your letter as necessary so that it is clear, complete, and courteous.
Answers will vary. Students should refer to Lesson 1.3 for revising strategies.

Exercise 49 Proofread and Publish

After you have carefully checked for grammar, usage, mechanics, and spelling errors and have fixed them, follow the advice given in the Writing Hint on page 97 about paper, type, and spacing. If you are working on a computer, first print out a copy of the résumé and the cover letter on inexpensive or scrap paper. Once you are pleased with the look of them, print out the final résumé and cover letter on good paper. Don't forget to sign the letter. Answers will vary. Students should refer to Lesson 1.4 for proofreading strategies as well as Chapters 13–16 for mechanical rules and suggestions.

Parts of Speech

STUDENT WRITING
Compare and Contrast Essay

Matisse and Picasso
Two Artists' Former Rivalry
Presented at Kimbell Art Museum
by Katherine Boone
high school student, Dallas, Texas

Spending an afternoon at the Kimbell Art Museum in Fort Worth may not sound like the ideal pastime for many; however, it is time well spent.

The exhibit, which runs until May 2, outlines the "gentle rivalry" between the two masters of modern art in chronological order. Separated into acts which span the years from their introduction in 1906 to Matisse's death in 1954, the tour is augmented by a hand-held audio guide that gives specifics about the paintings on display and the interaction between the artists.

The tour begins in Act One, which displays works by the artists from 1917 through the 1920s, a period in which Matisse took a brief hiatus from his artwork, while Picasso produced paintings similar to his contemporary's in style and substance in an attempt to "tease" him back to the art world. Much of the work in this act is answer/response, with Matisse taking much of the credit for many new ideas and styles. . . .

This act also displays bronze sculptures by both artists of human forms and faces, in which the similarity between the styles is astounding. The distorted features in the image of one artist are answered with nearly identical work by the other. To see such parallel genius at work is amazing, and the Kimbell takes great pains to arrange the works so that the similarities and differences are starkly juxtaposed.

Three paintings in this act which especially exhibit their blatant similarities are Picasso's *Repose*, Matisse's *Woman with Yellow Hair*, and Matisse's *Dream*. All are portraits of women done in similar settings and in similar poses.

As Act Two opens, the styles of the artists diverge significantly, but the thematic similarities remain as Picasso becomes more abstract and cubist, while Matisse paints with flowing lines and washed-out color.

Act Three chronicles the time during World War II when the artists could no longer keep in touch and often painted from imagination what the other would be doing. Again, the similarities are striking, though [each artist] could only guess at the other's inspiration. Both unwittingly maintained a theme of rocking chairs, among others, at this time. . . .

The paragraphs above are the beginning of a compare and contrast essay that is organized in a point-by-point method. Katherine Boone leads the reader step-by-step through the exhibit and through important stages of both artists' lives. Look back at the essay to see how Katherine uses words and phrases to help her reader follow the progress. She also uses examples to explain each point.

In this chapter, you'll take a close look at the different kinds of work that words do—the parts of speech. As you do the writing exercises in this chapter, you will apply what you learn about the parts of speech.

Allow time for students to discuss the student writing. Suggest that they identify its strengths and propose possible improvements. Use the model to introduce the concepts in the chapter.

Nouns

Nouns name everything you come across in life, including things you can imagine.

Nouns are words that name persons, places, things, or ideas.

PERSONS	cousin, Sammy Sosa, coach, ally, Yo Yo Ma
PLACES	school, highway, Phoenix, Lincoln Memorial
THINGS	calculator, speech, microwave, Kleenex
IDEAS	ambivalence, joy, legality, gladness, fascism

Names of ideas form a category of nouns known as **abstract nouns**. Names of persons, places, and things form a category known as **concrete nouns**. All concrete nouns identify objects that you can see, hear, smell, taste, or touch.

ABSTRACT	fear, cleverness, misery, civilization, honor
CONCRETE	trumpet, street, tortilla, Golden Gate Bridge

When you name particular persons, places, or things, you are using **proper nouns**. Always capitalize proper nouns. Some proper nouns contain two or more words; some are titles. Because **common nouns** are general, not particular, do not capitalize them.

COMMON	city, turnpike, attorney, war, scavenger
PROPER	Sioux City, New Jersey Turnpike, Supreme Court Chief Justice Marshall, the Civil War

Collective nouns name a group of people, animals, or things.

COLLECTIVE	squad, class, flock, club, association

Compound nouns consist of two or more words—sometimes hyphenated, sometimes written as one word, and sometimes written as two words. Check a dictionary whenever necessary.

COMPOUND	great-aunt, one-fourth, horseradish, postal worker, junior high school

A **noun phrase** is a noun and its modifiers.

NOUN	girl, children, tulip, chocolate
NOUN PHRASE	the young girl, several children, the yellow tulip, sweet as chocolate

Enriching Your Vocabulary

Scavenger is an alteration from the Middle English word *scawager*, which means "tax collector." The word *scavenger* suggests a person picking up dirt or refuse from the street. The pigeons acted like *scavengers* after the messy picnickers left the park bench.

Writing Hint

Nouns can signal possession. When you're working with plural nouns, add either an apostrophe or *'s*, depending on the last letter of the plural noun. If the last letter is *-s*, use just an apostrophe; if the last letter is not *-s*, use *'s*.

winners' blue uniforms

the **Kennedys'** fame

the **children's** shrieks

the **mice's** cheese

Exercise 1 Using Nouns

Complete each sentence by inserting the type of noun indicated. Make up any details that you need. Sample answers are given.

1. The [concrete noun] _____stadium_____ was filled with fans.

2. The [collective noun] _____committee_____ that planned the track meet worked hard.

3. [proper noun] _____Tanisha_____ won the 400-meter race handily.

4. The team from [proper noun] _____Kennedy High_____ won the mile relay.

5. Tony won the [compound noun] _____long jump_____.

6. One [collective noun] _____team_____ arrived late and missed the first two events.

7. One runner showed her [abstract noun] _____courage_____ by racing despite her injury.

8. During the storm, a [collective noun] _____committee_____ met to decide what to do.

9. When the meet resumed, many runners complained about the slippery surface of the [concrete noun] _____track_____.

10. Our coach's [abstract noun] _____joy_____ was complete when we won the overall competition.

Exercise 2 Revising and Editing a Paragraph

With a partner, improve the weak paragraph below by replacing the italicized words with specific nouns or noun phrases. Also feel free to add details, drop or add words, and combine sentences. Compare your response with that made by other pairs of classmates. Students' revisions will vary. Sample answers are given.

¹Last year in *a certain time* [August], along with *some people* and [my brothers,] their two small children *and pet* [, and their Labrador puppy], I climbed into *a place* [the Grand Canyon]. ²Wanting to get a jump on the other hikers, we left our *accommodations* [room at El Tovar Lodge] at 7:15 A.M., ate *food* [a hearty breakfast], and hit the *trail* [Bright Angel Trail]. ³We were feeling *a mood* [anxious] because *weather* [a thunderstorm] was in the forecast. ⁴But our luck held. ⁵On the way down, we spotted *animals* [deer, squirrels,] and *birds* [hawks]. ⁶We hiked through *trees* [scrubby brush] and over *different kinds of land* [rocky outcroppings]. ⁷When we arrived at *our destination some time* [Plateau Point two hours] later, we rested for *a while* [half an hour] and ate *what* [the sandwiches and fruit] we had brought with us. ⁸After talking about *things* [the views], we began the *walk* [tramp] back to the rim. ⁹When we finally got there, we felt *a mood* [exhilarated], despite our *condition* [exhaustion] [satisfaction]. ¹⁰What *a feeling*!

Pronouns

🖌 **Pronouns** are words that take the place of a noun or another pronoun.

Most—but not all—pronouns refer to something previously mentioned. The word or group of words to which the pronoun refers is called its **antecedent**. In the following sentences, arrows point to the antecedents of the pronouns.

Inez and **her** friend are newspaper staff members. **They** go to an editorial meeting each Tuesday. **It** is held in Mr. Chen's office.

🖌 The pronouns English speakers use the most are the **personal pronouns** and their **possessive forms**.

She was the first to arrive because **her** train was early.

🖌 Use **indefinite pronouns** to express an amount or to refer to an unspecified person or thing.

Many came despite the rain, and **few** were disappointed.

🖌 Use **demonstrative pronouns** to point to specific people or things.

This is the reserved section; **those** over there are available.

🖌 Use **relative pronouns** to introduce some subordinate clauses. (See Chapter 7 for more on subordinate clauses.)

Suki, **who** lives farthest from the school, has never been absent.

🖌 Use **interrogative pronouns** in questions.

To **whom** are you speaking? **What** did you say?

🖌 The pronouns that end in -*self* and -*selves* are either **reflexive** or **intensive**.

Use reflexive pronouns to refer to an earlier noun or pronoun. Use intensive pronouns to add emphasis.

I love **myself**. [reflexive]
The principal **himself** taught the class. [intensive]

Reciprocal pronouns express mutual action or relation.

Teammates rely on **one another** for support during a game.

Personal Pronouns, Including Possessive

I	me	my	mine
we	us	our	ours
you	you	your	yours
she	her	her	hers
he	him	his	his
it	it	its	its
they	them	their	theirs

Some Indefinite Pronouns

all	another
any	anybody
anyone	anything
both	each
either	everybody
everyone	everything
few	many
most	neither
nobody	none
no one	one
others	several
some	somebody
someone	

Demonstrative Pronouns

this	these
that	those

Relative Pronouns

who	whoever
whom	whomever
which	that	whose

Some Interrogative Pronouns

who? whom? whose?
what? which? how?

Reflexive and Intensive Pronouns

myself	yourself
himself	herself
itself	ourselves
yourselves	themselves

Exercise 3   Identifying Pronouns

Underline all the pronouns in these paragraphs, including possessive pronouns.
Hint: You'll find eighteen pronouns. Not all sentences contain pronouns.

¹Today, <u>everyone</u> knows about the Bering Sea, <u>which</u> separates Asia from North America. ²But during the last Ice Age, <u>it</u> was not a sea. ³The sea level dropped hundreds of feet; the sea floor became a plain. ⁴Many archeologists believe that people traveled on this plain, following <u>their</u> animals. ⁵Over time, temperatures gradually began to rise, causing the sea level to rise with <u>them</u>. ⁶The plain was slowly flooding. ⁷Families panicked. ⁸<u>They</u> found <u>themselves</u> needing to move to higher ground. ⁹<u>Many</u> headed eastward into the regions <u>we</u> know today as Alaska and Canada. ¹⁰<u>Some</u> then went southward into the area <u>that</u> is now Montana, Wyoming, and Colorado. ¹¹<u>Others</u> walked farther south into present-day Mexico and Central and South America. ¹²<u>This</u> happened about 17,000 years ago. ¹³<u>It</u> may have been the first great pilgrimage from the land <u>we</u> call Asia into the Americas. ¹⁴<u>What</u> did the newcomers find? ¹⁵How did <u>they</u> lead <u>their</u> lives? ¹⁶Archeologists still seek answers.

Exercise 4   Writing with Pronouns

Write ten engaging, complete sentences about a personal interest of yours—a hobby, a sport, a kind of music, etc. When you finish writing, underline all the pronouns in your sentences. Students' sentences will vary.

Exercise 5   Write What You Think

■ For more on persuasive writing, refer to **Composition, Lesson 3.3.**

A friend of yours plans to go to college. But she has an opportunity to spend a year overseas as an exchange student in either Japan, Italy, or Chile before college. Write a persuasive letter to her explaining why you think being a foreign exchange student for a year is or is not a good idea. If you do think it is an opportunity not to be missed, help her choose the country she should go to. When you've finished writing your letter, underline all the pronouns that you've used. Answers will vary, but ideally they will contain examples of each type of pronoun identified in the lesson. Look for grammatically complete sentences that begin with a capital letter and end with an appropriate end punctuation mark.

Verbs

All verbs help to make statements. You can't make a sentence without one.

● **Verbs** are words that express an action or a state of being. Every sentence has at least one action verb or one linking verb.

Some **action verbs** communicate an observable action; for example, they describe what people *do—glide, laugh, applaud.* But other action verbs tell us what people *feel—appreciate, love, dread.*

> Frank Lloyd Wright **designed** and **built** homes and other structures. His clients **admired** his style.

Verbs take a variety of forms to communicate time. (For more about verb tenses, see Lesson 8.4.)

> The hiker **shivers**. The hiker **shivered**. The hiker **was shivering**.

Some but not all action verbs take direct and indirect objects. (See Lesson 5.7.)

● **Linking verbs** do what their name says: They link the subject of a sentence with a word that tells more about it. (For more about subjects and predicates, see Lesson 5.2.)

> The surgeon **appeared** confident. The surgeon **is** an innovator.

Some words that can be action verbs in one context can be linking verbs in another context. If a form of *be* can substitute for the verb, then the verb is functioning as a linking verb.

> ACTION VERB   The performer **looked** nervously at the audience.
> LINKING VERB   The performer **looked** nervous.

● A **verb phrase** is a verb form preceded by one or more **helping** (or **auxiliary**) verbs. *Not* (*n't* in a contraction) is never part of the verb phrase.

> **Has**n't anyone here **seen** the remote? I **have been looking** for it for half an hour.

Generally, the more vivid a verb, the better.

> BLAND   John **is** on his way to work.
> VIVID   John **is dashing** to work.

Linking Verbs: Some Forms of *Be*

am	is	was	were
are	be	being	
can be		is being	
will be		could be	
should be		would be	
could have been			
might have been			

Some Other Linking Verbs

appear	seem
become	smell
feel	sound
grow	stay
look	taste
remain	turn

Some Helping Verbs

be (is, am, are, was, were, been)
have (has, had)
do (does, did)

can	may	could
must	might	shall
will	would	should

To write complete sentences rather than sentence fragments, use verbs or verb phrases, not just **verbals**. Although a verbal is formed from a verb, it is a part of speech that functions as a noun, adjective, or adverb, not as a verb. (For more about verbals, see Lesson 6.3.)

People ~~enjoying~~ *enjoyed* the play.

Exercise 6 Identifying Verbs

Underline every verb and verb phrase in the sentences. **Hint:** There are twenty.

1. Anyone <u>can create</u> music with the natural instrument we <u>call</u> the voice.

2. As musical expression <u>developed</u>, people <u>joined</u> voice groups.

3. Gregorian chant, or plainsong, which <u>arose</u> in the early Middle Ages, <u>was</u> one early form of choral performance.

4. In chant, all participants <u>sing</u> or <u>hum</u> one melody in unison; the technical term for this <u>is</u> monophony.

5. In the late Middle Ages, composers <u>experimented</u> and <u>gave</u> different voices different musical lines within the same piece of music.

6. Soon, variations in rhythm and harmony <u>led</u> to the diverse polyphonic music we <u>are</u> familiar with today.

7. If you have ever <u>participated</u> in a chorus, you <u>know</u> about different voice parts.

8. We <u>classify</u> women's voices as soprano (high), mezzo-soprano (middle), or alto (low).

9. A man <u>might sing</u> tenor (high), baritone (middle), or bass (low).

10. Choral music <u>produces</u> a rich blanket of sound, which either <u>stimulates</u> or <u>soothes</u> listeners.

Exercise 7 Revising and Editing a Paragraph

Strengthen the following weak paragraph by adding vivid verbs and precise nouns. Feel free to make up details, drop or add words, and combine sentences. Compare your revision with that of other pairs. Students' paragraphs will vary.

¹One day, I went to a choral concert. ²The program had music. ³The place where the music was was big and had many decorations. ⁴The place was packed. ⁵My seat was off to the side. ⁶I sat down and looked at the program that a person gave me. ⁷It had all the words to the songs. ⁸It also had stuff about the people who sang the music and the people who wrote the music and the people who played the music. ⁹I read some of it, and I guess that it helped me to like the music better. ¹⁰I had never heard any music like it before. ¹¹Different singers sang different things and sang some things over and over again. ¹²At the end, the people made a lot of noise to say how much they liked it, and I did too.

Adjectives

Adjectives can make nouns and pronouns come into focus.

🔊 **Adjectives** are modifiers. They give information about the nouns and pronouns they modify.

WHAT KIND?	**red** flower, **straight** road, **high-altitude** climb, **surprise** visit, **calamitous** fire
HOW MANY?	**four** days, **few** entries
HOW MUCH?	**more** space, **some** effort
WHICH ONE?	**third** response, **that** shirt, **worst** joke, **last** month

Writers sometimes use two or more adjectives to modify a single noun.

The **long, steep, strenuous** climb back to the rim loomed before them.

Her serves are **powerful** and **accurate**.

🔊 *A* and *an* are adjectives but are also called **indefinite articles**. They refer to any one member of a group and so are indefinite. Similarly, *the* is an adjective but is also called the **definite article**. It points out a particular noun.

🔊 **Proper adjectives** derive from proper nouns. Proper adjectives always begin with a capital letter.

Japanese food   **Confederate** troops   **Jacksonian** democracy

🔊 Most of the adjectives in the examples on this page come right before the word they modify. But adjectives can also follow a linking verb to modify the subject of a sentence; in this position, the modifier is called a **predicate adjective**.

The smoked salmon tastes **salty**.

The manager is **stern** but **fair**.

When a noun or a possessive pronoun modifies another noun, it sometimes is called an adjective.

motel room	**school** auditorium
mother's pie	**her** uniform
corn pudding	**its** melody

Enriching Your Vocabulary

Calamity stems from the Latin root *calamitas* meaning "destruction." The word *calamitous* describes an extraordinarily grave event. *Calamitous* floods in the Midwest left thousands of people without homes.

Writing Hint

Sometimes, for stylistic reasons, you may wish to use adjectives after the word they modify.

The stage set, **gloomy** and **mysterious**, made the audience gasp.

The cowboy, **dusty** and **exhausted**, straggled into town.

■ Refer to **Grammar, Lesson 5.8**, for more on predicate adjectives.

Exercise 8 Identifying Adjectives

Underline the adjectives, including all proper adjectives and articles, in the following paragraph. In this exercise, count nouns and possessives before nouns as adjectives. **Hint:** There are thirty-nine adjectives.

¹To detect movement, <u>an</u> <u>alarm's</u> sensors use radar. ²Radar is <u>a</u> device or system that emits <u>radio</u> waves to detect objects and determine <u>their</u> direction, distance, height, or speed. ³<u>The</u> echoes produced when <u>those</u> waves bounce off <u>the</u> object provide data on <u>the</u> <u>object's</u> <u>precise</u> location. ⁴<u>The</u> <u>earliest</u> <u>extensive</u> application of radar was as <u>a</u> <u>defense</u> system. ⁵During World War II, the British used radar effectively to detect <u>German</u> aircraft. ⁶But <u>the</u> waves, in <u>experimental</u> form, had caught <u>scientists'</u> attention much earlier. ⁷In 1887, Heinrich Hertz produced and detected <u>the</u> <u>first</u> ones on <u>a</u> <u>homemade</u> apparatus. ⁸<u>His</u> work led to <u>new</u> communications and provided <u>the</u> framework for <u>the</u> <u>eventual</u> invention of radar. ⁹Today, radar has <u>many</u> uses, from heating soup in <u>a</u> microwave to determining <u>the</u> speed of <u>a</u> fastball to figuring out whether <u>a</u> <u>weather</u> disturbance is <u>a</u> tornado or <u>a</u> hurricane. ¹⁰How <u>effective</u> would <u>air-traffic</u> controllers be without radar?

Eighteen of the adjectives underlined are articles.

Exercise 9 Editing Sentences to Give More Information

Edit the sentences below to give the readers more information and to create more interesting sentences. You may add details and drop or add words. Underline all of the adjectives you add.

EXAMPLE   The boy ate the meal.

The <u>hungry</u> boy grabbed the <u>full</u> plate and devoured <u>every</u> morsel .

1. The woman wore a coat.
2. A car sped by.
3. It was a clear night.
4. The sea was rough.
5. I sat under a tree and read.

6. Claire made a piece of pottery.
7. The team practiced on the field.
8. Alfred lives on that block.
9. The group waited in line to buy tickets.
10. The outcome of the tournament was in doubt.

Students' sentences will vary.

Adverbs

Like adjectives, adverbs add clarity to sentences.

● **Adverbs** modify, or tell more about, verbs, adjectives, and other adverbs by answering *when*, *where*, and *how* questions. **Intensifiers** are adverbs that answer the question *to what extent* or *how much*.

WHEN?	**Today**, we began rehearsals for the play.
WHERE?	They walked **here** from the station.
HOW?	The actor spoke **clearly** and **loudly**.
TO WHAT EXTENT?	We **thoroughly** enjoyed the performance.

Many adverbs, sometimes called **adverbs of manner**, end with the suffix *-ly*. However, many frequently used adverbs do not end in *-ly*.

Adverbs can modify prepositions and prepositional phrases. (See Lesson 4.7 for more on prepositions.)

They arrived **just** *after dinner*.
Her hand reached **almost** *to the top*.

Adverbs can also modify subordinate clauses and complete sentences.

I'll play the tape again **only** *if you want me to*.
Surely, he didn't mean to put the car in reverse.

Many negatives—for example, *not, n't, barely,* and *never*—are adverbs; they can interrupt parts of a verb phrase.

He *should* **not** *have* moved backward.

Exercise 10 Identifying Adverbs

Underline all the adverbs in each sentence below. **Hint:** One sentence has no adverbs.

1. A Greek mathematician named Philon traveled <u>about</u> and <u>then</u> wrote a paper in which he listed seven wonders of the ancient world.

2. Philon's paper was circulated <u>widely</u>.

3. Each structure was <u>still</u> standing or <u>partially</u> standing in 150 B.C., the date of Philon's trip.

4. The only wonder that survives <u>today</u>—the Great Pyramid—is located near Cairo, Egypt.

5. The Hanging Gardens of Babylon were <u>not</u> hanging gardens.

6. The Temple of Diana at Ephesus, Turkey, was <u>permanently</u> destroyed by the Goths in A.D. 262.

Some Common Adverbs That Do Not End in *-ly*

about	just	today
almost	late	tomorrow
already	more	too
also	never	well
always	seldom	why
around	still	yesterday
fast	then	yet
here	there	

Some Common Intensifiers

exceptionally	most
really	somewhat
extraordinarily	nearly
hardly only	so
least	quite	truly
less	rather	very

Editing Tip

Not all words that end in *-ly* are adverbs. For example, *ugly, lonely,* and *lovely* are adjectives; *comply* and *supply* are verbs.

7. After eleven years of digging, a British archeologist <u>finally</u> unearthed fragments of that temple's original columns in 1874.

8. Name some physical wonders of the twenty-first century.

9. Rising to a height of four hundred feet, the marble lighthouse on the Isle of Pharos was <u>truly</u> a remarkable sight.

10. The Colossus of Rhodes was <u>suddenly</u> toppled by an earthquake, and it lay in ruins for <u>almost</u> nine hundred years.

Exercise 11 Choosing the Correct Modifier

Underline the modifier in each parentheses that correctly completes each sentence.

1. Whales glide (graceful, <u>gracefully</u>) through the water.

2. When the police got the call, they moved (quick, <u>quickly</u>).

3. The time capsule was buried (near, <u>nearly</u>) one hundred years ago.

4. She hadn't slept, so she performed (bad, <u>badly</u>) on the test.

5. Sick for most of the night, she looked (<u>bad</u>, badly) in the morning.

6. Stand (correct, <u>correctly</u>) on the stage.

7. Chocolate chips on pizza taste (<u>terrible</u>, terribly). *Taste* is acting as a linking verb.

8. The young child spoke (polite, <u>politely</u>) to the guest.

9. If you continue to walk so (slow, <u>slowly</u>), we'll be late.

10. The (exceptional, <u>exceptionally</u>) graceful elephant rose on one foot.
Exceptional, an adjective, followed by a comma or *exceptionally*, an adverb, without a comma is correct; ask students to justify their choices.

Exercise 12 Editing Sentences to Add Adjectives and Adverbs

Working Together

Work with a partner to add adjectives and adverbs to the following sentences. (Ask yourself: *which one, what kind, how many, how much, when, where, how,* and *to what extent*.) In addition, replace vague or general nouns and verbs, and add other details to create interesting sentences. Compare your revisions with those of other pairs of students.

EXAMPLE   The cat stalked its prey.
The jaguar stealthily stalked the mouse, which was busily devouring its last meal.   Students' sentences will vary.

1. The athlete ran.

2. The girl smelled something.

3. A truck drove by.

4. The storm damaged the roof.

5. The train was crowded.

Mid-Chapter Review

Exercise A Identifying Nouns and Pronouns

The following sentences are about the names of unusual things. Underline all of the nouns you find. Circle all of the pronouns.

1. The plastic at the end of a shoelace is called an aglet.

2. A brassard is an armband with a distinctive design to identify someone.

3. The decaying organic matter found on the forest floor is known as duff.

4. A harp is the metal hoop that supports a lampshade all by itself.

5. The indentation at the bottom of bottles of wine is called a punt.

6. A quarrel is a small, diamond-shaped or square pane of glass in a latticed window—have you ever seen one?

7. The oblique line that separates parts of fractions is called a solidus.

8. Other names for it include slash, diagonal, and virgule.

9. Have you seen my mugs, which are shaped like stout men wearing three-cornered hats?

10. Those are called Tobies.

Exercise B Identifying Verbs

Underline all the verbs and verb phrases in the paragraph below.

¹It seems as if you are the only one in your lit class who is thoroughly enjoying the poetry lesson. ²Many of your classmates are squirming in their seats. ³Some are conversing privately. ⁴But you find the constant chatter and jokes a nuisance. ⁵Your immediate neighbors, in particular, are disturbing your concentration. ⁶Their irritatingly clever remarks drown out what the teacher is saying and what you are listening to. ⁷But these are your friends, and they are very popular kids. ⁸Still, their rudeness annoys you. ⁹Finally, you say, "Will you kindly be quiet?" ¹⁰Will they respond?

Exercise C Revising and Editing a Report

Improve the report on the following page. Enliven it with vivid verbs and specific nouns, but also consider using pronouns to avoid repeating nouns. Add adjectives and adverbs to make the report more descriptive. Make other changes to improve the piece. Keep in mind that there is no single way to improve a report and that some sentences may not need any work.

Students' revisions will vary.

[1]In late sixteenth-century England, Anglicanism was the state religion. [2]But Puritanism was a religion on the rise. [3]Puritans were groups of people who disagreed with some things about the Anglican Church. [4]These groups of people came to be known as Separatists. [5]Queen Elizabeth thought that these Separatists were bad. [6]She treated them as outcasts. [7]One group of Separatists formed in a place called Scrooby. [8]William Brewster and William Bradford were two people who led the Separatist people there. [9]According to things Bradford wrote, the Scrooby folks were watched and annoyed. [10]They were jailed, too.

[11]In 1607, the Scrooby group left England for Holland. [12]Holland was known for its religious freedom. [13]The group went there to seek a new life. [14]There were about a hundred in the group then. [15]They went first to Amsterdam and then on to Leiden. [16]Leiden was known as a place for people of all religious groups. [17]There they stayed until 1619. [18]By that time, British pressure on the Dutch government had forced the people to look elsewhere for a safe place. [19]It was time to move again. [20]The "New World" was supposed to be nice. [21]But a trip to America was hard and cost lots. [22]The Pilgrims knew that life there would be hard. [23]But they knew that in order to have their way of life, they had to give it a shot.

[24]In July 1620, fifty-three Separatists, led by Brewster and Bradford, left Leiden for Southampton, an English port. [25]At Southampton, the group got bigger. [26]There were now 120, including many who were not Separatists. [27]In the harbor was the *Mayflower* and the *Speedwell*. [28]They were being outfitted for the voyage. [29]When the *Speedwell* got a leak, all but eighteen boarded the *Mayflower*. [30]The *Mayflower* finally left England in September. [31]The voyage took sixty-seven days. [32]It was a hard trip. [33]Then the small ship went into what is now Provincetown Harbor on Cape Cod. [34]On December 26, it went to Plymouth Bay.

Combining Sentences: Inserting Single-Word Modifiers

Short, choppy sentences can be powerful when used occasionally, but when strung together, they are boring and jarring. Add rhythm and variety to your writing by varying your sentence lengths. One way to do so is to combine short sentences.

ORIGINAL   The sailboats were in the lagoon. These boats were small. They rocked. The rocking was dangerous. The water was rough. It was rising, too.

You can combine these six sentences by inserting key words from several of them into a base sentence.

COMBINED   The **small** sailboats rocked **dangerously** in the **rough**, **rising** waters of the lagoon.

The combined sentence sounds more sophisticated because it avoids both unnecessary repetition and stops and starts. Notice that the key words inserted into the base sentence work as **modifiers**—adjectives and adverbs. Here is another example of combining.

ORIGINAL   A restaurant will open in the port. It is new. It will open soon.

COMBINED   A **new** restaurant will **soon** open in the port.

Sometimes the key words change form when you combine sentences.

ORIGINAL   The restaurant's walls are decorated with paintings. They are paintings of the region. The paintings are of the sea. They were painted by local artists.

COMBINED   The **regional seascapes** on the restaurant's walls were painted by local artists.

ORIGINAL   The port is pretty. It stands out among many scenic towns along the coast.

COMBINED   The pretty port stands out among the many scenic **coastal** towns.

Step by Step

Combining Sentences

To combine a group of short sentences:

1. Find the sentence that gives the most information.

2. In the other sentences, look for single words that can be picked up and inserted into the sentence you chose in Step 1.

3. Insert the single words where they make sense. You may need to slightly change the words you're moving.

4. Read the combined sentence aloud to hear if it sounds natural.

Exercise 13   Combining Sentences

Combine the groups of sentences on the following page into single sentences with adjectives and adverbs. Drop some words, and change the form of others, as needed. See Answer Key.

EXAMPLE   William I was from Normandy. William I led a successful armed invasion
against England in 1066. He was ambitious.
William I was the ambitious Norman invader who conquered England in 1066.

1. William, known as William the Conqueror, achieved victory in the invasion.
   The victory had great importance.

2. William II was William's son. He was ruthless too.

3. William's grandson was Stephen, also a soldier. Stephen was triumphant as
   a soldier.

4. In the twelfth century, King Henry II quarreled with the Archbishop of
   Canterbury. The quarrel was loud. The quarrel was angry.

5. King Richard I, who reigned in the last decade of the twelfth century, went
   on crusades. The crusades were for religion. Richard was gallant.

Exercise 14 Revising and Editing a Paragraph

With a partner, improve the following paragraphs about the English king
Richard III for a history report. Look for opportunities to combine sentences.
Compare your new paragraphs with those of other pairs of students. Students'
paragraphs will vary.

[1]Some people view King Richard III as a monster with ambition. [2]They say
the ambition was unquenchable. [3]They assert that he killed all who stood in his
way. [4]They count the princes in the Tower of London among the victims. [5]The
victims were Richard's. [6]The princes were young. [7]William Shakespeare saw
Richard as evil. [8]Shakespeare saw Richard as ruthless.

[9]Others hold another view. [10]Their view is different. [11]They absolve Richard of
almost every crime of which he has been accused. [12]They claim that Richard was
conscientious. [13]They say that he was strong and successful. [14]They assert that
he had supporters. [15]The supporters were numerous. [16]The supporters were loyal.
[17]They say it is not certain that Richard had the princes killed. [18]The princes
were young.

[19]Opinion about Richard III varies. [20]That is obvious.

Prepositions

Prepositions link key words in your sentences; they never stand alone.

🔹 **Prepositions** connect a noun or pronoun (and its modifiers, if any) to another word in the sentence to form a prepositional phrase. (For more information about prepositional phrases, see Lesson 6.1)

> The crowd stood **along** the aisles.
> I spoke **on behalf of** the class.
> They dared to answer their cell phones right **under** the teacher's nose.

🔹 Some prepositions contain several words. They are **compound prepositions**.

> **In spite of** the snowstorm, we drove to the movies.
> I had to pay for the popcorn **in addition to** the movie.

A word that you may first identify as a preposition is actually an adverb *if it is not part of a prepositional phrase.*

> ADVERB   The bully bragged, "I've been **around**."
> PREPOSITION   We strolled **around the block**.

Exercise 15 Editing Sentences

Expand the sentences below by adding prepositional phrases. Use no more than four in each sentence. Make up all the details you need to create interesting sentences. Underline all the prepositions you've added to the sentences. Compare your sentences with those of other groups of students.   Students' sentences will vary.

EXAMPLE   Benny lost his gloves.

At the football game, Benny lost his gloves <u>by</u> accident, probably <u>under</u> his bleacher seat.

1. Andrew walked to school.
2. The dog barked.
3. Maria passed the baton.
4. Somebody was in the room.
5. She saw a dog's toy.
6. It's early.
7. Is the weather different?
8. The tree swayed.
9. Can you reach the pencil?
10. The chalk squeaked.
11. The polar bear yawned.
12. The bus stops here.
13. Bats hang upside down.
14. My tuba is heavy.
15. The cinema closed early.

Some Commonly Used Prepositions

about   above   across
after   against along
around   at   before
below   beside   between
beyond   but (meaning
                  except)
by   down   during
except   for   from
in   inside   into
like   near   of
on   out   outside
over   past   since
through throughout
to   toward   under
underneath   until
up   upon   within
with/without

Some Common Compound Prepositions

according to   in addition to
along with   in front of
apart from   in place of
aside from   in spite of
as to   instead of
because of   next to
behind   on behalf of
due to   out of
in the middle of

■ See Lesson 4.5 for more on adverbs.

Exercise 16 Choosing Prepositions

Underline all the prepositions in the parentheses below that make sense for the sentence. Notice how the meanings of the sentences change, depending on which preposition you choose.

1. We climbed steadily (<u>down</u>, <u>up</u>, <u>around</u>, across) the mountain.

2. (<u>Before</u>, Until, <u>After</u>, Beneath) our arrival at the top, we stopped to rest.

3. Upon reaching the pinnacle, we walked (up, <u>to</u>, <u>across</u>, <u>over</u>, beside, with, down, <u>around</u>) a spot where we could pitch our tents.

4. We placed our packs on the ground, opened them, and spread our things (<u>over</u>, under, <u>around</u>, beyond, <u>in</u>) the immediate vicinity.

5. (Since, <u>After</u>, <u>Before</u>, <u>In the middle of</u>) pitching our tents, we had lunch.

6. While eating, we noticed a bighorn sheep standing (<u>near</u>, behind, <u>in front of</u>, <u>next to</u>, between, <u>beside</u>) a huge boulder.

7. "What a magnificent animal!" we all thought (for, <u>to</u>, from, upon) ourselves.

8. Then we spotted two other sheep (<u>near</u>, <u>apart from</u>, <u>behind</u>, without, <u>beyond</u>) the first one we saw.

9. We had really come here to observe wolves (<u>in</u>, under, <u>throughout</u>, <u>in addition to</u>) the park.

10. We had heard about wolf watching (<u>from</u>, in, past, along) a newspaper.

Exercise 17 Distinguishing Prepositions from Adverbs

Fill in the blank with *PREP* if the underlined word is functioning as a preposition and with *ADV* if the underlined word is functioning as an adverb.

<u>PREP</u>   1. Why not seize the pleasure <u>at</u> once? —Jane Austen

<u>ADV</u>   2. Good painters imitate nature; bad ones spew it <u>up</u>. —Cervantes

<u>PREP</u>   3. Patriotism is the last refuge <u>of</u> a scoundrel. —Samuel Johnson

<u>ADV</u>   4. Peace is when time doesn't matter as it passes <u>by</u>. —Maria Schell

<u>ADV</u>   5. The best way <u>out</u> is always through. —Robert Frost

<u>PREP</u>   6. The darkest hour is just <u>before</u> the dawn. —Proverb

<u>PREP</u>   7. We trifle <u>with</u>, make sport of, and despise those who are attached to us, and follow those that fly from us. —William Hazlitt

<u>ADV</u>   8. A verbal art like poetry is reflective. Music is immediate; it goes <u>on</u> to become. —W.H. Auden

<u>PREP</u>   9. Prejudice is being down <u>on</u> something you're not up on. —Anonymous

<u>PREP</u>   10. Blest is the bride the sun shines <u>on</u>. —Old English Proverb

Conjunctions and Interjections

◖ Conjunctions join words or groups of words.

Coordinating conjunctions join words or groups of words that are equal in importance.

> I like the taste of asparagus **and** broccoli. I enjoy cauliflower **but** not spinach. In a choice between carrots **or** beets, I'd pick beets.

Correlative conjunctions function in the same way as coordinating conjunctions, but they always appear as pairs.

> **Either** a National League team **or** an American League team will win the World Series. I don't care **whether** one **or** the other wins, as long as the games are close.

Subordinating conjunctions connect adverb clauses to main clauses. (For more about adverb clauses, see Lesson 7.3.)

> The parade took place, **although** it rained the whole time.
> **Because** I had an umbrella, the wet weather didn't bother me.

◖ **Interjections** express mild or strong emotion.

Interjections have no grammatical connection to the rest of the sentence. They are set off by a comma or by an exclamation point.

> **Ouch!** That hurt!
> They have three pets: a dog, a parrot, and, **ugh!**, an iguana!

Coordinating Conjunctions			
and	but	or	nor
so	yet		

Correlative Conjunctions	
both . . . and	
not . . . but	
either . . . or	
not only . . . but also	
just as . . . so	
whether . . . or	
neither . . . nor	

Some Common Subordinating Conjunctions	
after	in order that
although	provided that
as far as	since
as long as	so that
as soon as	unless
as though	until
because	when
before	where
for	whereas
if	while

Some Common Interjections		
aha	ouch	wow
hey	yo	ugh
oh	nah	well

Exercise 18 ## Identifying and Classifying Conjunctions

Underline all the conjunctions and interjections in the sentences below. On a separate piece of paper classify the conjunctions as a coordinating, correlative, subordinating, or interjection.

1. My room at home needs <u>either</u> a paint job <u>or</u> new wallpaper. correlative

2. <u>Because</u> I prefer the look of paint, I'll go with paint, not wallpaper. subordinating

3. I'll choose among the colors periwinkle, taupe, <u>and</u> butter yellow. coordinating

4. My parents don't know <u>whether</u> to hire someone <u>or</u> to ask me to do the work myself. correlative

5. They'll hire a painter provided that he <u>or</u> she comes well recommended. coordinating

6. <u>Not only</u> would a painter do a better job than I would, <u>but</u> he or she would <u>also</u> do the job faster. correlative

7. She can paint away <u>while</u> I'm at school. subordinating

8. <u>Although</u> a good paint job is expensive, it's worth it to my parents. subordinating

9. They'll ask her fee for painting <u>both</u> my room <u>and</u> theirs. correlative

10. <u>Whoa!</u> <u>Unless</u> the painter's price is negotiable, my parents will ask me to do the painting after all. interjection, subordinating

Exercise 19 Using Conjunctions and Interjections

From the choices in parentheses, select and underline the conjunction or interjection that makes the most sense in the sentence.

1. Before 1975, women had served in the military, _____ in that year, Congress ended the tradition of male-only service academies. (for, since, <u>but</u>)

2. _____ women qualified, they now would be able to become officers. (<u>Provided that</u>, Or, Either)

3. The first women to make it into the U.S. Military Academy entered in 1976, _____ sixty-one graduated in 1980. (if, <u>and</u>, since)

4. The U.S. Merchant Marine had been the first academy to admit women _____ fifteen women joined in July 1974. (but, <u>when</u>, either . . . or)

5. The Air Force Academy accepted women as cadets starting in 1976, _____ women were barred from combat until 1980. (so, as though, <u>but</u>)

6. "_____," contend supporters, "women can be trained to perform any duties men can." (Until, Ugh!, <u>Well</u>)

7. "_____" say opponents of women in the military. (Aha!, <u>Nah!</u>, Well)

8. The opponents claim that women _____ upset morale _____ compromise safety. (neither . . . nor, <u>not only</u> . . . <u>but also</u>, whether . . . or)

9. Movies _____ television shows have featured women in the military. (nor, yet, <u>and</u>)

10. _____ women should participate in combat _____ not will remain a controversial issue. (Either . . . or, <u>Whether</u> . . . <u>or</u>, Both . . . and)

Exercise 20 Write What You Think

■ Refer to Composition, Lesson 3.3, for more on writing persuasively.

What is your opinion of the role of women in the military? Do you think female cadets should have the same training regimen and the same responsibilities and opportunities as male cadets? Write what you think. Support your opinions with facts.

Answers will vary. Give students full credit if they have stated an opinion and attempted to support their opinions. They should also have written grammatically complete sentences that begin with a capital letter and end with an appropriate end punctuation mark.

Determining a Word's Part of Speech

❧ A word's part of speech is determined by how the word is used in the sentence. Consider the word *round*.

NOUN	After the first **round**, the home team had the lead.
VERB	The students **round** the numbers to the nearest tenth.
ADJECTIVE	The **round** shape of the theater made all seats good seats.
ADVERB	He sent **round** for the veterinarian when his dog got sick.
PREPOSITION	We walked **round** the lake.

Exercise 21 Identifying Parts of Speech

Identify the part of speech of each underlined word as it is used in the sentence. You may use these abbreviations:

N = noun ADJ = adjective CONJ = conjunction
P = pronoun ADV = adverb INT = interjection
V = verb PREP = preposition

ADV 1. The fluent members of the Linguistic Society of America meet <u>annually</u>.

CONJ 2. Language development entails close study <u>and</u> hard work.

_N_ 3. Would you consider a <u>major</u> in anthropology with a focus on language?

PREP 4. Francis E. Sommer, a linguist, was fluent <u>in</u> ninety-four languages.

CONJ, CONJ 5. He learned Swedish, Sanskrit, <u>and</u> Persian <u>while</u> he was a schoolboy.

_V_ 6. He would <u>while</u> away his time by learning languages.

ADJ 7. Harold Williams, who spoke fifty-eight languages, was another <u>master</u> linguist.

_P, P_ 8. Williams could master conversation with every U.N. delegate in <u>his</u> or <u>her</u> native tongue.

ADJ 9. Linguistics professors say <u>language</u> skill is like musical talent.

ADV 10. One professor, who knows forty-eight languages, claims that one language spoken in Papua New Guinea is the <u>world's</u> toughest to master.

Enriching Your Vocabulary

The word *entail* comes from the prefix *en-* meaning "in" and the Old French word *taillier* meaning "to limit." In English the verb has come to mean "to involve." The castle restoration will *entail* considerable expense.

Revising and Editing Worksheet

Improve the following draft of a report. Consider adding specific nouns, replacing repeated nouns with pronouns, using vivid verbs, adding adjectives and adverbs, and introducing the best conjunctions and clearest prepositions. When you are finished revising and editing, proofread your paragraphs, and fix any spelling mistakes you find. Students' revisions will vary.

[1]It has been absent for nearly four hundred years. [2]Now Shakespeares' Globe Theatre has been resurrected. [3]Drawing on lots of scholarly research and archeological evidence. [4]Using Elizabethan building techniques, they have re-created the Globe. [5]They've done it authentic. [6]The process has been an adventure from the start. [7]They had fund-raising nightmares, lawsuits, and scholarly arguments. [8]They had other disasters, too. [9]But the result is a new Globe Theatre. [10]It would make Shakespeare hisself proud.

[11]A brewery is where the original Globe Theatre once was. [12]That spot is on the bank of the Thames River in London. [13]The bank is on the south. [14]Today's version is two hundred yards away. [15]Like the original, it has no roof. [16]Within its partial timbered walls, there are three tiers of wooden benches. [17]These going around an open yard and a platform stage. [18]On the stage, plays are performed as they were back then.

[19]All fifteen hundred seats were filled when a performance of Shakespeare's *Henry V* opened the Globe's first season. [20]The first season was 1997. [21]Richard Olivier directed. [22]He is the son of Sir Laurence Olivier. [23]Sir Laurence Olivier was famous. [24]The Globe production was pure Elizabethan: All the roles were performed by men wearing costumes from that time.

[25]The new Globe is the focus of a big-deal center that will eventually include a multimedia resource library, a bunch of buildings for education, places to eat and shop, and a three-hundred-seat indoor theater that is a copy of a 1617 design. [26]The cost of the entire project is about $45 million. [27]It cost about $900 to build the Globe in 1599.

Chapter Review

Exercise A **Identifying Parts of Speech**

Identify the part of speech of each underlined word as it is used in the sentence. You may use these abbreviations:

N = noun   ADV = adverb
P = pronoun   PREP = preposition
V = verb   CONJ = conjunction
ADJ = adjective   INT = interjection

ADJ   1. In the <u>last</u> half of the twentieth century, jumbo passenger jets shrank the globe.

PREP 2. Today's sophisticated giants evolved <u>from</u> smaller passenger airplanes.

_N_   3. In 1926, the <u>Ford 4-AT Tin Goose</u> carried thirteen passengers at a speed of 100 mph.

_V_   4. The Boeing 247, which <u>appeared</u> in 1933, was a marvel of engineering.

ADV   5. Although it held <u>only</u> ten passengers, the 247 could cruise at 155 mph.

CONJ 6. The Douglas DC-3 was an immediate success <u>when</u> it appeared in 1936.

ADV   7. The DC-3, which is still in use today, could reach speeds of <u>nearly</u> 200 mph.

_V_   8. The first airliner with a pressurized cabin <u>was</u> the 1940 Boeing Stratoliner.

PREP 9. The 1946 Lockheed Constellation sped its fifty-two passengers along <u>at</u> a speed of 300 mph.

ADJ   10. The <u>swept-back</u> wing, which appeared in a 1952 German plane, made speeds of 500 mph possible.

Exercise B **Using Parts of Speech**

Add a word or words to complete each of the following sentences. Also identify the part of speech of the words you add. Answers will vary. Sample answers are given.

1. American eating habits are changing because of the influence of _____ cultures. different, ADJ

2. New restaurants _____ elements of many countries and cultures. combine, V

3. For example, salsa has replaced ketchup as one of America's most
_____ condiments. popular, ADJ

4. Many cities _____ more Asian or Mexican restaurants than
steakhouses. boast, V

5. How would you like some chicken noodle soup flavored _____ with
Thai lemongrass? lightly, ADV

Exercise C Revising and Editing a Letter Beginning

Revise the draft of the opening paragraphs of a persuasive letter. Feel free
to make any changes that will make these paragraphs stronger and more
interesting. Replace words, add specific details, combine sentences, and
cut words or sentences. After revising and editing, proofread and correct
misspellings. You may want to finish the letter. Students' revisions will vary.

[1]Dear Mayor Washington:

[2]Their is a problem in our neighborhood. [3]I write to tell you about it.

[4]As you know, our neighborhood is very crowded. [5]The stores are

crowded. [6]The streets are Jammed. [7]The trains and buses are always

packed. [8]We don't need any new high-rise apartments. [9]We definitely

don't. [10]And new high-rises are exactly what we appear to be getting.

[11]Ouch!

[12]The end of our neighborhood has empty land. [13]The land is valuable.

[14]We should put that land to productive use. [15]But what would you think

of a park instead of the ten or so tall apartment buildings that Stump

Construction plans to build? [16]We need parks more than we do all that

extra traffic.

[17]My neighbors and I are now ready. [18]We are organized to protect the

quality of life here. [19]We've prepared a list of our complaints. [20]These

complaints are our biggest. [21]We want to meat with you to present it.

Parts of a Sentence

STUDENT WRITING
Narrative Essay

Working Pride
by Lacey Waldron
high school student, El Cajon, California

As I drove to my job interview on a sunny Saturday afternoon, my palms began to sweat. This was my first job interview, and I wanted to make sure I did everything perfectly. I thought to myself, "What should I say? How should I act?" As I came up to a white duplex that read "DR. McDONALD'S OFFICE," I started to panic. Looking at the clock, I realized I had ten minutes until I had to be in the office. I kept reminding myself that everything would be okay, but that was very hard to believe as my stomach began to turn in circles. After parking my car and fixing myself up, I slowly walked up to the office. Turning the knob of the large, oak door, it was time—time to suck up my fear and put my best foot forward. The first person that I met as I walked through the door was a lady named Mary. Mary seemed like she was a very kind hearted woman. She made me feel at home instantly. Before I knew it, a man who was skinny and had gray hair came walking out; it was Dr. McDonald.

I walked over and met him halfway, and he said, "You must be Lacey." I shook his hand firmly and remembered to make eye contact. I also remembered what my mom had advised me minutes earlier and told myself to relax. After a short interview, Dr. McDonald finished by saying, "I will call you and tell you when I want you to start working." I thanked him, shook his hand again, and walked out to my car.

"I GOT IT!" I said, "I GOT THE JOB!!" I couldn't wait to tell my mom the good news!

Getting my first job has really affected my life; it teaches me responsibility and gives me something to do rather than to get into trouble. My parents also seem to look at me as more responsible, and that's enough of a reward for me. Having money of my own has its ups and downs at times. But having the job that I am proud of is a valuable achievement that can never be forgotten.

Lacey Waldron organizes her personal narrative chronologically—in the order the events happened. She uses transition words and expressions such as *after, first,* and *before.* She also includes dialogue to make the reader feel close to the action. In the last paragraph, Lacey explains the significance of the event—what the incident meant to her.

Reread Lacey's essay and notice that each sentence is a little different from the one before. As you work on sentences in this chapter, think about how you can manipulate them communicate your ideas in an interesting way.

Allow time for students to discuss the student writing. Suggest that they identify its strengths and propose possible improvements. Use the model to introduce the concepts in the chapter.

Using Complete Sentences

◖ A **sentence** is a grammatically complete group of words that expresses a thought.

A sentence must perform two functions: (1) tell you the person, animal, or thing that the sentence is about and (2) tell you what that person, animal, or thing does or is.

Every sentence begins with a capital letter and ends with an end punctuation mark—a period, a question mark, or an exclamation point. (See Lesson 13.1.)

◖ A **sentence fragment** is a group of words that is not grammatically complete. Avoid sentence fragments when you write.

Don't let a fragment slip by just because it starts with a capital letter and ends with an end punctuation mark.

FRAGMENT   Enjoyed the concert enormously. [Who enjoyed it?]

FRAGMENT   We before. [What did "we" do "before"?]

FRAGMENT   Although we had heard the group before and enjoyed the concert enormously. [This thought is incomplete.]

SENTENCE   Although we had heard the group before and enjoyed the concert enormously, we still thought that the tickets were expensive.

A sentence always has one of four purposes.

◖ **Declarative sentences** make a statement. They end with a period.

The show lasted three hours.

◖ **Imperative sentences** make a command or a request. They end with either a period or (if the command shows strong feeling) an exclamation point.

Please sing "I Love My Sneakers More Than Her" again.

◖ **Interrogative sentences** ask a question. They end with a question mark.

Which is your favorite song?

◖ **Exclamatory sentences** express strong feeling. They end with an exclamation point.

Hey! That's my lap you're spilling soda on!

Writing Hint

Most sentences begin with a subject followed by a verb and add modifiers and complements at the end.

A frog leaped from behind the flowerpot on the stoop.

You can vary sentences by occasionally beginning with modifiers and withholding the subject and the verb until the end.

From behind the flowerpot on the stoop, a frog leaped.

Exercise 1 Identifying Sentences and Eliminating Sentence Fragments

Circle the number before each group of words that forms a complete sentence. Turn each sentence fragment into a complete sentence. Students' sentences will vary.

(1.) A new kind of basketball sneaker has arrived on the scene, and everyone is buying a pair.

(2.) There is nothing the wearer of this shoe will not be able to do.

3. Dribbling easily, which is something that many want, in these shoes.

4. To be able to dunk a basketball whenever they try.

(5.) According to the manufacturer, kids' dreams will come true simply by wearing these new sneakers.

6. Wearing them every day.

(7.) Some even want to wear them while sleeping.

8. Kids who desire success in one thing or another.

9. Wearing the sneakers, played the best basketball game of her life! Wow!

10. Just as the manufacturer claimed.

Exercise 2 Editing Fragments

Edit the paragraph below. If the numbered group of words is not a sentence, add or delete words to make it one. Be sure to add capital letters and end punctuation marks where necessary. Students' paragraphs will vary.

[1]From New York to Los Angeles, in recreation centers and on the streets, tap dancing is making itself heard. [2]From small children to senior citizens. [3]Tying up their shoes and clicking to the beat. [4]Americans are packing dance classes at studios and in senior centers. [5]Filling the seats on Broadway and in theaters everywhere. [6]Watching performances of shows such as *Tap Dogs*, *Riverdance*, and *Bring in da Noise, Bring in da Funk*. [7]In Manhattan, New Yorkers fill the avenues for Tap-O-Mania. [8]In 1989, the United States Congress set May 25 as National Tap Dance Day. [9]Which celebrated the birthday of Bill "Bojangles" Robinson. [10]Who was a masterful tap dancer. [11]In that year, only the nation's capital honored the occasion. [12]Today, twelve countries and more than forty cities. [13]Have joined in the festivity.

Subject and Predicate

Every sentence must have two parts: a subject and a predicate. The **subject** of a sentence names the person, thing, or idea that the sentence is about. The **predicate** of a sentence tells what the subject does, what the subject is, or what happens to the subject. A subject and a predicate may be a single word or a group of words.

SUBJECTS	PREDICATES
Joe	studies.
The president of the senior class	will study architecture in college.
The vice president	will study engineering.

💧 The **simple subject** is the key word or words in the subject. (When a proper noun or a compound noun is the simple subject, it may be more than one word.) The **complete subject** is made up of the simple subject and all of its modifiers (such as adjectives and prepositional phrases).

💧 The **simple predicate** is always one or more verbs or verb phrases that tell something about the subject. The **complete predicate** contains the verb or verbs and all modifiers (such as adverbs and prepositional phrases), objects, and complements.

From here on, when this book uses only the term *subject*, that word refers to the simple subject; similarly, the term *verb* will refer to the simple predicate. In the examples below, the highlighted words are the simple subject and the simple predicate.

■ For more on objects and object complements, see Lesson 5.7 and 5.9.

SUBJECT	PREDICATE
Pizza at Vinnie's	**tastes** better these days.
Mushrooms or **onions**	**are** extra and **cost** more.
Vinnie	now **charges** ten dollars for a pie.
That low **price**	**will** not **last** long.

Exercise 3 Identifying Subjects and Verbs

In each sentence, underline the subject (the simple subject) once and the verb (the simple predicate) twice. **Remember:** A sentence may have more than one subject and more than one verb.

EXAMPLE   Volleyball is a team sport.

1. A volleyball team fields six players at a time.

2. The left forward, right forward, and center forward stand closest to the net.

3. Each forward can play in the attack zone or in the back zone.

4. The server stands in the 3-meter square service area.

5. The center back stands to the server's left.

6. The left back is the third player in the back row.

7. The server plays the position of right back.

8. A volleyball court measures 18 meters long and 9 meters wide.

9. The net is 2.43 meters off the ground.

10. A referee sits atop a high chair to the side of the net.

11. A linesman stands in the clear space behind the end line.

12. Players rotate in a clockwise direction.

13. In other words, the players move to their right and back.

14. Or do I mean to their left and forward?

15. The term *clockwise* sometimes confuses and frustrates me.

Exercise 4 **Writing Complete Sentences**

On a separate piece of paper, with a partner or small group, rewrite the following notes (which are fragments) as complete sentences to form a brief biography of V. S. Naipaul. Compare your sentences with those of other pairs or groups.

> Born 1932 in Trinidad (island in West Indies)
>
> Family came earlier from India
>
> As youth: exposed to Asian & West Indian culture
>
> Scholarship to Oxford University; then stayed in England
>
> 1957: The Mystic Masseur (novel); 1959: Miguel Street (short stories)
>
> Both about West Indian life
>
> Both impress critics
>
> Then trips to India—to learn about heritage
>
> Rest of life: fiction, nonfiction (example of nonfiction—India: A Wounded Civilization, 1977)

Students' paragraphs will vary. See teacher pages for assessment rubrics.

Finding the Subject

Learning to identify the subject in every sentence you write helps you to select the right verb form so that you create subject–verb agreement.

■ Chapter 9 takes up subject–verb agreement in detail.

● In an **inverted sentence**, the verb (v) comes before the subject (s). You can use inverted order for poetic reasons or to build suspense.

         V   S
Over the castle's walls stormed the **knights**.
         V   S
Into the valley rode the **raiders**.

● The words *here* and *there* are very seldom the subject of a sentence. In a sentence beginning with *here* or *there*, look for the subject after the verb.

  V   S
Here is the front-door **key**.
  V   S   S
There are two **doors** on the side and **one** around back.

● The subject of a sentence is never part of a prepositional phrase.

  S   V
The **areas** of most geometric figures are simple to calculate.
[The subject is not *figures*. *Of most geometric figures* is a prepositional phrase modifying the word *areas*, the subject.]
  S   V
Neither of those two figures is a parallelogram.

● To find the subject of a question, turn the question into a statement.

  V S   V   S   V
Have **you** chosen your dress for the prom? [**You** have chosen your dress for the prom.]
        V   S   S V
What color is your **dress**? [Your **dress** is what color.]

● In a command or request (an imperative sentence), the subject is always *you* (the person being spoken to).
[**You**] Renounce your claim to the throne!
[**You**] Please leave the kingdom.

Even when you mention the name of the person being spoken to, the subject is still understood to be *you*. Do not confuse a **noun of direct address** with the subject of a sentence.

       S
Alex, [**you**] stop that this minute! [The word *you* is the understood subject of the verb *stop*. *Alex* is the noun of direct address.]

Writing Hint

Avoid beginning too many sentences with *there are*, *there is*, or *it is*.

WEAK	There is no one here.
STRONGER	No one is here.
WEAK	It is unlikely that she will vote.
STRONGER	She probably won't vote.

Enriching Your Vocabulary

The word *renounce* is made from the Latin roots *re-*, meaning "back," and *nuntiare*, meaning "to tell." To *renounce* something is to give it up. Julia *renounced* chocolate during Lent.

Identifying Subjects and Verbs

In each sentence, underline the subject (simple subject) once and the verb twice. If the subject is understood to be *you*, write the word *you* after the sentence. If the subject is a proper noun, underline the entire proper noun. **Remember:** A subject and a verb may be compound.

1. In the Caribbean, bananas appear in many dishes.
2. Casseroles, soups, and desserts feature this common fruit.
3. A favorite recipe is for banana fish.
4. It serves from six to eight people.
5. First, carefully read and collect the list of ingredients. (You)
6. There are two pounds of flounder, cod, or perch in this dish.
7. Two garlic cloves and two tablespoons of butter are necessary.
8. You will need a garlic press, too.
9. Sam, beat two eggs well. (You)
10. Also important is the juice of one lime.
11. A cup of diced tomatoes is essential.
12. The recipe also calls for a teaspoon of fresh thyme and a cup of cheddar cheese.
13. Four or five cups of salted water are also critical.
14. Above and beyond all this are the three plantains (bananas).
15. The instructions are straightforward and yield a delicious casserole.
16. Once in the oven, the dish takes thirty minutes.
17. The casserole must remain uncovered for ten to twenty minutes.
18. Only then should you cut into it.
19. Would your guests like it for lunch?
20. Guests for dinner appreciate it, too.

Exercise 6 **Write What You Think**

■ Refer to Composition, Lesson 3.3, for more on writing persuasively.

In many cultures, the traditional view is that the kitchen is a woman's domain. However, most of the world's most skilled and renowned chefs are men. Whose responsibility do you think it is to cook for a family? How do you account for the great number of leading male chefs? Write a persuasive paragraph putting forth your views. Support them with reasons and evidence. When you finish writing, underline all the subjects of your sentences once and the verbs twice. Students' paragraphs will vary but should contain complete sentences. Subjects and verbs should be underlined as specified.

Writing Complete Sentences

As noted in Lesson 5.1, you should avoid sentence fragments. You can use the following three strategies to correct fragments while revising and editing.

● **Attach it.** Join the fragment to a complete sentence before or after it.

FRAGMENT   Located along the Nile south of Egypt. Nubia was largely unknown to the ancient Greeks and Romans.

REVISED   Located along the Nile south of Egypt, Nubia was largely unknown to the ancient Greeks and Romans.

● **Add some words.** Introduce the missing subject, verb, or whatever other words are necessary to make the group of words grammatically complete.

FRAGMENT   The wealthy region. Wondrous goods such as ebony, ivory, panther skins traveled north in abundance.

REVISED   The wealthy region offered wondrous goods such as ebony, ivory, and panther skins that traveled north in abundance.

● **Drop or replace some words**. Drop the relative pronoun or subordinating conjunction that creates a fragment. (See Lesson 4.8 for more on subordinating conjunctions.)

FRAGMENT   The Nubian warriors who were very skilled with the bow and arrow.

REVISED   The Nubian warriors were very skilled with the bow and arrow.

> ### Step by Step
>
> **The Sentence Test**
>
> The answer to the following three questions must be *yes* for a group of words to be a sentence.
>
> 1. Does the group have a subject?
> 2. Does the group have a verb?
> 3. Does the group of words express a complete thought?

Exercise 7   Correcting Sentence Fragments

On a separate piece of paper, revise each numbered item to correct all sentence fragments. Use the three strategies just presented.   See Answer Key.

1. Nubia was an African empire. Rich in gold and emeralds.

2. In the Bible, its name is Kush. One of the many different names by which it was known.

3. The ancient Greeks called it Ethiopia. Which was what the Romans called it.

4. Nubia was located along the Nile. Stretching from Khartoum in Sudan north to present-day Aswan in Egypt.

5. Its land was extraordinarily hot and dry. Was an unlikely location for an empire.

6. Because Nubia had much less fertile land than Egypt.

7. Archeologists have identified at least six different Nubian cultures. That existed from 3800 B.C. through A.D. 600.

8. A rival to its northern neighbor, Egypt. Nubia conquered Egypt in about 730 B.C.

9. Nubian kings ruling Egypt for about sixty years.

10. The Nubian civilization reached the height of its political and economic power in about 200 B.C. Which lasted longer than the civilizations of ancient Greece and Rome.

Exercise 8 Eliminating Fragments

Improve the paragraph below. If the numbered group is not a sentence, add words or take away words to make it one. Be sure to add capital letters and end punctuation marks where necessary. Students' paragraphs will vary.

[1]Nubia was an ancient civilization once neglected by academics. [2]No longer the case. [3]In recent years, people beginning to recognize the many achievements of the Nubians, or Kushites. [4]This interest was signaled by several museum exhibits across North America in the 1990s. [5]Which celebrated the rich heritage of that neglected civilization. [6]There were exhibits at the Boston Museum of Fine Arts and at the Royal Ontario Museum in Toronto. [7]Among others. [8]In 1993, an exhibit called "Vanished Kingdoms of the Nile: The Rediscovery of Ancient Nubia" was hosted by the Oriental Institute in Chicago. [9]Been to any of these?

[10]The Nubians built great temples. [11]They created beautiful pottery. [12]Decorating it with drawings of animals and plants. [13]Some thin-walled pots were designed with geometric patterns and crosshatching. [14]On tombstones and altars, carved inscriptions using Egyptian hieroglyphics. [15]They made tools, pottery, and jewelry. [16]From clay, gold, ebony, and ivory. [17]Thanks in part to the exhibitions. [18]Awareness of the contributions of Nubian civilizations has grown.

Combining Sentences: Using Conjunctions

Unnecessary repetition of words and grammatical structures wastes space and sounds awful. Instead, try to use compound subjects, compound verbs, and compound sentences.

● Learn to tell the difference between (1) a compound sentence and (2) a simple sentence with a compound subject or compound verb.

         S   S   V   V

Regular cast members **and** understudies rehearse **and** show up for every performance. [simple sentence with compound subject and compound verb]

         S   V   S

Regular cast members receive most of the glory, **but** understudies

   V

also work hard. [compound sentence made up of two simple sentences—each with its own subject and verb]

● A **compound sentence** combines two or more simple sentences into a single sentence.

SIMPLE	Actors in plays have understudies. Understudies show up for every performance.
COMPOUND	Actors in plays have understudies; the understudies show up for every performance.

● Use these strategies to combine sentences into a compound sentence.

1. Use a comma and a coordinating or correlative conjunction.

SIMPLE SENTENCE	Seats in the front orchestra are expensive. Mezzanine seats usually cost less.
COMPOUND SENTENCE	**Just as** seats in the front orchestra are the most expensive, **so too** do mezzanine seats usually cost less.

2. Use a semicolon alone to combine the sentences.

COMPOUND SENTENCE	Seats in the front orchestra are the most expensive; mezzanine seats usually cost less.

3. Use a semicolon and a conjunctive adverb or a transitional expression to combine the sentences.

COMPOUND SENTENCE	Seats in the front orchestra are expensive; **however**, mezzanine seats usually cost less. [with conjunctive adverb]
COMPOUND SENTENCE	Seats in the front orchestra are expensive; **on the other hand**, mezzanine seats usually cost less. [with transitional expression]

> ## Writing Hint
>
> Use conjunctive adverbs and transitional expressions to create compound sentences.
>
> **SOME CONJUNCTIVE ADVERBS**
>
> | | |
> |---|---|
> | accordingly | moreover |
> | also | nevertheless |
> | besides | otherwise |
> | consequently | still |
> | furthermore | therefore |
> | however | |
>
> **SOME TRANSITIONAL EXPRESSIONS**
>
> | | |
> |---|---|
> | as a result | in summary |
> | for example | meanwhile |
> | most important | |
> | on the other hand | |

■ For a list coordinating and correlative conjuctions, see **Grammar**, Lesson 4.8.

Exercise 9 ## Compound Subjects, Compound Verbs

On a separate piece of paper, combine the sentences in each numbered item into a single sentence with a compound subject or a compound verb. You may need to change or omit words. In your revised sentences, underline the subject(s) once and the verb(s) twice. Do not underline the conjunction as part of the compound. See Answer Key.

1. Juan's first choice for college is a local school. Tom's last choice for college is a local school.

2. Rita's mother thinks highly of a college nearby. She would understand another choice by Rita.

3. Carmen dreams about Europe after graduation. Dolores dreams about Europe, too.

4. Pat spoke with the college adviser. Pat conducted research on the Internet about community colleges.

5. Jack will go to a state college. Suki will go to a state college. Elijah will go to a state college.

Exercise 10 ## Compound Sentences

On a separate piece of paper, with a partner or small group, combine the sentences in each numbered item into a single compound sentence. Choose from among the strategies discussed on page 133. See Answer Key.

1. The school soccer team has played poorly all season. It probably won't contend for the state championship.

2. The school basketball team has played well. The coach expects an invitation to a tournament.

3. The center on the basketball team has had a great season. His performance has attracted the attention of college and professional coaches.

4. The softball team has had a disappointing season. The lead pitcher attributes the losses to her knee injury.

5. The team's top swimmer has broken school records. Her teammates are urging her to try out for the Olympics.

Exercise 11 ## Creating Compound Sentences

On a separate piece of paper, write some notes about your pet peeves and the things that annoy you. Then, write as many compound sentences as you can based on your notes. Exchange papers with a partner or a small group to check that all your sentences are indeed compound sentences.
Answers will vary but should include compound sentences based on the notes.

Mid-Chapter Review

Exercise A Identifying Subjects and Verbs

In each numbered item, underline the simple subject once. Underline the verb or verb phrase twice. If the subject is understood to be *you*, write the word *you* after the sentence. **Hint:** Look for compound subjects and compound verbs.

EXAMPLE   Ernie and Carla love comics.

1. Superman first appeared in an issue of Action Comics in 1938.
2. He did not fly at that time.
3. However, he could leap an eighth of a mile and run faster than a freight train.
4. Batman made his first appearance in a 1939 edition of Detective Comics.
5. The character's original name was Bruce N. Wayne.
6. As an adult, Wayne donned his famous costume and vowed vengeance for the death of his parents.
7. He struck terror "into the hearts of the underworld."
8. Was Donald Duck as popular as Mickey Mouse in 1940?
9. There is a big business in comic-book sales these days.
10. Take care of old comics, and save them as collectibles. (You)

Exercise B Combining Sentences

On a separate piece of paper, combine the sentences in each numbered item. Your responses should be either a compound sentence or a simple sentence with a compound subject or compound verb. In your revised sentences, underline the subject(s) once and the verb(s) twice. Do not underline the conjunction when you use one. See Answer Key.

1. *It Happened One Night* won the Academy Award for best picture in 1934. Its stars won the year's acting awards.
2. In 1935, actor Victor McLaglen won for his work in *The Informer*. Director John Ford won for his work in *The Informer*.
3. The best picture of 1942 was *Mrs. Miniver*. William Wyler won an award for directing it.
4. Frank Capra won as best director for *It Happened One Night* in 1934. His *Mr. Deeds Goes to Town* won for best-directed picture in 1936. His *You Can't Take It with You* won for best-directed picture in 1938.
5. The Best Picture award in 1943 went to *Casablanca*. Its famous stars did not win awards that year.

Exercise C Writing Complete Sentences

On a separate piece of paper, rewrite the paragraphs below to correct any sentence fragments and to combine numbered items where appropriate. Check to see that every word group presented as a sentence has a subject and a verb and expresses a complete thought. Students' paragraphs will vary.

¹Should professional athletes be role models? ²Whatever that means. ³Do we expect too much from these young men and women? ⁴Events in their private lives become public information. ⁵Instantly. ⁶Think bad behavior by some athletes takes away from the integrity of their sports. ⁷Believe sportswriting should not deal with athletes' private lives. ⁸Still, athletes' off-court antics fill many columns of newspaper print. ⁹Articles about the sports themselves fill many columns.

¹⁰Athletes have become public figures. ¹¹Living their lives in full view. ¹²Like goldfish in bowls. ¹³Whenever an athlete behaves badly, he or she makes the nightly news. ¹⁴And gets prime space on the sports pages. ¹⁵Becomes a focus on the Internet. ¹⁶People eagerly read about the incident. ¹⁷People eagerly listen to it. ¹⁸They eagerly watch it.

¹⁹Maybe the huge salaries some athletes enjoy should require them to act as role models. ²⁰Perhaps good behavior is their responsibility. ²¹Because kids see them all the time in commercials. ²²In magazine ads, too. ²³Shouldn't team owners demand better behavior? ²⁴Shouldn't fans demand better behavior?

Exercise D Write What You Think

In a paragraph, answer one of the following questions. State your opinion clearly, and support it with reasons and examples. When you finish writing, check to see that your paragraph contains only complete sentences.

1. Who is your role model and why? You can identify someone from the sports field or from any other walk of life.
2. Are professional athletes overpaid? Give examples of salaries or earnings from one or more sports.

Answers will vary. Give students full credit if they have stated an opinion and attempted to support their opinions. Look for grammatically complete sentences that begin with a capital letter and end with an appropriate end punctuation mark.

Correcting Run-on Sentences

❧ A **run-on** sentence is made up of two or more sentences that are incorrectly run together as a single sentence. A run-on with no punctuation separating its sentences is called a **fused sentence**; a run-on with only a comma separating its sentences is called a **comma splice**.

Here are five strategies that effective writers use to avoid or to correct run-on sentences.

1. Separate them. Add end punctuation and a capital letter to separate the sentences.

RUN-ON   Corals are invertebrates, they are related to jellyfish.
CORRECTED   Corals are invertebrates. They are related to jellyfish.

2. Use a conjunction. Use a coordinating or correlative conjunction preceded by a comma.

RUN-ON   Corals form colonies that cover more than 200,000 square miles of sea floor, Australia's 1,250-mile-long Great Barrier Reef is one of their creations.
CORRECTED   Corals form colonies that cover more than 200,000 square miles of sea floor, **and** Australia's 1,250-mile-long Great Barrier Reef is one of their creations.

3. Insert a semicolon. Use a semicolon to separate the two sentences.

RUN-ON   Modern species of corals evolved about 230 million years ago they have changed little since then.
CORRECTED   Modern species of corals evolved about 230 million years ago**;** they have changed little since then.

4. Add a conjunctive adverb. Use a semicolon together with either a conjunctive adverb or a transitional expression. Be sure to put a comma after the conjunctive adverb.

RUN-ON   Coral reefs provide food for fish, they are home to starfish, crabs, eels, sea slugs, and sponges.
CORRECTED   Coral reefs provide food for fish**; in addition,** they are home to starfish, crabs, eels, sea slugs, and sponges.

5. Create a clause. Turn one of the sentences into a subordinate clause.

RUN-ON   Individual corals are the size of chocolate chips, they can build some of the largest solid structures on Earth.
CORRECTED   **Although individual corals are the size of chocolate chips,** they can build some of the largest solid structures on Earth.

Writing Hint

Four or more simple sentences in a row may *sound* like a run-on sentence even when, technically, they're not. To avoid this problem, use alternative structures.

ORIGINAL
The sky is gray. It's going to rain. I'm miserable. My new shoes will get soaked.

REVISED
The gray sky suggests rain. I'm miserable because my new shoes will get soaked.

Some Conjunctive Adverbs

anyway	next
in addition	nonetheless
incidentally	soon
indeed	then
likewise	thus

Some Transitional Expressions

after all	for example
at any rate	for instance
by the way	in addition
even so	in fact
on the other hand	

■ See Lessons 7.1 and 7.5 for more information on subordinate clauses.

Exercise 12 Editing Run-on Sentences

On a separate piece of paper, correct the run-on sentences below. Use a variety of strategies. See Answer Key.

1. A fragile layer of tissue coats coral reefs, this tissue is susceptible to diseases.

2. These diseases are old, in recent years they have intensified.

3. One ailment is called black-band disease it affects brain and star corals.

4. There are two types of white-band disease both threaten Caribbean coral.

5. Yellow-band disease is also known as yellow-blotch disease it attacks coral in the Caribbean too.

6. White pox gives some coral a white rash it was first identified in 1996 in the Florida Keys.

7. White plague was first noted in 1977 in 1995, a deadlier strain appeared.

8. Natural events, such as El Niño, have played a role in the destruction of coral reefs, increased tourism has played a role.

9. The coral in the Caribbean beckons me now I may stay on land I may watch underwater movies instead.

10. People should stay away maybe scientists can control the diseases.

Exercise 13 Revising a Friendly Letter

Work with a partner or small group to correct all the run-on sentences in the following letter to a friend. Use a variety of strategies. Compare your revision with that of other pairs or groups.

[1]Dear Max,

[2]Our senior class trip was a blast it was unique, too. [3]We went on a snorkeling excursion off the Florida Keys. [4]Whoa! [5]Did we ever see corals. [6]We swam all along the reef we saw corals of every color, we saw fish too. [7]Most fish were spectacular specimens, some were a little scary. [8]I think I saw a barracuda. [9]Mario spotted an octopus he didn't stick around to count all eight tentacles.

[10]The best part of the trip was that it was free Irma discovered a treasure chest full of jewels and pieces of gold, it was right there under a star coral. [11]We are all millionaires, none of us will have to worry about money so we'll simply spend the rest of our lives lying on the beach and snorkeling along the coral reefs. [12]Send suntan lotion! Students' letters will vary.

Direct and Indirect Objects

Besides a subject and a verb, many sentences include a **complement**, which completes the meaning of the sentence. This lesson reviews two kinds of complements: direct objects and indirect objects.

🖝 A **direct object** is a noun or pronoun that receives the action of an action verb. A direct object (DO) answers the question *whom* or *what* following the verb.

>   **DO**
> Jerome carried his **backpack** to school. [He carried—*what?*—a backpack. *Backpack* is the direct object.]
>   **DO**   **DO**
> We spotted the **ranger** and the **horse** by the falls. [We spotted—*whom* or *what?*—the ranger and the horse. *Ranger* and *horse* are the direct objects.]

When an action verb is followed by an object, the verb is called **transitive**. When an action verb stands without an object, the verb is called **intransitive**.

>   **DO**   **DO**
> The pitcher threw a **curveball** and then a **slider**. [Here, *threw* is a transitive verb.]
> He threw more powerfully than ever before. [Here, *threw* is an intransitive verb.]

Some sentences have not only a direct object but also an indirect object.

🖝 An **indirect object** (IO) is a noun or pronoun that answers the question *to whom* or *for whom* or *to what* or *for what* following an action verb.

>   **IO**   **DO**
> She gave **me** the **assignment**. [She gave the assignment—*to whom?*—to me. *Me* is the indirect object; *assignment* is the direct object.]
>   **IO**   **IO**   **DO**
> I gave the **wall** and **ceiling** one more **coat** of paint. [I gave one more coat—*to what?*—to the wall and ceiling. *Wall* and *ceiling* are indirect objects; *coat* is the direct object.]

The following two sentences have the same meaning, but structurally, only the first sentence has an indirect object—*Jack*. The second sentence includes *to Jack*, a prepositional phrase, not an indirect object.

>   **IO**   **DO**
> Please show **Jack** the test **scores**.
>   **DO**
> Please show the test **scores** to Jack.

It is not essential to their writing that students are able to differentiate between transitive and intransitive verbs. It is important, however, that they understand direct objects thouroughly.

Most people don't begin a question with *whom* when they write or speak informally. But in formal writing and speaking, begin a question with *whom* if that word is the object in a sentence.

INFORMAL **Who** are you calling?

                        DO
FORMAL **Whom** are you calling?

Exercise 14 Identifying Direct and Indirect Objects

Underline every direct object and indirect object. Label them *DO* for direct object and *IO* for indirect object.

1. Some of these companies financed British <u>colonies</u>. DO
2. In 1607, the Virginia Company started a <u>colony</u> in Virginia and called it Jamestown. DO; DO
3. The company sent 144 <u>men</u> there and promised <u>them</u> <u>wealth</u>. DO; IO; DO
4. Only 104 of the men survived the <u>voyage</u>. DO
5. The survivors settled swampy and inhospitable <u>land</u>. DO
6. About seventy more men lost their <u>lives</u> within a year. DO
7. They had expected <u>wealth</u>. DO
8. The environment caused <u>settlers</u> <u>malnutrition</u> and <u>disease</u> instead. IO; DO; DO
9. Captain John Smith's military discipline could not prevent the bad <u>conditions</u> and <u>starvation</u>. DO; DO
10. Nevertheless, Britain kept sending <u>Jamestown</u> more <u>settlers</u>. IO; DO

> **Hint**
>
> Objects may be compound, and a compound sentence may have an object after each subject and verb.

Exercise 15 Identifying Direct and Indirect Objects

In the paragraphs below, underline every direct and indirect object and label each one as *DO* or *IO*.

[1]The Jamestown colonists selected a <u>region</u> DO that was home to Algonquian tribes. [2]These Native Americans helped the struggling <u>colonists</u> DO. [3]Powhatan, the tribal leader, gave <u>them</u> IO <u>assistance</u> DO. [4]The colonists received <u>corn</u> DO and other <u>foods</u> DO from Powhatan's confederacy in exchange for tools, guns, and knives. [5]In 1614, Powhatan signed a <u>treaty</u> DO with the settlers. [6]He cemented the <u>arrangement</u> DO with the marriage of his daughter, Pocahontas, to John Rolfe.

[7]However, the relationship between the Algonquians and the settlers was not a smooth one. [8]Huge cultural differences caused the <u>neighbors</u> IO <u>stress</u> DO. [9]The confederacy attacked the <u>settlers</u> DO in 1622 and killed <u>more</u> DO than three hundred of them. [10]The Jamestown colony survived the <u>attack</u> DO and fought back.

> **Hint**
>
> Not every sentence has an object, and there are only three indirect objects.

Predicate Nominatives and Predicate Adjectives

Some action verbs take complements called direct and indirect objects (Lesson 5.7). This lesson reviews complements that follow *linking* verbs. These words are called subject complements.

🟥 A linking verb needs a **subject complement**—a noun, pronoun, or adjective—after it in order to express a complete thought.

> The woman standing next to the car is its **owner**.
> Yes, the owner is **she**.
> She appears **lost**.

🟥 A subject complement that is a noun or pronoun is called a predicate nominative (PN). A **predicate nominative** is a noun or pronoun that follows a linking verb (LV) and renames or identifies the subjects (S).

>   S   LV   PN   PN
> My favorite teams are the **Dodgers** and the **Mets**. [*Dodgers* and *Mets* are nouns that rename the subject, *teams*.]
>
>   S   LV PN
> The grand slam was **his**. [*His* is a pronoun that identifies the subject, *grand slam*.]

🟥 A subject complement that is an adjective is called a predicate adjective (PA). A **predicate adjective** is an adjective that follows a linking verb and modifies, or describes, the subject.

>   S   LV PA   PA
> The speech was **brief** but **powerful**. [*Brief* and *powerful* are adjectives that modify the subject, *speech*.]
>
>   LV   S   S   PA
> Were Juan and Lisa **angry**? [The adjective *angry* modifies the subjects, *Juan* and *Lisa*.]

Common Linking Verbs
All the forms of *be* are linking verbs: *am*, *is*, *are*, *was*, *were*, *have been*, and so on. These other verbs can also be linking verbs:

appear	seem
become	smell
feel	sound
grow	taste
look	turn
remain	

Enriching Your Vocabulary

The Latin noun *opus*, used on page 142, means a "work" and is commonly used in reference to musical compositions. *Opus* numbers often don't tell much about the date of composition of a piece of music.

Editing Tip

When you use a personal pronoun as part of a compound after a linking verb, do not use the object form of the pronoun. (See Chapter 10 for a review of the subject and object forms of pronouns.)

The winners are Li and ~~her~~ *she*.

Exercise 16 Identifying Predicate Nominatives and Predicate Adjectives

Underline every predicate nominative and predicate adjective in the sentences below. In the space provided, write *PN* for predicate nominative and *PA* for predicate adjective.

EXAMPLE   <u>*PA*</u>   *The movie was scary.*

<u> PN </u> 1. My radio is my <u>companion</u> each morning.

____PA____ 2. Did you ever notice how quickly the sky becomes <u>light</u> in the morning?

____PA____ 3. Does the sky turn <u>black</u> as quickly after sunset?

___PN, PN___ 4. That's not a <u>raven</u>; it's an ordinary <u>pigeon</u>.

____PN____ 5. My uncle and aunt are <u>biologists</u> who study marine life.

____PA____ 6. The composer's final opus was her <u>best</u>.

___PA, PA___ 7. On the menu, the dishes with a pepper symbol taste <u>hot</u> and <u>spicy</u>.

____PA____ 8. With awkwardness, I asked, "Are you <u>angry</u> with me?"

___PA, PA___ 9. The hiker suddenly felt <u>weak</u>; then she became <u>dizzy</u>.

____PN____ 10. Kevin is <u>one</u> of the best singers in the tenor section.

Exercise 17 **Writing a Description**

Imagine that you have won a contest sponsored by a leading architectural firm. As the winner, you have the opportunity to design the ideal small city. Work with a partner to generate ideas. Then write an essay proposing your plans for this place. When you've finished writing, underline and label all the predicate adjectives and predicate nominatives in your sentences.

• Where would your city be?

• What would it look like?

• What services, amusements, and cultural activities and spaces would it offer its citizens?

• What problems would your ideal city solve that your actual community presently has?

Answers will vary. Give students full credit if they have stated a plan and attempted to support their plan. See teacher pages for assessment rubrics.

Object Complements

The rarest complement is called an object complement.

◖ An **object complement** (OC) is a noun, pronoun, or adjective that follows the direct object (DO) and identifies or describes it.

<pre>
        DO   OC
The class elected me president.
                    S   V   DO   OC
Because of her tone, she made the committee hers.
        DO OC   OC
The news made him upset and frantic.
</pre>

The following verbs (and any of their synonyms) can take object complements:

appoint	consider	find	paint
call	cut	make	sweep
choose	elect	name	think

P.S. It's more important to know how to use the five complements mentioned in this chapter than to memorize their names.

Exercise 18 **Identifying Object Complements**

Underline the direct objects once and the object complements twice in each sentence below.

1. The student council president considers my help useful.

2. They have elected Roberta Sanchez class treasurer for the second time.

3. Doctors think the accident victim's situation hopeless.

4. The decorator said, "Paint the walls any color, but make the trim silver."

5. A team of volunteers swept the gym clean before the big party.

6. His attitude made the college adviser suspicious.

7. I consider the idea mine, and you should identify me in your research paper.

8. He saw my test score and called me brilliant.

9. I called him kind and generous.

10. Not everybody considers the cafeteria food tasteless.

Revising and Editing Worksheet

Revise the draft of the following paragraphs. Feel free to make any changes that will make these paragraphs stronger and clearer. Replace words; add details; combine sentences to create compound subjects, compound verbs, and compound sentences; and cut words and sentences. After revising and editing, proofread and correct misspellings.

[1]The late 1500s in England were a golden age. [2]England had a grate navy. [3]England became a sea power. [4]It was London that was the city where Queen Elizabeth I had her court. [5]And London could sparkle. [6]It had wealth. [7]It had energy. [8]And it had William Shakespeare.

[9]During her rain, Queen Elizabeth I considered literature important. [10]There were many writers in England then. [11]The most famous writer of the time was Shakespeare. [12]His lyric poetry became famous. [13]Many of his poems were sonnets. [14]His poetic dramas became famous, too. [15]For xample, *Romeo and Juliet*, *Macbeth*, and *Hamlet*.

[16]Many people today think Shakespeare was the best. [17]But lots of people think he is too hard. [18]Too many big words and long lines. [19]But every year still people put the plays on television and the movies. [20]And many life performances. [21]If they're too many big words and long lines, how come they put the plays on still today?

[22]All during the four hundred year since Shakespeares time, sometimes directors make the setting of his plays the day the audience is in. [23]For example, recently a movie director put *Romeo and Juliet* in the late twentieth century.

[24]The movie director of this *Romeo and Juliet* made his young actors superstars.

[25]This proves that Shakespeare and his language still speak to us.
Students' revisions will vary. You might have a Shakespearean Festival at which students share their favorite sonnets, poetry, and so on.

Chapter Review

Visit us at
www.sadlier-oxford.com

Exercise A Parts of a Sentence: Identifying
Subjects and Verbs

In each sentence, underline the subject (simple subject) once and the verb
twice. If the subject is understood to be *you*, write *you* following the sentence.

1. Fifty thousand <u>fans</u> <u><u>filled</u></u> the stadium.

2. The hot <u>sun</u> <u><u>beat</u></u> down on both the players and those in attendance.

3. Throughout the game, the <u>fans</u> <u><u>cheered</u></u> and <u><u>booed</u></u> equally loudly.

4. A sudden, unexpected <u>downpour</u> <u><u>soaked</u></u> the field and <u><u>stopped</u></u> play.

5. <u>Players</u> and <u>fans</u> alike <u><u>headed</u></u> for cover; the <u>fans</u> <u><u>amused</u></u> themselves at

    the food and souvenir stands.

6. <u><u>Bring</u></u> me a hot dog, please.   You

7. Finally, the <u>game</u> <u><u>resumed</u></u>, and a <u>cheer</u> <u><u>went</u></u> up.

8. The final three <u>innings</u> <u><u>were</u></u> nail biters; <u>players</u> and <u>fans</u> <u><u>were</u></u> tense.

9. The <u>game</u> <u><u>went</u></u> into extra innings.

10. The final <u>score</u>, 7 to 6, <u><u>left</u></u> the crowd disappointed.

Exercise B Identifying Complements

In each sentence, identify the italicized word(s). Above each word, write *DO*
(direct object), *IO* (indirect object), *PA* (predicate adjective), *PN* (predicate
nominative), or *OC* (object complement).

1. The following sentences give *information* about the 1950s.

DO (above *information*)

2. The person who invented the polio vaccine in 1952 was *Jonas Salk*.

PN (above *Jonas Salk*)

3. Americans used *credit cards* for the first time in 1950.

DO (above *credit cards*)

4. Some people were very *upset* when the Dodgers left Brooklyn in 1958.

PA (above *upset*)

5. In 1958, toy makers gave *us* the *Hula Hoop* and made *kids competitive*.

IO (above *us*), DO (above *Hula Hoop*), DO (above *kids*), OC (above *competitive*)

6. Elvis Presley sang his first hit *song* in 1954 and soon became *famous*.

DO (above *song*), PA (above *famous*)

7. One key invention of 1953 was the radial *tire*.

PN (above *tire*)

8. People ate *TV dinners* for the first time in 1954.

DO (above *TV dinners*)

9. Some of us remained *calm* when the Soviets launched Sputnik in 1957.

PA (above *calm*)

10. A key discovery of the 1950s was *DNA*.

PN (above *DNA*)

Exercise C **Combining Sentences**

On a separate piece of paper, combine the sentences in each numbered item into one sentence—a sentence with a compound subject, a sentence with a compound verb, or a compound sentence. You may change or omit words and insert punctuation. Students' sentences will vary.

1. The group met at the bus station. The group left for the white-water rafting trip at seven in the morning.

2. The group arrived at the starting place on the river on time. The guides were already there.

3. Most people were nervous. But not all were nervous.

4. The group members listened to safety instructions. They put on their life vests.

5. The raft glided through still waters. The raft tossed about in the rapids.

6. The passengers shrieked during rough spots. They hung on for dear life.

7. By the end of the first run, everyone thought the trip was fun. Everyone was ready for more adventure on the next run.

8. It was a safe trip. It was a scenic trip. It was relatively inexpensive.

9. I lost a sneaker on one run. It was a small price to pay for all the excitement.

10. We want a longer rafting trip next year. We'd better get more after-school jobs.

Exercise D **Writing Complete Sentences**

On a separate sheet of paper, with a partner or small group, rewrite the following high school sports reporter's notes (which are fragments) as complete sentences. Be sure to begin each sentence with a capital letter and add the appropriate end punctuation mark. Compare your sentences with those of other pairs or groups. Students' paragraphs will vary. See teacher pages for assessment rubrics.

> Big game, two undefeated teams
>
> Small gym—packed and noisy; tense atmosphere; much at stake
>
> Early lead by Jackson so Lincoln home crowd quiet
>
> Sudden comeback by Lincoln which awakens fans
>
> Tie game = overtime, much excitement
>
> Amazing show of sportsmanship when lights go out, no problems
>
> How game ends—last second shot for Lincoln victory

Phrases

Direct students to
chapter-specific
portfolio projects
on Sadlier-Oxford's
web site.

STUDENT WRITING
Expository Essay

The Specialist
by Pat Healy
high school student, Grosse Pointe Farms, Michigan

*The most important thing you can know about me is that I had polio when I was
a child. The least important thing you can know about me is that I had polio when
I was a child. It explains everything; it explains nothing.* —Scott Roberts

Library Media Specialist Scott Roberts is handicapped. His legs do not function,
so he gets around with crutches or a wheelchair. He will never be able to walk or
run. The rest of life, however, is fair game.

In the muffled silence of the library, the humming of Roberts's motorized
wheelchair cuts through the whispers of students who turn their heads toward the
sound. Roberts speeds through the rows of books, as students curiously wonder
who the man in the wheelchair is.

Today, Roberts wears a neatly pressed navy suit and a crisp white shirt. His red
striped tie doesn't have one wrinkle, and his polished glasses don't quite hide the
sparkle in his eyes. In many ways, Roberts instantly blends into a crowd. In others,
he could not be more noticeable. "I'm completely different from everyone else, but
I'm also exactly the same," Roberts said. "When people first meet me, I get a sense
that they're either attracted to me, or they're really uncomfortable and would rather
get away.". . .

From kindergarten through ninth grade, Roberts attended a school for physically
disabled students. He said he has mixed feelings about the experience. "It was
sometimes good, sometimes bad," he said. "It was good because I couldn't feel sorry
for myself, but bad because I didn't get to go to school with my brothers and sisters."

Everything changed for Roberts in tenth grade when he began going to Osborn
High School. He describes his reaction to the new school with a line from
Shakespeare's play, *The Tempest*: "A brave new world with such people in't!"

Every day, Roberts started school in a special classroom for handicapped
students. There, they could receive counseling or extra help.

"I got out of that room as quickly as I could," Roberts laughed. "It was 'brave
new world' time for me. I went exploring every day."

And explore he did. Roberts was active with student government and the Intra-
Metropolitan School Sportsmanship Council. He eventually became student
president of both. . . .

Roberts has been a librarian for the Grosse Pointe Schools for fifteen years, four
of them at Parcells Middle School, and eleven at North. His colleagues at South
have known him for years and are happy he's here. . . .

Allow time for
students to dis-
cuss the student
writing. Suggest
that they identify
its strengths and
propose possible
improvements.
Use the model
to introduce the
concepts in the
chapter.

The opening quotation of Pat Healy's expository essay grabs the reader's attention.
Pat supplies a physical description of Roberts, some background information, and
quotations. Each specific detail helps create an effective essay.

Pat's essay is also effective because he uses phrases to describe, to explain, and to
combine sentences. As you work on the exercises in this chapter, you will learn to
use phrases to improve your own writing.

Adjective and Adverb Phrases

◗ A **prepositional phrase** always begins with a preposition (PREP) and ends with a single object (a noun or pronoun) or a compound object (OBJ). It may also include adjectives (ADJ).

PREP OBJ   OBJ
for him and me

PREP   ADJ   ADJ   OBJ
on the old leather chair

Note: In some sentences, the object of the preposition actually falls before the preposition; as a writer, you have to decide which way a sentence sounds better. For example, which of the following two sentences do you prefer?

Use this red **pen** to write the note **with**.
Write the note **with** this red **pen**.

◗ An **adjective phrase** is a prepositional phrase that modifies a noun or a pronoun in the sentence.

Adjective phrases (like adjectives) answer these questions: *which one, what kind.*

A car **in the parking lot** has its lights on.
It is one **of the cars** in the first row.

◗ An **adverb phrase** is a prepositional phrase that modifies a verb, an adjective, or another adverb.

Adverb phrases (like adverbs) answer these questions: *when, how, where, to what extent.*

She arrived **before the performance**.
Her seat was the closest **of all the available seats**.

More than one prepositional phrase may modify the same word.
At once the crowd showed its approval **with a loud howl**. [Both phrases modify the verb *showed*.]

Remember: Some words function as either an adverb or a preposition depending on the sentence. If the word is part of a prepositional phrase, it is a preposition. If the word is alone, then it is an adverb. (See Lessons 4.5 and 4.7.)

Before doing the following exercises, you may wish to review the lists of prepositions and compound prepositions on page 115.

The word *undulate*, used in Exercise 2, means "to move as if in waves." It comes from the Latin word *unda*, which means "wave." The *undulating* motion of the boat made it difficult to get a steady read of the compass.

Enriching Your Vocabulary

The word *undulate*, used in Exercise 2, means "to move as if in waves." It comes from the Latin word *unda*, which means "wave." The *undulating* motion of the boat made it difficult to get a steady read of the compass.

Editing Tip

It's never *wrong* to use a comma after one introductory prepositional phrase, but it's not always *necessary.*

COMMA OR NO COMMA OKAY
By late morning, the sky brightened.

By late morning the sky brightened.

Do *not* use a comma when a verb immediately follows an introductory prepositional phrase.

NO COMMA
From the kitchen⁄came the pleasant aroma of bread baking.

Identifying Adjective and Adverb Phrases

Underline every prepositional phrase in the sentences below, and draw an arrow to the word each phrase modifies. Label the adjective phrases *ADJ* and the adverb phrases *ADV*. **Hint:** Some sentences have more than one prepositional phrase.

EXAMPLE   Many foreign words have moved into the English language. *ADV*

1. A faux pas is a blunder of a social nature.   ADJ

2. An ad hoc committee meets for a particular purpose.   ADV

3. We say an act is bona fide when we perform the act in good faith.   ADV

4. When someone acts with chutzpah, we mean that he or she acts with a certain amount of nerve.   ADV; ADV; ADJ

5. If you gather en masse, you gather in a large body.   ADV; accept *en masse* as an adverb phrase

6. When you take office in accordance with procedures, you are an officer de jure.   ADV; ADJ; accept *de jure* as an adjective phrase

7. When strained relations between countries ease, these countries experience détente.   ADJ

8. When you are standing on terra firma, you stand on firm ground.   ADV; ADV

9. When I am president pro tempore, I act only for the time being.   ADV; accept *pro tempore* as an adjective phrase

10. A person with a temperamental nature is a prima donna.   ADJ

Revising and Editing a Paragraph

Improve the following draft of a reporter's notes. The report will be televised with footage that shows what's happening, where and when it's happening, to whom it's happening, and how and why it's happening. Make up details for the report, and on a separate piece of paper, see how many prepositional phrases you can add. When finished, underline every prepositional phrase.
Students' revisions will vary.

[1]Parade progresses normally, marching bands play, elaborate floats. [2]What! [3]No!

[4]Huge balloon breaks from its mooring. [5]Undulating wildly, strikes lamppost, and stoplight.

[6]No! [7]Lamppost falls, and another. [8]People scurry frantically. [9]Is anyone hurt?

[10]Police sirens, distant, coming closer. [11]Parade marshals bark orders, calm onlookers. [12]Camera operators from TV stations are aiming left, right, up, down.

[13]Balloon hits building and bounces off it toward church steeple across street.

[14]Whoa! [15]It pops with a loud bang like a cannon's fire!

Appositives and Appositive Phrases

◖ An **appositive** is a noun or pronoun that identifies or explains the noun or pronoun that precedes it. An **appositive phrase** is an appositive plus all of its modifiers.

His wife, **Kathy**, is an attorney.

His wife, **a successful attorney**, is Kathy Stern.

If an appositive or an appositive phrase is *not* essential to the meaning of the sentence, it is called **nonessential**. Set off nonessential appositives and appositive phrases with commas.

Alex, **the tallest boy in the class**, is my closest friend.

London, **the capital of England**, is on the Thames River.

If an appositive phrase is **essential** to the sentence's meaning, do not set it off with commas.

My friend **Megan** is here. [I have other friends; Megan is the one I mean in this sentence.]

The writer **Charles Dickens** also lectured. [The reader needs to know which writer.]

Notice how converting a sentence to an appositive phrase allows you to combine sentences, save words, and introduce a new structure, which can give your writing variety.

ORIGINAL   I like poems by Wislawa Szymborska.
Szymborska is a winner of the Nobel Prize.

COMBINED   I like poems by Wislawa Szymborska, a winner of the Nobel Prize.

> ## Writing Hint
>
> Appositives and appositive phrases sometimes precede the noun or pronoun they modify. This placement emphasizes the appositive.
>
> **A talented pianist**, Zack began taking lessons when he was seven.
>
> A nonessential appositive that begins a sentence takes only one comma; a nonessential appositive within a sentence needs two commas.

Exercise 3   Identifying Appositives

Underline the appositives or appositive phrases in the following sentences. **Hint:** Some sentences contain more than one.

1. The writer William Sydney Porter is better known as O. Henry.

2. George Eliot was the pen name of the writer Mary Ann Evans.

3. Mark Twain, my favorite writer, once worked on riverboats.

4. Frederick Dannay and Manfred B. Lee, two men, wrote together as Ellery Queen.

5. The writer Charles Lutwidge Dodgson used the pen name Lewis Carroll.

6. The American statesman Benjamin Franklin sometimes used Poor Richard as a name.

7. Maxim Gorky, <u>a shorter name</u>, helped the Russian writer <u>Aleksei Maksimovich Peshkov</u> gain fame.

8. <u>An English novelist</u>, Alan Sillitoe writes about the hard lives of the working classes.

9. The great novelist <u>Joseph Conrad</u> wrote *Lord Jim*.

10. George Orwell was the pen name that the English writer <u>Eric Arthur Blair</u> gave himself.

Exercise 4 Writing Sentences with Appositives

On a separate piece of paper, rewrite the following sentences. Take the appositive or appositive phrase out of parentheses, and insert it at the caret (∧).

EXAMPLE   Chicago, ∧ is known as the Paris of the Prairie. (a city on Lake Michigan)
Chicago, a city on Lake Michigan, is known as the Paris of the Prairie.

1. In the 1970s, ∧ Hank Aaron broke Babe Ruth's home run record. (the decade of disco) *[the decade of disco,]*

2. In 1974, Richard Nixon ∧ resigned from office. (the thirty-seventh American President) *[, the thirty-seventh American President,]*

3. In 1986, the space shuttle ∧ exploded after liftoff. (*Challenger*) *[Challenger]*

4. The world was very upset at news of the 1986 nuclear accident ∧ . (the Chernobyl fires and explosions) *[, the Chernobyl fires and explosions]*

5. The year 1991 witnessed the breakup of the U.S.S.R. ∧ . (the huge Communist group of nations) *[, the huge Communist group of nations]*

Exercise 5 Combining Sentences with Appositives

On a separate piece of paper, combine the sentences in each numbered item with an appositive or an appositive phrase. Don't use commas for essential appositives; only use them for those that are nonessential. **Hint:** Clues tell you if the appositive provides essential information.   See Answer Key.

1. I watched my favorite television program tonight. *Nerds on the Run* is my favorite program.

2. Greg studied hard for Tuesday's test. The test is a science midterm.

3. I'm glad Ollie's is open again. Ollie's is the closest Chinese restaurant.

4. I received an e-mail from my friend in Thailand. Suki sent me the e-mail. (I have several friends living in Thailand.)

5. My sister's bird can laugh. Her bird is named Shakespeare. (She has only one bird.)

Participles and Participial Phrases; Absolute Phrases

A **verbal** is a verb form that functions as a different part of speech. Three types of verbals are participles, gerunds, and infinitives.

🔹 A **participle** is a verb form that acts as an adjective, modifying a noun or a pronoun. Like adjectives, a participle can come before or after the word it modifies.

■ For more on irregular verb forms, see **Usage, Lessons 8.2 and 8.3.**

Present participles end in -*ing*; **past participles** usually end in -*d* or -*ed*, but the past participles of irregular verbs have other endings.

> The **laughing** children clamored for more jokes. [present participle before the noun it modifies]
> The apples, **washed** and **polished**, are ready for the party. [two past participles after the noun they modify]

🔹 A **participial phrase** is made up of a participle and all of its modifiers and complements. The whole phrase acts as an adjective.

> **Singing at the top of her lungs**, Tanya impressed the judges. [present participial phrase before the noun it modifies]
> The violinist played an instrument **made by an expert craftsperson**. [past participial phrase after the noun it modifies]

When the present participle of *have* is followed by a past participle, a **present perfect participle** is formed.

> **Having eaten his fill**, William got up from the table.
> **Having been late often**, Mary lost her job.

🔹 An **absolute phrase** consists of a noun and either a participle or a participial phrase. It stands absolutely by itself—part of neither the subject nor the verb. Because absolute phrases are nonessential, they are always set off by commas. Use them to open your sentences, to conclude them, or to interrupt them.

> **Its paw broken**, the dog now limped along. [The participle *broken* modifies the subject of the phrase, paw, not *dog*, the subject of the independent clause.]
> Inez came in second, **first place going to the girl from Douglass**.

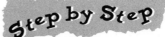

Step by Step

Commas With a Participial Phrase

1. Identify the phrase.

   The dog **sitting in the corner** is sick.
   Fido **sitting in the corner** is sick.

2. Decide if the phrase is essential to the meaning of the sentence.
   In the first example, *sitting in the corner* is essential; it tells *which dog is sick.*

   In the second example, *sitting in the corner* is not essential; the dog has been identified by name.

3. If the phrase is not essential, set it off with commas.

   Fido, **sitting in the corner**, is sick.

Exercise 6 Identifying Participial or Absolute Phrases

Underline the participial or absolute phrases in the following sentences.

1. <u>Beginning in 1660</u>, Samuel Pepys, an Englishman, kept diaries.

2. Pepys, <u>pronounced "peeps,"</u> was twenty-seven at the time.

3. Pepys made daily entries for nine years, <u>keeping the entries private</u>.

4. <u>Using a secret code</u>, he privately recorded events of his daily life.

5. At his death, the diaries were sitting on his bookshelf, <u>each volume neatly tied</u>.

6. The diaries, <u>left alone on the shelf for years</u>, eventually found their way to Magdalene College, Cambridge.

7. A student <u>named John Smith</u> deciphered Pepys's code.

8. Pepys's diaries, <u>proving very informative</u>, contained much information about life and customs in the seventeenth century.

9. One set of entries, <u>treasured by historians</u>, is a description of the great London fire of 1666, <u>a disaster not widely recorded</u>.

10. The diary is a useful source of information on the hundreds of buildings <u>destroyed in the fire</u>.

Exercise 7 Writing Sentences with Participial Phrases

On a separate piece of paper, write a complete sentence, using each of the numbered items as a participial phrase. Students' sentences will vary.

EXAMPLE   organized by professionals
The Himalayan trek, organized by professionals, was both safe and exhilarating.

1. breaking into laughter
2. leaning against the wall
3. removing his hat
4. shocked by the news
5. having entered the contest

6. announced in the morning
7. spread across the ground
8. having stopped by the fence
9. stretching across the field
10. known as a reliable worker

Exercise 8 Write What You Think

Write a paragraph in which you give your opinion about the following statement. Support your opinion with reasons and examples. Use participial phrases and absolute phrases to begin, interrupt and end sentences.

Under no conditions should the public ever read a diary written as a private record unless the writer has given his or her permission.

When you have finished writing, go back over your paragraph, and underline any participial or absolute phrases you may have used.

Mid-Chapter Review

Exercise A Identifying Adjective and Adverb Phrases

Underline every prepositional phrase in the sentences below. At the end of each line, write *ADJ* for a prepositional phrase acting as an adjective or *ADV* for a prepositional phrase acting as an adverb. **Hint:** Some sentences have more than one prepositional phrase.

EXAMPLE   According to Chinese records, paper was invented in A.D. 105. *ADV*

1. Supposedly, paper was invented by Cai Lun. ADV

2. Cai Lun's paper was made from tree bark.   ADV

3. In his technique of paper-making, the pieces of bark were soaked in water. ADV; ADJ; ADJ; ADV

4. This step continued for a long time. ADV

5. Then workers pounded the wet pieces of bark; they separated the outer from the inner bark. ADJ; ADV

6. After removal of the outer bark, workers mixed the pulp that remained with either lime or soda ash. ADV; ADJ; ADV

7. They then boiled the mixture for at least eight days and washed it. ADV

8. Next, they washed and strained the mixture and then pounded it into doughy sheets. ADV

9. They bleached the sheets, soaked them again, and placed them within a large vat. ADV

10. Next, they dipped a frame into the vat and drained the sheets, lifted this frame, and placed the sheets on heated wood or brick to dry. ADV; ADV

11. Paper-making in China was a closely guarded secret for many years. ADJ; ADV

12. Paper came to Europe a thousand years after the Chinese invention. ADV; ADV

Exercise B Identifying Appositives

Underline the appositives or appositive phrases in the following sentences.

1. At the zoo, I saw a baby kangaroo, a joey.

2. My friend, Steve, didn't know that a baby swan is called a cygnet.

3. I also spotted a poult, a baby turkey.

4. Steve didn't know a poult from a pullet, a baby hen.

5. On the other side of a ravine was a group of kangaroos, a troop.

6. Our zoo, a fabulous institution, has quite a collection of gaggles, parliaments, and rafters.

7. Rafters, groups of turkeys, make quite a racket.

8. Collections of owls, <u>parliaments</u>, neither argue nor wear wigs.

9. My sister <u>Carmela</u> wouldn't know a paddling from a skulk.

10. "A skulk is a group of foxes," my other sister, <u>Anna</u>, explained.

Exercise C Revising and Editing a Paragraph

Improve the following paragraph. Review the strategies presented in Lessons 5.4 and 5.6 for correcting fragments and run-ons. Make up details to add if you wish. When you have finished revising and editing, underline any prepositional phrases, appositive phrases, and participial phrases.

¹The British first tried to climb Mt. Everest. ²It was in 1921. ³Since then, more than 120 have died in the attempt, that's nearly one death for every person who reached the summit. ⁴Yet every year, tons of people try to make the climb. ⁵In 1993, the fortieth anniversary of the first successful climb. ⁶That year 294 climbers made an attempt. ⁷Since that time, traffic on Everest has been increasing. ⁸It has been doing so at an astonishing rate. ⁹Despite how much it costs and how long it takes. ¹⁰People hire guides. ¹¹They buy the right equipment. ¹²They get some training, too. ¹³No matter. ¹⁴This climb is so dangerous! ¹⁵Why do people do it?

Students' paragraphs will vary.

Exercise D Write What You Think

People continue to attempt to climb Everest and other great peaks. Consider the following statement.

> Some people believe that climbers should not be allowed to ascend Everest. They think it is unfair that rescuers must spend great amounts of money and expend much energy and expertise in helping climbers whose expeditions get into trouble. They also argue that the increased traffic on Everest is endangering its environment.

On a separate piece of paper, write one or more paragraphs in which you tell whether you agree or disagree with the statement. Support your view with reasons and examples. Answers will vary. Give students full credit if they have stated an opinion and attempted to support their opinions. They should also have written grammatically complete sentences that begin with a capital letter and end with an appropriate end punctuation mark.

MID-CHAPTER REVIEW

Gerunds and Gerund Phrases

◗ A **gerund**, a verb form ending in *-ing*, functions as a noun.

In a sentence, gerunds can be used in every way that nouns can be used.

Jogging is his favorite form of exercise. [subject]
Her least favorite pastime is **jogging**. [predicate nominative]
Do you enjoy **jogging**? [direct object]
Give **jogging** a try. [indirect object]
Some people call fast walking **jogging**. [objective complement]
I saw a video on the benefits of **jogging**. [object of a preposition]

◗ A **gerund phrase** is made up of a gerund and all of its modifiers and complements. The entire phrase functions as a noun.

Adjectives, adverbs, nouns, pronouns, and prepositional phrases can occur with a gerund to form a gerund phrase.

Watching movies is his favorite activity. [subject]
At the movies, he dislikes the **talking all around him**.
[predicate nominative]
He has tried **staring at talkers**. [direct object]
Then he gives **tapping them on the shoulder** a try.
[indirect object]
He calls talking at the movies **disturbing the peace**.
[objective complement]
He even bought a self-help video about **quieting one's neighbors**.
[object of a preposition]

Certain English verbs can't be followed by a gerund. Verbs such as *expect*, *plan*, *promise*, and *refuse* require an infinitive (see Lesson 6.5).

We **plan** to camp this summer.

We **promise** to behave ourselves.

Exercise 9 **Identifying Gerunds and Gerund Phrases**

Underline every gerund and gerund phrase in the sentences below. A gerund phrase may contain one or more prepositional phrases. Count these as part of the gerund phrase in this exercise. **Remember:** Not every *-ing* word is a gerund. A gerund functions as a noun in the sentence. **Hint:** A sentence may have more than one gerund or gerund phrase.

1. Eduardo likes <u>getting into his sleeping bag</u> and <u>telling ghost stories to his tentmates</u>.

2. <u>Sequestering himself</u> in the country always makes him feel independent and far from civilization.

Enriching Your Vocabulary

The word *sequester* means "to set apart" or "to withdraw." It comes from the Latin *sequestrare*, meaning "to entrust." The jury was *sequestered* to deliberate the verdict of the murder trial.

3. He loves the strong smells of a <u>cooking breakfast in the great outdoors.</u>

4. He brings his binoculars for <u>watching birds.</u>

5. <u>Being in the woods,</u> according to Eduardo, is ideal for <u>communicating with friends.</u>

6. <u>Talking,</u> <u>listening,</u> and <u>sharing</u> are all easier outdoors.

7. <u>Climbing mountain trails</u> is another thrilling experience he relishes.

8. In fact, he loves everything about <u>camping.</u>

9. He even likes the <u>buzzing of the mosquitoes.</u>

10. His least favorite part of the trip is <u>breaking camp.</u>

Exercise 10 Distinguishing Between Participles and Gerunds

On the line, write *PART* if the sentence contains a participle or participial phrase; write *GER* if it contains a gerund or gerund phrase. Then underline the word or phrase that you are identifying.

1. __GER__ <u>Programming a VCR</u> confounds many otherwise intelligent adults.

2. __GER__ Why does <u>dealing with machines</u> stump so many people?

3. __GER__ Younger people have much less trouble in <u>working with technology.</u>

4. __PART__ Why are young people <u>interested in technology</u>?

5. __GER__ <u>Growing up with computers in every household gadget</u> makes young people comfortable around technology.

6. __PART__ <u>Not intimidated by buttons on stereos,</u> they prepare personal music menus.

7. __PART__ Some young people are patient with <u>technologically challenged</u> adults.

8. __GER__ Teenagers help a parent with e-mail in exchange for <u>getting more time on the computer for themselves.</u>

9. __PART__ This phenomenon of adults <u>needing help</u> is temporary.

10. __PART__ After all, the future generations of adults will be people <u>raised electronically.</u>

Infinitives and Infinitive Phrases

🖌 An **infinitive** is a verb form that is almost always preceded by the word *to*. In a sentence, an infinitive can act as a noun, an adjective, or an adverb.

His grandfather likes **to complain**. [infinitive as noun]

At a family gathering, Grandfather is always the first one **to arrive**. [infinitive as adjective]

He is quick **to argue** with Uncle Sam. [infinitive as adverb]

We call the word *to* the **sign**, or **marker**, **of the infinitive**. *To* is part of an infinitive if it's followed by a verb. If it starts a prepositional phrase, then *to* is a preposition.

INFINITIVE	PREPOSITIONAL PHRASE
Maria really loves *to dance*.	Maria went *to the dance*.
We tried hard *to win*.	Give the trophy *to the winner*.

Sometimes the *to* of an infinitive is omitted but understood.

Jerome helped **[to] cook**.

🖌 An **infinitive phrase** is made up of an infinitive and all of its modifiers and complements.

To play the guitar in a band is Karen's dream.

It is fun **to play volleyball on the beach**.

Writing Hint

When a modifier comes between *to* and the *verb*, the infinitive is said to be **split**. Avoid split infinitives unless by doing so, the result is awkward or sounds unnatural.

To boldly go where no one has ever gone before

Exercise 11 Identifying Infinitives and Infinitive Phrases

Underline every infinitive and infinitive phrase in the following lines from literature.

1. I only ask <u>to be free</u>.—*Barnaby Rudge*

2. I believe, Sir, that you desire <u>to look at these apartments</u>. —*Bleak House*

3. He was very good to me.—*Bleak House*

4. 'Orses and dogs is some men's fancy. They're wittles and drink to me.—*David Copperfield*

5. The name of those fabulous animals (pagan, I regret <u>to say</u>) who used <u>to sing in the water</u> has quite escaped me.—*Martin Chuzzlewit*

6. All the wickedness of the world is print to him.—*Martin Chuzzlewit*

7. Oh! They're too beautiful <u>to live</u>, much too beautiful!—*Nicholas Nickleby*

Hint

Not every phrase beginning with *to* is an infinitive phrase. Some sentences contain no infinitives.

8. Only when one has lost all curiosity about the future has one reached the age to write an autobiography.—Evelyn Waugh

9. Beauty is truth, truth beauty,—that is all/Ye know on earth, and all ye need to know.—John Keats

10. We have no more right to consume happiness without producing it than to consume wealth without producing it.—George Bernard Shaw

Exercise 12 Revising and Editing a Biography

Underline the infinitives and infinitive phrases in the paragraphs below. Then work with a partner to correct sentence fragments and run-ons and to make any other changes you think will improve this biography of Charles Dickens.
Students' revisions will vary.

¹When you try to think of a writer, next to Shakespeare, who occupies the most important place in popular culture, you might name Charles Dickens. ²His works appeal to nearly everybody. ³With their unforgettable characters. ⁴Dickens's novels have already become plays and movies, and there are probably many more to come.

⁵Born to poor parents in Portsmouth on the southern coast of England in 1812. ⁶When his father was sent to debtor's prison. ⁷Young Charles was to spend time working in a factory. ⁸He worked there pasting labels. ⁹When he wasn't in the factory, he liked to wander, he walked through the streets of London. ¹⁰He saw bleakness and poverty all around him. ¹¹From his unhappy childhood experiences, Dickens learned to appreciate the plight of the poor.

¹²He became a law clerk when he was fifteen. ¹³He taught himself to write better, and he became a court reporter. ¹⁴He learned to observe things around him. ¹⁵He soon began to write sketches of everyday life. ¹⁶Which he contributed to several periodicals. ¹⁷He began to receive attention for his clever writing. ¹⁸In 1836, he published his first novel, *Sketches by Boz*. ¹⁹In the flurry of novels that followed, he showed a unique ability to express his passion for reform. ²⁰And to use humor and satire. ²¹Few writers since have been able to match his ability to portray modern industrial conditions. ²²As he did. ²³He did it so passionately. ²⁴He did it so poetically.

Combining Sentences: Inserting Phrases

🖊 Combine related sentences by inserting a phrase from one sentence into another sentence.

Sometimes, you must alter the words from one sentence to create a phrase for another sentence. Sometimes, you can simply pick up a phrase from one sentence and move it to another sentence.

ORIGINAL   Benny was traveling through Europe. He visited several circuses.

COMBINED   **Traveling through Europe**, Benny visited several circuses. [participial phrase]

ORIGINAL   Lisa plays in a band. The band is in New York. Janet and Rebecca are the other members of her band.

COMBINED   Lisa plays **in a band in New York with Janet and Rebecca**. [prepositional phrases]

ORIGINAL   We have time. We will buy the tickets at the ticket window. The ticket window is by the third-base line.

COMBINED   We have time **to buy the tickets at the ticket window by the third-base line**. [infinitive phrase containing two prepositional phrases]

ORIGINAL   My uncle enjoys something. He enjoys walking briskly.

COMBINED   **Walking briskly** is something my uncle enjoys. [gerund phrase]

Often there is more than one way to combine sentences. Here are two other versions of the last sentence.

COMBINED   To walk briskly is something my uncle enjoys. [infinitive phrase]

COMBINED   My uncle enjoys walking briskly. [gerund phrase at end]

In addition to creating a verbal or a prepositional phrase to put in another sentence, you can convert a sentence to an appositive phrase (see Lesson 6.2) and transfer it to another sentence.

ORIGINAL   My uncle lives in St. Louis now. He is an immigrant from Russia.

COMBINED   My uncle, **a Russian immigrant**, lives in St. Louis now.

Enriching Your Vocabulary

The adjective *apt* comes from the Latin *aptus*, which means "suited, fitted, or appropriate." The class valedictorian offered *apt* advice to the new graduates. *Aptitude*, as used on page 162, is derived from *aptus* and the suffix *-tudo* (condition or quality). Do you have an *aptitude* for a particular sport?

Writing Hint

Too many prepositional phrases in sentences can make them confusing and singsongy. Avoid this problem by breaking apart and rewording sentences.

The cashmere sweaters are **on the rack next to the ties on display in front of the shirt counter.**

The cashmere sweaters are displayed **on a rack.** They're **next to the ties.** You'll find the ties displayed **in front of the shirt counter.**

Exercise 13 · Combining Sentences by Inserting Phrases

Use phrases to combine the sentences in each numbered item. Don't forget to insert commas where they belong. See Answer Key.

EXAMPLE The SAT I is a three-hour exam. The exam is a test of verbal and mathematical abilities.

The SAT I, a test of verbal and mathematical abilities, is a three-hour exam.

1. The College Board and the Educational Testing Service are the producers of the SAT I. They produce other tests, too.

2. They also produce the SAT II tests. The SAT II tests are achievement tests in individual subjects.

3. In 1995, the College Board recalculated test takers' mean SAT I score. The mean score is the average score.

4. The scale of scores runs from 200 to 800. Scores are also given as percentiles.

5. In 1941, the mean score was about 500. This score reflected the results of only ten thousand students.

6. Then more and more students took the test. This resulted in lower individual scores.

7. Students want to score well. They must prepare carefully for the test.

8. Students are better at preparing now. This means higher scores.

9. Students take practice tests. The practice tests help them gain confidence. The confidence is for the real test.

Exercise 14 Writing Paragraphs

The information in the table is about mean, or average, verbal and math scores of college-bound seniors from 1988 to 1997. Use the information in the table to write one or more paragraphs about trends in the Scholastic Aptitude Test (SAT) scores over that ten-year period. Exchange papers with a partner, and make suggestions for improving each other's paragraphs. Try combining related sentences by inserting phrases. Students' paragraphs will vary. See teacher pages for assessment rubrics.

■ Refer to Composition, Lessons 3.4 and 3.5, to find strategies for writing an expository paragraph and essay.

SAT Mean Verbal and Math Scores of College-Bound Seniors										
	1988	1989	1990	1991	1992	1993	1994	1995	1996	1997
VERBAL SCORES	505	504	500	499	500	500	499	504	505	505
Males	512	510	505	503	504	504	501	505	507	507
Females	499	498	496	495	496	497	497	502	503	503
MATH SCORES	501	502	501	500	501	503	504	506	508	511
Males	521	523	521	520	521	524	523	525	527	530
Females	483	482	483	482	484	484	487	490	492	494

Source: The College Board

Revising and Editing Worksheet 1

Improve the following draft of a report to make it sound less choppy. You may combine sentences, rearrange sentences, change or omit words, and add new details. Write your revised report on a separate piece of paper. When you are finished revising and editing, proofread and fix any spelling mistakes you find. Revisions will vary.

¹The giant lizard lives on a group of four small islands in central Indonesia. ²The islands are named Komodo, Rinca, Gili Motang, and Flores. ³The lizzard is known as a Komodo dragon. ⁴The origin of its name is uncertain. ⁵Probably, the origin is a result of imagination. ⁶And exaggeration.

⁷It can grow to a length of nine feet or more. ⁸It can weigh up to two hundred pounds. ⁹It is a powerful predator. ¹⁰A predator is a hunter of other animals. ¹¹Then eating them. ¹²With its sharp teeth, strong and powerful claws, and unexpected agility. ¹³It has quickness, too. ¹⁴The Komodo dragon has a long, yellow, forked tongue. ¹⁵It uses it to sense the presence of prey. ¹⁶Prey can include large mammals. ¹⁷Like dear.

¹⁸There are many tales about the giant lizard. ¹⁹Tales about people-eating have been common. ²⁰The creatures have been blamed for several human deaths. ²¹These accounts may or may not be reliable. ²²However, researchers claim that the lizards are not likely to attack humans. ²³Humans are not the main item on their menus. ²⁴They prefer birds, deer, pigs, and water buffalo. ²⁵They also find other dragons tasty, they also enjoy a nice dish of poisonous snake. ²⁶Komodo dragons are scavengers, to. ²⁷Scavengers eat dead animals.

²⁸Today, the dragons are classified as an endangered species. ²⁹Indonesia protects their habitat. ³⁰By making much of it a national park. ³¹There are an estimated two hundred of these lizards living in zoos. ³²There are another three to five thousand loose in the wild. ³³According to zookeepers, these giants are surprisingly intelligent. ³⁴They possess an intelligence above any other reptile's.

Revising and Editing Worksheet 2

Improve the following draft of a report to make it sound less choppy. You may combine sentences, rearrange sentences, change or omit words, and add new details. Work with a partner or small group to revise these paragraphs. Write your revised report on a separate piece of paper. When you are finished revising and editing, proofread and fix any spelling mistakes you find. Compare your changes with those made by other pairs or groups of classmates. Revisions will vary.

[1]Paper reached Europe. [2]It was a thousand years after its invention in China. [3]It took a long time to get to Europe. [4]Because the process of paper-making was kept secret. [5]Knowledge of the process slowly made it's way west. [6]The Middle Eastern countries introduced paper to Europe and to India. [7]They did so in the twelfth century. [8]They brought the paper to Sicily. [9]Spain too.

[10]Until the nineteenth century in the West, rags were the most important ingredient in the paper-making process. [11]By the nineteenth century, the demand for paper increased greatly, more people were reading and writing. [12]Paper makers began to substitute wood for the rags. [13]Using wood lessened the quality of the paper. [14]Using wood made the paper less durable.

[15]The availability of large amounts of cheap paper had an enormous influence on Western civilization. [16]It caused the rapidly spread of printing. [17]It popularized education. [18]It proved essential to the administration of government. [19]But is paper here to stay, it once seemed so? [20]Until now. [21]Computers have begun to shake our faith in paper. [22]Computer technology makes it possible for a whole new approach to information storage. [23]Computers have challenged the supremacy of paper. [24]Will we have a bookless, magazineless, and newspaperless society some day? [25]It isn't here yet. You may wish to extend this exercise by asking students to write their reponses to the questions posed in the final pargarph.

Chapter Review

Exercise A Identifying Phrases

Underline each phrase in the following sentences. Then write one of these
abbreviations above the phrase:

PREP = prepositional phrase   INF = infinitive phrase
PART = participial phrase   APP = appositive phrase
GER = gerund phrase   ABS = absolute phrase

Remember: When a prepositional phrase is part of another kind of phrase,
you don't have to label the prepositional phrase separately.

1. Pancho Barnes made a name <u>for herself</u> [PREP] as the first woman stunt pilot <u>in</u>
   <u>motion pictures</u>. [PREP]

2. Barnes tried <u>setting new air-speed records</u>. [GER]

3. <u>In 1910</u>, [PREP] Blanche Scott became the first woman <u>to fly solo</u>. [INF]

4. <u>In 1912</u>, [PREP] Scott made her first cross-country flight, <u>a trip taking sixty-
   nine days</u>. [ABS or APP]

5. <u>Known as "the flying schoolgirl,"</u> [PART] Katherine Stinson was the first
   woman <u>to skywrite</u>. [INF]

6. Stinson was the fourth woman <u>in the world</u> [PREP] <u>to qualify</u> [INF] <u>for a pilot's</u>
   <u>license</u>. [PREP]

7. The first woman <u>to fly nonstop</u> [INF] <u>from the East</u> [PREP] <u>to the West</u> [PREP] across
   <u>North America</u> [PREP] was Laura Ingalls.

8. When Ruth Nichols graduated <u>from Miss Masters' School</u>, [PREP] she got an
   airplane as a graduation present.

9. <u>Breaking the women's speed record in both directions</u> [GER] was Nichols's
   accomplishment <u>for transcontinental flights</u> [PREP] <u>in 1929</u>. [PREP]

10. <u>Becoming the first woman</u> [GER] <u>to fly solo</u> [INF] <u>around the world</u> [PREP] was Jerrie
    Mock's claim <u>to fame</u>. [PREP]

Exercise B Combining Sentences

Use phrases to combine the sentences in each numbered item. Write your combined sentences on a separate piece of paper. Don't forget to insert commas where they belong. **Hint:** There is more than one way to combine most of these sentences. See Answer Key.

1. The 1941 film *Sergeant York* is about the life of the pacifist soldier Alvin York. Gary Cooper starred as York.

2. Oliver Stone's film *JFK* is about the assassination of President Kennedy in 1963. The director's interpretation is controversial.

3. The film *The Lion in Winter* won many Oscars when it was released in 1968. The film portrays a conflict between Henry II and Eleanor of Aquitaine.

4. *Gandhi* was the 1982 Best Picture of the Year. It tells about the life and times of Mohandas K. Gandhi.

5. In 1992, Spike Lee made a film biography of Malcolm X. Malcolm X was an African American leader.

6. Kirk Douglas starred in *Lust for Life*. This 1956 film adapted Irving Stone's biography of Vincent van Gogh.

7. *Out of Africa* is a film about the writer Karen Blixen. The film stars Meryl Streep and Robert Redford.

8. Gordon Parks made a 1976 film about the folk singer called Leadbelly. The folk singer's name was Huddie Ledbetter.

9. Steven Spielberg made a film about the courageous Oskar Schindler. This movie shows one person making a great difference.

10. The television miniseries *Shogun* aired in 1980. It introduced American audiences to the ways of imperial Japan.

Exercise C Write What You Think

Over the years, Hollywood has made many films based on historical events and real people. For many moviegoers, the view presented by these films is the only one they have about the event or people depicted. Since the filmmakers use dramatic license when telling their stories, they may distort the truth in order to make a more effective movie. Does this situation produce a problem?

Write a paragraph or two about whether or not you value movies made about real people and events. Try to use prepositional, verbal, appositive, and absolute phrases to express your ideas clearly. When you finish writing, underline all of the phrases you've used.

Answers will vary. Look for grammatically complete sentences that begin with a capital letter and end with an appropriate end punctuation mark.

Clauses

STUDENT WRITING
Expository Essay

What I Learned About Life
from Selling Shoes
by Katherine Ivers
high school student, Meriden, Connecticut

I know you're asking, "What could you possibly learn from selling shoes?" But the vast knowledge I have acquired from this minimum-wage job will last a lifetime.

Hired right before Christmas, I was about to receive a crash course in responsibility. Amid the decorations, elevator music, and hordes of customers, I learned my first lesson—patience. This virtue, unbeknownst to the six million crazed customers waving and shoving shoes in my face, is the only reason many of them were not bludgeoned to death by a high heel.

Another very important lesson is stress management. I faced the triple necessity of balancing honors courses at school, holding down a part-time job, and retaining a social life. . . .

I also learned to master quickly the art of budgeting time. I eat dinner, talk to my boss, and study for a trig quiz in fifteen minutes. Going to the bathroom can wait. In the shoe department, I learned something else that surprised me: Men and women are different! I never saw a man try on a pair of shoes and inquire whether they made his ankles look fat. On the other hand, I never saw a woman so anxious to get out of the mall that she purchased any shoe without trying it on. I learned to appreciate and adapt to these differences.

I learned, too, that physical fitness plays an important role. How many people get to do 8,432 knee squats a day? And, of course, there are the ever-present ladders and the constant reaching. From carrying sixteen boxes of size-twelve men's work boots over my head, I have developed biceps that even Arnold Schwarzenegger would envy.

Perhaps the most important lesson of all concerns responsibility. To choose between going to my job (that I love so much) or attending a party was a difficult decision. But I always try to make the right one. Who needs fun anyway?

My job in the shoe department has taught me, finally, a deep appreciation for the people who make a living by dealing with an often cranky—but always demanding—public. If we could all take the responsibility to understand and communicate with a positive attitude, we could have a more peaceful world.

In her essay, Katherine Ivers explains what she has learned from her personal experience. As you reread the essay, notice how she organizes her essay: she presents her least important lesson first and her most important lesson last. This careful organization encourages her audience to keep reading.

Katherine uses a noun clause as the title of her essay. She uses other kinds of clauses in her essay, adding variety to her sentences and connecting related ideas. In this chapter, you'll practice using clauses to express ideas clearly and to vary your sentences.

Allow time for students to discuss the student writing. Suggest that they identify its strengths and propose possible improvements. Use the model to introduce the concepts in the chapter.

Independent Clauses and Subordinate Clauses

● An **independent** (or **main**) **clause** has a subject (S) and a verb (V) and expresses a complete thought.

An independent clause can function all by itself as a **simple sentence**. Because of this power, the clause is called *independent*.

	S V
INDEPENDENT CLAUSE	They stayed for dinner.

	S S V
INDEPENDENT CLAUSE	Dave and Joanne came, too.

When you put two or more independent clauses together and join them with a conjunction (CONJ) or a semicolon, you have a **compound sentence**.

> CONJ
> I ate the lamb chop, **but** I left the asparagus on the plate.

> CONJ   CONJ
> I'd better clean my plate, **for** chocolate cake comes next, **and** I want a big slice.

● A **subordinate** (or **dependent**) **clause** has a subject and a verb but doesn't express a complete thought.

S V	S V
as we drove home	that gives instructions

S V	S V
if they are coming	because it was snowing

A subordinate clause can't stand alone. You must attach it to or insert it into an independent clause. Alternatively, you can drop the word that makes the word group subordinate. For example, if you take off the word *as* in the first word group above, what's left is an independent clause, or simple sentence.

You can place a subordinate clause at the beginning, middle, or end of a sentence.

> S V   S V
> **Because she knew the words**, Donna joined in. [Here, the subordinate clause comes before the independent clause.]

> S S V   V
> The Marx Brothers, **who made several movies**, have had a significant impact on American humor. [The subordinate clause falls between the subject and verb of an independent clause.]

> S V   S V
> Many people are partial to Harpo Marx, **who was the silent one**. [The subordinate clause comes after the independent clause.]

Enriching Your Vocabulary

The Latin word *minimus*, or "smallest," is the root of *minimize*, which is used in Exercise 2, and means "to reduce" or "to make smaller." You can *minimize* your interest payments by paying off your credit card every month.

Writing Hint

Be sure to put the more important idea of a sentence in an independent clause, where it will stand out.

Jackie, **who now swims faster and with less effort**, practiced every day.

To focus on Jackie's results, the following rewrite is more effective.

Jackie, who practiced every day, **now swims faster and with less effort**.

Exercise 1 Identifying Independent and Subordinate Clauses

On the blank for each numbered item, write *I* for an independent clause or *S* for a subordinate clause. On a separate piece of paper, revise every subordinate clause to make it a complete sentence. Sample revisions to subordinate clauses suggested.

____S____ 1. Trace gases and water vapor ~~that~~ affect atmospheric temperature.

____S____ 2. ~~Which is a~~ phenomenon known as the greenhouse effect.

(This) (is)

____I____ 3. The greenhouse effect is essential to life.

____I____ 4. It is what keeps Earth's temperatures within a reasonable range.

____S____ 5. ~~What~~ we've been hearing and reading about the greenhouse effect in recent years.

____S____ 6. ~~That~~ there is significant evidence that the world is getting warmer.

____S____ 7. Because of the greenhouse effect, the temperatures are increasing all over the planet

____I____ 8. Some causes of these increases are human products and activities.

Exercise 2 Revising and Editing Paragraphs

Revise the following paragraphs. Look for any subordinate clauses that incorrectly stand alone as sentences. When you are through revising and editing, proofread and fix spelling mistakes. Students' revisions will vary.

[1]The greenhouse effect, the destruction of the ozone layer, the pollution of the seas, and the loss of diversity among living things, which are problems that affect everyone on Earth. [2]What's more, these problems are interconnected. [3]Since it's clear that we're all in this together. [4]But, for many reasons, the concept is a tough one to act on.

[5]One reason has to do with the differences between wealthy and poor nations. [6]Because in poorer countries people care most about the basics of life—food, clothing, and shelter; they're survival is at stake, and survival comes first. [7]That is why they aren't as concerned as we are in the United States with the chemicals that help grow their foods. [8]Or with how to minimize industrial pollution from factories. [9]Even here in the United States, when jobs are at stake. [10]People put environmental issues second to economic ones.

Adjective Clauses

🔹 An **adjective clause** is a subordinate clause that functions as an adjective. It modifies a noun or pronoun.

Put an adjective clause directly after the word it modifies.
>Mike, **who is seven feet tall**, is the team's starting center.
>He is the player **whom the NBA scouts are watching closely**.
>They've come to watch him at our gym, **where he plays**.

The words in the side column often (but not always) signal the start of an adjective clause. These words are generally called **relative pronouns** and **relative adverbs**. (Most of these introductory words also function as other parts of speech.)

You can omit an introductory relative pronoun from a sentence if the sentence makes sense and sounds natural without one. Read aloud the sentences below to see for yourself how each sounds without the bracketed word.
>Where is the magazine **[that] I left on the table**?
>The college advisor is the person **[whom] you should call**.

If an adjective clause adds information that's necessary to the meaning that the writer intends, it is called an **essential clause**. When a sentence has the same meaning without an adjective clause, that clause is a **nonessential clause**. An essential clause does not need commas; a nonessential clause does.

ESSENTIAL CLAUSE (No commas)	NONESSENTIAL CLAUSE (Set off with commas)
Every player **who misses a free throw in practice** runs a lap.	Erin, **who missed two shots in practice**, ran two laps.
Arturo is looking for a lucky towel **that his mother gave him**.	The lucky towel, **which no one has seen**, has been missing for days.
Jackson is the team **that beat us twice last year**.	We are ready for the Jackson players, **who beat us twice last year**.

 You learned about essential and nonessential clauses when you studied appositives in Lesson 6.2. The same rules about commas apply to adjective clauses. In other textbooks, you may hear the term *nonrestrictive* used for *nonessential* and *restrictive* used for *essential*. These terms are synonyms.

Some Words That Introduce Adjective Clauses

Relative Pronouns
that	which
who	whom
whose	whoever

Relative Adverbs
when	where

Writing Hint

Too many adjective clauses in a row result in weak writing. Replace some of the clauses with phrases, or break up the sentence into separate, shorter sentences.

WEAK
Alex sent his sister, who is five years old and devoted to him, to the kitchen to fetch the cookies that were in a jar, which was located high up in a cabinet next to where the crackers were also stored.

BETTER
Alex sent his devoted five-year-old sister to the kitchen to fetch cookies, which were stored in a jar that was high up in a cabinet next to the crackers.

Underline the adjective clauses in the sentences below. **Hint:** Not every sentence has an adjective clause. Write *None* if the sentence does not have an adjective clause.

1. The calabash, <u>which grows on a vine</u>, is an oddly shaped gourd.

2. The gourd, <u>which comes in a variety of colors and textures</u>, has a hard rind.

3. East African women, <u>whose gardens produce calabashes</u>, make several useful household items out of them.

4. From calabashes, they make eating utensils, toys, and musical instruments. None

5. The women scoop out a calabash's insides and leave it in the sun, <u>where it dries and hardens</u>.

6. The next step is to decorate the calabash.   None

7. The decorator, <u>whoever she is</u>, has several choices to make.

8. She may simply stain the outer skin with vegetable dyes and then polish it to create a rich sheen.   None

9. Some women turn the gourd over to a craftsperson, <u>who carves or burns decorations into its surface</u>.

10. The designs may be purely geometric patterns, or they may show figures <u>that represent familiar stories or proverbs</u>.

Exercise 4 **Writing Sentences with Adjective Clauses**

Can you see into the future? Picture yourself—or perhaps a friend or classmate—ten years from now. What will you be doing? Where and how will you be living? On a separate piece of paper, write a descriptive paragraph that contains your predictions (or your hopes) for what your life will be like in ten years. In your paragraph, include at least three adjective clauses, and underline them.   Students' paragraphs will vary. See teacher pages for assessment rubrics.

Adverb Clauses

◖ An **adverb clause** is a subordinate clause that functions as an adverb. It modifies a verb, an adjective, or another adverb.

Adverb clauses, like adverbs, tell *how, how much, when, where, why, to what extent*, or *under what circumstances*. A comma always follows an introductory adverb clause.

> **Whenever he has time**, he practices the piano. [The clause modifies the verb *practices*; it tells *when* or *to what extent*.]

> He'll practice daily **unless there are too many other things to do**. [The clause modifies the adverb *daily*; it tells *under what circumstances*.]

> He was completely satisfied with his progress **after he'd played the piece several times**. [The clause modifies the adjective *satisfied*; it tells *when*.]

When the words in the side column signal the beginning of an adverb clause, they are called **subordinating conjunctions**.

An **elliptical adverb clause** omits some words. In the following examples, the bracketed words can be left out.

> Juan is younger **than Maria [is]**.
> I'm more concerned about the essay part of the test **than you are [worried about the essay part]**.
> Have you ever met anyone as funny **as Laura [is]**?

Some Words That Introduce Adverb Clauses (Subordinating Conjunctions)	
after	so that
although	than
as	though
as long as	unless
as soon as	until
as though	when
because	whenever
before	where
even though	wherever
if	whether
since	while

Editing Tip

Avoid clauses beginning with *when* or *where* after a form of *be*.

A hurricane ~~is~~ ^{occurs} when winds ~~get~~ above 75 miles per hour accompany ~~and it~~ rains.

Exercise 5 **Identifying Adverb Clauses**

Underline each adverb clause in the sentences below. Be sure to insert a comma after each introductory adverb clause. **Hint:** Not every sentence has an adverb clause. Write *None* if the sentence does not have an adverb clause.

1. <u>When Sojourner Truth was living as a slave</u> her name was

   Isabella Baumfree.

2. One day, she took her youngest son and escaped to freedom.   None

3. <u>After she changed her name</u> she began her campaign against slavery.

4. She chose the name Sojourner Truth <u>because she wanted to become</u>

   <u>a traveler spreading the truth.</u>

Enriching Your Vocabulary

The word *sojourn* comes from the Latin words *sub*, meaning "during," and *diurnum*, meaning "day." A day trip to hike on a nearby mountain could be called a *sojourn*.

5. Although Sojourner Truth was never taught to read or write she expressed her wisdom powerfully in her speeches.

6. She encouraged other former slaves when she heard them give gloomy speeches.

7. Wherever she spoke she had a profound effect on her audience.

8. Even though she was mistreated and often beaten Sojourner Truth kept up her fight.

9. While she worked as a nurse during the Civil War she urged President Lincoln to enlist free blacks to fight in the Union Army.

10. Sojourner Truth continued to fight for equality and for women's rights after the Civil War ended.

Exercise 6 **Writing Sentences with Adverb Clauses**

Work with a partner or small group to write a brief biography of Harriet Tubman based on the notes provided below. Your audience is seventh graders. Use adverb clauses to enrich your writing. Add details if you know them. When you have finished your draft, underline all of the adverb clauses you have used.

Biographies will vary. Check to see that students have inserted and underlined adverb clauses. Check that students have used complete sentences and correct punctuation. See that related ideas are grouped in paragraphs.

> Called Black Moses; born enslaved on plantation in Maryland
>
> Born in 1820; died in 1913
>
> Escaped before being sent farther south
>
> Returned several times to help other family members escape
>
> Used safe houses and hiding places of "Underground Railroad" to make 19 rescue trips
>
> Led more than 300 African Americans to freedom as "railroad conductor"
>
> $40,000 offered by slave owners for her capture; was never caught
>
> Received many honors, including medal from Queen Victoria of England
>
> Given a modest government pension for Civil War nursing services; used it to help establish home for destitute freed African Americans

Noun Clauses

◖ A **noun clause** is a subordinate clause that functions as a noun.

A noun clause, like a noun, can function as a subject, predicate nominative, direct object, indirect object, or object of a preposition. In the following examples, notice that noun clauses can have modifiers and complements. Like nouns, noun clauses can appear at the beginning, middle, or end of a sentence.

Whatever you do will be appreciated. [subject]
This is exactly **what I was looking for**. [predicate nominative]
I understood **why the play closed**. [direct object]
He will tell **whoever will listen** stories about his pet pig. [indirect object]
The committee gave a prize to **whoever entered the contest**. [object of preposition]

See the side column for a list of words that can introduce a noun clause. Sometimes, a noun clause's introductory word is understood.

Some listeners said **[that] Lincoln had a high voice**.
Lincoln did not think **[that] his Gettysburg Address would be so successful**.

Some Words That Introduce Noun Clauses

how	which
if	who
that	whoever
what	whom
whatever	whomever
when	whose
where	why
whether	

Editing Tip

Make sure that omitting an introductory word won't lead to a misreading.

Do people believe **that** the government has their best interests at heart?

Without the word *that*, a reader might think that *the government* is an object of *believe* when it really is a subject of a clause.

Exercise 7 Writing Sentences with Noun Clauses

On a separate piece of paper, write a sentence using each group of words as a noun clause. Exchange papers with a partner to check that you have written a noun clause, not an adjective or an adverb clause.   Students' sentences will vary.

1. that the hardest part of the test was over

2. what we have been shown

3. what I mean

4. whether we'll get to the game on time

5. whom the critics praise

6. whoever wins the World Series

7. how to program a VCR

8. why electric cars are in our future

9. that she is a soprano

10. whoever visits the site

Revising and Editing a Biology Report

Work with a partner to revise the following report. Express the ideas as clearly and directly as possible. Eliminate wordiness and repetition. When you finish, underline all the noun clauses that remain or that you've added. Compare your response with those made by other pairs.

Ponds and Lakes

[1]What I have learned is that the study of inland waters is called *limnology*. [2]Limnology is a division of the broader science of ecology, which is the study of how animals and plants coexist in an environment. [3]Limnologists concern themselves with the factors that affect the inland water environment, that create and maintain the conditions that support life in that environment of inland waters. [4]Limnologists would say to whoever would be interested that they focus not only on biology but also on geography, chemistry, weather, and climate.

[5]According to the science of limnology, a pond is different from a lake. [6]What a pond is is a quiet, shallow body of water that sustains the growth of rooted plants on its bottom and along its shore. [7]Ponds have uniform water temperatures from their wave-free tops to their mud-filled bottoms. [8]Pond temperatures change with changes in the air temperature.

[9]Lakes are different from ponds. [10]Lakes are larger than ponds. [11]Lakes have water. [12]The water is too deep for plant growth, except around the shore. [13]That is what limnologists say. [14]Water temperatures in lakes stay relatively stable from day to day. [15]Lakes that are where there are often low temperatures have what limnologists call "temperature layering" in the summer. [16]Whoever knows their lakes knows that when such a large expanse of water is exposed to the wind, the shores downwind are washed with waves, unlike ponds.

Revisions will vary.

Mid-Chapter Review

Exercise A Identifying Independent and Subordinate Clauses

On the blank for each numbered item, write *I* for an independent clause or *S* for a subordinate clause. On a separate piece of paper, revise every subordinate clause to make it a complete sentence. (To make revisions, you do not need to know anything about British history; just use your ability to write a complete and sensible sentence.) Answers will vary. Suggested corrections are shown.

_____I_____ 1. The nineteenth century began in England with a commercial boom.

_____S_____ 2. ~~When~~ the first British census was conducted in 1801.

_____S_____ 3. ~~Because~~ Admiral Nelson defeated the French and Spanish fleets at Trafalgar.

_____S_____ 4. Whose defeat in 1815 at Waterloo led to peace in Europe. ?

_____I_____ 5. Trade unions were legalized in 1825.

_____S_____ 6. ~~Because~~ the Factory Act of 1833 limited child labor.

_____I_____ 7. Slavery was abolished in the British Empire in 1834.

_____S_____ 8. ~~After~~ William IV died in 1837.

_____S_____ 9. ~~Which~~ *What* began in Ireland in 1845. ?

_____I_____ 10. There were revolutions throughout Europe in 1848.

Exercise B Identifying Adjective and Adverb Clauses

Underline each subordinate clause. On the blank for each numbered item, write *ADJ* for an adjective clause or *ADV* for an adverb clause.

___ADJ___ 1. The Crimean War, which pitted the British and French against the Russians, was fought from 1853 to 1856.

___ADV___ 2. After he published *The Origin of Species* in 1859, Charles Darwin gained worldwide attention.

___ADV___ 3. Queen Victoria was deeply grieved when Prince Albert, her husband, died in 1861.

___ADJ___ 4. The Confederacy, which lobbied the British government for support during the U.S. Civil War, never got this support.

___ADJ___ 5. The Suez Canal, which was a marvel of engineering, opened in 1869.

___ADV___ 6. When Prime Minister Disraeli bought Suez shares in 1875, Britain gained a controlling interest in the canal.

ADV   7. Because the British attempted to expand or maintain their empire, they ran into resistance.

ADV   8. When Victoria died in 1901, Edward VII ascended to the throne.

ADJ   9. An act of Parliament, which passed in 1911, limited the power of the House of Lords.

ADV   10. The British entered World War I after Archduke Ferdinand was assassinated at Sarajevo in 1914.

Exercise C **Writing Sentences with Noun Clauses**

On a separate piece of paper, write a sentence using each group of words as a noun clause. Check that you have written a noun clause, not an adjective or an adverb clause. Answers will vary.

1. that the seat next to me was taken

2. what she has learned

3. what I ate for breakfast

4. whether we'll get into that college

5. whom the colleges recruit

6. whoever loses the first game

7. how to eat a lobster

8. why basketball shorts go below the knees

9. that he has an after-school job

10. whoever studies the hardest

Exercise D **Identifying Adjective, Adverb, and Noun Clauses**

Each of the following numbered items is from Shakespeare's play *Macbeth*. Study the italicized clause in each item, and on the line, write *ADJ* if the words form an adjective clause, *ADV* if they form an adverb clause, and *N* if they form a noun clause. (The slashes indicate where one line of poetry ends and another begins.)

ADJ   1. This is the sergeant/*Who like a good and hardy soldier* fought/'Gainst my captivity.

ADJ   2. Good sir, why do you start, and seem to fear/Things *that do sound so fair?*

N   3. . . . *what seemed corporal* melted/As a breath into the wind.

N   4. Things without all remedy/Should be without regard: *what's done* is done.

ADV   5. *When our actions do not,*/Our fears do make us traitors.

Combining Sentences: Using Subordinate Clauses

🖋 You can combine two related sentences by turning one sentence into an adjective clause.

Change one sentence into an adjective clause that begins with *who*, *which*, *that*, or another word from the list of relative pronouns on page 171. Then place the adjective clause after a noun or pronoun in the remaining sentence. Don't forget the commas to set off nonessential adjective clauses.

ORIGINAL Latisha broke the school long-jump record. Latisha is Eddie's cousin.

COMBINED Latisha, **who is Eddie's cousin**, broke the school long-jump record.

ORIGINAL Latisha is an all-around athlete. College recruiters have been watching her performances.

COMBINED Latisha, **who is an all-around athlete**, has college recruiters watching her performances.

🖋 You can combine two related sentences by turning one sentence into an adverb clause.

Use a subordinating conjunction to create an adverb clause out of one sentence. Then attach the adverb clause to the remaining sentence. Choose a subordinating conjunction that shows how the ideas in the two sentences are related. For example, *because* and *since* show a cause-effect relationship; *while*, *when*, *whenever*, *before*, *after*, and *until* show a chronological relationship.

ORIGINAL Storms raged along the coast. Several beach houses were damaged.

COMBINED **When storms raged along the coast**, several beach houses were damaged.

COMBINED Several beach houses were damaged **when storms raged along the coast**.

ORIGINAL Some inhabitants remained. Many evacuated to safety.

COMBINED **Although some inhabitants remained**, many evacuated to safety.

COMBINED Many evacuated to safety, **although some inhabitants remained**.

Writing Hint

If a paragraph contains several sentences in a row with adjective clauses, change one or more of the clauses to appositive phrases (see Lesson 6.2).

Latisha, who is Eddie's cousin, broke the school long-jump record. ~~Latisha,~~ *An*
~~who is an~~ all-around *she* athlete, has college ^ recruiters watching her performances. She broke several other school records, which were also city records.

Exercise 9 Combining Sentences Using Adjective Clauses

Work with a partner to combine each pair of sentences into a single sentence by using an adjective clause. Put the less important idea in the adjective clause. Write your responses on a separate piece of paper, and underline the adjective clause in your combined sentences.   See Answer Key.

EXAMPLE   Sandra Cisneros is a critically acclaimed author. She was born into a large Mexican American family.

Sandra Cisneros, <u>who was born into a large Mexican American family</u>, is a critically acclaimed author.

> **Hint**
>
> Set off nonessential adjective clauses with commas.

1. Cisneros attended the Writers Workshop at the University of Iowa. She learned to become a writer there.

2. At the Writers Workshop, Cisneros improved her writing skills dramatically. The Writers Workshop has a terrific reputation.

3. Her Mexican American heritage provided her with a source of ideas for her fiction. Her heritage made her stand out among other young writers.

4. Cisneros wrote a group of stories about her childhood. She put them in her first book, entitled *The House on Mango Street.*

5. Her next book won critical acclaim and earned her popular recognition. It was entitled *Woman Hollering Creek.*

Exercise 10 Combining Sentences Using Adverb Clauses

Work with a partner to combine each pair of sentences into a single sentence with an adverb clause. Put the less important idea in the adverb clause. Write your responses on a separate piece of paper, and underline the adverb clause in your combined sentences.   See Answer Key.

1. *Bless Me, Ultima*, by Anaya, won as the best novel written by a Chicano in 1972. Anaya wrote many other books.

2. Anaya became a full professor at the University of New Mexico. He taught in junior and senior high schools first.

3. Anaya had taught creative writing at the university for nineteen years. He retired in 1993.

> **Hint**
>
> Set off an introductory adverb clause with a comma.

4. Anaya has been described by *Newsweek* as "the most widely read Mexican American." Until recently, his work was not known by many readers on the East Coast.

5. Anaya remains by nature a quiet person. His fame has given him a feeling of great satisfaction.

Four Types of Sentence Structure

We classify sentences according to the number and kind of clauses they have. You need to know about the four types of sentence structures so that your paragraphs and longer papers offer variety to the reader.

● A **simple sentence** has one independent clause and no subordinate clauses.

Simple sentences are not necessarily short and uncomplicated. A simple sentence may have a compound subject (s), a compound verb (v), and many different phrases.

>   S
> The origin of the word *patsy*, like the origin of many English words and
>   V
> phrases, is not clear.

● A **compound sentence** has two or more independent clauses and no subordinate clauses.

>   S   V   S
> Most dictionaries list the source of *patsy* as "origin unknown"; it
>   V
> comes from the Italian word *pazzo*, or "fool."

● A **complex sentence** has one independent clause and at least one subordinate clause.

>   S   V   S   V   S
> The term *slapstick* comes from *slapsticks*, which were two sticks that
>   V
> could create a loud noise.

● A **compound-complex sentence** has two or more independent clauses and at least one subordinate clause.

>   S   V   S V
> Hubbard Keary invented the word *smog*, which is a blend of *smoke*
>   S
> and *fog*, during a winter of pollution in Des Moines, and it first
> V
> appeared in a newspaper headline.

Writing Hint

A complex sentence with the same subordinator before and after a main clause sounds bogged down. Try to add variety.

If you keep trying, your writing will improve ~~if you~~ , so make a special effort.

Exercise 11 Identifying Sentence Structure

The sentences on the following page are about word and phrase origins. Identify the sentence structure of each sentence. On the blank before each numbered item, write *S* for simple, *Cd* for compound, *Cx* for complex, and *Cd-Cx* for compound-complex.

Cx	1. Since *ante* means "before" in Latin and *bellum* means "war," *antebellum* simply means "before war." *Since* is understood in this elliptical sentence.
Cd	2. *Antebellum*, in the United States, refers to the pre-Civil War period; in Great Britain, it refers to periods before the Boer War and before both world wars.
Cx	3. *Apartheid*, which was the South African policy of segregation, derived from two Dutch words—*apart*, meaning the same as the English word, and *heid*, meaning "hood."
S	4. Theories about the origin of April Fool's Day, the day for pranks, abound.
Cd-Cx	5. One account traces April Fool's Day to Roman mythology; another links it to the time when the Gregorian calendar, which is the one we use today, replaced the Julian one.
Cx	6. Abraham Lincoln, who attended a *blab school*, learned his lessons by reciting them over and over, in unison, with his classmates.
S	7. The expression *bite the bullet* comes from the medical profession.
Cx	8. During surgery, when no anesthesia was available, wounded soldiers bit on bullets to deal with their pain.
S	9. The first *blazers* belonged to some Cambridge students in England in the nineteenth century and were of a bright, blazing red color.
Cd-Cx	10. *Levis* derive their name from Levi Strauss, the gold rush clothing merchant; he added rivets to the corners of pockets to prevent tearing when the miners filled them with ore.

Exercise 12 **Expanding Sentences**

Expand each of the following simple sentences by making up interesting details. After each new sentence you write, identify its structure by adding *S* for simple, *Cd* for compound, *Cx* for complex, and *Cd-Cx* for compound-complex sentence structure. Compare your expanded sentences with those of a partner or small group.   Answers will vary.

EXAMPLE   Jerome is seven years old.

Jerome, who is seven years old, can stand on his head and recite poetry. **Cx**

1. Tamika enjoys poetry.

2. Walt Whitman is her favorite poet.

3. Carlos prefers comics.

4. He has a collection of comic books.

5. Patrick is a couch potato.

6. He watches TV programs.

7. Patrick likes watching commercials.

8. Margaret listens to music.

9. She carries her own CD player.

10. She can't hear her friends.

Effective Sentences: Parallel Structure

🖌 To achieve parallel structure, use the same grammatical structure for two or more similar ideas.

NOT PARALLEL I enjoy **beef**, **chicken**, and **eating fish**. [After the verb, the first two items are nouns, but the third is a gerund phrase.]

PARALLEL I enjoy **beef**, **chicken**, and **fish**. [All three items are nouns.]

The principle of parallelism applies to clauses.

NOT PARALLEL The teacher said **that I should write more** and **to talk less**.

PARALLEL The teacher said **that I should write more** and **that I should talk less**.

PARALLEL The teacher said **to write more** and **to talk less**.

🖌 Use parallel structure with correlative constructions such as *both . . . and*, *either . . . or*, and *not only . . . but also*.

NOT PARALLEL It was *both* **a hot day** *and* **humid**. [The first complement is a noun phrase; the second is an adjective.]

PARALLEL The day was *both* **hot** *and* **humid**. [two adjectives]

NOT PARALLEL I want to explain *both* **who I am** *and* **my beliefs**.

PARALLEL I want to explain *both* **who I am** *and* **what I believe**.

To make your meaning clear in a parallel construction, repeat articles, prepositions, or pronouns whenever necessary.

After the game, I spoke with the coach and team captain. [Are they the same person?]

After the game, I spoke **with** the coach and **with** the team captain. [Now it is clear that the coach and captain are two different people.]

Readers have trouble with lists—especially a list of instructions—if the items aren't parallel.

Directions for Grandparents' Day at my school:

1. Take bus #3 uptown to 75th St.

2. Walk 2 blocks east. ***Ring bell***

3. ~~Bell~~ on main door of building with flag (on right side of street).

Exercise 13 ## Revising Sentences to Create Parallel Structure

On a separate piece of paper, revise each of the following sentences so that it has parallel structure. **Hint:** There is more than one way to revise each one. See Answer Key.

1. The Middle East has witnessed decades of turmoil and being in a constant state of crisis.

2. Before the Gulf War, the United States and its allies tried persuasion and to use diplomacy.

3. Jordan borders Saudi Arabia, Iraq, and it is also a neighbor of Syria.

4. In Egypt, you can see pyramids, you can ride along the Nile, and explore the streets of Cairo.

5. On Israel's Mediterranean beaches, you can try snorkeling and to swim.

6. In Iran, you can visit the ancient city of Isfahan, which is centrally located, and Tehran, a city on the coast.

7. In Israel, people live in modern cities, in small towns, and they have farms.

8. In Saudi Arabia, you can find schools for the children of American workers and where other students can go, too.

9. Some Americans like to work for oil companies in the Middle East for the high salaries and because they like the lifestyle.

10. Visitors to Middle Eastern countries can visit communities that haven't changed much over time, and ever-changing ones.

Exercise 14 Write What You Think

■ Refer to **Composition, Lesson 3.3,** for strategies for writing persuasively.

Do you agree or disagree with the following statement? Respond by writing a paragraph that not only states your opinion but also offers the reasons you hold your opinion.   Answers will vary. Responses should include reasons for agreeing or disagreeing with the statement—humanitarian or ethical reasons, economic reasons, political reasons.

The United States should always do whatever it takes to bring peace to troubled regions of the world.

Exercise 15 Parallel Structure

On a separate piece of paper, respond to each question below by giving a three-part answer. Then exchange papers with a partner, and check each other's answers for three parallel structures.   Answers will vary.

EXAMPLE   What did you wash last weekend?
Last weekend, I washed the car that went through many storms, the dog that played in a puddle, and the laundry that had piled up in my room.

1. What do you see when you look around the room you are now in?

2. What do you hear when you listen to the sounds in the room?

3. What are your goals?

4. What would you like to learn more about?

5. What would you consider a good summer job?

6. Why do you go to school?

7. Why do you or don't you look forward to your birthday?

8. Why are holidays important?

Varying Sentence Beginnings, Structures, and Lengths

● For variety, begin some of your sentences with a subordinate clause.

Subordinate clauses give you a tool for varying sentence beginnings. Keep clauses and noun clauses in mind as a variety of ways for expressing an idea. Here is the same idea expressed in several different ways.

ORIGINAL
Ulysses S. Grant died on July 23, 1885, less than a month after he completed his memoirs.

PREPOSITIONAL PHRASE
On July 23, 1885, after he completed his memoirs, Ulysses S. Grant died.

PARTICIPIAL PHRASE
Resting from his work on his memoirs, Ulysses S. Grant died on July 23, 1885.

ADVERB CLAUSE
Shortly after he completed his memoirs, Ulysses S. Grant died on July 23, 1885.

NOUN CLAUSE
What Ulysses S. Grant did just before he died on July 23, 1885, was complete his memoirs.

● When you write a paragraph or longer paper, vary the sentence structures and the lengths of sentences.

If all your sentences have the same forms and the same number of words, you will bore your readers. Use phrases and clauses in some sentences but not all, and provide a mix of long and short sentences.

> ### Writing Hint
>
> It never hurts to count the words in each sentence of a paragraph you write. If all the sentences are about the same length (say, twenty-two words), consider rewriting to create one very short sentence (say, eight words).

Exercise 16 Varying Sentence Beginnings

On a separate piece of paper, rewrite each of the following sentences to change the structure with which it begins. Do not change the meaning of the sentence. Answers will vary.

1. Girls officially played Little League baseball, starting in 1975.

2. President Gerald Ford signed legislation on December 26, 1974, to open the Little League baseball program to girls.

3. The Little League charter was amended to replace the word *boys* with *young people*.

4. Changes in the Little League charter occurred after parents filed numerous lawsuits to open the leagues to girls.

5. Women's baseball is more popular in Europe than in the United States, even with the increase of girls in the Little League here.

> ### Enriching Your Vocabulary
>
> The verb *amend* means "to correct, change, or alter." From the same root, and similar in meaning, is the verb *emend*. *Amend* is more general in usage than *emend*, which usually refers to text.

Work with a partner to revise the following report on the history of women's basketball. Write on a separate piece of paper. Your audience is the readers of your school newspaper. In your revision, try to vary some sentences' beginnings and structures. Combine sentences, and find other ways to eliminate unnecessary repetition and monotony. Revisions will vary.

[1]Women first played basketball at Smith College in 1892. [2]Smith College is in Northampton, Massachusetts. [3]Senda Berenson introduced the game. [4]She was the director of physical education at Smith. [5]The first women's intercollegiate basketball game was between teams from Berkeley and Stanford. [6]It took place on April 4, 1896. [7]Male spectators were barred from the game.

[8]Berenson drew up the first rules for women's basketball. [9]She did so in 1899. [10]These were the sport's first official rules. [11]According to Berenson's basketball rules, players could dribble only three times. [12]They could hold the ball for three seconds or less. [13]These rules remained the standard for nearly three-quarters of a century.

Exercise 18 **Writing a Paragraph**

Use the notes below along with other ideas that you may have to write a one-paragraph school newspaper article about the opening of a new school gymnasium. Write your paragraph on a separate piece of paper. Put the ideas into a sensible order, and try to vary your sentence beginnings, structures, and lengths. Students' paragraphs will vary. See teacher pages for assessment rubrics.

> Seats 1,500 for basketball
>
> Can serve many purposes, some simultaneously
>
> Came in under budget
>
> Money raised by student body and by community efforts
>
> Can seat 2,000 for concerts
>
> Has state-of-the-art locker rooms and other facilities
>
> Has state-of-the-art security system
>
> Opening day ceremony: May 25
>
> Former student, now mayor, to speak

Revising and Editing Worksheet 1

Improve the following story beginning. Correct sentence fragments, and try to vary sentence structures and beginnings. When you are finished revising and editing, proofread your paragraphs, and fix any spelling or comma mistakes you find. Write your improved story beginning on a separate piece of paper.

[1]The two boys had been in Nova Scotia. [2]They were camping there. [3]It was the summer following their senior year. [4]Before they were to pack their bags, go away to college, and seeing less of each other. [5]Ben and Tony had borrowed Ben's father's car. [6]They were lucky to have the car. [7]They filled it with all the camping gear that anyone who went camping where it gets cold which is not unusual in the summer would need. [8]But they didn't know Ben would get sick. [9]He had a fever. [10]While Tony drove them back home. [11]Which was far. [12]Ben simply stayed asleep or half asleep in the back seat.

[13]Late one evening is when they found themselves in a small town in New Brunswick, Canada. [14]Niether had been there before. [15]It was raining. [16]It was cold. [17]It would be too much trouble to set up their tent. [18]Because Ben was sick, they decided to spend some of their remaining money on a hotel room. [19]They found an old one. [20]It was a little shabby. [21]Also it was small.

[22]Late that night, while Tony slept like a baby. [23]Ben was up and down. [24]At about two in the morning, he was up. [25]He was standing at the sink. [26]The sink was in the room. [27]He was soaking his tea shirt in cold water. [28]He planed to hold it against his forehead that felt like it was on fire. [29]Then, suddenly, there was a loud rapping at the door.

[30]"Open up. Its the police." [31]That woke Tony.

[32]"The police!" Ben said. [33]"What do they want?"

[34]He opened the door and let the two officers in. [35]He still had the wet T-shirt in his hands. [36]Tony stood up, too.

[37]"Which one of you is Ben Anker?" [38]The boys looked at each other. [39]They had puzzled looks on their faces.

Revisions will vary but should contain only complete sentences and correct spelling. Check that students have varied sentence structures, beginnings, and lengths. Students may wish to finish the story on their own.

Revising and Editing Worksheet 2

Work with a partner to revise the following report on America's rainforests. Correct sentence fragments, and try to vary sentence structures and beginnings. You may combine sentences, add or leave out details, and replace or drop words. Remember to fix spelling mistakes, too. Write your revised report on a separate piece of paper. Compare your revision with those of other pairs of students.

¹From northern California to southeast Alaska lies an ancient forest. ²It carpets the land. ³It is a forest of Douglas fir, red cedars, Sitka spruce, and hemlock. ⁴Which are huge trees of spectacular proportions. ⁵It rivals any forest on Earth in size and grandeur. ⁶It is cool. ⁷It is wet. ⁸It is forever green. ⁹The North American temperate rainforest is where we have treasure that may be in trouble.

¹⁰You read alot about the severe difficulties facing rainforests that are in tropical parts of the world, which include Central and South America, which you know humankind can not afford to lose. ¹¹Losing them can jeopardize life on the planet. ¹²But the rainforests right here in North America also have significant value. ¹³The trees alone are an extraordinary resource. ¹⁴They are a treasure, too. ¹⁵And under the canopy of these great trees lie immense biological resources. ¹⁶For example, their is the wild Pacific yew that, some claim, has been demonstrated to cure certain kinds of cancer. ¹⁷Who knows what else in the way of untapped medical value the forests contain?

¹⁸Unfortunately, some policies in the United States and Canada have put this region in danjer. ¹⁹Nearly 90 percent of the original forest is gone. ²⁰Since they explored the forest in the nineteenth century, timber barons have been logging it. ²¹Cutting down trees. ²²Eroding and depleting the soil. ²³There has been a disappearance of natural habitat. ²⁴It has been wholesale. ²⁵In some parts, industry has protected the forests. ²⁶But more needs to be done. ²⁷America's temperate rainforests deserve better.   Revisions will vary but should contain only complete sentences and correct spelling. Check that students have varied sentence structures, beginnings, and lengths. Students may wish to finish the story on their own.

Chapter Review

Exercise A Identifying Independent and
Subordinate Clauses

On the blank for each numbered item, write *I* for an independent clause or *S*
for a subordinate clause. On a separate sheet of paper, revise every
subordinate clause to make it a complete sentence. Answers will vary. Sample
revisions suggested.

EXAMPLE ___*S*___ When someone invented the ballpoint pen.

*When someone invented the ballpoint pen, sales of
fountain pens decreased.*

___S___ 1. ~~When~~ Pluto was discovered in 1930.

___S___ 2. ~~When~~ color cartoon film showed up for the first time in 1932.

___I___ 3. In 1933, people first played the game Monopoly.

___S___ 4. ~~Because~~ the first mass-market paperback books came out in 1935.

___S___ 5. The helicopter, which was a key invention in 1936~~,~~ , is still in use today.

Exercise B Identifying Types of Clauses

On the blank for each numbered item, identify the underlined clause in
each sentence by writing *ADJ* for adjective clause, *ADV* for adverb clause, or
N for noun clause.

EXAMPLE ___*ADJ*___ Kathy Waller, <u>who holds the record for the length of an
apple peeling</u>, took 11¹/₂ hours to create her peeling.

___ADJ___ 1. The record for apple peeling, 172 ft. 4 in., <u>which is held by
Kathy Waller</u>, was achieved in 1976.

___ADV___ 2. Greg Mutton must have been extremely tired <u>after he broke
the bathtub racing record in 1987</u>.

___ADV___ 3. <u>When a team from Scotland wheeled a hospital bed 3,233
miles</u>, it broke the bed-pushing record.

___ADJ___ 4. The record for brick balancing, <u>which involves balancing bricks
on one's head</u>, is seventy-five bricks for nineteen seconds.

___ADV___ 5. <u>After students from a Washington high school had worked
eight hours</u>, they had washed a total of 3,844 cars—a record.

___N___ 6. <u>What made him do it</u> is a mystery, but V. Jeyaraman clapped
his hands for more than fifty-eight hours without stopping.

___N___ 7. Tell <u>whoever has a sense of humor</u> that the record for jokes
told in one hour is 345.

___ADV___ 8. <u>Even though he may not have liked eating oysters</u>, Mike Racz
opened a hundred of them in 2 minutes, 20.07 seconds.

CHAPTER REVIEW

Exercise C Identifying Sentence Structure

Identify the sentence structure of each. On the blank before each number, write *S* for simple, *Cd* for compound, *Cx* for complex, and *Cd-Cx* for compound-complex.

____Cx____ 1. If you enjoy listening to the blues, you may know that Jelly Roll Morton first published a blues tune in 1905.

____Cx____ 2. Some say that the expression *bring home the bacon* derives from contests for catching greased pigs.

____Cd____ 3. The word *brunch* is a blend word; Lewis Carroll's *slithy*, a combination of *slimy* and *lithe*, is another example.

____Cd-Cx____ 4. Some sources report that *buddy*, meaning "friend," is more than a century old, but other dictionaries, which disagree, claim that it is probably baby talk for "brother."

____S____ 5. The expression *by the skin of my teeth* comes from the Book of Job in the Bible.

____Cd-Cx____ 6. When you call someone *every name in the book*, that book is neither the Bible nor the phone book; it is the dictionary.

____Cx____ 7. A *can of worms*, which has long been an expression used by people in the advertising business, refers to a problem that is complicated and hard to solve.

____Cx____ 8. A person *who can't see the forest for the trees* is concerned with insignificant issues and is unable to grasp the larger problems.

Exercise D Editing to Create Parallel Structure

On a separate piece of paper, edit each sentence so that it has parallel structure.

1. The historical period between the ninth and thirteenth centuries is called the Middle Ages, sometimes the Dark Ages, and it's the Medieval Period.

2. Some scholars describe the period as scientifically undeveloped, backward when it comes to art, and infested by the Black Plague.

3. Other scholars describe the Middle Ages as teeming with ideas, it had exploded with energy, and flowering with regard to economic growth.

4. Gothic cathedrals, originating in the Middle Ages, are both astonishingly tall and brilliant in lighting.

5. Students at the universities in Paris that began during the Middle Ages learned what the great philosophers wrote, to recite the Church teachings, and arguing for their ideas.

See Answer Key.

Cumulative Review

Exercise A Identifying Parts of Speech

On the blank before each number, identify the part of speech of each underlined word as it is used in the sentence. Use these abbreviations:

N = noun   ADJ = adjective   CONJ = conjunction
PRON = pronoun   ADV = adverb   INTER = interjection
V = verb   PREP = preposition

___N___ 1. In the world of <u>camping</u>, there are several kinds of tents.

___ADJ___ 2. The largest is the <u>family</u> tent.

___PREP___ 3. Several tents come <u>with</u> canopies.

___PRON___ 4. <u>Some</u> even have windows.

___V___ 5. Guy ropes attached to stakes <u>stabilize</u> the tents.

___V___ 6. The guy ropes <u>attach</u> to the grommets on the tent roofs.

___N___ 7. Some tents have mud walls and sewn-in <u>floors</u>.

___ADV___ 8. Have you ever slept <u>peacefully</u> in a pup tent?

___ADV___ 9. A dome tent looks like but is <u>not</u> a pop-up tent.

___CONJ___ 10. Other types of tents include Baker tents, tourist tents, wall tents, <u>and</u> wagon tents.

Exercise B Identifying Phrases

On the blank before each numbered item, identify each underlined phrase by writing one of these abbreviations in the space provided: ·

PREP = prepositional phrase   INF = infinitive phrase
PART = participial phrase   APP = appositive phrase
GER = gerund phrase

___APP___ 1. Ms. Miller, <u>the French teacher</u>, is a gourmet cook.

___GER___ 2. Mr. Ruben tried <u>playing the bagpipes</u>.

___APP___ 3. Mr. Angelos, <u>the soccer coach</u>, has a pilot's license.

___PREP/PREP___ 4. <u>In the summer of 1998</u>, Ms. Scott hiked on the Appalachian Trail <u>for thirty-nine days</u>.

___APP/PREP___ 5. The science teacher, <u>Ms. Jackson</u>, has a tree farm <u>in Vermont</u>.

___INF___ 6. Mr. Wong, the art teacher, was the first person from our school <u>to display his artwork</u> at the museum.

___PREP___ 7. The new social studies teacher was immediately a favorite <u>with her students</u>.

PREP   8. When you get a compliment <u>from Ms. Feldstein</u>, you never forget it.

PART   9. <u>Working through the weekend</u>, Mr. Gonzales and Ms. Reilly got everything ready for the science fair.

GER   10. This spring, Ms. Mann plans on <u>accompanying the senior class</u> to Italy.

Exercise C **Identifying Clauses**

On the blank before each numbered item, identify the underlined clause in each sentence by writing *ADJ* for adjective clause, *ADV* for adverb clause, or *N* for noun clause.

ADJ   1. The Negro baseball leagues, <u>which were founded in 1920</u>, came to an end when the major leagues were integrated.

ADV   2. <u>Before these leagues were formed</u>, independent teams made up of black players competed with one another.

ADV   3. For the most part, <u>wherever the Negro baseball leagues played</u>, crowds showed enthusiasm.

ADJ   4. Players such as Josh Gibson, Oscar Charleston, and Buck Leonard, <u>who were Negro League stars</u>, never played in the major leagues.

N   5. <u>Whatever went on in Negro League baseball</u> was largely ignored by the white communities.

ADV   6. <u>Although it was ignored by the white community</u>, Negro League baseball was a major attraction in the black communities.

ADJ   7. The Eastern Colored League, <u>which lasted from 1923 to 1928</u>, was one of several Negro baseball leagues.

N   8. Any fan could see <u>how some of the black ballplayers excelled</u>.

ADJ   9. Jackie Robinson, <u>who was the first person to break the color barrier</u>, soon had black colleagues in the majors.

ADV   10. <u>After the best Negro League players joined Major League teams in the early 1950s</u>, all the Negro leagues began to fold.

Grammar Test

Exercise 1 Identifying Errors

Directions: Each of the numbered items either is totally correct or contains an error in one of the underlined word(s) or in punctuation. In the answer section to the right of each item, circle the letter of the underlined word(s) or punctuation mark that contains the error. If the sentence is correct, circle *D* for NO ERROR.

EXAMPLE   It was <u>really</u> cold on the <u>first</u> day of the World Series, and the   A B Ⓒ D
                    A   B

Players struggled to stay warm.   <u>NO ERROR</u>
C   D

1. At the start <u>of the contest</u>, the umpires, players, and   1. A B Ⓒ D
                 A   B

    <u>coaches'</u> took their places on the field.   <u>NO ERROR</u>
    C   D

2. The pitchers <u>beginning</u> to warm up in the bullpens, and <u>some</u> players   2.Ⓐ B C D
                 A   B

    tossed the ball around <u>on the sidelines</u>.   <u>NO ERROR</u>
                           C   D

3. The <u>one-time</u> great player, <u>who's</u> whole family was in the stands,   3. A Ⓑ C D
        A   B

    <u>threw</u> out the first ball.   <u>NO ERROR</u>
    C   D

4. <u>the</u> first batter completed <u>his</u> practice swings and stepped   4.Ⓐ B C D
    A   B

    <u>up to the plate</u>.   <u>NO ERROR</u>
    C   D

5. He fixed <u>his</u> hat, <u>tugged</u> at his <u>sleeve,</u>   5. A B C Ⓓ
             A   B   C

    and tapped the plate with his bat.   <u>NO ERROR</u>
                                         D

6. The pitch came, and the batter pulled it foul down the <u>third-base</u>   6. A Ⓑ C D
                                                           A

    line, <u>bare</u> <u>missing</u> a home run.   <u>NO ERROR</u>
          B   C   D

7. The manager, <u>of the home team,</u> gave signals to his catcher, <u>who</u> then   7.Ⓐ B C D
                 A   B

    <u>passed</u> them on to the pitcher.   <u>NO ERROR</u>
    C   D

8. A problem for <u>pitchers</u> is <u>when</u> the batter knows   8. A Ⓑ C D
                  A   B

    what kind of pitch <u>is coming</u>.   <u>NO ERROR</u>
                       C   D

Exercise 2 Correcting Errors

Directions: Each numbered item either may or may not be correct. If the numbered item contains no errors, circle D in the answer section for NO ERROR. If the numbered item contains errors, circle the letter of the correctly written revision.

EXAMPLE   Anna love to eat. She eats quick, too.   (A) B C D
          A. Anna loves to eat. She eats quickly, too.
          B. Anna loves to eat. She eats quick, too.
          C. Anna love to eat. She eats quickly, too.
          D. NO ERROR

1. Both Ian and his sister doing gymnastics.   1.(A) B C D
   A. Both Ian and his sister do gymnastics.
   B. Ian and his sister both doing gymnastics.
   C. Ian and his sister do both gymanstics.
   D. NO ERROR

2. James spotted an antique car. While waiting for the bus.   2. A B (C) D
   A. James spotted an antique car. While he was waiting for the bus.
   B. James spotted an antique car waiting for the bus.
   C. While waiting for the bus, James spotted an antique car.
   D. NO ERROR

3. Did you forget to call? Or is the error mine's?   3. A (B) C D
   A. Did you forget to call? Or is the error mine.
   B. Did you forget to call? Or is the error mine?
   C. Did you forget to call or is the error mines?
   D. NO ERROR

4. I called the library and got a recorded message, I guess it was closed.   4. A B (C) D
   A. I called the library and got a recorded message. I guess it was closed.
   B. I called the library and got a recorded message, I guess the library
      was closed.
   C. I called the library and got a recorded message. I guess the library was
      closed.
   D. NO ERROR

5. The package arrived today. The one we had been waiting for.   5.(A) B C D
   A. The package that we had been waiting for arrived today.
   B. The package arrived today. The one we waited for.
   C. The day we had been waiting for arrived with a package.
   D. NO ERROR

6. Gomez the coach of the Tigers has a new four-year contract.   6. A (B) C D
   A. Gomez the coach of the Tigers had a new four-year contract.
   B. Gomez, the coach of the Tigers, has a new four-year contract.
   C. Gomez who is the coach of the Tigers has a new four-year contract.
   D. NO ERROR

7. To who are you writing that letter.   7. A B (C) D
   A. To whom are you writing that letter.
   B. To who are you writing that letter?
   C. To whom are you writing that letter?
   D. NO ERROR

8. Luke sometimes studies with Pat, whose in two of his classes.   8.(A) B C D
   A. Luke sometimes studies with Pat, who's in two of his classes.
   B. Luke sometimes studies with Pat. Whose in two of his classes.
   C. Luke studies with Pat sometimes, whose in two of his classes.
   D. NO ERROR

Exercise 3 Combining Sentences

Directions: On a separate piece of paper, combine the sentences in each numbered item into a single sentence. There is more than one way to combine most sentences. See Answer Key.

EXAMPLE   Walt Whitman was a poet. He was American. He was an important
           poet who revolutionized American literature.
           *Walt Whitman was an important poet who revolutionized
           American literature.*

1. Whitman was a journalist. He was an essayist. He was a poet.

2. Whitman held a variety of jobs. Those jobs included teacher, printer, and newspaper writer.

3. He spent a great deal of time observing and walking. He frequently went to the theater. He often went to the opera, too.

4. Whitman's brother was wounded at the battle of Fredericksburg. It was a Civil War battle. Whitman went there to care for him. The experience awakened him to the horrors of war.

5. "When Lilacs Last in the Dooryard Bloom'd" was Whitman's elegy on Lincoln. He wrote it in 1865. It was famous.

Exercise 4 Identifying Parts of a Sentence

Directions: Answer each numbered question by circling, in the answer section, the letter of the sentence that contains the named sentence structure.

If no sentence contains that structure, circle *D* for NONE OF THE
SENTENCES.

EXAMPLE   Which sentence contains a **direct object**?   A Ⓑ C D
         A. The first Norman castles in England were made of wood.
         B. The Normans conquered England.
         C. Wooden castles were defenseless against fire.
         D. NONE OF THE SENTENCES

1. Which sentence contains a **compound object of a preposition**?   1.Ⓐ B C D
   A. I waited for Steve, Maria, and Noah.
   B. She waited to hear the results.
   C. For whom are those letters and cards meant?
   D. NONE OF THE SENTENCES

2. Which sentence contains a **gerund phrase**?   2.Ⓐ B C D
   A. Using the Internet is a breeze for some.
   B. To get better at the piano is Tina's goal.
   C. Singing relaxes her.
   D. NONE OF THE SENTENCES

3. Which sentence contains an **adjective clause**?   3. A B Ⓒ D
   A. Inez wants to be an actress.
   B. What Inez wants most of all is to be admired for her work.
   C. Ms. Fisher, who is her acting teacher, gives her lots of encouragement.
   D. NONE OF THE SENTENCES

4. Which sentence contains an **adverb clause**?   4. A Ⓑ C D
   A. Gary, who works for the Parks Department, is a landscape architect.
   B. Wherever he works, he impresses people with his knowledge and
      concern for the city.
   C. One of his bosses, whom nobody likes, is about to retire.
   D. NONE OF THE SENTENCES

5. Which sentence contains a **participial phrase**?   5. A Ⓑ C D
   A. It was snowing all week.
   B. Snow drifts, piling higher by the minute, blocked doorways and
      covered steps.
   C. "I'm simply freezing," Alan declared.
   D. NONE OF THE SENTENCES

6. Which sentence contains a **predicate nominative**?   6.Ⓐ B C D
   A. Alaska is the largest state.
   B. It has the tallest mountains in North America.
   C. It has some of the coldest temperatures, too.
   D. NONE OF THE SENTENCES

Using Verbs

Direct students to
chapter-specific
portfolio projects
on Sadlier-Oxford's
web site.

STUDENT WRITING
Persuasive Essay

Refugees Still Wait for Change
by Gene Liu
high school student, San Francisco, California

The Universal Declaration of Human Rights, hailed as the "Magna Carta for humanity," turns fifty this year, at a time when Americans seem to have strayed from its objective of achieving worldwide freedom and liberty.

In December, I attended the commemoration of the original document—the first comprehensive agreement among nations on the specific freedoms and rights of all human beings. The document included freedom from torture and slavery and freedom of religion, expression, and assembly, as well as the right to education, medical care, and fair trials.

Speakers at the ceremony relayed gruesome accounts of situations overseas where such liberties were absolutely unavailable. The most moving story was about a Bosnian refugee couple captured by ethnic-cleansing Serbian troops in the early 1990s and sent to a concentration camp.

In 1993, the pair escaped with a wave of fugitives to Germany. When their German refugee visas expired last year, the couple came to the United States in hopes of obtaining citizenship here. However, by December, the United States had reached its limit on the number of refugees it accepts per year. The couple faced the daunting reality of deportation.

This case clearly illustrates how the challenges the Declaration addressed fifty years ago have not been met today. Governments continue to persecute, torture, and murder individuals because of religion and ethnicity. At the center of the human rights dilemma is the problem of refugees, who suffer significant abuse to their natural human rights. They are forced to abandon their homes, communities, and countries in fear of persecution and abuse. . . .

[S]tatistics from Amnesty International indicate that most refugees eventually become economically self-sufficient. The human rights organization has found that most refugees do not become life long welfare recipients. Finances aside, the bottom line remains: helping refugees escape turmoil and affliction is simply the only humane thing to do. Americans must not turn their backs to the persecuted nor force them to leave because of an inhumane technical detail like a quota.

On this, the Declaration's fiftieth anniversary, I say the most fitting celebration of it would be a public and vigorous renewal of the commitment to the Declaration by the nations that signed it. And we should rededicate ourselves to turning that commitment into reality by doing our part to alleviate the world's refugee problem.

Allow time for
students to dis-
cuss the student
writing. Suggest
that they identify
its strengths and
propose possible
improvements.
Use the model
to introduce the
concepts in the
chapter.

Gene Liu places the thesis statement for his persuasive essay in his first paragraph. He supports it with specific examples, facts, statistics, and a call to action.

As you reread the essay, notice how Gene changes verb tenses as he shifts from his opinion today to his experiences in the past. Using verb tenses precisely helps your reader understand the progression of your thoughts. As you write the exercises in this chapter, you'll practice using verbs and verb tenses correctly.

Regular Verbs

● All verbs have four basic forms, or **principal parts**: the present, the present participle, the past, and the past participle.

Depending on how a verb forms its past and past participle, it is a regular verb or an irregular verb.

● **Regular verbs** add -*d* or -*ed* to the present to form the past and past participle.

Principal Parts of Verbs			
PRESENT	**PRESENT PARTICIPLE** (Use with *am, is, are, was, were.*)	**PAST**	**PAST PARTICIPLE** (Use with *has, had, have.*)
talk	(is) talking	talked	(had) talked
swallow	(is) swallowing	swallowed	(had) swallowed
care	(is) caring	cared	(had) cared

The **present participle** works with a helping verb, a form of the verb *be* (*am, is, are, was,* or *were*) to make a verb phrase.

> I **am learning** Greek. Ralph **was learning** French last year.

The **past participle** works with a helping verb, a form of the helping verb *have* (*has, have,* or *had*), to make a verb phrase.

> I **have requested** a transfer. Ralph **had requested** one earlier.

Spelling rules require you to drop the final -*e*, change -*y* to *i*, and double consonants under certain conditions: *cope, coping, coped; hurry, hurried; drop, dropping, dropped.* (For more about spelling rules, see Lesson 16.2.)

A few regular verbs have alternate past and past participle forms: *dreamed/has dreamed* or **dreamt/has dreamt**; *burned/has burned* or **burnt/has burnt**; *has proven* or **has proved**.

Exercise 1 Using the Principal Parts of Regular Verbs

To complete each sentence, write on the blank the correct past form or past participle form of the verb in parentheses. Some sentences have more than one verb in parentheses. **Remember:** After a form of the helping verb *have*, use the past participle.

> EXAMPLE   In 1900, the Boxers (rebel) __*rebelled*__ against the Europeans in China, and many other events of interest (occur) __*occurred*__ that year.

1. In 1900, Americans once again (elect) __elected__ William McKinley as President.

2. Meanwhile, in South Africa, the British and Boers (clash) __clashed__ and war (rage) __raged__.

3. In 1900, Conrad's novel *Lord Jim* (appear) __appeared__, and so did Chekhov's *Uncle Vanya*.

4. In that same year, American writer Stephen Crane (die) __died__.

5. In 1900, Sigmund Freud and Bertrand Russell (introduce) __introduced__ new written works.

6. That year, Picasso (paint) __painted__ *Le Moulin de la Galette*, and Gauguin (report) __reported__ on his travels through Tahiti.

7. The births of American composer Aaron Copland and German composer Kurt Weill also (mark) __marked__ 1900.

8. In 1900, many people had (learn) __learned__ to dance the cakewalk.

9. It was also the year that F. E. Dorn (discover) __discovered__ radon, and R. A. Fessenden first (transmit) __transmitted__ human speech using radio waves.

10. During excavations in Crete in 1900, archeologists (uncover) __uncovered__ evidence of an ancient Minoan culture.

Exercise 2 **Revising a Story Beginning**

Revise the story beginning so that it describes an event that happened in the past. Use the past form and past participle form of the italicized verbs. Compare the original version and your version. Does the story sound better to you in the present tense or in the past tense? Work with a partner or small group to finish the story.

[1]The old green Ford *pulls* (pulled) into the elevated parking area and into a spot right along the edge. [2]It *is* (was) all alone; there *are* (were) no other vehicles there. [3]Then the car's front doors *open* (opened), and two men in lab coats *appear* (appeared). [4]They slowly *walk* (walked) to the edge of the bluff and *look* (looked) down at the old covered bridge that *arches* (arched) over the swiftly moving stream. [5]No sounds *disturb* (disturbed) them; nothing *interrupts* (interrupted) their concentration. [6]A silent breeze *tickles* (tickled) the leaves. [7]Then, one of the men *points* (pointed) to a spot on the other side of the stream, just to the left of the bridge. [8]There, next to the dying elm, they *spot* (spotted) it. [9]It *waits* (waited) for them, *taunts* (taunted) them. [10]They *stare* (stared) at one another for a moment and then *stroll* (strolled) down the path to the bridge and across it to the other bank.

Irregular Verbs 1

Irregular verbs do not form their past or past participle by adding *-d* or *-ed* to the present form the way regular verbs do. (See Lesson 8.1.) In some cases, the irregular past and past participle are the same—but not always. This lesson and the next one cover sixty-six irregular verbs that are often used incorrectly.

◆ Use the principal parts of these common irregular verbs correctly when you write or speak.

The most irregular English verb is *be*, because it has singular and plural forms in both the present and the past tenses. Notice that the word *be* itself is not one of its principal parts.

Principal Parts of Common Irregular Verbs			
PRESENT	PRESENT PARTICIPLE (Use with *am, is, are, was, were.*)	PAST	PAST PARTICIPLE (Use with *has, had, have.*)
[be] is, are	(is) being	was, were	(had) been
become	(is) becoming	became	(had) become
begin	(is) beginning	began	(had) begun
bite	(is) biting	bit	(had) bitten
blow	(is) blowing	blew	(had) blown
break	(is) breaking	broke	(had) broken
bring	(is) bringing	brought	(had) brought
build	(is) building	built	(had) built
burst	(is) bursting	burst	(had) burst
buy	(is) buying	bought	(had) bought
catch	(is) catching	caught	(had) caught
choose	(is) choosing	chose	(had) chosen
come	(is) coming	came	(had) come
cost	(is) costing	cost	(had) cost
do	(is) doing	did	(had) done
draw	(is) drawing	drew	(had) drawn
drink	(is) drinking	drank	(had) drunk
drive	(is) driving	drove	(had) driven
eat	(is) eating	ate	(had) eaten
fall	(is) falling	fell	(had) fallen
feel	(is) feeling	felt	(had) felt
find	(is) finding	found	(had) found
forget	(is) forgetting	forgot	(had) forgotten; (had) forgot
freeze	(is) freezing	froze	(had) frozen
get	(is) getting	got	(had) gotten; (had) got

Writing Hint

When you prepare a résumé or business letter, or when you fill out a job application, check your verbs. Then check them again. People in the business world expect the standard English forms of irregular verbs. They develop negative opinions about people who don't use them.

RESPONSIBILITIES
brought
~~brung~~ eight-year-olds to camp by bus

drew
~~drawed~~ daily schedule on board

◆ Don't even think about putting the regular verb ending *-d* or *-ed* on irregular verbs.

INCORRECT	The book costed ten dollars at last week's sale.
CORRECT	The book cost ten dollars at last week's sale.

P.S. All dictionaries list the principal parts of irregular verbs. The entry word is in its present form, and the past, past participle, and present participle are listed after the pronunciation or part of speech.

catch (kach) *vb* **caught**, **catching**

You can be sure that the verb is a regular verb if only the present verb form appears in a dictionary entry.

Exercise 3 Using Irregular Verbs

For each verb in parentheses, write the past form or past participle form as required by the sentence.

1. Have the players (bring) __brought__ their uniforms with them today?

2. Greg thawed the pizza that he had (freeze) __frozen__.

3. Have you (break) __broken__ the new vase I (buy) __bought__ yesterday?

4. She had (forget) __forgotten__ the steps for parallel parking.

5. Before the hike, we had (drink) __drunk__ our fill.

6. At the car dealer, they (choose) __chose__ a red convertible.

7. After the beaver had (build) __built__ its dam, the wind (blow) __blew__ a tree down on top of it.

8. The dam (burst) __burst__, and the water (begin) __began__ to flow through it.

9. Have you ever (eat) __eaten__ a flower salad?

10. He was quite surprised when he (bite) __bit__ into the burrito and (feel) __felt__ something very hard.

11. She had (draw) __drawn__ a map to show where she had (fall) __fallen__.

12. Jack had (be) __been__ the first in line for the playoff tickets.

13. He (get) __got__ four tickets for his efforts.

14. Sherman had (drive) __driven__ ten miles before he realized that he had (choose) __chosen__ the wrong direction.

15. Larry (catch) __caught__ a cold just before the performance.

16. Once a tenor, Larry (become) __became__ a baritone.

17. As soon as I (come) __came__ into the room, Li (find) __found__ an excuse to leave.

18. The wind had (blow) __blown__ over the scarecrow, and the crows were devouring the crop.

19. Julie had (do) __done__ her best, but Toni (get) __got__ the role.

20. Cal (find) __found__ the place where all the lost socks were hiding.

Irregular Verbs 2

To the twenty-five irregular verbs in Lesson 8.2, this lesson adds forty-one more.

🔖 Use the principal parts of these common irregular verbs correctly when you write or speak.

Principal Parts of Common Irregular Verbs			
PRESENT	**PRESENT PARTICIPLE** (Use with *am, is, are, was, were.*)	**PAST**	**PAST PARTICIPLE** (Use with *has, had, have.*)
give	(is) giving	gave	(had) given
go	(is) going	went	(had) gone
grow	(is) growing	grew	(had) grown
hold	(is) holding	held	(had) held
hurt	(is) hurting	hurt	(had) hurt
keep	(is) keeping	kept	(had) kept
know	(is) knowing	knew	(had) known
lay [to put or place]	(is) laying	laid	(had) laid
lead	(is) leading	led	(had) led
lend	(is) lending	lent	(had) lent
lie [to rest or recline]	(is) lying	lay	(had) lain
lose	(is) losing	lost	(had) lost
make	(is) making	made	(had) made
meet	(is) meeting	met	(had) met
put	(is) putting	put	(had) put
ride	(is) riding	rode	(had) ridden
ring	(is) ringing	rang	(had) rung
rise	(is) rising	rose	(had) risen
run	(is) running	ran	(had) run
say	(is) saying	said	(had) said
see	(is) seeing	saw	(had) seen
sell	(is) selling	sold	(had) sold
send	(is) sending	sent	(had) sent
set	(is) setting	set	(had) set
show	(is) showing	showed	(had) shown
shrink	(is) shrinking	shrank, shrunk	(had) shrunk, shrunken
sing	(is) singing	sang	(had) sung
sink	(is) sinking	sank, sunk	(had) sunk
sit	(is) sitting	sat	(had) sat
speak	(is) speaking	spoke	(had) spoken
stand	(is) standing	stood	(had) stood
steal	(is) stealing	stole	(had) stolen
swim	(is) swimming	swam	(had) swum
swing	(is) swinging	swung	(had) swung
take	(is) taking	took	(had) taken
tell	(is) telling	told	(had) told
think	(is) thinking	thought	(had) thought
throw	(is) throwing	threw	(had) thrown
wear	(is) wearing	wore	(had) worn
win	(is) winning	won	(had) won
write	(is) writing	wrote	(had) written

Editing Tip

Watch out for three troublesome pairs of verbs: *lay, lie*; *raise, rise*; and *sit, set*. The direct object test below can help.

WITH DIRECT OBJECTS

The chicken **lays** an egg.

I **raise** my hand.

I **set** the table.

WITHOUT DIRECT OBJECTS

I **lie** down.

I **rise** early.

I **sit** down.

Using Irregular Verbs

On a separate piece of paper, write the past form or past participle form for each verb in parentheses as required by the sentence.

1. People in southern Louisiana and other places have (grow) used to the taste of hot pepper sauces. grown

2. Hot sauce sales have (rise) to $180 million yearly. risen

3. Vendors have (show) as many as twenty hot sauces at the national food festival. shown

4. Inez (ride) twenty miles just to buy a particular hot sauce. rode

5. When Gordon tried a red savina, the hottest pepper on Earth, the hair (stand) up on his head. stood

Exercise 5 **Revising and Editing a Paragraph**

Cross out any incorrect verb, and write the correct one above it. Make any other changes you think will improve the letter. Revisions may vary. Sample revisions are given.

¹As president of the senior class, I have ~~speaked~~ *spoken* to you often of my concern

that not enough of us are fluent in a second language. ²I regret that we have

~~fell~~ *fallen* short of my goal to be the first totally bilingual graduating class.

³You know why I'm pushing language study. ⁴The world has ~~shrinked~~ *shrunk or shrunken*. ⁵The

pendulum has ~~swinged~~ *swung*. ⁶The economies of the world have ~~became~~ *become* one global

economy, and we have ~~feeled~~ *felt* the results of other countries' politics.

⁷Many young people in the world have ~~meeted~~ *met* the challenge of speaking two

or more languages. ⁸Too many of us up until now have ~~throwed~~ *thrown* away an

opportunity to study languages. ⁹My older friends in this state and others have

~~tell~~ *told* me of trouble in getting jobs because of their language handicap.

¹⁰They originally ~~sayed~~ *said*, "English has become a universal language, so

everyone can understand me." ¹¹But then they ~~comed~~ *came* to see that young

Americans with two languages have ~~took~~ *taken* the better full-time and part-time jobs.

¹²If you have ~~hurted~~ *hurt* yourself up to now, it's not too late to sign up for summer

language school. You may wish to have students write what they think about the following statement.

To graduate from high school, students must take at least three years of a foreign language and must pass a test proving they can read, write, and speak that language fluently.

Mid-Chapter Review

Exercise A Using Regular Verbs

On a separate piece of paper, rewrite each sentence using the correct past form or past participle form of the verb in parentheses.

1. The Scoville heat unit is the method we have (use) *used* for rating hot sauces.
2. This unit dates back to 1912, when Wilbur Scoville (devise) *devised* a test to measure the heat in chilies.
3. Have you ever (learn) *learned* about Scoville units?
4. Scoville (determine) *determined* that a jalapeño pepper had from 2,500 to 5,000 heat units. He then measured a red savina and (find) *found* that it contained 577,000 units!
6. Later, someone (compare) *compared* the red savina with pepper oil extract; the latter was six times hotter.

Exercise B Using Irregular Verbs

Complete the chart below by filling in the missing principal parts. Then write two sentences for each verb on a separate piece of paper. Use the past form for one sentence and the past participle for the other. Students' sentences will vary.

Principal Parts of Verbs			
PRESENT	PRESENT PARTICIPLE	PAST	PAST PARTICIPLE
1. become	2. (is) becoming	became	3. (had) become
4. catch	(is) catching	5. caught	6. (had) caught
7. bite	8. (is) biting	bit	9. (had) bitten
buy	10. (is) buying	11. bought	(had) bought
12. choose	(is) choosing	13. chose	14. (had) chosen
drive	15. (is) driving	16. drove	17. (had) driven
feel	18. (is) feeling	19. felt	20. (had) felt
21. freeze	(is) freezing	22. froze	23. (had) frozen
24. grow	25. (is) growing	grew	26. (had) grown
keep	27. (is) keeping	28. kept	29. (had) kept
30. lose	(is) losing	31. lost	32. (had) lost
hold	33. (is) holding	34. held	35. (had) held
36. ride	37. (is) riding	rode	38. (had) ridden
39. send	40. (is) sending	41. sent	(had) sent

Exercise C **Revising and Editing Paragraphs**

In each sentence, correct any mistakes you find in the use of past and past participle verb forms. **Hint:** Not every sentence has a verb error, and some have more than one.

¹Sometimes historical events ~~maked~~ ^{made} such a powerful impact on earlier writers that they ~~tryed~~ ^{tried} to describe the events. ²World War I had precisely that effect. ³After a series of indecisive early battles, the war had ~~became~~ ^{become} a trench war; huge opposing armies entrenched themselves on opposite sides of a four-hundred-mile battle line. ⁴The German army ~~builded~~ ^{built} trenches on one side. ⁵The British, French, and Belgians ~~are~~ ^{were} only a short distance away. ⁶Gunfire ~~bursted~~ ^{burst} from both sides relentlessly. ⁷Seven thousand British solders ~~become~~ ^{became} casualties each day.

⁸The slaughter and destruction inspired the British poets Siegfried Sassoon and Wilfred Owen, who were also soldiers, to address their wartime experiences. ⁹Both poets ~~thinked~~ ^{thought} of their poems as realistic reports of activity along the front. ¹⁰Sassoon ~~choosed~~ ^{chose} to shock his readers with the horrors he had ~~saw~~ ^{seen}. ¹¹He called his work trench poetry. ¹²Owen ~~want~~ ^{wanted} only to stir compassion for the plight of the ordinary soldier. ¹³Sassoon was wounded in battle; Owen ~~losed~~ ^{lost} his life.

Exercise D **Write What You Think**

On a separate piece of paper, write one or more paragraphs discussing what you think about the thesis statement below. State clearly whether you agree or disagree with the statement. Support your view with reasons and examples. When you finish writing, check your paper to correct any inappropriate verb forms.

All conflicts between nations should be settled only through negotiations and diplomacy.

Paragraphs will vary. Give students full credit if they have stated an opinion and attempted to support their opinions. Look for grammatically complete sentences that begin with a capital letter and end with an appropriate end punctuation mark.

Verb Tense

◖ A **verb tense** expresses the time an action was performed.

Verbs have three **simple tenses** (present, past, and future) and three
perfect tenses (present perfect, past perfect, and future perfect).

The Six Verb Tenses		
TENSE	**WHAT IT SHOWS**	**EXAMPLE**
Present	action happening in the present; action that happens repeatedly	I **start**. The tide **rises** and **falls**.
Past	action completed in the past	I **started**.
Future	action that will happen in the future	I **shall start**. I **will start**.
Present perfect	action completed recently or in indefinite past	I **have started.**
Past perfect	action that happened before another action	I **had started** before they arrived.
Future perfect	action that will happen before a future action or time	By the time you return, I **will have started**.

Each verb tense also has a **progressive form**, to show
ongoing action.

The Progressive Forms for the Six Tenses	
PROGRESSIVE FORM	**EXAMPLE**
Present progressive	**(am, is, are) starting**
Past progressive	**(was, were) starting**
Future progressive	**will be starting;** **shall be starting**
Present perfect progressive	**(has, have) been starting**
Past perfect progressive	**had been starting**
Future perfect progressive	**will have been starting;** **shall have been starting**

One more verb form is the **emphatic form**, which takes the
word *do*:

I **do** start on time every day. He **does** start on time.
She **did** start on time.

◖ Keep verb tenses consistent whenever possible.

ORIGINAL   Ed walked into the strange room. He has no idea what
he is looking at.

CONSISTENT Ed **walked** into the strange room. He **had** no idea what
he **was looking** at.

Writing Hint

Professional writers in the
humanities follow the
style of the Modern
Language Association and
use the present tense
when reporting research.

In his 1998 book, Harold
Bloom **credits** Shakespeare
with teaching us human
behavior.

Writers in the sciences
follow the style of the
American Psychological
Association and use the
past or present perfect.

Jones **studied** and **wrote**
about the effect of peers on
teenagers.

Editing Tip

Avoid awkward or
complicated verb forms
by looking for simpler
ways to express yourself.
                    to surprise
They had wanted ~~to have
surprised~~ their dad.
              had
If I ~~would have~~ slept more,
I'd be less cranky.

Of course, sometimes the meaning requires you to shift tenses.

Erin **left** late for work this morning; her boss **will return** tomorrow.

None of us **have been** to the new mall, but everyone **wants** to go.

Exercise 6 Using Verb Tenses

Replace the italicized verbs with the past or past perfect forms to show actions completed in the past.

[1]In 1868, the plastic industry *begins* [began] in America. [2]Plastic *substitutes* [substituted] for ivory, which *is* [was] in short supply. [3]A billiard ball manufacturer *offers* [offered] a huge cash award for a substitute material for ivory, from which he *makes* [made] billiard balls. [4]John Wesley Hyatt, a printer from Albany, New York, *comes up* [came up] with a product he *calls* [called] "celluloid." [5]Actually, Hyatt *doesn't invent* [didn't invent] the product himself; he *produces* [produced] it from a compound that a British professor *invents* [invented] about eighteen years earlier. [6]Hyatt *buys* [bought] the patent rights to the professor's product and *manufactures* [manufactured] it in the United States. [7]Celluloid, the world's first plastic, *becomes* [became or had become] a household word in America by 1890.

Exercise 7 Using Progressive Verb Tenses

Replace the italicized verbs in the paragraph to show ongoing action. Use the clues in the parentheses after each sentence.

[1]Look at Luis over there; he *eats* [is eating] a bag of potato chips. (present progressive) [2]In fact he *polished off* [was polishing off] the bag the last time I looked. (past progressive) [3]If he hasn't already finished, he *finishes* [will be finishing] very soon. (future progressive) [4]I'll bet that while he *munches* [is munching] those chips, he is not aware that the potato chip is America's favorite snack food. (present progressive) [5]I'll bet also that Luis, who *was eating* [has been eating] potato chips nearly all his life, is unaware that the chip was invented by accident by a chef in Saratoga, New York. (present perfect progressive) [6]The chef, who *had made* [had been making] a batch of French fries for customers at his restaurant, purposely made them too thin for one difficult diner. (past perfect progressive) [7]But the diner loved them, and millions of others *have loved* [have been loving] them since! (present perfect progressive)

Using the Active Voice

Verbs have voice—either the active voice or the passive voice.

◗ When a verb is in the **active voice**, the subject of the sentence performs an action. When a verb is in the **passive voice**, the subject receives an action.

A verb in the passive voice always involves a form of the helping verb *be*.

ACTIVE	Corrine **collected** the mail.
PASSIVE	The mail **was collected** by Corrine.
ACTIVE	Corrine **collects** the mail in the morning.
PASSIVE	The mail **is collected** in the morning by Corrine.
ACTIVE	Corrine **has thrown** out the junk mail.
PASSIVE	The junk mail **has been thrown** out by Corrine.

◗ When you write, use the active voice whenever you can.

Effective writers prefer the active voice because it is stronger and more economical. Writers use the passive voice, however, when they don't know the performer of the action or when they want to emphasize the action, not the performer.

The stadium **was filled** to capacity with excited fans. [The receiver of the action, not the performer, is emphasized.]

The murder **was committed** on the deserted island after dark. [The performer of the action is unknown.]

Exercise 8 Using the Active Voice

On a separate piece of paper, rewrite the sentences to use the active voice whenever possible. If the passive voice is acceptable, explain why.   See Answer Key.

EXAMPLES   The novel *Silas Marner* was written by George Eliot.
George Eliot wrote the novel <u>Silas Marner</u>.

The archaeopteryx, an extinct bird, was discovered in Germany.
Keep the passive voice. The performer is not as important as the discovery itself.

1. In 1861, the state of Kansas was formed.

2. *Great Expectations* was written by Charles Dickens in 1861.

3. The Opera House in Paris was designed by Charles Garnier.

4. Daily weather forecasts were begun in Great Britain.

5. In 1862, Forts Henry and Donelson were captured by Union forces under Grant.

6. In that same year, *Les Misérables* was penned by Victor Hugo.

7. In London, the Albert Memorial was designed by Gilbert Scott.

8. In 1863, Mexico City was captured by the French.

9. New Zealand's first railroad was opened.

10. Pasteurization was invented by Louis Pasteur in 1864.

Exercise 9 Revising and Editing a Paragraph

On a separate piece of paper, improve the following paragraph by changing as many verbs as possible into the active voice. If you leave some examples of passive voice, be ready to explain why. Combine sentences, creating subordinate clauses or phrases as you revise. Revised paragraphs will vary.

[1]A comeback has been made by the moose. [2]According to the *New York Times*, in 1900 in America, "Moose had been all but wiped out in much of their range by hunting and by conversion of their forest habitat to farms. [3]Now hunting is tightly controlled, and many of the farms have reverted to forest." [4]The newspaper report goes on to say, "Natural predators like wolves have been eliminated from much of the north woods." [5]But the most important reason for the comeback is that logged forests have been replaced by young second-growth forest. [6]The moose have been provided a bountiful food supply by the new forests. [7]The population of moose in the northern part of the continent has been tripled in the last fifty years. [8]In northern Maine alone, the number of moose has been increased fifteen times from the number a hundred years ago. [9]Moose sighting is now popular, and moose have a reputation for tolerating humans near them. [10]But they should be approached with caution at all times.

Mood

● The **mood** of a verb shows the speaker's or writer's *intent*—whether to state a fact, opinion, or inquiry; to make a request or to command; or to state a wish, requirement, or condition contrary to fact.

Most speakers and writers have no problem with two of the three moods—the indicative and the imperative—which account for most of the verbs used in everyday communication.

● The **indicative mood** states a fact, an opinion, or a question.
The baseball team **practices** during spring training.
She **believes** the 1998 Padres **do** not **get** enough credit.
What **does** she **think** of the Yankees?

● The **imperative mood** gives a direct command or request.
Practice bunting and hitting to the opposite field.
Please **pick** me up at six for the game.

Using the third mood—the subjunctive—can cause problems, perhaps because it occurs in English relatively infrequently, usually only in formal speaking and writing.

● The **subjunctive mood** states a wish, requirement, or condition contrary to fact.

In a *that* clause expressing a requirement, necessity, or wish, the subjunctive calls for using the infinitive form of a verb without the word *to*. Use this form whether the subject is singular or plural.
It is necessary **that** the batter **improve** his statistics.
The manager insists **that** the batter **practice** bunts.
The manager requests **that** the pitcher **be** on time.
My goal is **that** he **become** a better pitcher.

In a wish or a contrary-to-fact clause beginning with the word *if*, the subjunctive calls for using *were* instead of *was* whether the subject is singular or plural.
I wish I **were** a better catcher.
If he **were** a better pitcher, I'd be a better catcher. [This is an example of a contrary-to-fact clause; he is *not* a better pitcher.]

P.S. Don't let these terms—*indicative, imperative,* and *subjunctive*—intimidate you. With a little practice, you'll learn to use the subjunctive as easily as the other two moods.

The Latin word *imperare* means "to command" and is the root of the word *imperative*, meaning "necessary or commanding." It is *imperative* that the driver's ed teacher know how to change a tire.

Not all *if* clauses deal with contrary-to-fact matters; some *if* clauses deal with facts and so require the indicative mood, not the subjunctive mood.

If that cake **was** fattening, the french fries were even more so.

Exercise 10 Using the Indicative and the Subjunctive

Based on the contexts that sentences 1–5 provide, fill in the blank with an indicative or subjunctive form of a verb of your own choice. For sentences 6–10, choose between *were* and *was*. Answers will vary. These are sample answers with notes for the teacher.

EXAMPLE   Ed's parents suggested that she ___hire___ a tutor.

1. Her parents urged that she ___take___ a part-time job. (subjunctive)

2. The teacher suggested that the student ___borrow___ a computer. (subjunctive)

3. The coach recommends that the captain ___improve___ his attitude. (subjunctive)

4. The coach thinks the captain ___is___ self-centered. (indicative)

5. The teacher's goal is that the student ___write___ better. (subjunctive)

6. If I ___were___ a billionaire, I'd give money to charity. (subjunctive)

7. If he ___were___ a friend, he'd help me out. (subjunctive)

8. If the movie ___was___ so bad, maybe you'll trust reviews from now on. (indicative)

9. If the movie ___were___ available, I'd rent it. (subjunctive)

10. At noon I heard that he ___was___ in the school building. (indicative)

Exercise 11 Revising and Editing a Paragraph

On a separate piece of paper, improve the following paragraph by changing, as necessary, some indicative forms of verbs to subjunctive forms. See Answer Key.

   ¹Whether she's dreaming or not, my friend claims that she has been granted two wishes that will come true. ²First of all, she wishes that each individual stops bickering with others. ³Then her goal is that each person picks a non-profit organization to help. ⁴She thinks it is necessary that each of us takes an active role in making our own piece of the world better. ⁵If she was able to improve the whole world with her two wishes, she would.

Exercise 12 Writing Sentences with the Subjunctive

Write a paragraph telling what a friend wishes for himself or herself or for the world. Make sure the sentences are related to one another so that they make a sensible paragraph. Limit yourself to the following sentence structures, and use the subjunctive mood: Paragraphs will vary. Encourage students to vary their sentences by putting extra clauses or phrases into the beginning, middle, or end of the sentences. Have students exchange papers with a partner, and check each other's work for the correct use of the subjunctive.

My friend wishes that _____.

He (*or* She) insists that _____.

For him (*or* her), it is necessary that _____.

His (*or* her) goal is that _____.

Revising and Editing Worksheet 1

Work with a partner or small group to improve the following report on the origin of the handshake. Focus especially on verb usage, but make any other changes you think will improve the report. You may combine sentences, change or omit words, and rearrange sentences. After you revise and edit, proofread your report, and fix any spelling mistakes you find. Write your revised report on a separate piece of paper, and compare your response with those made by other pairs or groups of classmates.

Revisions will vary but should use verbs correctly.

[1]On the ceiling of the Sistine Chapel in rome, the Italian artist Michelangelo has painted in the early sixteenth century a handshake. [2]The handshake, a custom of greeting, has originated nearly five thousand years ago. [3]It begun in ancient egypt. [4]Where it was symbolizing the transfer of authority from a god to a king. [5]In fact, the Egyptian hieroglyph for the verb "to give" had been a picture of an extended hand.

[6]About four thousand years ago, in Babylonia, kings were required to grasp the hands of a statue of Marduk. [7]Marduk was being that civilizations chief god. [8]This act was taken place every year during the New Year's festivities. [9]It serves to provide that king with power for another year. [10]This practice catched on. [11]When the Assyrians conquered Babylonia, their kings, to, were adopting that ritual. [12]They have no interest in offending any gods.

[13]Some folklorists claim that the handshake has far earlier origins. [14]They say that the right hand, the one used in a handshake, was traditionally the one in which men holded there weapons. [15]When strangers are content that they were in no danger, they put away their weapons and will have extended their right hands as a symbol of good will. [16]This explanation is making sense for another reason. [17]It explains why women, who were rarely the warriors, never, until recently, have been developing the custom of shakeing hands.

Revising and Editing Worksheet 2

Improve the following report on an American dance craze. Focus especially on verb usage, but make any other changes you think will improve the report. After you revise and edit, proofread your report, and fix any spelling mistakes you find. Write your revised report on a separate piece of paper.

Revisions will vary but should use verbs correctly.

[1]Throughout the decade of the twenties, one dance craze after another taked the country by storm. [2]The most popular of those dances was the Charleston.

[3]Music scholars have traced the origins of the Charleston back to Africa, where the dances of the Ashanti people have featured similar movements in their dances. [4]In the American South, a dance known as the Jay-Bird and the Juba dances of plantation times had been similar to the Charleston. [5]Charleston steps were done in Haiti, to, according to anthropologists. [6]Judging from it's name, its likely that the version of the dance that arrived in New York had came by way of Charleston, South Carolina.

[7]The Charleston was first introduced in the musical *Lisa*. [8]But it didn't gain popularity until the hit song "Charleston" was wrote for the 1923 musical *Runnin' Wild*. [9]The Charleston will have featured whole-body shimmying movements, forward and backward fast-kicking steps, and slapping hands on the knees. [10]Audiences never saw these complex rhythms danced before. [11]The Charleston had been causeing a sensation.

[12]People raced to learn the Charleston. [13]Dance studios couldnt keep up with the demand for lessons. [14]People from all walks of life, including the Duke of Windsor, learn the dance. [15]In fact, one lingering image of the Roaring Twenties is that of young women with short "bobbed" haircuts, wearing fringed skirts, dancing the Charleston. [16]Because the dance has required the birdlike flapping of all four limbs, these women become known as flappers.

[17]There were other dance crazes at that time, both in the United States and in Europe. [18]But none equaled the popularity of the Charleston.

Chapter Review

Exercise A Using Irregular Verbs

Write the form of the verb in parentheses that correctly completes
the sentence.

EXAMPLE   The debate (begin) on time. **began**

1. When Jana (bite) into the pie, she found a surprise. bit

2. Have you (eat) lunch yet? eaten

3. I (feel) bad when there were no more chocolates left. felt

4. Alfredo (buy) that tennis racquet at a yard sale. bought

5. Len hit the ball right at her; she should have (catch) it. caught

6. Yesterday, we (drive) the whole way home without stopping. drove

7. The bagels had been (freeze) and had to thaw. frozen

8. He lived nearby and (be) the first to arrive. was

9. I (find) the earring I thought I had lost. found

10. When the skyscraper was (build), it was the tallest structure in the city. built

11. Have you (choose) the outfit you're going to wear? chosen

12. Barbara (give) it her best shot. gave

13. The plant (grow) best when we placed it on the window sill. grew

14. We (know) that no one would eat the cauliflower dip. knew

15. She (lend) her tape recorder to Iris. lent

16. He (lie) on the couch and finished his book. lay

17. Then he (lay) the book on the coffee table. laid

18. The fortunes of the team (sink) when the pitcher got injured. sank

19. Have you (speak) to Ben since Monday? spoken

20. I (wear) my lucky sweater to the finals last week. wore

Exercise B Using Verb Tenses

Change the italicized verb to the verb tense specified in parentheses. You
may refer to the charts in Lesson 8.4. Write your answers on a separate piece
of paper.

1. James *eat* all his vegetables before he started in on his beef. (past perfect) had eaten

2. Sheila *finish* her homework and now can begin calling her friends.
   (present perfect) has finished

3. The two girls were dismayed when they noticed that they *wear* the same dress. (past progressive) were wearing

4. Next week, all students *take* the achievement tests. (future) will take

5. We *sit* right behind two people with big hair. (past) sat

6. While we *wait* impatiently, he *take* his time. (past progressive) were waiting, was taking

7. Although she *write* all along, the letters never arrived. (past perfect progressive) had been writing

8. By next Tuesday, I *show* my paintings to all the art teachers. (future perfect) will have shown

9. Alex *run* the marathon for ten years. (present perfect progressive) has been running

10. Alex *lose* last year's race to a future Olympian. (past) lost

Exercise C Revising and Editing a Paragraph

Improve the paragraph below on a separate piece of paper. Decide on a tense to use, and make the verbs consistent throughout. Use the active voice whenever possible, and make any other verb changes you think will improve the paragraph.   Paragraphs will vary.

    [1]Have computers becoming too hard to use? [2]This is what some psychologists think. [3]They believe the home computer is too complicated because it is trying to do too many things: word process, manage e-mail, surf the Internet, and so on. [4]To have gotten their point across, the psychologists ask us to have imagined a kitchen in which one appliance opens cans, made coffee, and is beating eggs. [5]Surely, they say, all three jobs won't be done well by the one appliance. [6]Furthermore, low cost, performance, and simplicity are cared about by consumers, they say. [7]So the psychologists were suggesting replacing the one home computer with several smart electronic devides. [8]They insist that each smart device performs only one task and each such device was simple to use. [9]Maybe there would be something to this theory about simplicity. [10]If the typical home computer was simpler now, maybe more technophobes would buy one.

Exercise D Write What You Think

Write a paragraph or two in which you agree or disagree with the following statement. Give your opinion clearly, and support it with reasons and examples.

> The public, the government, and private industry must work together to make sure that anyone in the United States who wants one would be able to get an up-to-date computer.

Reread your paragraphs to check for verb usage.

Subject-Verb Agreement

Direct students to chapter-specific portfolio projects on Sadlier-Oxford's web site.

STUDENT WRITING
Narrative Essay

My Piano Recital
by Anh Van Vu

high school student, Houston, Texas

The soothing melody of Beethoven's *Moonlight Sonata* soared through my ears. It was so relaxing, yet my body tensed with anxiety. I stood nervously behind the dense, maroon curtains and glanced out across the stage. An elegantly dressed girl about my age sat at a grand piano; I could see her fingertips gliding over the black and white keys in front of her.

"She makes it seem so easy," I whispered to myself. "I wonder if I'll look and sound that way."

As the last chords of the music echoed, my body froze. The girl stood up from the bench and bowed deeply as the audience applauded. It was finally my turn. A part of me wanted to run home and hide under my bed. I didn't have to be here, I didn't have to come, I didn't have to say yes, but I knew I had chosen to perform. Now wasn't the time to chicken out. As the applause died down, the girl onstage walked toward me. I could hear my heart drumming loudly, and butterflies began to rise in my stomach. The girl had a proud smile pasted on her face, and when she passed me, I heard her say two words of encouragement: "Good luck!"

"Well, here goes nothing," I said to myself.

I stepped onto the stage and walked slowly toward the piano. My footsteps echoed softly. The bright lights nearly blinded me, making it difficult to see the audience. When I reached the piano, I automatically slid onto the bench and into position. The sounds of whispering and people shuffling around gave way to complete silence. I stared at my trembling fingers, and, for a moment, my mind went blank. Finally, I took a deep breath and began to play Chopin's *Nocturne in E-flat Major*. The rich tones of the piano rang out. One by one, each muscle in my body loosened and relaxed. I sat with ease on the bench, and my fingertips danced over the row of black and white keys as if they had a mind of their own. They glided over the keys while my mind drifted into the music.

When I reached the end of the piece, the audience started clapping. I rose from the bench and gave a deep bow. My mouth curled into a proud smile. Inside, I felt relieved that it was over and happy I had done so well. As the applause died down, I pivoted and glided to the other side of the stage. I saw a young boy standing nervously behind the dense, maroon curtains staring fearfully out at the stage. When I walked by, I passed to him the two words that were given to me for encouragement: "Good luck!"

Allow time for students to discuss the student writing. Suggest that they identify its strengths and propose possible improvements. Use the model to introduce the concepts in the chapter.

Anh Van Vu organizes her narrative essay chronologically. She includes dialogue to grab the reader's attention. The sensory details about the audience and about her nervousness draw the reader into her essay and add suspense.

Because she wrote her essay in the first person, the subject of most of Anh's sentences is *I*. Her verbs are, therefore, first-person singular, agreeing with her subjects. You will learn more about subject-verb agreement as you do the lessons and exercises in this chapter.

Agreement with Intervening Phrases and Clauses

In talking about grammar, we say there are three **persons**. The subjects *I* and *we* are **first person**. The subject *you* is **second person**. A noun subject or *he, she, it,* or *they* is **third person**.

◖ A third-person *singular subject* takes a *singular verb*. A third-person *plural subject* takes a *plural verb*.

TENSE	PERSON	NUMBER	
		SINGULAR SUBJECT	PLURAL SUBJECT
Present	*1st*	I swim and splash.	We swim and splash.
	2nd	You swim and splash.	You swim and splash.
	3rd	She **swims** and **splashes**. Henry **swims** and **splashes**.	They **swim** and **splash**. The boys **swim** and **splash**.
Present Perfect	*3rd*	She **has swum**.	They **have swum**.
Present Progressive	*3rd*	Henry **is swimming**. **Is** Henry **swimming**?	The boys **are swimming**. **Are** the boys **swimming**?

Table title: **Subject-Verb Agreement**

The verb *be* is more complicated. The verb *be* must agree with first-, second-, *and* third-person subjects not only in the present tense but also in the past tense.

◖ A prepositional phrase that comes between the subject and verb is called an **intervening phrase**. The subject of a verb never appears in an intervening phrase.

Make sure the verb (v) agrees with the subject (s), not with the object of a preposition.

```
S    PREP. PHRASE        V
One of my teachers is leaving this year.
```

```
              S          PREP. PHRASE          V
The other teachers at the high school are staying.
```

◖ A clause that comes between the subject and verb is called an **intervening clause**. The subject of a sentence is never within an intervening clause.

```
S              INTERVENING CLAUSE          V
Jawann, who is my teacher and my friend, is the first to arrive.
```

A negative construction following the subject doesn't affect the number of the subject.

```
       S              V
This book, not those, is a mystery.
```

Forms of Be

Singular
I **am** late.
I **was** late.
You **are** late.
You **were** late.
He **is** late.
He **was** late.

Plural
We **are** late.
We **were** late.
You **are** late.
You **were** late.
They **are** late.
They **were** late.

Editing Tip

Many speakers say *don't* when standard English grammar calls for *doesn't*. In school and business, remember that a third-person singular subject, *he* or *she*, needs the third-person singular form of the verb *do*, which is *does* + *n't*.

She ~~don't~~ *doesn't* know a thing about cooking.

Underline the subject of each sentence and the verb in parentheses that agrees with the subject.

1. <u>Toothbrushes</u> (has, <u>have</u>) a long history.

2. The "<u>chew stick</u>," which was used by Egyptians more than five thousand years ago, (<u>is</u>, are) the earliest toothbrush we know about.

3. Some <u>tribes</u> in Africa (uses, <u>use</u>) it even today.

4. <u>Members</u> of a tribe (chooses, <u>choose</u>) their sticks only from certain trees, known as "toothbrush trees."

5. The <u>American Dental Association</u>, which studied these ancient tools still in use, (<u>has found</u>, have found) that these frayed sticks are used today in parts of the United States, too.

6. <u>People</u> who live in the South (calls, <u>call</u>) them twig brushes.

7. <u>Dentists</u> in the study (says, <u>say</u>) that these twig brushes can be every bit as effective as modern nylon-bristle brushes.

8. Bristled <u>toothbrushes</u>, like the one in your bathroom, (has been, <u>have been</u>) around for five hundred years.

9. <u>These</u>, not the chew stick, (traces, <u>trace</u>) their origin to China, where hog bristles fastened onto bamboo shoots were early tooth-cleaning tools.

Exercise 2 Revising and Editing a Paragraph

For each mistake in subject-verb agreement in the following paragraph, cross out the incorrect verb, and write the correct one above it.

[1] ~~Is~~ (Are) our high schools adequately preparing students for the work world? [2] Opinions on this subject ~~varies~~ (vary). [3] Some schools in the nation ~~focuses~~ (focus) their attention on the needs of their college-bound students. [4] Those in this camp ~~offers~~ (offer) enriched programs to prepare graduates for college studies and professional careers. [5] Other schools, on the other hand, ~~emphasizes~~ (emphasize) courses geared to preparing graduates for the rigorous and ever-changing demands of jobs in industry. [6] But manufacturers who employ these graduates ~~claims~~ (claim) that new workers ~~is~~ (are) unprepared for using the machinery and technology. [7] These supervisors in industry ~~says~~ (say) that a student comes to them not only without the necessary skills in computing but also without basic writing and math skills.

Agreement with Indefinite Pronouns

An **indefinite pronoun** expresses an amount or refers to an unspecified person or thing. When used as a subject, some indefinite pronouns are always singular, some are always plural, and some can be singular or plural, depending on their context.

● In the present tense, the present perfect, and the present progressive, use a singular verb when the subject is a singular indefinite pronoun. Use a plural verb when the subject is a plural indefinite pronoun.

SINGULAR   **Much** of the audience **is expecting** to win a small prize.

SINGULAR   But **somebody walks** away with a grand prize.

PLURAL   **Few** of the entrants **expect** to win.

● The following indefinite pronouns can be either singular or plural, depending on the word they refer to: *all, any, enough, more, most, none,* and *some.*

```
  S              V
```
All of her free time **has gone** into piano practice. [singular]
```
  S              V
```
All of his performances **include** Mozart. [plural]

```
  S            V
```
Any of the food **tastes** delicious. [singular]
```
  S            V
```
Any of the tennis courts **are** available. [plural]

```
  S              V
```
Enough of the work **is** easy. [singular]
```
  S              V
```
Enough of the workers **are** union members. [plural]

```
  S              V
```
Some of the rainfall **is** heavy. [singular]
```
  S              V
```
Some of the storms **are** coming this way. [plural]

P.S. Most of the time, choosing the correct verb for an indefinite pronoun will occur to you naturally. But when you need to look up a rule, check this page.

Always Singular

anybody	neither
anyone	nobody
each	no one
either	one
everybody	somebody
everyone	someone
much	such

Always Plural

both	many
few	several

The pronoun *none* is especially tricky. Use a singular verb only when you can think of the subject as "none of it." Use a plural verb when you can substitute "none of them."

None of the story **sounds** believable. [None of *it* sounds believable.]

None of the stories **sound** believable. [None of *them* sound believable.]

Exercise 3 **Writing Complete Sentences**

On a separate piece of paper, write a complete sentence for each numbered item, using the group of words as the subject of the sentence. Use present tense, present perfect, or present progressive verbs. Then check your sentences for correct subject-verb agreement. Read your sentence aloud to yourself for extra practice in hearing how correct agreement sounds. Students' sentences will vary.

EXAMPLE   Some of the actors
Some of the actors are terrific!

1. Several of the students

2. All of my teachers

3. None of the questions

4. Much of the concert

5. One of the best movies

6. More of the kids

7. Few of the events

8. Nobody in the building

9. Many of the players

10. No one in the audience

Exercise 4 **Choosing the Correct Verb**

Underline the subject of each sentence and the verb in parentheses that agrees in number with the subject. Then, with a partner, write five more sentences that practice subject-verb agreement. For each, give a choice of two present tense, present perfect, or present progressive verbs in parentheses. Exchange sentences with another pair of students. Students' sentences will vary.

1. Several of the countries in the world (is sending, are sending) athletes to the summer Olympics.

2. Not all of the athletes (has been, have been) professionals.

3. Some of the events (takes, take) place in a swimming pool.

4. Most of the participants (trains, train) hard for their events.

5. Each of the athletes (has, have) world-class skills.

6. Every one of them (marches, march) in the opening ceremonies.

7. Many of the viewers (prefers, prefer) the track-and-field events.

8. Few of the American viewers (is, are) familiar with the rules of team handball.

9. All of it (seems, seem) simple to the players.

10. All of the water polo players (is, are) good swimmers.

11. Everybody in the arena (has enjoyed, have enjoyed) the spectacle.

12. Some of the runners (had been, have been) injured by racing.

13. Nobody in the races (wants, want) to risk injury.

Mid-Chapter Review

Exercise A Subject-Verb Agreement

Improve the paragraph below. Correct any errors you find in subject-verb agreement. Make any other revisions that you think will improve the paragraph. **Hint:** Not every sentence has an agreement error.

¹Many of the major league baseball teams ~~recruits~~ *recruit* new players from Puerto Rico and from countries in Central and South America and in the Caribbean. ²Several look for players from Japan; some ~~seeks~~ *seek* players in Korea, too. ³Some even pursue players who leave Cuba. ⁴Clearly, few of the teams ~~is~~ *are* unaware of the vast talent pool in these places. ⁵Most ~~has~~ *have* professional scouts in those countries. ⁶One of the primary reasons for sending scouts ~~are~~ *is* to save money. ⁷Another is that the talent pool for American players ~~seem~~ *seems* to be dwindling. ⁸Find out whether one of your favorite teams ~~are~~ *is* pursuing talent from outside the United States. Students' revisions may vary but should have correct subject-verb agreement. Sample revisions are given.

Exercise B Revising and Editing a Passage

Edit the following paragraphs. Correct any errors you find in subject-verb agreement. Make any other revisions that you think will improve the paragraphs. **Hint:** Not every sentence has an agreement error. Students' revisions may vary. Sample revisions are given.

¹What ~~does~~ *do* you know about sleep? ²According to a recent national survey, people in this nation ~~seems~~ *seem* to know very little about ~~is~~ sleep. ³Only 144 of the 1,027 people surveyed by the National Sleep Foundation in late 1997 and early 1998 ~~was~~ *were* able to pass a twelve-question "sleep I.Q. test." ⁴When you consider that an estimated 100,000 car crashes each year ~~results~~ *result* from drivers falling asleep at the wheel, this ignorance about sleep habits ~~are~~ *is* serious.

⁵The typical adult ~~need~~ *needs* eight to nine hours of sleep each night. ⁶Most ~~gets~~ *get* no more than seven hours, and a lot of others get even less. ⁷Many of the respondents in the survey ~~says~~ *say* they get very sleepy during the day and that their drowsiness ~~affect~~ *affects* their activities. ⁸Some of the participants say

they have a sleep-related problem, such as snoring or insomnia. ⁹Some

say

~~says~~ they twitch or have muscular discomfort. ¹⁰However, only one in

has

twenty ~~have~~ consulted a doctor or sleep specialist about the problem.

Exercise C Choosing the Correct Verb

Underline the verb in parentheses that agrees with the subject.

1. A person's sleep needs (is, <u>are</u>) biological.

2. You (is, <u>are</u>) incapable of teaching yourself to need less sleep.

3. Some of the adults I know (needs, <u>need</u>) only six hours a night.

4. Others (snoozes, <u>snooze</u>) for ten hours.

5. Most of my adult friends (requires, <u>require</u>) at least eight hours a night.

6. In fact, a few of them (sleeps, <u>sleep</u>) more than ten hours out of every twenty-four.

7. How much sleep (does, <u>do</u>) monkeys get? Ten hours!

8. Scientists in this field (estimates, <u>estimate</u>) that Americans accumulate an annual sleep debt.

9. What (<u>is</u>, are) the average annual sleep debt among Americans?

10. That annual sleep debt, believe it or not, (<u>averages</u>, average) about five hundred hours per person.

Exercise D Writing a Paragraph

On a separate piece of paper, write at least one paragraph about your own sleep habits. Are they regular? If so, in what way? Do you get enough rest? Do you usually sleep through the night, or do you wake up frequently? Do you think you accumulate a sleep debt each year? Are you ever tired in the late afternoon or during some other time of day? Respond to these questions and others you can think of. When you finish, read your paragraph aloud to yourself, and listen for correct use of subject-verb agreement.

Students' paragraphs will vary. See teacher pages for assessment rubrics.

Agreement with Compound Subjects

A **compound subject** can have singular subjects, plural subjects, or a combination of singular and plural subjects.

● When singular subjects are joined by *and*, they take a plural verb.

    The giant armadillo, the cheetah, **and** the red wolf **are** endangered species.

    Have both the wild yak **and** the California condor **made** the list as well?

● When singular subjects are joined by *or* or *nor*, they take a singular verb.

    Neither the African lion **nor** the blue whale **is** an endangered species.

    Has either Ted **or** Elise **written** a report on endangered animals in America?

● When a singular subject and a plural subject are joined by *or* or *nor*, the verb agrees in number with the subject closer to it.

    Neither pythons **nor** the painted frog **is** found in North America.

    Does either the giant panda **or** camels **live** in North America outside of zoos?

    Do either camels **or** the giant panda **live** here?

P.S. Newspaper reporters and editors don't always follow this rule about *or* and *nor*. Try to be consistent in *your* writing.

● When *many a(n)*, *every*, or *each* precedes a single or compound subject, the subject takes a singular verb.

    Every zoologist **cares** about endangered species of plants and animals.

    Many a plant and animal **is** in danger in our rain forests.

Editing Tip

A compound subject that names only one thing or person takes a singular verb.

Peas and carrots **is** Fran's least favorite vegetable dish.

My teammate and best friend **is** also my roommate.

Exercise 5 Choosing the Correct Verb

Underline the simple subject(s) of each sentence and the appropriate verb in parentheses. **Hint:** Not every sentence has a compound subject.

    EXAMPLE   Neither <u>you</u> nor <u>he</u> (<u>wants</u>, want) the forests to disappear.

1. Shortsighted government <u>policies</u>, <u>burning</u>, and <u>chain saws</u> (is, <u>are</u>) causing our rainforests to disappear.

2. Biological <u>extinction</u> and <u>annihilation</u> of traditional native lifestyles (is, <u>are</u>) two results of tropical deforestation.

3. The lush, fertile <u>forest</u> and the tropical <u>climate</u> (supports, <u>support</u>) more species of plants and animals than all other regions of earth combined.

Enriching Your Vocabulary

The verb *annihilate* comes from two Latin roots: *ad* meaning "to" and *nihil* meaning "nothing." It is used to mean "demolish" or "to bring to nothing." When the enemy was *annihilated*, the soldiers staked their claim.

4. At least 545 <u>species</u> of birds, 792 <u>kinds</u> of butterflies, and 100 <u>types</u> of dragonflies (lives, <u>live</u>) in one Peruvian wildlife preserve.

5. <u>Many</u> a plant and animal (have, <u>has</u>) yet to be named.

6. <u>Cancer</u> and <u>leukemia</u> (is, <u>are</u>) diseases for which certain tropical plants provide medication.

7. Unfortunately, neither <u>rainforests</u> nor tropical <u>vegetation</u> (<u>is</u>, are) being protected from destruction.

Exercise 6 **Writing a Passage**

On a separate piece of paper, write a passage about recess in elementary schools. Base your passage on the following notes and some of your own ideas. Use present tense, present perfect, or present progressive verbs. Then get together in a small group to read your paragraphs aloud and check one another's subject-verb agreement. Students' paragraphs will vary; check for subject-verb agreement. See teacher pages for assessment rubrics.

> *Recess under fire: a waste of time?*
>
> *Child's play—important or not?*
>
> *Some schools eliminating recess*
>
> *Pressures to increase academic performance; more time needed for core subjects*
>
> *Fear of accidents*
>
> *Fear of strangers appearing in school yards*
>
> *Many child development experts disagree. Cite importance of recess time for exercise, social interaction.*
>
> *Some cite need for kids to gain sense of independence.*

Exercise 7 **Write What You Think**

■ Use the suggestions in **Composition, Lesson 2.1,** to help you write a clear and unified paragraph.

On a separate piece of paper, write a paragraph (in the present tense, present perfect, or present progressive) that expresses your view on this statement.

Students in kindergarten through sixth grade need recess only once a week. This compromise provides more time for studies as well as some opportunity for exercise.

Support your position with reasons and examples. When you finish, check for complete sentences and for subject-verb agreement.

Answers will vary. Give students full credit if they have stated an opinion and attempted to support their opinions. Look for grammatically complete sentences that begin with a capital letter and end with an appropriate end punctuation mark.

Agreement with Subject Following Verb and Collective Nouns

Some Common Collective Nouns

army	flock
audience	group
class	herd
club	orchestra
committee	(the) press
crowd	(the) public
family	team

Sometimes, verbs follow subjects in sentences—for example, in sentences that are questions and in sentences beginning with *here* and *there*.

🔹 A verb (v) must agree with the subject (s) even when the subject follows the verb. Be careful, *here* and *there* are never the subject in a sentence.

       V   S
Where **are** the **sleeping bags** I brought up from the basement?

     V   S
Here **are** Tami's favorite **dolls**.

     V   S
Here**'s** one **doll**. [*Here's* is a contraction involving the singular verb *is*.]

                    V   S
On the back porch by the grill **are** the old **newspapers**.

🔹 A verb agrees with the subject of a sentence, *not* with the predicate nominative (PN).

                  S V PN
The toddler's favorite **toy is** blocks.

    S   V   PN
The **films** by the new director **were** the winner.

🔹 **A collective noun**, which names a group of people or things, may be either singular or plural depending on how you are using it.

Use a singular verb when you think of a collective noun as one single unit. Use a plural verb when you think of a collective noun as multiple members.

    The **team is** on a winning streak. [*Team* refers to a single unit and takes a singular verb.]
    The high school varsity **team are** going to five different colleges next year. [*Team* here refers to multiple members in the group and takes a plural verb.]

Writing Hint

Technically, *data* and *media* are plural words. However, in common usage, *data* can be used as a singular word when it refers to a pool of information and *media* can be singular when it refers to the media industry. In other cases, think of *data* and *media* as only plural.

Data on smoking **is** impressive.

Data from many schools **are** in.

The **media loves** scandals.

My favorite **media are** TV and the Web.

Exercise 8 Choosing the Correct Verb

Underline the verb in parentheses that agrees with the subject.

1. Where (is, <u>are</u>) those copies I made?

2. There (<u>is</u>, are) a particular group of stores I like to visit.

3. The army (<u>helps</u>, help) during times of natural disasters.

4. This audience (<u>is</u>, are) one of the most enthusiastic we've had.

5. The orchestra (<u>performs</u>, perform) tonight at the hall.

6. In a small house along the river (<u>lives</u>, live) an elderly woman.

7. The audience (is, <u>are</u>) entering the theater through three doors now.

8. The media (pools, <u>pool</u>) their resources at times.

9. Under the stairs (<u>is</u>, are) the gift I must hide.

10. At the sound of the lion's roar, the herd of wildebeasts (<u>leaps</u>, leap) away in all directions.

11. All the data (<u>proves</u>, prove) I'm right.

12. (Has, <u>Have</u>) the data come in from China and from Taiwan?

13. The final act (is, <u>are</u>) the jugglers and clowns.

14. The group (<u>holds</u>, hold) its meeting in the community center.

15. When (is, <u>are</u>) your brothers, sisters, and cousins coming?

Exercise 9 Writing Complete Sentences

On a separate piece of paper, write a complete sentence for each numbered item, using the collective noun given as the subject of the sentence. Use present tense, present perfect, or present progressive verbs. Then check your sentences with others in your group for correct subject-verb agreement. Read your sentences aloud to one another for extra practice in hearing the sound of correct agreement. Sentences will vary; check for subject-verb agreement.

EXAMPLE   jury
The jury consists of twelve members.

1. audience

2. class

3. crowd

4. committee

5. group

6. flock

7. team

8. family

9. club

10. (the) public

Other Problems in Agreement

You must watch subject-verb agreement in both independent clauses and in subordinate clauses.

◗ In an adjective clause, the verb agrees with the word to which the relative pronoun refers.

In the following examples, the arrows show which word the relative pronoun refers to. When the relative pronoun refers to a singular noun or pronoun, use a singular verb in the adjective clause. When the relative pronoun refers to a plural noun or pronoun, use a plural verb in the adjective clause.

The **story, which is** hard to believe, **comes** from a reliable source.
The **stories, which are** hard to believe, **come** from a reliable source.

◗ A noun that ends in -*s* and refers to two parts working together is plural, like most nouns that end in -*s*. But some nouns ending in -*s* are singular. Other nouns ending in -*s* can be singular or plural depending on context.

Mumps is a common childhood disease.
Her **slacks are** on the chair next to the bed.
The **acoustics** in Carnegie Hall **are** superb.
Acoustics is a science of interest to musicians.

◗ The title of a work of art (painting, literature, music, and so on) is always a singular subject and takes a singular verb.

Hannah and Her Sisters **is** a film by Woody Allen.
Calder's *Horizontal Spines*, which **is** a sculpture, **makes** me smile.

◗ Use a singular verb with a subject that names an amount or time thought of as a unit. Use a plural verb when the amount or time refers to multiple items.

Twenty **dollars is** the price of the ticket. [a single amount]
The twenty **dollars weigh** down my pocket. [multiple bills]
Two **weeks makes** a fortnight. [a single time period]
These two **weeks are going** to be busy. [multiple items]

P.S. You can always check problematic nouns in a dictionary to find a note about when they're singular and when they're plural.

Singular Nouns
mathematics   news
measles   physics
mumps

Plural Nouns
binoculars   scissors
eyeglasses   slacks
pants

Singular or Plural
acoustics   statistics
economics   tactics
politics

Writing Hint

Learn the difference between "one of the" and "the only one of the."

He's one of the **students** who **drive**. [*Who* refers to *students*, a plural noun.]

He's the only **one** of the students who **drives**. [Here, *who* refers to *one*, a singular pronoun.]

Exercise 10 | Choosing the Correct Verb

Underline the verb in parentheses that agrees with the subject.

1. Geoffrey Chaucer, who lived and wrote in the medieval period, (is, are) best known for *The Canterbury Tales*.

2. Christopher Marlowe is one of the writers who (was, were) alive in Shakespeare's day.

3. Alan Sillitoe is one of those twentieth-century writers who (crafts, craft) stories about the English working class.

4. "Intimations of Immortality" (is, are) the short title of a Wordsworth poem.

5. Politics (has, have) been on the minds of many British authors.

6. The fourteen years at the beginning of the twentieth century (is, are) commonly known as the Edwardian Age.

7. Military tactics in World War I (is, are) the topic of poems by several British poets.

8. The poets Byron, Shelley, and Keats, who (appears, appear) in high school literature texts, (has, have) loyal followings.

9. The only one of Keats's poems that (affects, affect) me (is, are) "To Autumn."

10. Fifty dollars (is, are) a very reasonable price for a first edition of a Graham Greene novel.

Exercise 11 | Writing Complete Sentences

On a separate piece of paper, write a complete sentence for each numbered item, using the word or group of words given as the subject of the sentence. Use present tense, present perfect, or present progressive verbs, and check your sentences for correct subject-verb agreement. Read your sentences aloud to yourself for extra practice in hearing the sound of correct agreement.

EXAMPLE   scissors

The scissors are on the desk.

Sentences will vary; check for subject-verb agreement.

1. measles
2. pants
3. six months
4. *Friends* (the TV series of the 1990s)
5. ten pounds
6. three inches
7. acoustics
8. two gallons
9. Geoffrey Chaucer's *The Canterbury Tales*
10. physics

Revising and Editing Worksheet 1

Read the following paragraphs carefully. Correct errors in subject-verb agreement. Make any other changes you think will improve the passage. Write your revised paragraphs on a separate piece of paper. When you have finished revising and editing, proofread your work, and correct any spelling mistakes you find. **Hint:** Not every sentence contains an agreement error.

Students' revisions will vary. Sample revisions are given. Encourage students to find out more about Jonathan Swift.

¹*Gulliver's Travels*, published in 1728, ~~are~~ _{is} the Irish writer Jonathan Swift's fictional masterpiece. ²In the first part of the story, Lemuel Gulliver, one of the men who ~~is~~ _{are} traveling on a merchant ship, ~~tell~~ _{tells} about his shipwreck on the island of Lilliput, which ~~are~~ _{is} the home of people only a few inches tall. ³All of the other items on the island ~~is~~ _{are} one-twelfth the size Swift's readers expect. ⁴Here, on Lilliput, ~~is~~ _{are} opportunities for Swift to satirize English politics. ⁵(Politics, of course, ~~are~~ _{is} the art and science of government.) ⁶For example, a group ~~argues~~ _{argue} among themselves about whether to break eggs at the big end or the small end.

⁷In the next part of the story, Gulliver ~~find hisself~~ _{finds himself} in Brobdingnag, where ~~everone~~ _{everyone} he meets ~~are~~ _{is} as big as the Lilliputians are small. ⁸The king, after learning about life where Gulliver ~~come~~ _{comes} from, ~~conclude~~ _{concludes} that the life ~~their~~ _{there} must be awful. ⁹He says that all of the English people ~~seems~~ _{seem} hateful.

¹⁰In the third part of the book, Gulliver visits the island of Laputa. ¹¹Here, neither the philosopher nor the scientist ~~escape~~ _{escapes} Swift's satire. ¹²Gulliver finds that the wise men of Laputa ~~is~~ _{are} so wrapped up in contemplation that they can't accomplish the simplest practical tasks. ¹³Some of these men ~~tries~~ _{try} the dumbest projects, such as extracting sunshine from cucumbers.

¹⁴The last pages of the book ~~tells~~ _{tell} about the Houyhnhnms and the Yahoos. ¹⁵Houyhnhnms ~~is~~ _{are} horses, whose society ~~are~~ _{is} rational and clean. ¹⁶The Yahoos, beasts in human form, ~~is~~ _{are} filthy and ~~acts~~ _{act} brutally. ¹⁷Gulliver sadly recognizes these Yahoos as similar to the English people. ¹⁸He is disgusted. ¹⁹When he finally ~~return~~ _{returns} home_, ²⁰Gulliver ~~withdraw~~ _{withdraws} from his family.

Revising and Editing Worksheet 2

Read the following paragraphs carefully. Work with a partner to correct errors in subject-verb agreement. Make any other changes you think will improve the passage. Write your revised passage on a separate piece of paper. Compare your revision with that of other pairs of classmates. When you have finished revising and editing, proofread your work, and correct any spelling mistakes you find.

                                                                      comes
   ¹*Frankenstein*, a tale of intrigue and terror, ~~come~~ from the pen of Mary
                           was
Wollstonecraft Shelley, who ~~were~~ a nineteenth-century English author.
                                                              has   which
²Everyone from countries all around the world ~~have~~ heard of this story. ³~~Which~~
                                                         tale
has inspired several film versions. ⁴The seeds for this ~~tail~~ of the supernatural
were
~~was~~ a nightmare that Shelley had.

                                                                   are
   ⁵In the book, a man named Walton, one of the men who ~~is~~ exploring the
            has   relate
Arctic, ~~have~~ written letters. ⁶The letters by Walton ~~relates~~ the story of an

idealistic student, Frankenstein, who has discovered how to give life to

inanimate matter. ⁷From bones he collects, Frankenstein creates the form of a
                              gives
human being and ~~give~~ it life. ⁸The creature is strange-looking, huge, and very
                                          comes   fears
strong. ⁹Every man and woman who ~~come~~ across the creature ~~fear~~ it.

   ¹⁰As a result, the creature is lonely and unhappy. ¹¹It wants a female
                        but fails
counterpart. ¹²~~Fails~~ to persuade Frankenstein to create a bride for him. ¹³The

creature vows to hurt Frankenstein. ¹⁴Indeed, Frankenstein's brother, friend, and
              die
fiancé ~~dies~~ by the creature's hand. ¹⁵Consequently, Frankenstein, along with
           pursues
others, ~~pursue~~ the creature to the Arctic in order to destroy it. ¹⁶But after telling

his story to Walton, Frankenstein dies. ¹⁷The creature claims that Frankenstein is
its   ends its
~~it's~~ final victim. ¹⁸Then the creature ~~end~~ ~~it's~~ own existence.
                                                      beginning
   ¹⁹*Frankenstein* is considered by some as the ~~begining~~ of modern science
                                                              maintain
fiction. ²⁰Others see it as one of the noble-savage myths, which ~~maintains~~ that

bad treatment can corrupt an essentially good nature.
                                                              are
   ²¹Have you seen any of the Frankenstein movies that ~~is~~ available on video?
Students' revisions will vary. Sample revisions are given. Students might research
the humorous variations of the Frankenstein theme.

Chapter Review

Exercise A **Choosing the Correct Verb**

Choose the verb in parentheses that agrees with the subject.

1. None of the content in these ten sentences (is, are) familiar to all Americans.

2. Morning television news (goes, go) back to at least 1947, the year of the premiere of the *Today* show.

3. The only one of the American newspapers that (was, were) by and for African Americans first appeared on a March 16.

4. (Doesn't, Don't) Bruce Willis or Glenn Close have a birthday on March 19?

5. From December 26 to January 1, many an African American (observes, observe) the festival of Kwanzaa.

6. The word *kwanzaa* comes from one of the languages that (is, are) prominent in Africa.

7. The unity of African American families (is, are) celebrated during Kwanzaa.

8. The former slave and evangelist Sojourner Truth (is, are) remembered on November 26.

9. Tampa's Big Guava Festival, the Mount Rushmore Completion Anniversary, and the anniversary of the first time an African American athlete played in the National Basketball Association (falls, fall) on October 31.

10. (Does, Do) a Walt Disney show or *Seinfeld* claim October 27 as the date of its premiere?

Exercise B **Revising and Editing for Subject-Verb Agreement**

For each mistake in subject-verb agreement in the following paragraphs, cross out the incorrect verb, and write the correct one above it. Correct all spelling errors as well.

¹Is visits to the dentist a painful experience? ²Thanks to new laser technology, this situashion may not prevail. ³The nature of visits to dentists' offices are changing. ⁴However, neither the patient nor the dentist are complaining. ⁵The forty million in the country who hasn't been to the dentist in ages is getting ready to return. ⁶High-tech developments, including the laser, is the reason. ⁷To the rescue come the laser.

[Editing marks shown above the text: "Are" above "Is"; "situation" above "situashion"; "that is, the" above "The"; "is" above "are"; "is" above "are"; "haven't" above "hasn't"; "are" above "is"; "are" above "is"; "comes" above "come"]

^{is}

⁸Using lasers, every dentist ~~are~~ soon going to zap pockets of decay

^{damaging}

without ~~damageing~~ the surrounding tooth. ^{is}

⁹Here ~~are~~ more great news:

^{use}

When dentists in the modern age ~~uses~~ lasers, painkillers of any kind ^{will be} ~~is~~

^{are}

unnecessary. ¹⁰In other words, shots with a long hypodermic needle ~~is~~ on

^{Doesn't}

the way out. ¹¹~~Don't~~ it sound as if families will flock to the dentist?

^{hopes} ^{Is}

¹²Many a dentist ~~hope~~ so. ¹³~~Are~~ "Many Pleasant Visits to Dentists" a good

title for an article about these changes?

Exercise C Writing Complete Sentences

On a separate piece of paper, write a complete sentence for each
numbered item, beginning your sentence with the given word or group of
words. Use present tense, present perfect, or present progressive verbs, and
check your sentences for correct subject-verb agreement. Students' sentences
will vary.

1. One of the reasons
2. Every member of the group
3. The only one of the parents who
4. A flock of pigeons
5. The press
6. Everybody who was there
7. The clowns in the circus
8. Some of the people
9. Pat, not Luis,
10. The media
11. One of the players who
12. Either Ed or his sisters
13. Below the window
14. The acoustics
15. Neither Jo nor Mei
16. The film *The Ten Commandments*
17. Both he and I
18. None of the players
19. Six gallons of paint
20. Three dollars

Exercise D Writing a Summary

Using present tense verbs, on a separate piece of paper, write a summary
of a movie or TV program you've seen, or of a book, short story, or play
you've read. Assume your audience has *not* seen or read the work. Include
specific and descriptive details. Feel free to include your opinions and
responses. Include comparisons with other works to clarify points or to
make your writing more vivid. When you've completed your summary,
review it carefully to make sure that the subjects and verbs agree.
Answers will vary. See teacher pages for assessment rubrics.

Using Pronouns

STUDENT WRITING
Expository Essay

Crew's . . . Fun!
by Rachel Kamins
high school student, Middletown, Connecticut

I was sitting in a boat on the Connecticut River one afternoon, bundled in six layers of clothing, contemplating my doom. My knees were squinched up to the level of my shoulders, my back was sore from being repeatedly slammed into the stern, and my gloves were still in the locker room on land. Every now and then, the arctic waters which were leaping around me jumped the gunwhales and spattered me with frigid drops.

Breaking this pleasant reverie came this question from the mouth of one of the eight bodies grunting and straining before me: "Why do we like doing this?"

To tell the truth, I have often wondered the same thing myself. What in heaven's name about the sport of crew actually attracts thinking people?

As one of these walking anomalies, I think I can actually explain the attraction of crew. At least I can explain why I like it—and that's not just because as a coxswain I get to sit around and watch people kill themselves all afternoon. Well, not entirely.

The initial attraction for me was the idea of a river. Even though it's the vile, sewage-filled Connecticut, it still looks great on a sunny day. And the scenic view from the middle of the river, especially up in Cromwell and down past Portland, is nature at its best. Tree-covered islands, boat-filled marinas, craggy rocks, and rolling hills—that's what keeps me coming back.

I also like how the sport itself looks. First of all, the equipment is downright smooth. A brand new Vespoli racing shell is like St. Patrick's Cathedral to me. Secondly, there's no athlete like a crew athlete.

The best is when all of the elements of crew come together—the boats, the rowers, and rowing. The motion of the stroke is a complex combination of pushing, sliding, pulling, and leaning, but it just looks like a beautiful, ritualistic, fluid cycle. And to see eight people doing it at once, in sync, is just mesmerizing. I often find myself staring at the river during regattas, hypnotized by the swing of the crews as they pass.

I think the most wonderful opportunity provided by crew is the chance to overcome [the physical pain of the sport.] The knowledge that one has pushed one's body to the limit and beyond—creating, in fact, new limits—is wonderfully triumphant. Accomplishing the previously impossible. One has such supreme control over the body that one can make it work when it no longer has the ability. These are awesome feelings.

Of course, athletes can get this sensation from more sports than crew, such as running and swimming. But the unique aspect of crew is that one can accomplish this simultaneously with seven other athletes and friends. When a team has come together to follow through on a commitment against all adversity, the members of that team have a connection that can't be produced by any other activity.

The purpose of Rachel Kamins's essay is to explain the reasons she enjoys her sport. Notice the transition words she uses to lead you through her explanation.

Reread the essay and pay particular attention to Rachel's pronouns. How many can you find? You'll get many opportunities to use pronouns in the exercises in this chapter.

Using Subject Pronouns

Subject Pronouns	
SINGULAR	**PLURAL**
I, you, he, she, it	we, you, they

🔹 Use a **subject pronoun** when the pronoun functions as the subject (**s**) of a sentence or a clause.

  s   **s**
Marjorie and **I** are scheduling the performances.

  s
We have considered several plans.

🔹 Use a subject pronoun when the pronoun functions as the predicate nominative (**PN**) of a sentence or clause.

Remember: A **predicate nominative** is a noun or pronoun that follows a form of the verb *be* and renames or identifies the subject.

         PN **PN**   **PN**
The students handling the props are Warren, Crystal, and **I**.

        PN   **PN**
The teacher advisors are Mr. Li and **she**.

> ## Writing Hint
>
> Most people answer "It's me" when someone asks, "Who's there?" But the preferred response for speeches, essays, and grammar tests is "It's I." Use a subject pronoun after a form of the verb *be*. "It is **I**." "It is **we**."

Exercise 1   Choosing the Correct Pronoun

Underline the pronoun in parentheses that correctly completes each sentence.

 EXAMPLE The people who planned our trip are Ms. Chan and (him, <u>he</u>).

1. My friend Michelle and (me, <u>I</u>) will visit England this summer.

2. (Us, <u>We</u>) are going with seniors interested in British history.

3. The person who made all the arrangements for the trip is (her, <u>she</u>).

4. Our faculty chaperones for the trip are Mr. Gomez and (<u>she</u>, her).

5. (Them, <u>They</u>) will take some students to visit the universities in Cambridge and Oxford.

6. Michelle and (me, <u>I</u>) will stay in London.

> ## Step by Step
>
> Here's how to choose the pronoun for a compound predicate nominative.
>
> The first in line will be Al and (me, I).
>
> 1. Turn the sentence around so that the pronouns are the subject.
>
>   (Me, I) will be the first in line.
>
> 2. Say the sentence with just the pronoun.
>
>   **Me** will be the first in line. [sounds wrong]
>   **I** will be the first in line. [sounds right]
>
> 3. Place the pronoun that sounds right in the original sentence.
>
>   The first in line will be Al and **I**.

7. (Her and me, <u>She and I</u>) plan to visit several sights.

8. Who will get to the Tower of London first—Michelle or (me, <u>I</u>)?

9. It will be Mr. Gomez and (her, <u>she</u>) who will be responsible for us.

10. I dreamt that the English prince was (me, <u>I</u>).

Exercise 2 Editing a Paragraph

Edit the following paragraph to correct all errors in pronoun usage.

¹Michelle, Gabriel, and ~~me~~ [I] visited Hampton Court on Tuesday. ²We pretended that the residents of the castle, twelve miles up the Thames River from London, were Michelle's family and ~~her~~ [she]. ³We learned about Cardinal Thomas Wolsey; in 1514, the owner of Hampton Court was ~~him~~ [he]. ⁴Over the years, ~~him~~ [he] and other owners made many changes to the palace and grounds. ⁵Gabriel and ~~me~~ [I] examined the tennis court built in about 1625. ⁶Meanwhile, Michelle explored on her own, imagining how she would redecorate if the owner really were ~~her~~ [she]. ⁷Then Michelle, Gabriel, and ~~me~~ [I] marveled at the gardens, at the Great Gatehouse, and at the paintings above the King's Staircase.

⁸On Wednesday, Chui and ~~me~~ [I] went to Brighton, a seaside town, to see the Royal Pavilion. ⁹~~Her and me~~ [She and I] were astonished by this fantasy palace, with its domes, pinnacles, and minarets. ¹⁰The builder, George IV, was a regent with unique tastes, wasn't ~~him~~ [he]? ¹¹Chui and ~~me~~ [I] liked the music room best. ¹²~~Her and me~~ [She and I] especially enjoyed its Chinese landscapes and water-lily chandeliers.

Exercise 3 Write What You Think

■ Refer to **Composition, Lesson 3.3,** to find suggestions for writing persuasively.

People have many different opinions about travel and sightseeing. Think about one of the following statements. Then, on a separate piece of paper, write a paragraph or two expressing your opinion about the statement. Support your opinion with examples and reasons. When you finish writing, check to see that you have used subject pronouns appropriately.

• Teenagers who live in the United States should travel to Europe, Asia, Australia, or Africa before they graduate from high school.

• Teenagers who live in the United States should explore other cities and states.

Answers will vary. Give students full credit if they have stated an opinion and attempted to support their opinions. They should also have written grammatically complete sentences that begin with a capital letter and end with an appropriate end punctuation mark.

Using Object Pronouns

Object Pronouns	
SINGULAR	**PLURAL**
me, you, him, her, it	us, you, them

◖ Use an **object pronoun** when the pronoun functions as the direct object (**DO**), indirect object (**IO**), or object complement (**OC**) of a sentence or a clause.

                    IO   IO   DO
My father gave Dolores and **me** the keys to the car.

                    DO
We thanked **him** for the keys.

                              DO   DO OC   This usage is
The family counselor made **you** and **me us**.   very rare.

◖ Use an object pronoun when the pronoun functions as the object of a preposition (**OP**) in a sentence or clause.

                              OP   OP
Dad handed the keys to Delores and **me**.

           OP   OP
For both of **us**, driving Dad's car was a big responsibility.

P.S. Don't become confused by the many terms that include the word *object*. Just get a general sense of how an object differs from a subject.

> **See Grammar, Lesson 5.7,** for more on direct and indirect objects and **Lesson 5.9** for more on object complements.

Editing Tip

Avoid this common error: "between you and I." Always say or write, "between you and me."

Exercise 4 ## Choosing the Correct Pronoun

Underline the pronoun in parentheses that correctly completes each sentence.

1. Every actor in his heart believes everything bad that's printed about (he, <u>him</u>). —Orson Welles

2. There is nothing which (<u>we</u>, us) receive with so much reluctance as advice. —Joseph Addison

3. Everything intercepts (we, <u>us</u>) from ourselves. —Ralph Waldo Emerson

4. A man in passion rides a horse that runs away with (he, <u>him</u>). —Thomas Fuller

5. We shape our buildings; thereafter, they shape (we, <u>us</u>). —Winston Churchill

Step by Step

To decide whether to use a subject pronoun or an object pronoun:

1. Decide what function the pronoun performs in the sentence.

2. If the pronoun is a subject or a predicate nominative, use the subject pronoun.

3. If the pronoun is a direct object, an indirect object, an object complement, or the object of a preposition, use the object pronoun.

6. Audiences are the same all over the world, and if you entertain (they, <u>them</u>), they will respond. —Liza Minnelli

7. Woe to (he, <u>him</u>) inside a nonconformist clique who does not conform to nonconformity. —Eric Hoffer

8. We cannot despair of humanity since (<u>we</u>, us) ourselves are human beings. —Albert Einstein

9. Happy are (them, <u>they</u>) that hear their detractions and can put them to mending. —William Shakespeare

10. (Him, <u>He</u>) who hesitates is sometimes saved. —James Thurber

Exercise 5 Editing Sentences

Improve the following sentences. Look carefully at subject pronouns and object pronouns. Cross out each pronoun that is used incorrectly, and write the correct pronoun above it. If a sentence is correct, write *C* after it.

EXAMPLE   Specialists have studied what economic principles high school graduates
they
need to understand; ~~them~~ have identified twenty principles.

Hint

First, check to see what function the pronoun performs in the sentence.

1. Edina knows that people can't have all the goods and services ~~them~~ want.
 they

2. James and ~~her~~ have learned that they must make choices.
 she

3. For ~~she and he~~, making choices means weighing costs and benefits.
 her and him

4. Thinking in terms of more and less, not in terms of everything or nothing, is a new idea to ~~she~~ and her friends.
 her

5. When positive and negative incentives are presented to people, they respond predictably to them. C

6. People trade products and services when they expect some benefit. C

7. ~~Her, him, and me~~ know that people and nations should concentrate on what they do best and then trade with others.
 She, he, and I

8. Kim and ~~them~~ have learned that when buyers and sellers form a market, they determine prices.
 they

9. You and ~~me~~ know that prices reflect supply and demand in the market.
 I

10. When sellers compete, prices drop; that pattern is what Suki and I now understand. C

11. ~~Him and us~~ also know that when buyers compete, the prices go up.
 He and we

12. Carl and ~~me~~ understand that institutions affect markets. Among ~~they~~ are banks, corporations, and labor unions.
 I   *them*

13. With money, you and ~~me~~ borrow, trade, invest, and save; we also use money to compare the value of goods and services.
 I

Who or Whom?

Deciding between *who* and *whom* is the same as deciding between *he* and *him* or between *she* and *her*.

Subject Pronoun	Object Pronoun
who	whom

◗ Use the subject pronoun *who* when the pronoun functions as a subject or predicate nominative in a sentence or in a clause.

Who will represent the school in the debate?
[*Who* is the subject of the sentence.]
The winner is **who**? [*Who* is the predicate nominative.]

Let your ear help you decide between *who* and *whom*. Consider replacing the pronoun in a question with *he* or *him*. If *he* sounds right in the sentence, use the subject pronoun *who*. If *him* sounds right, choose the object pronoun *whom*.

If you have to choose between *who* and *whom* in a subordinate clause, ignore the rest of the sentence. Focus only on how *who* or *whom* functions within the subordinate clause. If you need to, reverse the word order in the clause to determine what function the pronoun performs.

The student **who** was chosen to go into space is in my class. [*Who* is the subject of the adjective clause.]
Do you know **who** their second choice was? [*Who* is the predicate nominative of the noun clause.]

◗ Use the object pronoun *whom* when the pronoun functions as the direct object, indirect object, or object of a preposition in a sentence or in a clause.

Whom did Sarah choose as her partner? [*Whom* is the direct object of *did choose*.]
For **whom** did you buy this shirt? [*Whom* is the object of the preposition *For*.]

Sometimes, a pronoun is both the object of a preposition in the main clause of a sentence and the subject or predicate nominative in a subordinate clause in the sentence. In such a case, always use the pronoun *who*, not *whom*.

Before the ballgame, the pitcher and the catcher talk about who the other team's best hitters are.

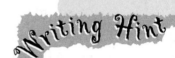

Writing Hint

Most people don't use *whom* at the beginning of a question.

Who did you see?

In formal writing and speaking, however, and on grammar tests, use *whom* whenever the pronoun functions as an object.

Whom did you see?

Step by Step

When you need to choose between *who* and *whom*:

1. Decide what function the pronoun performs in the sentence.

2. Use *who* if the pronoun functions as a subject or a predicate nominative (even if the pronoun is *also* the object of a preposition).

3. Use *whom* if the pronoun functions as a direct or indirect object or as the object of a preposition.

Exercise 6 Choosing the Correct Pronoun

Underline the pronoun in parentheses that correctly completes each sentence.

EXAMPLE   Jackie Robinson was an athlete (<u>who</u>, whom) inspired millions.

1. Robinson, (<u>who</u>, whom) was the first black athlete to play in the major leagues, played second base and other positions.

2. Robinson, (who, <u>whom</u>) teammates praised, was feared by opponents for his hard work.

3. Some players (who, <u>whom</u>) Robinson came across in his career were less than friendly to him.

4. Robinson, (<u>who</u>, whom) had been a football, basketball, and track star at UCLA, eventually made his mark on the baseball diamond.

5. Scouts thought that there were other baseball stars of the Negro Leagues (<u>who</u>, whom) were equal in talent to Robinson.

6. Brooklyn Dodgers owner Branch Rickey, (who, <u>whom</u>) other baseball executives criticized, brought Robinson to the major leagues in 1947.

7. Other Negro League players, many of (who, <u>whom</u>) were past their playing primes, eventually made it to the major leagues.

8. The African American player (<u>who</u>, whom) was the first to compete in the American League was Larry Doby.

9. Doby, (<u>who</u>, whom) played for the Cleveland Indians, also experienced both support and prejudice.

10. Today, reporters write about (<u>who</u>, whom) plays well without regard to race.

Exercise 7 Revising and Editing a Paragraph

Improve the following paragraph about Maya Angelou. Correct all errors in pronoun usage. **Hint:** One sentence contains no errors.

[1]When you think of people who have succeeded against all odds, ~~whom~~ who comes to mind? [2]Consider Maya Angelou, a poet who has earned international respect for her insightful work. [3]Angelou, ~~whom~~ who is a writer, director, and educator, has also had a successful career as a singer, actress, and dancer. [4]Angelou, ~~whom~~ who is the great-granddaughter of a slave, has written several volumes of poetry that explore the themes of economic, racial, and sexual oppression. [5]Her writing captures the aspirations of other African American women, ~~who~~ whom she celebrates in her work.

Mid-Chapter Review

Exercise A Choosing the Correct Pronoun

Underline the pronoun in parentheses that correctly completes each sentence.

EXAMPLE   Jackie and (me, I) are deciding what summer jobs to pursue.

1. Jackie, (who, whom) is a great swimmer, wants a waterfront job.

2. A camp sent (she, her) and (I, me) some brochures.

3. (She, Her) and (I, me) filled out applications.

4. I asked Angelo and Fred what (they, them) plan to do.

5. Angelo, (who, whom) is from a family of chefs, plans to work in the family restaurant.

6. Fred, for (who, whom) work is something to be avoided at all costs, plans to sleep the entire summer.

7. I then asked Carmela and (she, her) what their plans were.

8. Carmela said that she has an aunt (who, whom) is a potter.

9. Rita, with (who, whom) my brother goes to school, plans to volunteer at a soup kitchen.

10. By May, most of (we, us) will have our summer plans in order.

Exercise B Revising and Editing a Passage

Improve the following paragraphs. Correct any errors you find in pronoun usage. Make any other changes that you think will improve the paragraph. Then, proofread to correct any errors in spelling. **Hint:** Not all sentences contain errors, but some may have more than one. Answers may vary. Sample answers are given.

¹People ~~whom~~ [who] are seeking jobs can look for employment opportunities in printed or online want ads. ²By placing advertisements, individuals and companies inform you and ~~I~~ [me] of their goods and services. ³The earliest advertisers were criers ~~whom~~ [who] hustled about in the streets promoting their wares. ⁴Most of ~~they~~ [them] shouted about the advantages of their fabrics, pots, and livestock. ⁵What ~~there~~ [their] approach lacked in subtlety and cleverness, it made up for in loudness.

[6]Historians believe that written advertising had its start with a "wanted" poster in Egypt about three thousand years ago. [7]At that time, a man ~~whom~~ who owned a slave ~~whom~~ who had run off offered gold as a reward for the slave's return. [8]Although none of ~~we~~ us today knows whether or not the slave was captured, we do know that posters in marketplaces and in temples became a popular way to inform people about new developments.

[9]After the invention of the printing press in Europe in about 1450, modern print advertising began. [10]Then, fliers could be printed in large numbers. [11]~~Them~~ They could not only be posted in public places but also be inserted in printed materials. [12]The people ~~whom~~ who placed the ads studied sales patterns to learn which locations or publications resulted in the greatest response. [13]Newspapers were the outright winners.

[14]By the 1670s, newspaper owners, ~~whom~~ who realized that ad revenue could greatly increase their income, began to print separate advertising supplements. [15]These were the forerunners of the inserts that bombard ~~we~~ us in today's Sunday papers. [16]Eventually, advertising became so popular that it commanded as much space as the news.

[17]When the Internet gained millions of users in the 1990s, advertisers came after ~~we~~ us in that medium as well. [18]Esther Dyson and Stewart Brand have opinions about advertising on the Internet. [19]Look for what ~~her~~ she and ~~him~~ he have to say.

[Exercise C] Write What You Think

In a paragraph or two, answer one of the following questions. State your opinion clearly, and support it with reasons and examples. When you finish writing, check to make sure you've used appropriate subject pronouns and object pronouns.

• In what ways does advertising make our lives better or worse?
• Should advertising be banned from school grounds?

Answers will vary. Give students full credit if they have stated an opinion on one of the two questions and attempted to support their opinions. They should also have written grammatically complete sentences that begin with a capital letter and end with an appropriate end punctuation mark.

Pronoun Problems

An appositive (see Lesson 6.2) can be a pronoun referring to a noun or a noun referring to a pronoun. In both instances, you must choose the correct form of the pronoun—either a subject pronoun or an object pronoun.

Possessive pronouns are listed and discussed in Lesson 4.2.

🔹 For a pronoun appositive, use a subject pronoun if the word the appositive refers to is a subject or a predicate nominative. Use an object pronoun if the word the appositive refers to is a direct object, an indirect object, or the object of a preposition.

The best actors, Elaine and **he**, have the lead roles.

[*He* refers to *actors*, the subject of the sentence.]

The leads are the best actors, Elaine and **he**. [*Actors* is now a predicate nominative.]

The director gave the leads to the best actors, Elaine and **him**.

[*Actors* is the object of the preposition *to*.]

The director gave the best actors, Elaine and **him**, the leads.

[*Actors* is the indirect object of the sentence.]

🔹 When the pronoun *we* or *us* is followed by a noun appositive, choose the pronoun form you would use if the pronoun were alone in the sentence.

We actors found the endless rehearsals tedious.

[You would say, "**We** found the endless. . . ."]

🔹 In an **incomplete construction** (also called an elliptical construction), choose the pronoun form (subject or object) you would use if the sentence were completed.

Usually, an incomplete construction is a comparison, one that comes at the end of a sentence and starts with the word *than* or *as*. In the following examples, the omitted words appear in brackets. When you write an incomplete construction, say the missing words to yourself as a check for pronoun choice.

Yan is two inches shorter than **she** [is].

My aunt likes my cousin more than [she likes] **me**.

🔹 Reserve pronouns ending in *-self* or *-selves* for referring to or intensifying another word in the sentence. By itself, a pronoun ending in *-self* or *-selves* cannot be a subject or an object of a sentence.

Kendra and ~~myself~~ are in the band. *(I)*

The prize goes to the team from Adams and to ~~ourselves~~. *(us)*

Enriching Your Vocabulary

The Latin root of *tedious*, *taediosus*, means "disgusting" or "offensive." The English word, not quite as strong, means simply "boring" or "tiresome." The *tedious* lecture on using the spell check feature lasted far too long.

Editing Tip

Avoid unnecessarily shifting pronouns from one person to another in a given sentence.

One must prepare for tests as thoroughly as ~~you~~ *one* can.

I want to be a writer, but ~~you~~ *I* need more confidence.

Exercise 8 Choosing the Correct Pronoun

Underline the pronoun in parentheses that correctly completes each sentence.

EXAMPLE   The judges gave the prize to the cleverest dog, (him, he).

1. (Us, We) dog owners love to show off our pets' new tricks.

2. I think my spaniel is smarter than (him himself, he himself) thinks.

3. The smartest dogs, Alexander and (her, she), make Lassie look like a dolt.

4. I prefer loyal and calm dogs such as beagles. Yes, I prefer (they, them) and retrievers.

5. The things that a mutt can do sometimes astound (us, we) judges.

6. I can't take my dog Lucy and her pup on vacation, but the dog camp will please even the most ornery campers, (her, she) and Baby Lucy.

7. Three dogs—Sam, Dottie, and (him, he)—play together all day.

8. The camp gave a special treat to the quietest dogs, (her, she) and (him, he).

9. The two dogs that bark the most, Baby Lucy and (her, she), are only puppies.

10. Do you think Lucy and her pup would like a postcard from (myself, me)?

Exercise 9 Revising Sentences

The following sentences contain errors with pronouns. Cross out a pronoun that is incorrect, and write the correct pronoun above it. **Hint:** Watch for incomplete constructions, unnecessary shifts, and other pronoun misuses.

1. We don't trust Amelia, but we trust Willie less than ~~she~~ ^{her}.

2. Darnell and ~~myself~~ are the newest players on the team.

3. ^{We} ~~Us~~ tenors think we have the best voices in the choir.

4. Not only Margaret but also Fatima and ~~her~~ ^{she} performed in recitals.

5. As you go through life, you learn that ~~one's~~ ^{your} plans often go astray.   #5—Accept answer with consistent use of *one*.

6. The boys predicted the winners, Tina and ~~she~~ ^{her}.

7. My male hamster is smarter than your female hamster; my hamster knows more tricks than ~~her~~ ^{she}.

8. One never finishes cleaning up as early as ~~she~~ ^{one} thinks ~~she~~ ^{one} will.   #8—Accept answer with consistent use of *she* or *he*.

9. The team from Greeley or ~~ourselves~~ ^{we} will get the highest marks in the band contest.

10. Jonathan has played the violin longer than ~~me~~ ^I.

Agreement with Antecedent

The word that a pronoun refers to is its **antecedent**. Pronouns and antecedents must agree in **gender** (male, female, or neuter) and in **number** (singular or plural).

◖ Use a plural pronoun to refer to two or more antecedents joined by the word *and*.

> *Mary*, *Ruth*, and *Helen* were the most popular female names in the United States in 1900. **Their** counterparts in England that year were *Florence*, *Mary*, and *Alice*.

◖ Use a singular pronoun to refer to two or more singular antecedents joined by *or* or *nor*. When a singular antecedent and a plural antecedent are joined by *or* or *nor*, use a pronoun that agrees with the nearer antecedent.

> In 1900, a John, a Robert, **or** a Joseph found **his** name to be very popular. Will the name *Jennifer* **or** other popular names lose **their** appeal one day?

◖ Use a singular pronoun when the antecedent is a singular indefinite pronoun: *anybody, anyone, each, either, everybody, everyone, much, neither, nobody, no one, one, somebody, someone, such.*

> **Anyone** with the name Robert can say that **his** name was the most popular boy's name in the United States in 1925, 1940, and 1950.

When a singular indefinite pronoun refers to both males and females, use the expression "his or her."

> **Everybody** is interested in where **his or her** name came from.

In an adjective clause, the personal pronoun agrees with the word to which the relative pronoun refers.

> **Some who** give **their** children an unusual name later apologize.
> **One who** gives **his or her** child an original name is proud.

Exercise 10 **Choosing the Correct Pronoun**

Underline the pronoun in parentheses that agrees with its antecedent. **Hint:** First, find the antecedent(s).

> EXAMPLE   Kristen, Stacey, and Courtney use (her, <u>their</u>) calculators to do the assignment.

1. Damon and his girlfriend Felicia always eat (his, <u>their</u>) favorite foods.

2. Neither of the girls taking the swim test finished (<u>her</u>, their) lunch.

For a discussion of subject-verb agreement and indefinite pronouns, refer students to Lesson 9.2.

Writing Hint

Sometimes in a formal situation, *his or her* sounds awkward, but you can't use *their* with a singular antecedent. Avoid this problem by rewording your sentence. One way is to make the sentence plural.

~~Each student~~ *Students* must pick up ~~his or her~~ *their* bus passes tomorrow.

Each student must pick up ~~his or her~~ *a* bus pass tomorrow.

3. Either the twins or James will bring (his, their) football.

4. Did Tanisha or Jessica remember (her, their) homework?

5. Someone named Lee, whom I don't know, picked me for (his or her, their) team.

6. Miguel, Dave, and Naseem sent (his, their) gift by an overnight service.

7. Many a parent helps (his or her, their) child fill out a college- or job-application form.

8. Did the dancers or the soprano, Lena, practice (her, their) part?

9. Somebody has left (his or her, their) cell phone at my house.

10. Antoine, Sean, and Jermaine know (his, their) roles.

11. Several members of the club and its president will present (his or her, their) views at the next meeting.

12. Neither Mr. Wilson nor Mr. Johnson will be in town to watch (his, their) son graduate.

13. Each of the members of the band dressed in (his or her, their) best for the performance.

14. Everyone who donates to the clothing drive will receive thanks for (his or her, their) gesture.

15. Tom, Steve, or Fiona will read (their, his or her, her) story at the ceremony.

Exercise 11 Writing an Opinion About a Name

Think about your first name, the first name of a friend or relative, or any first name. Write one or more paragraphs in response to the following question.

■ Use the questions for peer editors in **Composition, Lesson 1.3,** as you read one another's work.

What do you like or dislike about the name you've chosen to explore? Consider writing about the meaning of the name, where it may have come from, and what it makes you think of.

Support your opinion with examples and reasons. To do so, you may have to conduct some research in books about names. When you have finished, give your writing to a partner for his or her comments. Do not give your writing to someone with the name you wrote about.

Answers will vary. Give students full credit if they have stated an opinion and attempted to support their opinions. They should also have written grammatically complete sentences that begin with a capital letter and end with an appropriate end punctuation mark. Check that students' sentences contain correct pronoun-antecedent agreement.

Clear Pronoun Reference

Pronouns are helpful only if your readers or listeners can figure out their meanings.

🔹 Avoid an ambiguous reference, which occurs when a pronoun appears to refer to either of two antecedents.

Rewrite the sentence to make your meaning clear.

UNCLEAR	When the Millers greeted their visiting relatives, **they** smiled and laughed. [Who did?]
CLEAR	The Millers smiled and laughed when they greeted their visiting relatives.
CLEAR	The Millers greeted their smiling and laughing visitors.

🔹 Avoid using the words *it, this, that,* and *which* without a clearly stated antecedent.

Replace the pronoun with a noun, or make sure the pronoun points clearly to a noun.

UNCLEAR	Not many people showed up to watch the game, **which** was disappointing. [What was disappointing, the game or the low turnout?]
UNCLEAR	Not many people showed up to watch the game. **This** was disappointing. [same problem as before]
UNCLEAR	Not many people showed up to watch the game. **It** was disappointing. [same problem as before]
CLEAR	Not many people showed up to watch the game. The low attendance was disappointing.
CLEAR	The game drew low attendance. **It** was a disappointing game.

🔹 Except in very informal writing, avoid using *you* or *they* without saying what the word refers to.

UNCLEAR	Math can be practical. For example, they say that a straight line is the shortest distance between two points. [Who says?]
CLEAR	Math can be practical. For example, **mathematicians** say that a straight line is the shortest distance between two points.
UNCLEAR	They are advertising a new headache pill. You don't want to take it on an empty stomach. [very informal]
CLEAR	An **advertisement** for a new headache pill is running. A **patient** should not take the pill on an empty stomach. [clearer subjects]

Revising Sentences

The following sentences contain unclear pronouns. On a separate piece of paper, rewrite the sentences to avoid these errors. **Hint:** Multiple revisions for each one are possible. Answers will vary. Sample answers are given.

EXAMPLE   They say that Bright toothpaste works best.
Dentists say that Bright toothpaste works best.

the proof
1. He tried to explain ~~to his father how to prove a theorem~~, which was

difficult, for his father to understand.

audiences expect
2. At circuses, ~~they expect the audience~~ to howl with laughter.

                                                        He   the altos
3. Mr. Rosen separated the altos from the sopranos and practiced with ~~them~~.

inhabitants
4. In some places, ~~they~~ never know when the next tornado will suddenly

appear.

5. He does not believe that I broke the record. ~~This is a fact~~. I did, in fact, break it.
Car mechanics   your
6. ~~They~~ say that you should change the oil in ~~a~~ car every six months.

7. First the politicians passed, then the floats, and then three bands.

~~It was loud~~. The bands were playing loudly.

8. I took a sheet of paper out of the envelope ~~and then folded it~~. I folded the paper.

their trip to
9. When I read my friends' postcard about the Rocky Mountains, I wished
those peaks
~~they~~ were here.

management asks
10. At many hotels, ~~they want~~ you to check out by noon.

Exercise 13 **Creating Your Own Exercise**

On a separate piece of paper, write ten sentences that have unclear pronouns. Include at least two of each of the following:

• sentences in which a pronoun refers to either of two antecedents

• sentences in which *it, this, that,* or *which* lacks a clearly stated antecedent

• sentences in which *you* or *they* has no antecedent

Swap papers with a partner, and rewrite each other's sentences so that their meanings are clear. Check each other's answers. Students' sentences will vary.

Revising and Editing Worksheet 1

USAGE
Chapter 10

Read the following paragraphs carefully. Correct errors in pronoun usage. Make any other changes that you think will improve the passage. Write your revised paragraphs on a separate piece of paper. When you have finished revising and editing, proofread your work, and fix any spelling mistakes you find.

Answers will vary. Sample revisions are given.

¹Although many countries have wonderful food markets, ~~they~~ [travelers] say that the vast one in Ho Chi Minh City in Vietnam is superior for ~~their~~ [its] varied, attractive, and fresh products. ²Everywhere ~~you look~~ [in that market], vendors are washing, cutting, peeling, and selling food, and shoppers are enjoying ~~them~~ [it]. ³When ~~me and~~ Brian [and I] were ~~their~~ [there], we saw fruits neither of ~~we~~ [us] had ever heard of~~.~~ [, such as] ⁴~~Like~~ durian, dragon fruit, and jackfruit. ⁵Brian spotted even more unusual foods than ~~me~~ [I].

⁶There was much ~~for you~~ to notice at this market, which was already getting crowded by 7:30 in the morning. ⁷Brian and ~~myself~~ [I] saw ducks and chickens, [which were] squawking in ~~there~~ [their] cages, and vendors ~~whom~~ [who] were squatting and eating their *pho*, a meat soup, for breakfast. ⁸Nearby were jars of herbs and spices. ⁹~~Us~~ [We] tourists were dazzled by the fragrances. ¹⁰~~It was~~ [The smells were] amazing. ¹¹~~And huge, too.~~ [In addition, the market was huge,] ¹²~~The market,~~ with its many blocks of stalls and canvas storefronts~~,~~ [. The crowds] began to thin out by mid-morning. ¹³The vendors, for ~~who~~ [whom] the workday was winding down, were cleaning their stalls.

¹⁴Equally amazing to ~~we~~ [us] tourists was the fact that ~~they~~ [the vendors] didn't use refrigerators in the market~~.~~ ¹⁵~~D~~espite the fact that temperatures never dipped below 90 degrees. ¹⁶Foods were stocked, covered, or layered so that ~~it~~ [they] all stayed cool. ¹⁷There was, however, ice for the squid and some other fragile items. ¹⁸~~They~~ [Vendors] kept the fish in pools of water~~,~~ and ~~they~~ kept changing ~~them~~ [the water.] ¹⁹They slaughtered only enough poultry to sell that day. ²⁰Anyone who visits a market like this one will never forget ~~their~~ [his or her] experience. ²¹The memory will live for ~~myself~~ [me] for the rest of my life.

Chapter 10 • Using Pronouns **251**

Revising and Editing Worksheet 2

Read the following paragraphs carefully. Work with a partner to correct errors in pronoun usage. Make any other changes that you think will improve the passage. Write your revised paragraphs on a separate piece of paper. Compare your revision with that of other pairs of classmates. When you have finished revising and editing, proofread your work, and fix any spelling mistakes you find.   Answers will vary. Sample revisions are given.

¹The film *Chariots of Fire* came out in 1981. ²~~They gave it~~ [It won] three Academy Awards, including one for best picture. ³~~It~~ [The picture] introduced ~~you~~ [the public] to ~~it's~~ [its] stars—Ben Cross, Ian Charleson, and Nigel Havers. ⁴Several well-known actors appeared in the film, ~~which was a key factor~~ [helping to make it a success]. ⁵For director Hugh Hudson, it was his first film.

⁶*Chariots of Fire* ~~tell~~ [tells] the absorbing and unusual true tale of two runners, Eric Liddell and Harold Abrahams. ⁷Both of ~~who~~ [whom] competed successfully in the 1924 Olympics games in Paris. ⁸This [film describes the] compelling drama of the struggles the two faced leading up to ~~it~~ [those games]. ⁹Liddell was a devout Scottish missionary. ¹⁰Abrahams, a Jewish [was] student at Cambridge University. ¹¹Liddell stuck to ~~their~~ [his] principles when confronted with the choice of whether or not to race on Sunday, his holy day. ¹²Abrahams, ~~who~~ [whom] anti-Semitic forces targeted, was determined to compete on his own terms, despite the university's disapproval of ~~himself~~ [him]. ¹³Both overcame ~~his~~ [their] crises to run and win ~~there~~ [their] races.

¹⁴You'll love this compelling story. ¹⁵The sets and costumes seem real, as do the running scenes. ¹⁶~~They~~ [The filmmakers really] put considerable effort into ~~it~~ [giving the film an authentic appearance]. ¹⁷~~More authentic than other films~~. ¹⁸And the music, which is by now familiar to ~~ourselves~~ [most of us], is terrific. ¹⁹Next time ~~your~~ [you're] at the video store, rent ~~it~~ *Chariots of Fire*.

Exercise A Choosing the Correct Pronoun

Underline the pronoun in parentheses that correctly completes each sentence.

1. Sarah Josepha Hale, (who, <u>whom</u>) the publisher appointed in 1828, was the first woman to edit a major publication for women.

2. The publisher of *Ladies Magazine* and (<u>she</u>, her) worked in Boston.

3. Hale probably enjoyed saying, "The editor is not a man but (<u>I</u>, me)."

4. Hale believed education was important for a man and for (<u>her</u>, herself) too.

5. Hale, to (who, <u>whom</u>) education was very important, had received her own schooling at home.

6. In 1837, Louis Godey, after (who, <u>whom</u>) another women's magazine was named, became the owner of the magazine Hale worked for.

7. *Godey's Lady's Book* was the magazine named for (himself, <u>him</u>).

8. A theme that Godey and (<u>she</u>, her) promoted was that women, through "secret, silent influence," could affect the lives of men and children.

9. If you could meet Hale and Godey today, what would you say to (he and she, <u>her and him</u>)?

10. Between (she and he, <u>her and him</u>), they brought out an important publication.

Exercise B Correcting Pronoun Errors

Correct all pronoun errors in the following sentences. Cross out the incorrect pronouns, and write the correct ones in the space above each sentence. If a sentence is correct, write *C*.

1. Evan and ~~me~~ ^I are meeting our friends later.

2. Helen, ~~who~~ ^{whom} a community college admitted, will also work for her father.

3. I suggest that George and ~~her~~ ^{she} meet at the car dealership.

4. We asked Gloria and them about having us over. C

5. ~~Him~~ ^{He} and his brother were the first to start using that expression.

6. My father says the argument is between my sister and ~~himself~~ ^{him}.

7. ~~Who~~ ^{To whom} do we send the bill ~~to~~? *or Whom do we send the bill to?*

8. Sherry, Tamisha, and ~~her~~ ^{she} made the track team.

9. Do you know who the Prime Minister of England is? C

10. ~~Us~~ We guys were the last to find out about the changes.

Exercise C Agreement with Antecedents

Fill in each blank with a pronoun that agrees with its antecedent(s).

1. Either Tyrone or Felix will bring ____his____ extra racquet to the courts.

2. The four friends have ____their____ own opinions on things.

3. Neither the two Gong sisters nor Lucy brought ____her____ lunch today.

4. Either Lola or Nola gave up ____her____ seat on the bus.

5. Nick, Paul, and Tony called in ____their____ orders at the same time.

6. The woman who gave ____her____ account of the fire was articulate.

7. Each of the participants brought _his or her_ own instrument.

8. Neither Chuck nor Ted drove ____his____ car to the beach.

9. Every entrant must send in _his or her_ name to the committee by Tuesday.

10. Jake and Lydia rehearsed ____their____ parts together.

Exercise D Revising Sentences

Each of the following items lacks clear pronoun reference. On a separate piece of paper, rewrite the sentences to avoid these errors of ambiguity.
Hint: Multiple revisions for each are possible.

Answers will vary. Sample answers are given.

1. The evening was a hot and sticky August night. ~~It~~ The weather was uncomfortable.

2. In zoos, ~~they~~ visitors expect the animals to be in suitable environments.

3. Ms. Walker removed the book from the shelf and wiped ~~it~~ the dust from its cover.

4. ~~In the mountains, they~~ People who live in the mountains always know when the first snow will come.

5. When the World Series winners paraded past their fans, they waved enthusiastically. from the cars in which they rode.

6. She tried the door, ~~to the store, which was closed~~. which was locked. The store was closed.

7. I took my telescope, and went to the window, ~~and~~ I looked through ~~it~~ the telescope.

8. I took the place mats off the tables, and ~~cleaned them~~. Then I cleaned the tables.

9. When I met her new friend in her big house, I wished I had ~~one~~ a house like that.

10. At basketball games, ~~they~~ coaches ask for time-outs.

Using Modifiers

Direct students to
chapter-specific
portfolio projects
on Sadlier-Oxford's
web site.

STUDENT WRITING
Narrative Essay

Thank You
by Molly Gondek
high school student, Rocky Hill, California

Did I miss something? Why were these people so motivated to do this? My stomach turned as the leader of my youth group read us a flyer about Habitat for Humanity. The idea of waking up at seven o'clock on the first Saturday of summer vacation for a day of hammering and a night of nursing the resulting blisters did not appeal to me. I am not a fan of being dirty. Needless to say, after hearing, "Come on, Molly, it will be fun!" I reluctantly volunteered.

By no means was I counting down the days to that dreaded Saturday. My panic reached its peak as we drove to the site. The horror began when I heard, "Move the stripped roofing shingles that surround the house."

My morning included many worries. "Will I step on a nail and be rushed to the hospital? Will these directors leave us alone and stop instructing the most 'productive' method of completing the task? Is there a place to wash up a little?"

Amazingly, I made it to lunch break which came and went much too fast. Soon I returned to the grueling work. I was in dire need of a break when a thirteen-year-old boy (a member of the family moving into the house) brought me a cup of water. After I said a polite thank-you, he responded, "No, thank *you*." In three words, my whole viewpoint changed. After introductions, we started talking about his future home. His face lit up as he told me his decorating plans for his very first room. He told me of his mother's death and of living with his aunt and cousins in a car. Not once did a tear flow from this boy's eyes as he related his misfortune and his missed opportunities. Pure joy radiated from him.

I can barely remember any more about the day. I cannot even remember the boy's name. But his beaming face is vivid in my mind. His innocence shocked me. He helped me be more appreciative. How could I complain about the dirt and the nails?

That night, soaking my sore feet, I looked around. I had gained a greater appreciation and a clearer view of life's important matters.

From the very first sentences, Molly Gondek's narrative essay has a lively tone. She uses humor, dialogue, and sensory details to tell her story. Molly ends her essay by explaining the significance of the event.

As you reread the essay, pay attention to the modifiers—the adjectives and adverbs. Modifiers add color and freshness to your writing. As you do the exercises in this chapter, you'll practice adding modifiers to your writing—and using them correctly.

Allow time for students to discuss the student writing. Suggest that they identify its strengths and propose possible improvements. Use the model to introduce the concepts in the chapter.

Degrees of Comparison

Suppose you attended the Jumping Frog Jubilee at the Calaveras County Fair and you wanted to compare the leaps of three competing frogs. To express yourself, you would need the three **degrees of comparison**: **positive**, **comparative**, and **superlative**.

POSITIVE   Frog One's jump is **long**.

COMPARATIVE   Frog Two's jump is even **longer**. [Use the comparative to compare two items.]

SUPERLATIVE   Frog Three's jump is the **longest**. [Use the superlative to compare three or more items.]

Here are the rules for forming the comparative and superlative degrees.

● **One- and two-syllable modifiers** Add -*er* and -*est* to most one- and two-syllable modifiers. A dictionary will alert you to spelling changes.

old, old**er**, old**est**   fast, fast**er**, fast**est**
quick, quick**er**, quick**est**   hard, hard**er**, hard**est**
shallow, shallow**er**, shallow**est**   lazy, laz**ier**, laz**iest**

If an -*er* or -*est* modifier sounds strange, use *more* and *most* before the positive degree.

earnest, **more** earnest, **most** earnest

● **-ly adverbs** Use *more* and *most* for all adverbs that end in -*ly*.

slowly, **more** slowly, **most** slowly

● **More than two syllables** For modifiers of three syllables or more, use *more* and *most* to form the comparative and superlative degrees.

delightful, **more** delightful, **most** delightful
terrible, **more** terrible, **most** terrible

● **Decreasing degrees** For all modifiers (regardless of number of syllables), use *less* and *least* for decreasing degrees of comparison.

strong, **less** strong, **least** strong
urgently, **less** urgently, **least** urgently

● **Irregular modifiers** A few modifiers form their degrees of comparison irregularly. See the side column above for a list of these modifiers.

℘.℘. Most of the time the correct forms of comparative and superlative modifiers will occur to you automatically.

Irregular Degrees of Comparison

good	better	best
well	better	best
bad	worse	worst
ill	worse	worst
many	more	most
much	more	most
little	less *or* lesser	least
far	farther [*for physical distances*]	farthest
far	further [*for nonphysical advancement*]	furthest

Writing Hint

Since *good* is always an adjective—never an adverb—do not use *good* to modify an action verb.

Sammy bats ~~good~~ *well*.

Besides working as an adverb, *well* is also an adjective that means "in good health."

She didn't look good. [attractive]

She didn't look well. [healthy]

Editing Tip

A double comparison incorrectly uses both -*er* or -*est* and *more* or *most*. Avoid double comparisons. Use either the word *more* (or *most*) or the suffix -*er* (or -*est*).

This mountain is ~~more~~ higher than the other one.

Editing Sentences

Cross out any incorrect modifiers, and write the correct form in the space above or at the end of the line.

1. We just took the ~~most~~ hardest test in art history class, but I think I did ~~good~~. *well*
2. The essay part was the ~~most long~~ of all the parts. *longest*
3. The exam was so difficult that all of us worked ~~quietlier~~ than on any previous test. *more quietly*
4. The ~~difficultest~~ questions were the ones about modern architecture. *most difficult*
5. I had forgotten that, of all architects, Louis Sullivan was ~~more~~ responsible for pioneering the design of skyscrapers. *most*
6. I'd read about Frank Lloyd Wright, Le Corbusier, and Mies van der Rohe, but I couldn't tell you who was the ~~talentedest~~ architect of the three. *most talented*
7. All I knew was that Wright, Le Corbusier, and van der Rohe were ~~importanter~~ architects than their contemporaries. *more important*
8. Our teacher suggested that those three architects designed especially ~~good~~ *well* and were ~~artisticker~~ than all the others. *more artistic*
9. She said that all three had a poetic vision of the world, so they advanced ~~more~~ further with their designs than most.
10. She also pointed out their faults, including the fact that in Wright's ~~most early~~ houses, the flat roofs leaked. *earliest*

Forming the Comparative and Superlative

Write the comparative and superlative degrees for each of the following modifiers on a separate piece of paper.

1. formidable *more formidable, most formidable*
2. modest *more modest, most modest*
3. agile *more agile, most agile*
4. good *better, best*
5. curious *more curious, most curious*

6. busy *busier, busiest*
7. generous *more generous, most generous*
8. far [distance] *farther, farthest*
9. fearful *more fearful, most fearful*
10. convincing *more convincing, most convincing*

Answers will vary. Check for the correct use of different degrees of comparison. You might have students check for examples of degrees of comparison in local newspapers. See teacher pages for assessment rubrics.

Writing an Advertisement

Imagine that you are a realtor, someone who sells houses and apartments. You are writing an ad for a house or apartment that you have been hired to sell. On a separate piece of paper, write a description that will persuade prospective home-buyers that your property is the best they'll see. Use at least five comparative or superlative modifiers in your ad.

Using the Degrees of Comparison

🔹 Use the **comparative degree** to compare two things. Use the **superlative degree** to compare three or more things.

COMPARATIVE   Maria's hair is **longer** than Bonita's.

SUPERLATIVE   Sol's route is the **longest** of all ten ice-cream truck routes.

In dialogue and in casual conversation, you may hear someone use the superlative form when comparing only two things.

Of the two flavors, the chocolate fudge is the **best**.

When you write standard English, however, use the comparative form.

Of the two flavors, the chocolate fudge is **better**.

🔹 **Avoid illogical comparisons** Use the word *other* or *else* to compare something with others in its group.

ILLOGICAL   The Sears Tower is taller than any building in Chicago. [The Sears Tower cannot be taller than itself too!]

LOGICAL   The Sears Tower is taller than any **other** building in Chicago.

ILLOGICAL   Alex studies harder than anyone in the class.

LOGICAL   Alex studies harder than anyone **else** in the class.

🔹 **Avoid unclear comparisons** Add whatever words are necessary to make a comparison clear.

UNCLEAR   Ken is more interested in hiking than Fiona.

CLEAR   Ken is more interested in hiking than Fiona is.

CLEAR   Ken is more interested in hiking than in Fiona.

UNCLEAR   The temperature in Miami is usually higher than Maine.

CLEAR   The temperature in Miami is usually higher than the temperature in Maine.

Editing Tip

Use *fewer*, not *less*, when referring to plural nouns.
      fewer
I've noticed ~~less~~ eagles than last year.

      fewer
Some regions have ~~less~~ people than livestock.

Exercise 4 **Correcting Modifiers**

Review these sentences for use of modifiers. Write the sentence correctly on a separate piece of paper.

EXAMPLE   Is the accident rate among teenage drivers higher than adults?

Is the accident rate among teenage drivers higher than that of adult drivers?

1. Lauren likes drag racing more than her brothers. _{do}

2. Of the five siblings, Lauren is the ~~more~~ ^{most} accomplished racer.

3. She is the ~~younger~~ ^{youngest} of the five children, all of whom love cars.

4. Of her two oldest brothers, Jim is the ~~best~~ ^better^ mechanic.

5. But Lauren has more interest in cars than all the ^other^ members of her family.

6. Lauren is one of a growing number of young women who are becoming more interested in cars than young men ^are^.

7. Until very recently, the auto business has been more a man's business than a ~~woman~~.   woman's

8. Car manufacturers have aimed their advertising more directly at men than at anyone ^else^.

9. In the past, ~~less~~ ^fewer^ women than men were interested in car shopping.

10. Today's women are ~~most~~ ^more^ likely than women in the past to purchase a car.

Exercise 5 Write What You Think

Some commentators claim that the automobile reshaped the world in the twentieth century. In a paragraph or two, answer one of the following questions. Support your opinion with reasons and evidence.

• What will be the most important law about automobiles in the twenty-first century?

• How would you feel about raising the driving-license age to nineteen?

When you have finished, give your writing to a partner for his or her comments. Both of you should check the paragraphs for correct modifiers.

Exercise 6 Writing a Paragraph

Write a paragraph in which you compare two or more objects, people, animals, or places. Here are some possible topics, but feel free to choose your own.

■ You may wish to refer to the strategies for writing a compare and contrast essay in Composition, Lesson 3.4.

two athletes	two musicians	two schools
three movies	three magazines	three friends
three cars	three vacations	three part-time jobs

As you draft or revise, include at least four comparative or superlative forms in your paragraph, and underline them.

Paragraphs will vary; check for the correct use of different degrees of comparison, the correct use of *less* and *fewer*, and the avoidance of double comparisons. See teacher pages for assessment rubrics.

Double Negatives and Absolute Adjectives

Some Negative Words

barely	none
hardly	no one
never	not (-n't)
no	nothing
nobody	scarcely

● Using two negative words together when one will do results in the error called a **double negative**.

Usually, only one negative word is necessary to express a negative idea. Count the contraction *-n't* (for the word *not*) as a negative word.

You can usually correct a double negative in more than one way.

INCORRECT I couldn't never have done it without your support.
CORRECT I could never have done it without your support.
CORRECT I couldn't ever have done it without your support.

INCORRECT Didn't nobody agree to clean up?
CORRECT Didn't anybody agree to clean up?
CORRECT Did nobody agree to clean up?

INCORRECT I haven't got no time for nothing except studying.
CORRECT I have no time for anything except studying.
CORRECT I haven't got any time for anything except studying.

As shown above, in eliminating a negative, you often replace a word—for example, replace *never* with *ever*, and *nobody* with *anybody*.

● Some adjectives—such as *excellent*, *perfect*, *faultless*, *flawless*, *ideal*, *immaculate*, and *unique*—don't take comparative or superlative forms. These are **absolute adjectives**. They are already "the most" they can be. For example, if something is *flawless* ("without a flaw"), it can't be "more flawless"; if something is *unique* ("one of a kind"), it can't be "most unique."

> Her description of the event was flawless. She made it clear that the moment was unique.

Editing Tip

When it is essential to your meaning, two *not's* in a row are acceptable in standard English; likewise, *not* followed by a negative prefix is sometimes permitted.

I won't *not* give in, but I need time to think about the matter.

He's not unattractive.

Enriching Your Vocabulary

The noun *inkling* in Exercise 7 comes from the Middle English word *ingkiling*. The word and its root both mean "a hint" or "a suspicion." The detective had an *inkling* that the heiress was murdered by the butler.

Exercise 7 Editing Sentences

Review these sentences for their use of modifiers. Watch for double negatives and for the incorrect use of absolute adjectives. If you find an error, rewrite the sentence correctly. If a sentence is correct, write *C*.

1. In the Verde Valley in central Arizona are remnants of two distinct

   Native American cultures that once flourished there. C

2. The first of these ~~very~~ unique cultures, the Hohokam, was made up of farmers, who moved into the valley in the seventh century.

3. The Sinagua, who didn't know ~~no~~ ^{any} Hohokam, lived in pit houses in the nearby foothills and on the plateau beyond them.

4. None of the Hohokam ~~didn't stay~~ ^{stayed} in the valley; they migrated north to lands made fertile by the eruptions of a volcano.

5. At that point, the Sinagua, who wouldn't ~~never~~ ^{ever} miss such an opportunity, began using the irrigation system the Hohokam had left behind.

6. You can't ~~hardly~~ blame them.

7. Then the Sinagua began constructing above-ground dwellings, much like those ~~way super~~ perfect "apartment houses" that the Anasazi had built.

8. Anthropologists ~~don't~~ have no inkling why the Sinagua abandoned their sites in the early 1400s.

9. If you ever visit this area, you ~~wouldn't never~~ ^{won't} want to miss the Sinaguan sites, including Montezuma Castle, a five-story cliff dwelling.

10. Montezuma Castle is an odd name for the ruin, since the building ~~doesn't have~~ ^{has} nothing to do with Montezuma, and it's not ~~no~~ ^a castle.

Exercise 8 Editing a Paragraph

Correct all double negatives in the paragraph below as well as any errors with other modifiers.

¹The saguaro cactus doesn't grow ~~nowhere~~ ^{anywhere} except in the Sonoran Desert of Arizona and Mexico and in the Baja Peninsula. ²You ~~can't~~ ^{can} hardly miss them; they're the ones with the arms. ³It is not unexpected for these giants to reach heights of sixty feet and to live for more than 150 years. ⁴These cacti survive in the desert because of their ~~very~~ unique ability to retain moisture. ⁵Through a ~~most~~ flawless system of expanding pleats, the saguaro can store as much as eight tons of moisture after a rainy season. ⁶That statement ~~ain't~~ ^{is} no lie. ⁷These sturdy, majestic giants couldn't ~~hardly~~ live without this uncanny ability.

Misplaced Modifiers

A **misplaced modifier** is a word, phrase, or clause that's in the wrong place. It modifies a word that is different from the one it's meant to modify.

Misplaced modifiers may be confusing and misleading; they may force a reader to reread the sentence to understand its meaning. Also, misplaced modifiers may unintentionally make humorous interpretations possible.

> The weary traveler boarded the train with a long face.
> At the meeting, we discussed filling swampland with local politicians.

◗ Correct a misplaced modifier by moving it as close as possible to the word it is meant to modify or by changing some words.

MISPLACED	Passing over the stadium, the pitcher saw an airplane.
CORRECTED	The pitcher saw an airplane passing over the stadium.
MISPLACED	The manager screamed at the umpire in the dugout.
CORRECTED	The manager in the dugout screamed at the umpire.
CORRECTED	The manager screamed at the umpire from the dugout.
MISPLACED	Modern and yet traditional, everyone loves the new ballpark.
CORRECTED	Everyone loves the modern, yet traditional, new ballpark.

Notice that in the two preceding examples, the correction involves new constructions altogether.

Writing Hint

Make sure that the adverb *only* modifies the word you mean it to modify. Place *only* directly before the word or phrase it modifies.

MISPLACED
I only practice in the morning. [This implies that you don't do anything else in the morning.]

CORRECTED
I practice only in the morning. [Now it's clear that when you practice, you do so in the morning.]

Exercise 9 Editing Headlines

Rewrite each of the following newspaper headlines so that it makes sense.

VALUABLE COIN WITH TWO HEADS FOUND BY BUS DRIVER
1. VALUABLE COIN FOUND BY BUS DRIVER WITH TWO HEADS

CAR GOING 50 MILES PER HOUR CRASHES INTO LAMPPOST
2. CAR CRASHES INTO LAMPPOST GOING 50 MILES PER HOUR

CHILD STAR, ALONG WITH HIS MOTHER, BUYS MANSION
3. CHILD STAR BUYS MANSION ALONG WITH HIS MOTHER

PHILANTHROPIST DIES AT AGE OF 97 IN HOUSE IN WHICH SHE WAS BORN
4. PHILANTHROPIST DIES IN HOUSE IN WHICH SHE WAS BORN AT

   AGE OF 97

PLANE DELIVERS FOOD AND MEDICINE NEEDED BY HUNGRY AND SICK VILLAGERS
5. HUNGRY AND SICK, PLANE DELIVERS FOOD AND MEDICINE

   NEEDED BY VILLAGERS

Enriching Your Vocabulary

A synonym for *philanthropic* is the seldom used word *eleemosynary*, which stems from the Greek *eleos*, meaning "mercy." The mission of the church was primarily *eleemosynary*; all donations went directly to the poor.

SMITH'S BEHAVIOR AS BOSS CONDEMNED

6. AS BOSS, SMITH'S BEHAVIOR CONDEMNED

CRAWLING UNDER HIS PORCH, MAN FINDS COMPLETE MASTODON SKELETON

7. MAN FINDS COMPLETE MASTODON SKELETON CRAWLING

UNDER PORCH

JUDGE SENDS POLITICIAN, FOUND GUILTY OF PERJURY, TO PRISON

8. FOUND GUILTY OF PERJURY, JUDGE SENDS POLITICIAN TO PRISON

WOMAN DONATES ARTIFACT FOUND IN BACKYARD TO MUSEUM

9. WOMAN DONATES ARTIFACT TO MUSEUM FOUND IN BACKYARD

MAJOR DISCOVERY OF LOST CITY FROM 12TH CENTURY LEAKED TO PRESS

10. MAJOR DISCOVERY OF LOST CITY LEAKED TO PRESS FROM 12TH CENTURY

Exercise 10 Editing A Story Beginning

Work with a partner to correct misplaced modifiers in this story beginning. Compare your changes with those made by other pairs. Answers may vary. Sample answers are given.

During our social studies class,
¹I told my friends about how I got the game-winning hit during our social

Since I am
studies class. ²As a good storyteller, my friends listened intently. ³I told them

when I stepped
how I saw teammates on all three bases stepping up to the plate. ⁴I only missed

only   I had
the first pitch by a hair. ⁵After two swings and misses, the pitcher eyed me

He leaned
menacingly, leaning forward from the pitching-mound rubber. ⁶He threw a

, which I was awaiting,   in that moment,
fastball right down the middle of the plate which I was awaiting. ⁷Luckily, I

had been
remembered all the hitting hints that I was taught in that moment.

Exercise 11 Continuing a Story

On a separate piece of paper, continue the story started in Exercise 10. Use your imagination. You should work with a partner, but neither one of you needs to know much about baseball to pick up where the story leaves off. Then, exchange papers with another pair. Check each other's work for misplaced modifiers, double negatives, and absolute adjectives.
Continuations will vary; discuss insertions and corrections of misplaced modifiers with students. See teacher pages for assessment rubrics.

Dangling Modifiers

A **dangling modifier** is a word, phrase, or clause that doesn't clearly and logically modify any word in the sentence.

> While watching TV, the cable went out.

In the sentence above, the introductory phrase is a dangling modifier because it appears to modify the word *cable*. Since a cable cannot watch television, the modifier is not misplaced; it simply doesn't make sense.

BETTER   While **we** were watching TV, the cable went out.

🖋 Correct a dangling modifier by rewording the sentence to add a word or words that the modifier can modify.

DANGLING   While chatting with friends, the subject of college came up.
CORRECTED   While chatting with friends, I brought up the subject of college.

DANGLING   Riding in the plane, many towns could be seen far below.
CORRECTED   From the plane, passengers could see many towns far below.
CORRECTED   Riding in the plane, we could see many towns far below.

DANGLING   To understand events today, a knowledge of American history is essential.
CORRECTED   To understand events today, one must have a knowledge of American history.
CORRECTED   A knowledge of American history helps a person to understand events today.

You may sometimes correct a dangling modifier in more than one way, as the two preceding examples show.

Exercise 12   Editing Sentences

On a separate piece of paper, write each sentence to correct all dangling modifiers. If a sentence is correct, write *C*.

Answers will vary. Sample revisions are given.

While she was
1. Lying still in bed, the loud storm outside scared her.

we began
2. To get ready for guests, the party preparations ~~began~~ early.

I brought up
3. While talking with teammates, the topic of college coaches ~~came up~~.

4. If you want to understand the rules of rugby, you should watch several games.   C

When he was
5. Carrying grocery bags home, his hat blew off.

I was
6. While trying to do my math homework, someone in the next room began to play the drums.

7. Having promised to return after dinner, ~~were made~~ [I made] my friends anxious when I didn't show up until much later.

8. After driving in the rainstorm for hours, [I noticed that] the rain stopped, and [that] visibility got much better.

9. Anticipating very tough questions, she was relieved at how easy the biology test was.   C

10. Annoyed by ~~his~~ [the manager's] constant complaints, the ~~manager got tossed~~ [umpire tossed the manager] out of the game.

 Working Together

Exercise 13 **Editing an Anecdote**   Answers will vary. Sample answers are given.

Work with a partner to correct dangling modifiers in this anecdote. Compare your changes with those made by another pair.

[1]Entering the small, dimly lit restaurant, ~~many of the tables were empty.~~ [we saw many empty tables.]
[2]While [we were] hanging up our coats, ~~our table was prepared.~~ [the staff prepared our table.] [3]Despite the fact that other tables offered privacy, we were seated right next to a table of three. [4]After a long day of walking all over the big city, ~~little energy remained~~ [we had little energy left] for conversation. [5]We sat silently and looked at our menus. [6]Then, looking around the room, ~~a chill ran~~ [I felt a chill run] down my back.

[7]Sitting at the table next to us, not more than five feet away, ~~could be seen~~ [were] two celebrities. [8]Holding my breath, ~~my sister had to be told.~~ [I had to tell my sister.] [9]I kicked her under the table and nodded in their direction. [10]She gasped. [11]~~Having clued her in~~ [Not yet clued in] to our famous neighbors, my mother wondered what we two were pretending not to stare at.

[12]"What are you two gawking at? . . . Oh, my!"

[13]I guess she figured it out. [14]They were *major* celebrities. [15]Soon the whole family was in the know. [16]~~While~~ [Although] pretending to read the menu and even to carry on our own little conversation, ~~all~~ attention [we focused all our] ~~was focused~~ on the discussion at the next table. [17]After ~~going~~ [we went] on with this charade for what seemed like hours, the waiter arrived and took our order. [18]I don't think I tasted any of my food that night, but I now know that I am a good listener.

Revising and Editing Worksheet 1

Carefully read the following essay about a famous mystery writer. Correct errors in the use of modifiers, and make any other changes you think will improve the piece. Write your revised essay on a separate piece of paper. When you have finished revising and editing, proofread your work, and fix any spelling mistakes you find. Answers will vary. A sample revision is given.

[1]Agatha Mary Clarissa Christie, ~~more~~ better known as Dame Agatha Christie, was ~~not only~~ a ~~writter~~ [writer] of English detective novels but also [not only] of plays. [2]Although [her play] *The Mousetrap* (1952) set a world record for its continuous run at the Ambassador Theatre in London, she is best known for writing novels[.] ~~good.~~ [3]~~Writing~~ [Written] over a period of many years, her detective novels have sold more than one hundred million copies. [4]Many feature the egotistical detective Hercule Poirot or the elderly Miss Jane Marple.

[5]~~Appearing first~~ in *The Mysterious Affair at Styles* (1920), people were [first] introduced to Poirot. [6]~~Nobody~~ [People] didn't know ~~nothing~~ [anything] about Miss Jane Marple until she made her first appearance in *Murder at the Vicarage* (1930). [7]With *The Murder of Roger Ackroyd* (1926), considered by some to be a ~~most~~ perfect novel, Christie achieved recognition. [8]~~Following~~ [After writing] that book, she wrote dozens more, many of which sold extremely ~~good~~ [well]. [9]~~Translated~~ [Because her books have been Translated] into one hundred languages, ~~the whole world has read her books.~~ [people all over the world have read them.]

[10]Several of Christie's novels ~~has~~ [have] been made into films. [11]Perhaps the ~~better~~ [best] of them is *Witness for the Prosecution*. [12]Nobody who has ~~saw~~ [seen] this movie will ~~never~~ [ever] forget ~~it's~~ [its] many unexpected twists and turns. [13]While recalling this film, ~~other~~ [I find that other] movie versions of her novels come to mind[.] ~~,~~[14]~~Like~~ [such as] *Murder on the Orient Express* and *Murder on the Nile*. [15]Christie was made a Dame of the British Empire before her death ~~in 1976, in 1971.~~ [in 1971,] [1976] [16]~~Appearing after her death in 1977,~~ Dame Agatha Christie wrote her autobiography[, which appeared in 1977.]

Revising and Editing Worksheet 2

Carefully read the following essay about two other famous mystery writers. Work with a partner to correct errors in the use of modifiers and to make any other changes you think will improve the piece. Write your revision on a separate piece of paper, and compare your revision with those made by other pairs of classmates. When you have finished revising and editing, proofread your work, and fix any spelling mistakes you find. *Answers will vary. A sample revision is given.*

[1] When ~~discussing~~ *people discuss* famous British mystery writers, the names of Dorothy Sayers and P. D. James inevitably come up. [2] If it weren't for these novelists, we wouldn't ~~never~~ *ever* have heard of the two exceptional (but fictional) sleuths Lord Peter Wimsey, of Oxford, and Inspector Adam Dalgleish, of Scotland Yard. [3] ~~Its~~ *It's* challenging to determine which sleuth is ~~best.~~ *better.*

[4] Sayers, who earned a degree in medieval literature from Oxford University, was among the ~~most earliest~~ *first* women to have graduated from there. [5] After introducing Wimsey, the dashing gentleman scholar, in 1923, ~~he appears~~ *Sayers put him* in one or two ~~Sayers~~ mysteries each year for the next fifteen years. [6] In *Strong Poison*, Sayers introduces Lord Peter to the ~~most~~ perfect woman for him, Harriet Vane.

[7] Wimsey is an aristocrat who ~~only became~~ *becomes* a detective *only* after he ~~discovered~~ *discovers* after graduation that he ~~had~~ *has* a gift for crime detection. [8] This Oxford graduate with a private income is charming, witty, and a lover of books. [9] His servant, Bunter, ~~who~~ aids him in his investigative efforts. [10] While ~~solving~~ *Lord Peter solves* crimes in the Oxford area, ~~the assistance of~~ Inspector Parker ~~is helpful.~~ *assists him.*

[11] P. D. James wrote the first of her mystery novels in 1962. [12] Her books are noted for their ~~most~~ unique characterizations and their vivid sense of atmosphere. [13] Her detective hero, Adam Dalgleish, is actually one of ~~two of~~ this writer's *two* protagonists; Cordelia Gray, a private sleuth, is the other. [14] Dalgleish, in contrast to Wimsey, has climbed up the ladder in Scotland yard, ~~no aristocrat.~~ *is no aristocrat. He* [15] Whereas Lord Peter is cool and detached, Dalgleish is an emotional poet. [16] But, like Lord Peter, Dalgleish's investigative methods are thoughtful and ~~most~~ flawless.

Chapter Review

Exercise A   Using the Degrees of Comparison

Review the following sentences for the correct use of modifiers. If you find an error, cross out the word or phrase, and rewrite it correctly in the space above. If a sentence contains no errors, write *C*.

1. In Seattle in 1998, a competition took place for the world's smallest kite. C

2. Seattle is the ~~most~~ largest city in Washington.

3. Kites in the competition had to soar either at a ten-degree angle of flight or more ~~steeplier~~. steeply

4. One kite was no bigger than a mosquito. C

5. There were no ~~less~~ than twenty kites in the competition. *(fewer)*

6. Most of the miniature kites flew ~~good~~. *(well)*

7. One of the ~~most~~ prettiest kites looked like a birch leaf.

8. All of the kites, from the ~~most~~ tiniest to the greatest, had to be small enough to fit in the palm of the hand.

9. The judges included a test pilot, a mechanical engineer, and an administrator. Which one was the ~~stricter~~? strictest

10. The winner, although not the ~~smaller~~ of all the kites, may get a mention in the Guinness Book of World Records. *(smallest)*

Exercise B   Editing Sentences

On a separate piece of paper, rewrite each sentence to correct all misplaced modifiers and dangling modifiers. See Answer Key.

1. Hanging from a hook in his locker, the pitcher took his cap.

2. The player's shoes hurt his feet, which were too small.

3. The slumping batter learned a new trick from an instructor that would help him.

4. Practicing in the batting cage, it began to rain.

5. Overweight and slow, the coach says our team needs to shape up.

6. As manager, Reilly's desk was always piled with scouting reports.

7. The rookie got on the bus with a big smile.

8. To keep the field in good condition, the grass needs lots of attention.

9. Leaving at 7 P.M., management will have a plane for the players.

10. The team was only bought by Mrs. Leary.

11. While running after a fly ball, there was some commotion in the stands.

CHAPTER REVIEW

12. In the sports magazine's editorial, they applauded the team for trading players.

13. Young but talented and aggressive, all sportswriters like our team's chances of winning.

14. Being young and inexperienced, people think we will make crucial mistakes.

15. Generally speaking, only mature teams win championships.

Exercise C   Editing Sentences

Review these sentences for the correct use of modifiers. If you find an error, rewrite the sentence correctly on a separate piece of paper. If a sentence is correct, write *C*.

1. So you think ~~there isn't~~ ^there's^ nothing about money you don't know?

2. The ~~most~~ oldest written records of money are from ancient Mesopotamia (now southern Iraq).

3. ~~Describing payments in silver,~~ historians have discovered inscribed Mesopotamian tablets. ^describing payments in silver.^

4. The ~~most~~ earliest coins date from the seventh century B.C. in what is now Turkey.

5. ~~Measuring precious metals,~~ ancient Egyptian wall paintings show the weights that were used. ^to measure precious metals.^

6. Money in eighteenth-century Burma was pancake-shaped disks called "flower silver."   C

7. The people of Yap, an island in the Pacific, paid their debts with enormous, ~~most~~ round stone disks.

8. ~~Made from tiny red feathers glued together and tied to coils of vegetable fiber, the islanders of Santa Cruz, in the Pacific, used these huge coils as money.~~

For the islanders of Santa Cruz in the Pacific, money took the form of huge coils that were made from tiny red feathers glued together and tied to coils of vegetable fiber.

9. From the fifteenth century to 1948 in Nigeria, ~~they had~~ ^people^ used copper rings ^,^ ~~as money~~ called *manillas*. ^, as money.^

10. ~~Known as wampum,~~ some North American Indians used belts of beads ^,^ as payment. ^, known as wampum,^

Exercise D   Creating Your Own Exercise

Misplaced and dangling modifiers can be funny. Work with a partner or small group to create a paragraph, at least ten newspaper headlines or sentences with misplaced and dangling modifiers. Then, exchange your efforts with another group. Correct each other's deliberate errors.

Students' misplaced and dangling modifiers will vary; discuss all corrections.

Choosing the Right Word

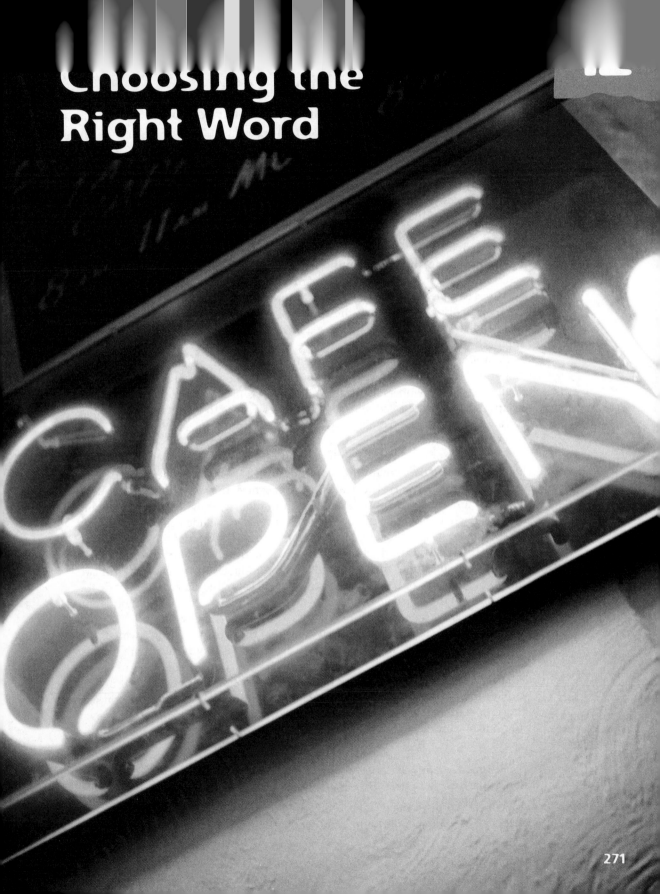

Direct students to
chapter-specific
portfolio projects
on Sadlier-Oxford's
web site.

STUDENT WRITING
Expository Essay

Food for Thought . . . or Maybe Not?
by Jason Farago
high school student, Scarsdale, New York

Lucky you—you've just finished your early morning Greek class, and now you have first period free! Oh, how I envy you. I didn't have time to eat this morning, but you have the luxury of making up for the breakfast you forgot to devour earlier by heading down the staircase to our gossipfest of a cafeteria. There you can enjoy everybody's favorite A.M. delight:

French Toast Stix.

Whence came this anomalous final letter on *stix*? Originally reserved for waitresses and notetakers too lazy to learn stenography, the "x" in place of "ks" or "cks" has become a way to make a word avant-garde, or interesting. Students raised more by Madison Avenue than their parents, the same students who scoff at signs such as "Ice Cream Shoppe" or "Ye Olde Taverne," can identify with this MTV approach to spelling: If it's correct phonetically, write it.

Above the bagels, muffins, and French toast stix appears a sign that, presumably, describes the food under it: *Hot & Healthy*. Anyone who attended his seventh-grade English classes remembers the lecture about the eggplant who does three hundred sit-ups a day and the salad who jogs ten miles a week, both of which would be considered "healthy foods." Of course, the proper word choice is *Hot & Healthful*—unless the sign describes the women who serve the food.

My Poland Spring bottle runneth over with interesting linguistic choices in the high school cafeteria. Perhaps the most intriguing is the text on the awning of the entrance: *Scarsdale Café*. The reader will recognize the definition of *café* as a relatively upscale coffeehouse, usually with outdoor seating. Modern usage and francophilia have modified this once-exclusive term to include what one originally called *bistro*, *restaurant*, *ice cream parlor*, *coffee shop*, and worst of all, *refectory*. The word *café* originally evoked certain senses: smells of freshly brewed espresso, sounds of cappuccino machines that foam milk, visions of tables for four set up with two chairs, both facing out toward the street. . . . This vision hardly matches the atmosphere of the Scarsdale Café, complete with help-yourself cinnamon buns and chicken nuggets on demand. . . .

Language and cuisine share so many traits that they are forever intertwined. The latter has a considerable influence on the former; idioms abound about grapevines, rotten eggs, and cooks who spoil broth. The close relationship between food and language causes words used in the high school cafeteria to receive special notice. Perhaps the next time you visit this school's fine dining establishment, you will notice how interesting the choice of words is. Maybe you'll even discuss it over your lunch—just not with your mouth full. That's disgusting.

Allow time for
students to dis-
cuss the student
writing. Suggest
that they identify
its strengths and
propose possible
improvements.
Use the model
to introduce the
concepts in the
chapter.

Jason Farago's humorous essay discusses the linguistic problems he finds on food signs in the school cafeteria. His essay is effective because he includes many examples.

As you work through the lessons of this chapter, remember to apply Jason's canny observations about choosing the right word.

From *a* to *anyway*

🌢 **a, an** Use *a* before a word that starts with a consonant sound. Use *an* before a word that starts with a vowel sound.

   a television, **a** home run, **a** university, **a** eulogy, **a** one-sided match

   an elevator, **an** upset, **an** X-ray, **an** honest response

🌢 **accept, except** *Accept* is a verb that means "to receive willingly" or "to agree to." *Except* is a preposition that means "but."

   The school agreed to **accept** the company's offer of used computers.

   All students **except** ninth-graders will have access to them.

🌢 **adapt, adopt** *Adapt* means "to adjust to" or "to make fit for a different use." *Adopt* means "to take by choice as one's own."

   When I **adapt** to the climate, I will **adopt** a new way of dressing.

🌢 **advice, advise** *Advice*, a noun, means "a recommendation" or "an opinion." *Advise* is a verb meaning "to offer advice."

   My **advice** is to speak up for yourself.

   I **advise** you to speak to the boss about the promotion.

🌢 **affect, effect** *Affect* is a verb that means "to influence." The noun *effect* means "the result of an action"; the verb *effect* means "to cause" or "to bring about."

   Lack of sleep may **affect** your grades.

   What are the **effects** of the cutbacks in service?

   Time-outs are meant to **effect** a change in the way a team performs.

🌢 **all ready, already** *All ready,* an adjective, means "completely ready." *Already* is an adverb meaning "previously."

   I have **already** packed my suitcase and am **all ready** to leave.

🌢 **all right** *All right* is always two words. There's no such word as *alright.*

   Is it **all right** to invite her?

🌢 **all the farther, all the faster** Use *as far as* and *as fast as*.

   One mile is **as far as** she can run. She runs **as fast as** she can.

🌢 **all together, altogether** *All together* means "in a group." *Altogether* is an adverb that means "completely" or "in all."

   I worked on the school newspaper for four years **altogether**.

   I kept the papers **all together** in my drawer.

Enriching Your Vocabulary

The root of *eulogy* is the Greek *eulogia,* meaning "praise." Every Memorial Day, the mayor delivers a *eulogy* extolling the selfless devotion of those who have died in defense of this country.

The word *eulogy* starts with the consonant sound /y/; *one-sided* starts with the sound /w/; *honest* starts with the vowel sound /ô/.

Writing Hint

Although *affect* usually works as a verb, you may occasionally see it or use it as a noun. As a noun, it means "a feeling" or "an emotion," as in the following sentence.

The psychologist was concerned about the flat **affect** of the patient who had just learned of his sister's death.

💧 **allusion, illusion** An *allusion* is "an implied or indirect reference."
An *illusion* is "an unreal impression."

    The poem contained an **allusion** to World War II.

    The magician created the **illusion** that the woman was floating.

💧 **amount, number** Both words refer to a quantity. Use *amount* with nouns
that cannot be counted (for example, *water* or *sand*). Use *number* with nouns
that can be counted (for example, *books* or *calories*).

    The **amount** of junk mail that we receive is staggering.

    The **number** of people at the party kept increasing.

💧 **and etc., etc.** *Etc.* means "and so forth." Never use the word *and* before *etc.*

    We brought sandwiches, chips, drinks, cookies, fruit, ~~and etc~~.   *Etc.* is the abbreviation of
                                         the Latin words *et cetera.*

💧 **anyway, anyways** The word *anyway* does not end with an *-s*.

    I didn't make the team, but I went to the games **anyway**.

Exercise 1 **Revising and Editing a Report**

Review the following paragraphs to correct all errors in word choice.

                                  adapt
¹Prehistoric people struggled to ~~adopt~~ to their environment, but they did

                                    an
little to change it. ²Mere survival was ~~a~~ ongoing concern. ³The focus on survival

                     anyway
persisted, ~~anyways~~, until about thirty thousand years ago, when art began in

the form of cave paintings. ⁴On cave walls in Altamira, Spain, and Lascaux,

                                  number
France, people painted a great ~~amount~~ of bison, reindeer, and other animals.

                 all right
    ⁵It is ~~alright~~ to say that the Lascaux paintings constitute history's first art

                                                 Except
gallery. ⁶The group includes deer, horses, jungle cats, large bulls, ~~and~~ etc. ⁷~~Accept~~

for the smaller figures, the animals are not colored, just outlined in black. ⁸Those

smaller figures were probably "spray painted" by a technique that involved

                                        adapted
blowing pigment through hollow bones or reeds ~~adopted~~ for that purpose.

    ⁹The paintings at Altamira also demonstrate very skillful execution. ¹⁰From

artifacts found at this site, scientists have deduced that those people were not

           already
~~all ready~~ living in the caves but were using them solely to paint and maybe to

                  a number
perform ~~an amount~~ of religious ceremonies.   Students' revisions may vary.
                                                     Sample revisions are given.

From *anywheres* to *different from*

● **anywheres, everywheres, nowheres, somewheres** These words are spelled incorrectly. They do not have an *-s* at the end.

> There were people **everywhere**. **Somewhere**, there must be a seat.

● **at** Don't use the word *at* after *where*.

> Where is the party ~~at~~?

● **bad, badly** Use *bad*, which is always an adjective, after a linking verb. Use *badly*, an adverb, to modify an action verb.

> He plays **badly**. I feel **bad** about his poor playing.

● **being as, being that** Neither of these is standard English. Don't use either. Use *since* or *because*.

> **Because** she lived in Paris, she speaks French.

● **beside, besides** *Beside* means "by the side of." *Besides* means "in addition to." *Besides* as an adverb means "moreover."

> We rested **beside** the falls. **Besides** me, John and Dolores were there.
> We were hungry; **besides**, we were tired of lugging our packs.

● **between, among** Use *between* to refer to two people or things. You can also use *between* when discussing three or more items if you think that only two will be compared at a time. Use *among* to refer either to a group of people or things or to three or more people or things.

> **Between** you and me, we'll get the job done in an hour.
> Can you tell the difference **between** a saguaro, a cholla, and a prickly pear?
> We chose from **among** several routes.

● **borrow, lend, loan** *Borrow* means "to take something temporarily that must be returned." *Lend*, the opposite of *borrow*, means "to give something temporarily." Don't confuse *loan* and *lend*. *Loan* is always a noun; it's the thing that's *lent*.

> Jerome asked to **borrow** ten dollars. I agreed to **lend** him the money. He said that he would repay the **loan** within a week.

● **bring, take** *Bring* refers to a movement toward or with the speaker. *Take* refers to a movement away from the speaker. *Bring* is related to *come*; *take* is related to *go*.

> **Bring** your CDs when you come over. Don't **take** any of mine when you go home.

Editing Tip

Most of the time, when you say or write *feel*, you should follow it with *bad*, not *badly*.

> I feel ~~badly~~ **bad** that you can't come to the party.

"Feeling bad" is about emotions; "feeling badly" is about the sense of touch.

can, may Use *can* to show the ability to do something. Use *may* to show permission to do something or the possibility of doing something.

I know you **can** sing loudly and brightly, but you **may** not do so in this choir.

cite, site, sight *Cite* is a verb that means "to call upon officially" or "to quote by way of example." *Site*, a noun, is "a place." *Sight* is a noun that means, among other things, "something worth seeing" or the "process of seeing."

The attorney **cited** several prior cases in her argument.

We arrived at the **site** of the excavation and were met with an impressive **sight**.

complement, compliment *Complement* means "something that completes or makes perfect." *Compliment* means "to praise."

She **complimented** me by saying that my tie **complemented** my jacket.

could (might, should, would) of Use *have*, not *of*, with these helping verbs.

Ariel **should have** worn her best dress to the graduation.

data *Data* is the plural form of *datum*. It is frequently used, informally, with a singular verb. Formally, it is plural.

The financial **data** are almost ready; when do you need **them**?

different from When comparing two nouns, use *from*, not *than*, after *different*.

Mars is **different from** Earth.

Exercise 2 Choosing the Right Word

Underline the word in parentheses that correctly completes each sentence.

The following two questions relating to Exercise 2 may be used as a writing prompt.

• Can you get a good job without a college education?

• Should everyone be required to go to college?

Ask students to state an opinion and support it with facts, examples, and reasons.

1. Felicia is deciding (among, <u>between</u>) state schools and private schools.

2. Helen is looking at the data that (has, <u>have</u>) come in.

3. Parents worry about whether they (<u>can</u>, may) afford college tuition.

4. The (cite, <u>site</u>) for the new gymnasium has been chosen.

5. (Beside, <u>Besides</u>) local colleges, Leslie is looking at some that are out of town.

6. Edgar can (sight, <u>cite</u>) ten colleges that he thinks will accept him.

7. Angela hopes she can get somebody to (<u>lend</u>, loan) her the money.

8. Lincoln University is (<u>among</u>, between) the five schools she applied to.

9. (Being as, <u>Because</u>) Will has an interest in science, he's applying to schools known for their science faculty.

10. Lenny believes that taking a year off first and traveling will (<u>complement</u>, compliment) his formal studies.

From *discover* to *it's*

● **discover, invent** *Discover* means "to find something for the first time." *Invent* means "to think up and produce something new."

The campers **discovered** a shortcut through the woods.
In 1920, Earle Dickson **invented** the first Band-Aid.

● **disinterested, uninterested** *Disinterested* means "fair," "free of bias," or "impartial." *Uninterested* means "showing no interest."

For an independent prosecutor to be effective, he or she needs to be **disinterested** in the outcome of the investigation.
She was **uninterested** in the outcome of the World Series.

● **emigrate, immigrate** To *emigrate* means "to move away" from one country to settle in another." To *immigrate* means "to come into a country to settle there."

When the famine hit Ireland, many people **emigrated** from that country.
Many Irish **immigrated** to the United States after the famine began.

● **explicit, implicit** *Explicit* means "fully revealed" or "unambiguous." *Implicit* means "understood even though not directly expressed."

The player was **explicit** about his reaction to the umpire's call; he screamed, "You're blind!"
The player showed only an **implicit** reaction to the call; he stared at the ground and then walked silently away.

● **farther, further** *Farther* refers to physical distance. *Further* refers to additional degree or time.

Which is **farther** from Boston—Springfield or Providence?
They said that nothing could be **further** from the truth.

● **fewer, less** *Fewer* refers to nouns that can be counted. *Less* refers to nouns that can't be counted.

I eat **fewer** donuts than I used to but not **less** meat.

● **good, well** *Good* is always an adjective, never an adverb; *good* after *feel* often means "happy" or "content." *Well*, however, can be both an adjective and adverb. The adverb *well* means "done in a satisfactory way." The adjective *well* means "in good health."

It felt **good** to feel **well** after two weeks with a fever.
Now he will work to play **well** again.

● **had ought, hadn't ought** Drop the *had*; use just *ought* and *ought not.*

They **ought not** to have left without saying, "Good-bye."

Enriching Your Vocabulary

The adjective *explicit* comes from the Latin verb *explicare*, meaning "to disentangle." In English, it means "definite" or "readily observable." The coach gave *explicit* directions for getting to the away game.

This list (page 278) warns you not to use the nonword *irregardless*. Another nonword is *hisself*; there is no such word. Use *himself.*

He built the model ~~hisself~~. **himself**

🖊 **hopefully** *Hopefully* is an adverb and is used to describe doing something "with hope." Do not use *hopefully* to replace *I hope that . . . .*

> We stood at the backstage door **hopefully**.
> **I hope that** we'll see the star of the play.

🖊 **imply, infer** To *imply* is "to suggest or hint." To *infer* is "to understand a hint or suggestion."

> A movie director might **imply** a theme in a film. The viewer must **infer** the theme from the plot, setting, characters, or point of view.

🖊 **in, into** *In* indicates condition or location, whereas *into* suggests movement from the outside to the inside.

> I waited to get **into** the stadium. Once I was **in** the stadium, I found my seat.

🖊 **irregardless, regardless** Always use *regardless*; *irregardless* isn't a word.

> Will the manager be fired, **regardless** of his track record?

🖊 **it's, its** *It's* is a contraction for "it is" or "it has." *Its* is a possessive pronoun.

> **It's** painful to watch the car begin to lose **its** value as soon as it leaves the showroom.

Exercise 3 Choosing the Right Word

Underline the word in parentheses that correctly completes each sentence.

Suggest that students work with partners to make up mnemonic devices for one or more of the easily confused words in this lesson or the preceding ones. Mnemonic devices will vary. To help students get started, provide the device for remembering the distintion between *lend*, a verb, and *loan*, a noun: "Friends, Romans, countrymen, *lend* me your ears. (OK, folks, I'm returning your ears. Thanks for the *loan*.)"

1. I (discovered, invented) a book of etymology buried under the house.

2. The expression *the coast is clear* goes (farther, further) back than Shakespeare's use of it in *Henry VI*.

3. The word *brokenhearted* interests me. I can trace (its, it's) use to 1526.

4. The expression *the best-laid plans of mice and men*, which came (in, into) the language in the eighteenth century, was penned by the Scottish poet Robert Burns.

5. A book that sells (fewer, less) copies than most will never be a *best-seller*, another term of American origin that was first recorded in 1905.

6. The term *bigfoot*, which first appeared in 1958, is an (explicit, implicit) reference to Sasquatch, that huge hairy figure reported to exist in the California mountains.

7. (Irregardless, Regardless) of its original meaning, a *big wheel* today is also known as a *bigwig*, *big shot*, *big cheese*, *big fish*, and *big dog*.

8. The book of etymology aged (good, well) because it had been in a metal box.

From *lay* to *seldom*

◖ **lay, lie** *Lay*, which means "to set something down," always takes a direct object. *Lie*, which means "to place oneself down" or "to stay at rest in a horizontal position," does not take a direct object.

> **Lie** on the blanket, and I will **lay** the sun block, books, and drinks beside you.

■ See **Usage**, Lesson 8.3, for more on *lay* and *lie*.

◖ **like, as, as if, as though** Don't use the preposition *like* to introduce a subordinate clause; instead, use *as*, *as if*, or *as though* before a subordinate clause.

> He left after dinner, **as** he said he would.
> She looks **as if** she's truly happy. It's not **like** her to be happy.

◖ **loose, lose** *Loose* means "not tight." *Lose* means "to misplace."

> You may **lose** your earring because it is too **loose**.

◖ **most, almost** *Almost* means "very nearly but not exactly." *Most* means "the greatest in quantity."

> We're **almost** finished; **most** of the books are packed.

◖ **off, off of** Don't use *of* after the prepositions *inside*, *outside*, and *off*. Also, use *from*, not *off* or *off of*, when you're referring to the source of something.

> I took the apples **off** ~~of~~ the table and put them **inside** ~~of~~ the cabinet.
> I got the car keys **from** my father.

◖ **passed, past** *Passed* is the past tense of *pass* and means "went or gone by." *Past*, as a noun, means "a former time." As a preposition, it means "beyond."

> Driving **past** the mall, we **passed** our friends in their car.

◖ **percent, percentage** *Percent* is an adverb that means "per hundred." *Percentage*, a noun, means "a part of a whole expressed in hundredths."

> Eighty **percent** of the population voted for her; that's a huge **percentage**.

◖ **precede, proceed** *Precede* means "to come before." *Proceed* means "to continue."

> A speech will **precede** the dinner; then the festivities can **proceed**.

Step by Step

To decide whether to use *principal* or *principle*:

1. Decide if you need an adjective or a noun.
2. If you need an adjective, use *principal*.
3. If you need a noun, use *principle* only if you mean "a fundamental rule or truth."

principal, principle *Principal*, as an adjective, means "of chief importance." As a noun, it means "a chief person, such as the head of a school" or "an amount on which interest is computed." *Principle*, always a noun, means "a fundamental rule or truth."

Our **principal** runs our school smoothly. The **principal** reason for her success is her fairness.

When faced with tough issues, she always sticks to her **principles**.

The investor earned eight percent on his **principal**.

■ The principal parts of the verb *rise* are in Usage, Lesson 8.3.

raise, rise *Raise*, which means "to lift up," always takes a direct object. *Rise*, which does not take a direct object, means "to go up" or "to get up."

At camp, we **raise** the flag right after we **rise** each morning.

real, really *Real* is an adjective that means "actual." *Really* is an adverb that means "actually" or "genuinely."

The election results were a **real** surprise. We were **really** excited.

reason is because Don't use *because* after *reason is*.

The **reason** for my hunger **is that** I haven't eaten since breakfast.

I am hungry **because** I haven't eaten since breakfast.

seldom, seldom ever Strictly speaking, *ever* is redundant after *seldom*.

She is **seldom** on time.

Exercise 4 Revising and Editing a Paragraph

Cross out the words that are used incorrectly, and write the correct words above them. **Hint:** Some sentences have more than one error. Revisions will vary. Sample revisions are given.

¹Alex used to play the piano ~~most~~ (almost) every day. ²Now he seldom ~~ever~~ does. ³The reason he gives is ~~because~~ (that) he thinks he plays ~~like~~ (as if) he has ten thumbs. ⁴He claims the reason for cutting back is ~~because~~ (that) unless he plays ~~real good~~ (really well), he doesn't want to play at all. ⁵However, his friend Andrew disagrees with him and his ~~principals~~ (principles). ⁶He says that Alex should ~~precede~~ (proceed) to play just for the pleasure he gets ~~off of~~ (from) it and not to be the best pianist there is. ⁷The ~~percent~~ (percentage) of players who play ~~real~~ (really) well is small. ⁸He urges Alex to ~~loose~~ (lose) his attitude and start playing regularly again.

From set to which

▸ **set, sit** *Set* means "to place" or "to put." *Set* takes a direct object except when it refers to the sun. *Sit*, which means "to occupy a seat," does not take a direct object.

   Let's **set** the beach chairs down and **sit** for a while as the sun **sets**.

■ See **Usage**, Lesson 8.3, for more on *set* and *sit*.

▸ **shall, will** Although the old distinction between these words is no longer observed by most people, use *shall* in polite questions.

   I **shall** be glad to help.   *Or*   I **will** be glad to help.
   Shall we help?

▸ **slow, slowly** *Slow* is an adjective. Other than in the expressions *Drive slow* and *Go slow*, which have become acceptable because of their wide use on road signs, don't use *slow* as an adverb. *Slowly* is always an adverb.

   She is a **slow** driver who drives **slowly** around curves.

▸ **some, somewhat** *Some* is an adjective. *Somewhat* is an adverb meaning "rather" or "a bit." Don't use *some* as an adverb.

   Some movie producers are filled with avarice; in hope of a big hit, many produce **somewhat** inferior films.

▸ **stationary, stationery** *Stationary* is an adjective meaning "fixed," "still," or "in one place." *Stationery* is a noun that means "letter paper."

   The word processor was **stationary** on the desk. The **stationery** was in the printer.

▸ **sure, surely** In formal writing, avoid using *sure* when you mean "surely," "certainly," or "without a doubt."

   He **certainly** [or **surely**] didn't mean to hurt your feelings.
   I am **sure** of one thing: My grades are good.

▸ **than, then** *Than* is a conjunction that introduces a subordinate clause, the second part of a comparison. *Then* is an adverb meaning "therefore" or "next in order or time."

   I study harder **than** she does. **Then** why don't I get higher test scores? I'll watch how she takes notes in class; **then** I'll adopt her system.

▸ **these, those, them** Don't use *them* as an adjective. Use *those* or *these*.

   Have you seen all of **those** videos? I've seen only **these** three.
   I watched **them** at my friend's house.

Enriching Your Vocabulary

The noun *avarice* comes from the Latin noun *avaritia*, meaning "greed." A synonym is *cupidity*. Both mean "greed for riches." One of the seven deadly sins, *avarice* usually afflicts misers and wealthy people.

this here, those there In standard English, *this*, *that*, *these*, and *those* are used alone. Drop *here* or *there*.

I'll change **this** ~~here~~ old light bulb.

try and Don't use *and* with *try*. Use *to*.

I'll **try to** get there on time, but if you're early, **try to** find us two seats.

way, ways *Ways* is sometimes used informally in place of *way*, but in formal speaking and writing, use *way* to refer to a distance.

By the evening, they were a long **way** from home.

when, where When you define a word, don't use *when* or *is when*. *Where* refers to a place. Don't use *where* to mean "that."

Multiplying **is** ~~when~~ ~~you do~~ repeated addition.

that
I heard ~~where~~ violence on TV causes kids to be violent.

■ See Usage, Lesson 10.3, for more on *who* and *whom*.

which, that, who, whom Each of these relative pronouns has its own job. Use *which* or *that* to refer to things—preferably, *which* when the clause is nonessential and *that* when the clause is essential. Use *who* and *whom* to refer to people—*who* to a subject or a predicate nominative, and *whom* to an object.

Our team is going to the state finals, **which** begin next Tuesday.

The game **that** I want to see is against Woodhaven High.

Mr. Lopez, **who** has twenty years' experience, coaches the boys.

Mr. Lopez, **whom** I admire, inspires hard work.

Exercise 5 **Writing Correct Sentences**

On a separate piece of paper, write an interesting and complete sentence for each of the words below. Underline the word in your sentence, and then exchange papers with a classmate. Check to see whether your partner has used his or her underlined words correctly. Then, if necessary, revise your own sentences.

1. set
2. sit
3. who
4. sure
5. somewhat

6. slowly
7. way
8. stationary
9. than
10. then

Sample sentences:
1. She <u>set</u> the chess set on the table.
2. From where I <u>sit</u>, I can see the whole game.
3. My brother was the only one <u>who</u> liked the movie.
4. The detective was <u>sure</u> the woman was guilty.
5. I was <u>somewhat</u> nervous about driving on the snowy roads.

6. Unsure of herself, she moved <u>slowly</u>.
7. Considering how little he knew at first, he has come a long <u>way</u>.
8. The kitchen phone is <u>stationary</u>, so I can't walk around with it.
9. His mother is a better player <u>than</u> his father.
10. First, they chose their pieces, <u>then</u> he made the first move.

In the following draft of an essay, correct errors in the choice of words, and make any other changes that you think will improve the paragraphs. Write your revised report on a separate piece of paper. When you have finished revising and editing, proofread your work, and fix any spelling mistakes you find.

[1]Alan Sillitoe's angry accounts of working-class lives ~~sure~~ *surely* introduced an ~~all together~~ *altogether* new vitality into post–World War II British fiction. [2]His father was ~~a~~ *an* illiterate and often unemployed laborer. [3]Sillitoe ~~hisself~~ *himself* began working in 1932 at the age of fourteen. [4]The ~~cite~~ *site* of his work was a bicycle factory. [5]He later served with the Royal Air Force in Malaya. [6]Then he was hospitalized for more ~~then~~ *than* a year. ~~[7]The reason was~~ because he had contracted tuberculosis. [8]~~Anyways,~~ while time ~~past~~ *passed* in the hospital, Sillitoe began reading extensively. [9]It was then that he ~~invented~~ *discovered* his interest in writing.

[10]Sillitoe's first novel, an immediate success, was *Saturday Night and Sunday Morning*. [11]~~Its~~ *It's* a fictional biography that tells the story of Arthur Seaton, ~~a~~ *an* angry young laborer, [12]~~Whose~~ weekend life has the ~~affect~~ *effect* of providing him with escape from the drudgery of his daily job. [13]The film version of *Saturday Night and Sunday Morning*, ~~staring~~ *starring* Albert Finney as Seaton, ~~come~~ *came* out in 1960.

[14]Another of Sillitoe's works, *one* that ~~farther~~ *further* explores the theme of alienation ~~between~~ *among* working people, is *The Loneliness of the Long Distance Runner*. [15]~~Its~~ *It's* the title story in a short-story collection and perhaps Sillitoe's best-known work. [16]*The Loneliness of the Long Distance Runner* is a first-person account of a brash and angry teenager ~~whom~~ *who* rebels against ~~a~~ *an* establishment that, he believes, has treated him ~~bad~~ *badly*.

[17]Alan Sillitoe has ~~writen~~ *written* several other works. [18]Essays, volumes of poetry, and even plays and screenplays. [19]He has written children's books also. [20]*Raw Material*, written in 1972, is semiautobiographical.

Students' revisions will vary. Sample revisions are given.

Revising and Editing Worksheet 2

In the following draft of a book review, correct errors in the choice of words, and make any other changes that you think will improve the paragraphs. Work with a partner to revise and edit the paragraphs. Write your revised review on a separate piece of paper, and compare your revisions with those made by your classmates. When you have finished revising and editing, proofread your work, and fix any spelling mistakes.   *Students' revisions will vary. Sample revisions given.*

[1]Think about all the things that have been ~~discovered~~ [invented] and that ~~effect~~ [affect] our lives today—from canals to batteries. [2]~~Whom discovered~~ [Who invented] them? [3]If you want to read an ~~all together~~ [altogether] fascinating book about several of the world's oldest and most wonderful ~~discoveries~~ [inventions], I ~~advice~~ [advise] you to pick up *Ancient Inventions* by Peter James and Nick Thorpe, ~~its~~ [It's] great. [4]~~Its written real good, two~~ [and it's well-written, too]. [5]If you can't find it in the library or in a bookstore, ask a friend to ~~loan~~ [lend] you a copy.

[6]What we can gain from studying earlier ~~inventions~~ [discoveries] in medicine, transportation, communication, and other fields, ~~irregardless~~ [regardless] of when ~~it~~ [they] happened, ~~hadn't~~ [not] ought to go unnoticed. [7]Modern scientists have ~~sure~~ [surely] gotten ~~off of~~ [from] the ancients ~~alot~~ [a considerable number] of ideas on topics ~~like~~ [as far ranging as] brain surgery, automated doors, chewing gum, perfume, ~~and~~ etc. [8]~~Anyways,~~ [T]his ~~here~~ book tells an astonishing ~~amount~~ [number] of amazing stories about human ingenuity ~~everywheres~~ [everywhere] around the globe. [9]You'll love it, and the reason is ~~because~~ [that] it lets you appreciate the ongoing human spirit of curiosity and experimentation. [10]~~Beside, its~~ [Besides, it's] fun to read all the data that ~~appears~~ [appear] on each page.

[11]With concrete example after example, the authors are ~~implicit~~ [explicit] in stating that the human brain has not evolved at all in the last fifty thousand years. [12]Many readers don't know that ~~there~~ fact. [13]Reading this book made it ~~real~~ [really] clear to me that modern people are no smarter ~~then~~ [than] ancient people; they just benefit from thousands of years of accumulated knowledge and experimentation. [14]It has taught me that we have so much to learn from ~~passed~~ [past] explorations by ancient scientists and inventors.

Chapter Review

Exercise A **Choosing the Right Word**

Underline the word in parentheses that correctly completes each sentence.

1. The playwright made several (allusions, illusions) to real events.

2. A larger (amount, number) of people attended (than, then) were expected.

3. She felt (bad, badly) when the other applicant got the job.

4. Will you please (lend, loan) me the cab fare?

5. Jed and Kai kept their feelings about each other (among, between) them.

6. The pear was a perfect (complement, compliment) to the cheese.

7. The case needed (a, an) (disinterested, uninterested) third party.

8. With her new car, she gets (fewer, less) miles to the gallon.

9. As soon as we stepped (in, into) the greenhouse, we felt the humidity.

10. I (implied, inferred) from her stare that she was not pleased.

11. She played (good, well) up until her last-second shot at the basket.

12. In composing his speech for graduation, he did (good, well).

13. (Irregardless, Regardless) of the outcome, it has been a great game.

14. For someone (that, who) loves pizza, (this, this here) pie will hit the spot.

15. The sign warned hikers to (precede, proceed) at their own risk.

16. The new (principal, principle) has strong (principals, principles).

17. The earthquake caused the ground to (real, really) (raise, rise) up.

18. The dentist asked me to (set, sit) in (that, that there) chair.

19. The gym had a new (stationary, stationery) bicycle.

20. Each new song at the concert was better (than, then) the one before it.

21. We opened the cage door (slow, slowly) and slipped in the food.

22. The rain increased (some, somewhat) after lunch.

23. He jumped (off, off of) the raft.

24. The children are (laying, lying) on the couch, asleep.

25. Even children understand the (principal, principle) of hot air
    (raising, rising).

26. In a theory (seldom, seldom ever) debated, some archeologists and
    scientists place balloon flight much (further, farther) in the past.

27. You may have heard (that, where) the Nazca lines in Peru were the work
    of ancient astronomers.

Exercise B **Revising and Editing a Paragraph**

Cross out the words that are used incorrectly, and write the correct words above them. **Hint:** Some sentences have more than one error; one has no errors.   Revisions may vary. Sample revisions are given.

¹~~Its~~ [It's] no ~~allusion~~ [illusion] ~~,~~ [.] there's a beeper in many a high school kid's pocket.

²We can ~~site~~ [cite] two good reasons for this development: Parents can use the beepers to keep in touch with their kids, and, ~~beside that~~ [besides], kids think they are cool. ³But ~~irregardless~~ [regardless] of parental plans, the reality is that as soon as kids get their beepers, they ~~loose~~ [lose] contact with their folks. ⁴The reason is ~~because~~ [that] a huge ~~percent~~ [percentage] of them use the beepers only to stay in contact with their pals, a communication they need to maintain.

⁵~~Being as~~ [Like] any trend ~~between~~ [among] teens, the beeper universe has its own conventions and language. ⁶The language is a ~~real~~ [really] simple one ~~being that~~ [because] the beepers that most kids have transmit only numbers, not words. ⁷Teens' beeper vocabulary has increased ~~some all ready~~ [somewhat already]. ⁸For example, ~~most~~ [almost] all kids know that 911 means "call me right away" and that 101 means "I've got an easy question." ⁹But some groups develop their own syntax, ~~adapt~~ [adopt] their own code, and even assign an identifier for each person. ¹⁰~~Anyways~~ [Anyway], do you have a beeper? ¹¹If so, is your beeptalk rightside up, upside down, or sideways?

Exercise C **Writing Correct Sentences**

On a separate piece of paper, write an interesting and complete sentence for each of the words below. Underline the word in your sentence, and then exchange papers with a classmate. Check to see if your partner has used his or her underlined words correctly. Then, if necessary, revise your own sentences.   Answers will vary.

1. accept	6. percentage	11. raise	16. beside
2. except	7. amount	12. rise	17. stationary
3. all ready	8. number	13. lie	18. emigrate
4. already	9. than	14. lay	19. badly
5. slow	10. then	15. besides	20. infer

Cumulative Review

Exercise A Using Verbs Correctly

On a separate piece of paper, correct all of the errors in verb usage in the following sentences. Look for incorrect verbs and verb forms, unnecessary shifts in verb tense, and unnecessary use of the passive voice.

1. When he ~~bite~~ [bit] into the sandwich, he found a surprise. *or* When he bites into the sandwich, he finds a surprise.

2. Have you ~~ate~~ [eaten] your lunch yet?

3. I would feel bad if I ~~was~~ [were] you.

4. She bought something every time she ~~goes~~ [went] to a yard sale. *or* She buys something every time she goes to a yard sale.

5. The ball was thrown right to her; she should have ~~catched~~ [caught] it.

6. The principal requests that Ms. Smith ~~teaches~~ [teach] usage of verbs.

7. ~~The earring I thought I had lose was then finded by me~~. I found the earring I thought I had lost.

8. When the bridge was ~~builded~~ [built], it ~~would be~~ [was] the longest one in the city. *or* When the bridge is built, it will be the longest one in the city.

9. Have you ~~choosed~~ [chosen] what you're going to wear?

10. She ~~loaned~~ [lent] her CD player to me, which I then ~~had~~ gave to my cousin.

Exercise B Subject-Verb Agreement

Underline the verb in parentheses that agrees with the subject.

1. May 1, which is Cartoon Appreciation Day and International Tuba Day, (<u>is</u>, are) the beginning of quite a month.

2. On May 2, Italy honors the anniversary of the death of Leonardo da Vinci—the artist, scientist, and inventor—(<u>doesn't</u>, don't) it?

3. I know someone who (<u>observes</u>, observe) Be Kind to Animals Week.

4. On May 5, which is Cinco de Mayo, one of my friends (<u>celebrates</u>, celebrate) the 1862 victory of Mexican troops over France's Napoleon III.

5. (<u>Does</u>, Do) your Dutch mother or Dutch aunts celebrate the 1945 liberation of the Netherlands from Nazi forces on May 5?

6. Mother's Day and my birthday (occurs, <u>occur</u>) on May 6.

7. Either actor George Clooney or British Prime Minister Tony Blair (<u>claims</u>, claim) to share his birthday, May 6, with baseball great Willie Mays.

8. May 7 (<u>is</u>, are) the anniversary of the birth of composer Johannes Brahms and of the premiere of Beethoven's Ninth Symphony.

9. No Socks Day or the Poke Salad Festival (<u>is</u>, are) celebrated in Blanchard, Louisiana, on May 8 every year.

10. Sentence 9 is the only one of these facts that (<u>surprises</u>, surprise) me.

Exercise C Correcting Pronoun Usage

On a separate piece of paper, rewrite correctly each sentence that contains an error in pronoun usage. If a sentence is correct, write *C*. Answers may vary. Sample answers are given.

1. Maria gave Celia the sweater ~~she~~ Celia loved.

2. The band teacher gave ~~we~~ us musicians the schedule for this semester's concerts.

3. Not many people came to last year's concert. ~~It~~ That poor showing was too bad.

4. Either Angela or Raymond has college in ~~their~~ his or her plans.

5. Do you know ~~whom~~ who is going to buy a car?

6. Why don't you like the singer ~~who~~ whom I tell everyone to listen to?

7. The two best-liked seniors, Meg and ~~her~~ she, are coming to the party.

8. Did you see ~~where they~~ the article that gave the debating team high marks?

9. Everyone in the boys club who volunteers gets a medal. C

10. ~~Us~~ We members of the track team work out nearly every day.

Exercise D Using Modifiers Correctly

On a separate piece of paper, correct the sentences that contain errors with modifiers. If a sentence is correct, write *C*.

1. Researchers found that in 1999 ~~less~~ fewer teenagers had access to the Internet than originally thought.

2. ~~Estimating~~ Researchers estimate that soon about three-fourths of the nation's teens will be online, a lot of kids use the Internet.

3. Compared with all other age groups, soon teens will be using the Internet in ~~a higher~~ the highest proportion.

4. Some teens think that taking their place in front of the computer screen is the most ~~wonderfulest~~ wonderful thing they can do.

5. Many think that carrying on conversations with several other kids by computer is ~~more~~ better than carrying home stuff from the mall.

6. ~~Expensive and controversial,~~ some parents worry about expensive and controversial online communication.

7. Some teens ~~only~~ use computers only for homework.

8. The computer may be more popular than any other invention. C

9. ~~As a substitute for television,~~ some kids turn to cyberspace, as a substitute for television.

10. For some teens, the ~~most~~ ideal use of cyberspace is socializing.

You may wish to use the following statements as a writing prompt.
• All people under eighteen should be limited to no more than four hours' access to the Internet a week.
• The Internet will teach teenagers responsibility. Students should support their opinions with examples and reasons.

Usage Test

Exercise 1 Identifying Errors

Directions: Each of the numbered items either is correct or contains an error in one of the underlined parts of the sentence. In the answer section to the right of each item, circle the letter of the underlined sentence part that contains the error. If the sentence is correct, circle *E* for NO ERROR.

EXAMPLE   Leonardo da Vinci must have <u>rised</u> some eyebrows when he <u>proposed</u>
                                     A   B

the idea of contact lenses in the sixteenth century. In his *Code on the*

Eye, this multitalented Italian artist, sculptor, engineer, and architect

<u>described</u> a method for correcting vision by placing against the eye a
C

short tube sealed at <u>its</u> end with a flat lens.   <u>NO ERROR</u>
                     D   E

Ⓐ B C D E

1. Da Vinci's tube <u>was filled</u> with water which, when it <u>come</u> into contact
                   A   B

   with the eye, <u>refracted</u> the light waves in the same way that a <u>curved</u>
                 C   D

   lens did.   <u>NO ERROR</u>
               E

1. A Ⓑ C D E

2. <u>Who</u> would've <u>dreamed</u> that such a modern idea had <u>it's</u> origins four
   A   B   C

   hundred years ago? Today, the high water content of soft lenses <u>mirrors</u>
                                                                    D

   da Vinci's use of water.   <u>NO ERROR</u>
                              E

2. A B Ⓒ D E

3. The first practical contact lenses <u>was</u> <u>developed</u> in 1877 by A. E. Fick, a
                                      A   B

   man <u>who</u> was a Swiss doctor. <u>They</u> were hard lenses.   <u>NO ERROR</u>
       C   D   E

3. Ⓐ B C D E

4. Fick's lenses, <u>which</u> covered not only the cornea but also the entire
                  A

   eyeball, <u>were</u> for the vain only, because <u>they</u> were thick and
            B   C

   uncomfortable <u>to wear</u>.   <u>NO ERROR</u>
                 D   E

4. A B C D Ⓔ

5. From Fick's lenses, we <u>will learn</u> two things: Vision <u>can be corrected</u> when
                         A   B

   lenses <u>are placed</u> directly on the eye, and the eye <u>can tolerate</u> a foreign
          C   D

   glass object.   <u>NO ERROR</u>
                   E

5. Ⓐ B C D E

6. <u>Until 1936</u>, glass was the standard material <u>used</u> to make hard contact

     A   **B**

   lenses. In that year, a German company <u>introduced</u> a hard plastic lens,

                                  C

   which soon <u>has become</u> the industry standard. <u>NO ERROR</u>

                 D   **E**

6. A B C (D) E

7. But the era of modern contact lens design was the <u>1940s, when</u>

                                                       A

   American opticians <u>made</u> a <u>breakthrough</u>: the first lens that <u>only</u>

                          B   **C**   **D**

   covered the cornea. <u>NO ERROR</u>

                         E

7. A B C (D) E

8. Since the 1940s, scientists <u>have been working</u> to change the chemical

                                       A

   and physical <u>composition</u> of lenses <u>to try and</u> to make them more

                   B   **C**

   <u>closely</u> resemble the composition of the eye. <u>NO ERROR</u>

    D   **E**

8. A B (C) D E

Exercise 2 Correcting Errors

Directions: In the following sentences, the underlined part may contain one or more errors. In the answer section to the right of each item, circle the letter of the choice that correctly expresses the idea in the underlined part of the sentence. If you think that the original wording is correct, circle *D* for NO ERROR. **Hint:** A sentence may have more than one error.

EXAMPLE   <u>All ready wealthy beyond his dreams,</u> the basketball star agreed to play for minimum wage.
         A. Already wealthy beyond his dreams,
         B. All ready wealthier beyond his dreams,
         C. All ready wealthy past his dreams,
         D. NO ERROR

(A) B C D

1. <u>Neither you nor me can do</u> this job alone.
   A. Neither you nor me can be doing   B. Neither you nor I can do
   C. Neither me nor you can do   D. NO ERROR

1. A (B) C D

2. <u>Ivan sighted four sources</u> in his research paper.
   A. Ivan sited four sources   B. Ivan sighted four sauces
   C. Ivan cited four sources   D. NO ERROR

2. A B (C) D

3. <u>From between the pool of contestants</u>, one good candidate is sure
     to emerge.
   A. From among the pool of contestants
   B. From outside the pool of contestants
   C. From among the two contestants   D. NO ERROR

3. (A) B C D

4. <u>Maeve complimented me</u> when I showed up in school wearing the scarf my grandmother made for me.

   A. Maeve complemented me   B. Maeve had complimented me

   C. Maeve complimented I   D. NO ERROR

4. A   B   C   (D)

5. <u>The President or the Secretary of State stay</u> in that hotel.

   A. The President or the Secretary of State stays

   B. The President or the Secretary of State are staying

   C. The President or the Secretary of State staying

   D. NO ERROR

5. (A)   B   C   D

6. The generals chose the officer, <u>who were a reliable soldier</u>, for the mission.

   A. who are a reliable soldier   B. whom were a reliable soldier

   C. who was a reliable soldier   D. NO ERROR

6. A   B   (C)   D

7. <u>Neither Edgar nor Belinda are going</u> on the class outing.

   A. Neither Edgar or Belinda are going

   B. Neither Edgar nor Belinda is going

   C. Either Edgar or Belinda are going

   D. NO ERROR

7. A   (B)   C   D

8. <u>Who did the drama teacher pick</u> to play Biff?

   A. Whom did the drama teacher pick

   B. Who all did the drama teacher pick

   C. Whoever did the drama teacher pick

   D. NO ERROR

8. (A)   B   C   D

Exercise 3   Identifying Errors

Directions: In each numbered group of sentences, one or more of the sentences may contain usage errors. In the answer section to the right of each item, circle the letter of every sentence that contains an error. If you think all four sentences are correct, Circle *E* for NO ERROR.

   EXAMPLE   A. Manny and Omar plan to try out for the team.

             B. Neither of the two have a chance.

             C. Neither know how much competition there is.

             D. Manny, of the two, has a better chance.

             E. NO ERROR

A (B)(C) D   E

1. A. He and I are on the school paper together.

   B. Just between you and me, our band needs work.

   C. Of the two of them, she is the ~~best~~ skater. better

   D. Miguel or Suki ~~are~~ representing our grade at the conference. is

   E. NO ERROR

1. A   B   (C)(D)   E

2. A. She is the most ~~unhappiest~~ person I've ever met.   *unhappy*
   B. He is less experienced than I thought he was.
   C. I am most interested when I'm not tired.
   D. His project was ~~more~~ unique ~~than the others~~.
   E. NO ERROR

2. (A) B C (D) E

3. A. Helen had drawn directions, but Paul lost them.
   B. I invited them to join ~~I~~ for lunch.   *me*
   C. Everyone is responsible for cleaning ~~their~~ paint brushes.   *his or her*
   D. Both the Democrats and the Republicans are planning to attend.
   E. NO ERROR

3. A (B)(C) D E

4. A. We ~~hadn't~~ hardly begun when the problems started.   *had*
   B. I'm eating fewer hot dogs than I used to eat.
   C. The first check-out line is for ten or ~~less~~ items.   *fewer*
   D. Sarah went home to care for her sister, who is sick.
   E. NO ERROR

4. (A) B (C) D E

5. A. We barely knew one another.
   B. North High's team is as good as South's team.
   C. She was not unexpected when she appeared at the party.
   D. He edited his paper and made it ~~more~~ perfect ~~than it had been~~.
   E. NO ERROR

5. A B C (D) E

6. A. He knows more about fly-fishing than anyone.   *else*
   B. I plan to ~~loan~~ my bowling ball to Sid.   *lend*
   C. The two candidates shook hands and smiled.
   D. As a pet, Cuddles was ideal.
   E. NO ERROR

6. (A)(B) C D E

7. A. When Ben pulled his car out of the drive, he crashed into a trash can.
   B. ~~Flabby and out of shape,~~ Tom's doctor told him to begin a course
      of conditioning.   *because Tom was flabby and out of shape*
   C. Hauling a large suitcase, her knee scraped against the doorway.   *When she was*
   D. Strictly speaking, pigeons are a nuisance to city dwellers.
   E. NO ERROR

7. A (B)(C) D E

Exercise 4 Correcting Errors

Directions: Look back at each item in Exercise 3, and double-check your
answers. Make sure you have identified all of the sentences with errors. On a
separate piece of paper, rewrite correctly all of the incorrect sentences in
each numbered item. Write the entire sentences. If you decided that all four
of the sentences in a numbered item are correct, write *C* for CORRECT.

Punctuation: End Marks and Commas

STUDENT WRITING
Expository Essay

Food Committee Takes Another Stab
by Mark Boucher
high school student, Pennington, New Jersey

The 1997–1998 Food Committee met for the first time Tuesday to evaluate menus, food preparation, fat/caloric content of meals, and food service in general.

The group is composed of Dean of Students Martin Doggett, Food Service Director and Executive Chef Roland Young, and eight students.

The students made several suggestions to improve the quality and variety of the menus. They proposed more nonsugared cereals in the Abbott Dining Center, the prompt refilling of the drink dispensers, a reinstitution of the yogurt bar, and better replenishment of the deli bar during meals. They also recommended a reduction in the number of fried foods served. Many asked for menu adjustments, and the executive chef plans to review the current menu cycles.

In addition, the company in charge of food service has promised to work toward a labeling system for all entrees. This would give students and faculty a variety of health information, including calories, carbohydrates, and fat content; it would allow them to make better-informed choices about the food they eat.

The students also proposed a series of nutrition workshops in the houses. These workshops would be geared toward specific groups, such as athletes or people trying to lose weight. In general, the students are pleased with the food service, and the meeting was very productive and organized, according to Doggett. "The students made several reasonable suggestions," he said. "It was not just bashing the [food service company]." They praised the service at the Tuesday sit-down dinners and Friday sit-down lunches.

As you reread Mark Boucher's expository essay, notice how often he gives examples to support his general statements. When he gives more than two examples in a row (a series), he separates them with a comma. You'll get practice using commas in a series and in lots of other ways as you do the exercises in this chapter.

Allow time for students to discuss the student writing. Suggest that they identify its strengths and propose possible improvements. Use the model to introduce the concepts in the chapter.

End Marks and Abbreviations

- Use a **period** at the end of a statement (declarative sentence).

  The Beatles might have worked together again if John Lennon had lived**.**

- Use a **question mark** at the end of a direct question (interrogative sentence). An indirect question ends with a period.

  DIRECT   Who was the band's first drummer**?**

  INDIRECT   Inez asked me who the band's first drummer was**.**

- Use an **exclamation point** at the end of an exclamation (exclamatory sentence).

  Wow**!** That woman can sing**!** or Wow, that woman can sing**!**

- Use either a **period** or an **exclamation point** at the end of a command (imperative sentence).

  Call to find out where she's performing next**.**

  Don't be late for the concert**!**

- Use a **period** after many abbreviations.

Papers and reports for school or work should, in general, not contain abbreviations. **Exceptions:** You may use abbreviations of time (such as A.M. and B.C.) and of certain titles before and after names (such as *Ms.* and *M.D.*) Students may wish to use small caps for abbreviations of time. Capital letters are also acceptable.

Abbreviations and Periods				
CATEGORY	**EXAMPLE**			
Initials and Titles	Mr. D. T. Williams, Jr.		Harriet C. Gomez, Ph.D.	
	Dr. Kyle E. Tang	Mrs. Elena Hart	Jo Keen, M.D.	
Times	A.M.	P.M.	B.C.	B.C.E.	A.D.
Others	Inc.	Co.	Assn.	etc.	vs.

Don't use periods with acronyms. An **acronym** is a word formed from the first letter(s) of several words, such as *laser* (from "*l*ight *a*mplification by *s*timulated *e*mission of *r*adiation").

The modern tendency is to omit the period following common abbreviations such as *ft* (foot *or* feet) and *lb* (pound), metric measures such as *cm* (centimeter) and *kg* (kilogram), and chemical elements such as *He* (helium). Some other abbreviations that don't take periods include *mph* (miles per hour), *AM* and *FM* radio, *FBI*, *IRS*, and postal abbreviations for states (*ME*, *AZ*, *NJ*).

- Use punctuation correctly in bibliographies.

  Palmer**,** Pete**,** and John Thorn**.** *Total Baseball***.** New York: Warner**,** 1989**.**

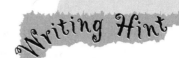

When you use an unfamiliar abbreviation, first give the full name or expression followed by the abbreviation in parentheses.

In 1816, African American Methodist ministers organized the African Methodist Episcopal (AME) church. The AME took a leading role in the struggle to end slavery.

Use only one period with an abbreviation at the end of a sentence. However, don't omit a comma, question mark, or exclamation point following an abbreviation.

The play ended at 11 P.M.

What happened in Crete in 1200 B.C.**?**

Punctuation in bibliographical entries is modeled in Lesson 3.8, page 84.

Proofread the following sentences to add missing punctuation and to replace abbreviations that do not belong in a school report. **Hint:** Some sentences require more than one punctuation mark.

1. The first Doric and Ionic columns appeared in Greece in the first century b.c.

2. D.H. Lawrence wrote poignant short stories.

3. A majority of the ~~srs.~~ seniors will take the Scholastic Aptitude Test (SAT) *or S.A.T.* in ~~Nov.~~ November

4. Besides "Mr. Pym Passes By," what did A.A. Milne write?

5. A plague took its toll on Athens from 430 to 423 b.c.

6. Oh, no! I've forgotten who won in 1988. Who was it?

7. In 1705, young composer J.S. Bach walked 200 ~~mi~~ miles to attend a concert.

8. In 1967, the musical *Cabaret*—by J. Masteroff, J. Kanter, and F. Ebb—opened in New York.

9. She asked if I know what K.F. Gauss and Wilhelm E. Weber invented in 1833.

10. Don't forget periods for ~~bks.~~ books in your bibliography. *or* !

Review the following paragraph to add end marks and other periods as needed. If you're not sure whether an abbreviation takes a period, check a dictionary.

[1]The Web site for the Modern Language Association (MLA) is worth visiting. *or M.L.A.*

[2]M.LA is perhaps best known as the authority on documentation. *or M.L.A.* [3]Its Web site

provides up-to-date directions and examples of how to cite sources in a research

paper. [4]The most basic citation is for a book by one author, an example of

which follows. [: acceptable]

[5]Peterson, Robert. *Only the Ball Was White* (New York: Oxford, 1992).

[6]The site also provides guidelines for citing online documents as well as

movies and TV. and radio shows.

[7]The MLA style advice is also available in print. *or M.L.A.* [8]One advantage the Web site

has over the print version of the style guide is that the former is always there,

be it 6 a.m. or 10 p.m. [9]Students don't have to ask themselves, "Where did I put

that book?" [10]To explore what the MLA Web site offers, go to www.mla.org. *or M.L.A.* <http:// >

Commas in a Series

Commas, the most frequently used punctuation mark, signal a slight hesitation but not a complete stop. Mainly, their purpose is to prevent misreading. In the next few lessons, you'll review the most important rules for using commas.

■ See also **Mechanics, Lesson 14.2,** which explains when to use semicolons rather than commas for a series.

🖊 Use commas to separate items in a series.
Some rule books do not require the last comma in a series.
A **series** contains three or more similar items in a row.

> New York, Detroit, and Chicago have professional teams in baseball, football, basketball, and hockey.

When a coordinating conjunction (such as *and* or *but*) connects items, don't insert commas unless the items are independent clauses.

> I took the ice cream out to defrost **and** left it on the counter **but** forgot about it.
> I took the ice cream out to defrost, **but** my brother put it back, **and** it froze again.

🖊 Use a comma to separate two or more adjectives that precede and modify the same noun.

> Visiting the Holocaust Memorial Museum in Washington is a powerful, memorable experience.

Don't use a comma when the last adjective in a series is really part of a compound noun.

> Which new compact disk player did you get? [*Compact disk player* is a compound noun, so don't use a comma after *new*.]

To decide whether to put a comma between two adjectives preceding a noun, try *and* between the two adjectives. If *and* makes sense, use a comma.

> He gave a quick *and* dismissive answer. [makes sense]
> He gave a quick, dismissive answer. [use comma]

If *and* doesn't make sense, don't use a comma.

> He walked some *and* large dogs. [doesn't make sense]
> He walked some large dogs. [no comma]

Exercise 3 Adding Commas to Sentences

Walter copied the quotations on the following page from a reference book. In his haste, he left out commas. Insert all necessary commas. If a sentence does not need a comma, write *C*.

Writing Hint

Some publications omit the comma after the next-to-last item in a series.

She hates broccoli, beans and asparagus.

This book advises *always* using a series comma before the conjunction because it's never wrong to do so.

Another test for the use of a comma between adjectives is to reverse the position of the adjectives. If the adjectives can be reversed, use a comma.

Enriching Your Vocabulary

The word *obsolescence*, used on page 298, means "the state of being obsolete." *Obsolete* comes from the Latin *obsolescere*, meaning "to go out of use." The *obsolescence* of ten-year-old computers has forced many owners to replace their systems.

1. There are three modes of bearing the ills of life: by indifference, by philosophy, and by religion. —Charles Caleb Colton

2. I sing of brooks, of blossoms, birds, and bowers. —Robert Herrick

3. Some books are to be tasted, others to be swallowed, and some few to be chewed and digested. —Francis Bacon

4. You will find that deep place of silence right in your room, your garden, or even your bathtub. —Elisabeth Kübler-Ross

5. I reject get-it-done, make-it-happen thinking. —Jerry Brown

6. Dancing is the loftiest, the most moving, the most beautiful of the arts. —Havelock Ellis

7. War's a brain-spattering, windpipe-splitting art. —Lord Byron

8. What does education often do? It makes a straight-cut ditch of a free, meandering brook. —Henry David Thoreau

9. Happy families are all alike; every unhappy family is unhappy in its own way. —Leo Tolstoy C

10. For a while I thought history was something bitter, old men wrote. —Jacqueline Kennedy Onassis

11. The four stages of man are infancy, childhood, adolescence, and obsolescence. —Art Linkletter

12. Only in growth, reform, and change, paradoxically enough, is true security to be found. —Anne Morrow Lindbergh

13. There is nothing more enticing, disenchanting, and enslaving than the life at sea. —Joseph Conrad

14. My personal hobbies are reading, listening to music, and silence. —Edith Sitwell

15. Style is character. A good style cannot come from a bad, undisciplined character. —Norman Mailer

Exercise 4 Checking a Paper for Punctuation

Take a paper you've written recently, and review it carefully. Focus particularly on end punctuation marks and commas. Check to see whether you have used these punctuation marks correctly. If you decide to make any changes in punctuation, be prepared to explain your decision. Students' recent papers will vary as will their corrections, but they should focus particularly on end marks and commas, and they should also be prepared to explain their decisions.

Commas with Compound Sentences and Introductory Elements

■ See **Mechanics,** Lesson 13.5, for a discussion on using commas following introductory words such as *yes*, *no*, and *well*.

🖊 Use a comma before a coordinating conjunction that joins two independent clauses.

> Miguel wants to swim at the beach**,** and Sonia will sunbathe and read her book. [compound sentence with two declarative clauses]
> Does Miguel know how to swim**,** and will Sonia remember to bring her book? [compound sentence with two interrogative clauses]
> Sonia, keep an eye on Miguel in the water**,** and use sunblock on your skin. [compound sentence with two imperative clauses]

Generally, you do not need a comma between parts of a compound subject or a compound verb. The sentence below, however, uses a comma within the compound verb to prevent a misreading.

> I worry about his common sense**,** and am relying on you to guide him.

🖊 Use a comma after an introductory adverb, participle, phrase, or clause.
> **Unfortunately,** the tennis star missed the ball. [introductory adverb]
> **Horrified,** the tennis star glared at the referee. [introductory participle]
> **Horrified by the call,** the tennis star glared at the referee. [introductory participial phrase]
> **In brief,** we won. [introductory prepositional phrase]
> **To the delight of our coach in her final year,** we won. [series of introductory prepositional phrases]
> **To help her with math,** Diane hired a tutor. [infinitive phrase]
> **His hair blowing in the wind,** the diver stood at the edge of the high cliff. [introductory absolute phrase]
> **As soon as we sat down to dinner,** the phone started ringing. [introductory adverb clause]

🖊 Use a comma before a concluding adverb clause only if it expresses the idea of contrast or if the sentence might be misread without it.

> I watched quietly **as my brother put on his tie**. [no comma necessary before adverb clause]
> I watched quietly**, even though I could have helped him**. [comma before adverb clause expressing contrast]

When the subject follows the verb, do not use a comma after one or more introductory prepositional phrases.

In the attic under a pile
ᵛ
of old clothes **are** the
ˢ
paintings.

Exercise 5 Revising Sentences

On a separate piece of paper, revise each sentence so that it begins with an introductory phrase, adverb, or adverb clause. Add commas where necessary. **Hint:** You may need to add, drop, or change some words. See Answer Key.

EXAMPLE   We will win the game if we practice diligently.
If we practice diligently, we will win the game.

1. Six American high school students astonished the judges at a world mathematics competition in Hong Kong.

2. All the students on the team achieved perfect scores on the exam for the first time in the history of the competition.

3. The American team claimed victory over sixty-eight other countries to bring home a win from the International Mathematical Olympics.

4. Every member of the American team answered all six questions correctly— a remarkable accomplishment.

5. The mathematics exam took a grueling nine hours to complete because of its difficulty.

6. The test was brief, consisting of only six questions.

7. Each question, however, was a complicated problem testing algebra, geometry, or numbers theory.

8. An American team has not won the competition since 1986, when Americans tied with Russian students.

9. Some teams, such as the one from China, train for the test by living together and studying year-round.

10. The Americans, hailing from New York, Massachusetts, Maryland, and Illinois, were coached by Walter Mientka, a professor of mathematics at the University of Nebraska.

Exercise 6 Write What You Think

Successes like that of the math team in Hong Kong make Americans proud of our educational achievements. Write a brief essay explaining the academic successes of your school or the schools in your community. You may choose to focus on a particular club or on the successes of a specific individual.

Where possible, use examples and statistics to support your statements. When you've finished writing, review your work to see if you've used commas and end punctuation correctly. Then share your work with your classmates.

Students' paragraphs will vary. Give students full credit if they have stated an opinion and attempted to support their opinions. Look for grammatically complete sentences that begin with a capital letter and end with an appropriate end punctuation mark.

Commas with Sentence Interrupters and Nonessential Elements

You learned about setting off an introductory element with a single comma in Lesson 13.3. Likewise, you must set off an **interrupter** that occurs within a sentence with a pair of commas.

🔹 Use a pair of commas around a noun of direct address and around a parenthetical or transitional expression.

Did you know**,** Orlando**,** that leathercraft is a major industry in Morocco?
Moroccan leather goods**,** by the way**,** make wonderful gifts.
Tourists in Morocco**,** therefore**,** love to shop for leather goods.

🔹 Use a pair of commas around a nonessential, or interrupting, phrase or clause.

An **essential** phrase or clause is necessary to the meaning of the sentence. A **nonessential** phrase or clause adds information, but the sentence makes sense without it.

My cousin **Zev** visited Morocco last summer. [no comma around essential appositive phrase; it tells *which* cousin]
He saw leather goods in markets**, or souks,** throughout Morocco. [commas around nonessential appositive phrase]

Some French teens **traveling with him** spent all their time in the souks. [no comma around essential participial phrase]
Zev**, looking for the larger picture,** visited mosques**, or houses of worship**. [commas around nonessential participial phrase and comma before nonessential appositive phrase]

The mosques **that are his favorite** are in Marrakech**, which is in the foothills of the Grand Atlas,** and in Rabat. [no commas around the essential adjective clause; commas around the nonessential adjective clause]

🔹 Use commas to set off **contrasting expressions**.

Leather bags and purses**, not book covers or desk accessories,** are the most popular Moroccan exports.

Do not, however, use commas with correlative conjunctions.

While in Morocco, Zev ate **not only** couscous **but also** tajine.

Exercise 7 **Adding Commas to Sentences**

Review the following sentences, adding commas where they are needed. Write *C* if the sentence is correct.

1. Sumerian writing which developed about six thousand years ago involved cutting pictographs onto clay tablets.

2. A pictograph also called a hieroglyph is a picture representing a word or idea.

3. Ancient Egyptian calendars regulated by the sun and moon had 360 days.

4. Each month by the way had thirty days.

5. Sumerian wedge-shaped cuneiform writing appeared about 5500 years ago. C

6. Five thousand years ago, Egyptian musicians played not only lyres but also clarinets. C

7. Wheeled vehicles incidentally first appeared in Sumeria more than five thousand years ago.

8. During the period from 3000 to 2500 B.C. the Phoenicians settled two cities, Tyre and Sidon along the Mediterranean Sea.

9. The Great Wall of Uruk which had nine hundred towers was built by Sumerians between 3000 B.C. and 2500 B.C.

10. Rodney who loves dogs would be interested to know that Egyptians domesticated dogs nearly five thousand years ago.

11. The ancient Sumerians who also wrote poetry and knew about the healing qualities of mineral springs used oil-burning lamps.

12. The Sumerians developers of a numerical system based on six and twelve, began using metal coins by 2500 B.C.

13. During the period between 2500 B.C. and 2000 B.C. Egyptians began using papyrus and moreover started their first libraries.

14. Bows and arrows were used as weapons in warfare for the first time during that same period. C

15. The Egyptians not the Sumerians built pyramids.

Exercise 8 **Describing an Ancient Setting**

Imagine yourself spending a day in an ancient civilization such as Egypt or Sumer. What do you think you'd see around you? Imagine what daily life might have looked like and sounded like. Think about what it might have smelled like and what the weather would have been like. Brainstorm ideas with others in a group. Then write two descriptive paragraphs filled with details of your imagined journey. Check your sentences for correct end marks and commas. **Share your passages with classmates.** Students' paragraphs might include descriptions of buildings, street life, people, modes of transportation, foods, colors, fabrics, and so on. See teacher pages for assessment rubrics.

Other Comma Uses

■ **See Mechanics,
Lesson 14.1, for more
on setting off long
quotations with
colons.**

🍃 Use commas to set off interjections, such as *well*, *yes*, *no*, and single-word adjectives that begin a sentence.

> Well, have you seen *Microscopic*, the hit movie about the sinking of the world's smallest boat?
> Yes, I did.
> Ugh, I'll never see it.
> Curious, we stood in line for two hours to get in.
> Disappointed, we left even before the boat sank in the tub.

🍃 Use commas to separate parts of a reference, parts of an address, geographical terms, and parts of a date.

> The Beatles performed in Liverpool, England, at first.
> Turn to *The History of Art*, page 722, for more on that topic.
> Our favorite scene was Act I, scene 3, because of its humor.
> June 27, 1927, is the birth date of Captain Kangaroo (Bob Keeshan).

You do not need a comma between month and date or between month and year.

> Who else was born on June 27?
> Justice Thurgood Marshall resigned from the Supreme Court in late June 1991.

🍃 Use commas following the greeting of a friendly letter and following the closing of both friendly and business letters.

> Dear Suki,   Sincerely,   Dear Aunt Thelma,   With love,

🍃 Use commas to set off short, direct quotations.

> "I can't think of two TV shows that I like," Ralph complained.
> "Prime time television," he claimed, "has gone down the tubes."

🍃 Use a comma to set off tag questions.

> I told you that I scratched the new car, **didn't I**?
> You don't happen to have Theo's address, **do you**?

Don't use commas every time you see quotation marks. Quoted words or phrases that serve as subjects, predicate nominatives, or direct objects do not need commas.

"Yesterday" is her favorite Beatles song.

But my favorite is "In My Life."

Eddie sighs whenever he hears "While My Guitar Gently Weeps."

Exercise 9 **Adding Commas to Sentences**

Proofread the following sentences, adding commas where they are needed. **Hint:** A sentence may require the insertion of more than one comma. Write *C* if the sentence is correct.

1. Yes, the play put all the students to sleep.

2. Well, our class didn't have the background to appreciate this revival of the March 1938 comedy.

3. So do you think New York New York is the best place to see theater productions?

4. Michael Richards (Kramer on *Seinfeld*) was born on August 24, 1950.

5. By Act III, scene 2, of *Waiting to Nap* everyone in the audience was asleep.

6. "Wake up, you dolts," Richard said. "You don't know what you're missing!"

7. I warned you not to attend, didn't I?

8. We saw the same play in March 1999 and didn't like it then.   C

9. No, I don't remember seeing it; I must have been asleep.

10. I read the *Playbill*, page 14, to learn about the background of this theater.

Exercise 10   Revising a Friendly Letter

Review the friendly letter below. Add commas, periods, and other end punctuation marks where necessary. Remove unnecessary commas.

Students' revisions will vary. Sample revision shown.

May 25, 2000

Dear Michelle,

or State U!

Well, am I glad that you've decided on State U. Man, are you going to love it

or here!

here. I began a whole new life on September 4, 1999, the first day of classes.

You could say that the curtain went up on Act II, scene 1, of my life on that

day. "Let It Be," was the perfect song to wake up to that day.

Binghamton, New York, is so different from Maplewood. It snows here every

day in the winter. But in the spring, we have classes outside. That sounds

great, doesn't it?

or campus!

I can't wait to see you next September. 3. I'll say, "Hey, welcome to campus."

As always,

Karen

Exercise 11   Writing a Friendly E-mail

On a separate piece of paper, write a real or simulated e-mail to a friend you haven't seen or spoken to in a while. Tell him or her about what's been happening in your life. Share the details of some of your recent experiences. Inform your friend of some of the things you've been thinking about lately. Write about any plans you have. When you have finished your draft, check it for end punctuation and the correct use of commas. *Students' e-mail letters will vary. E-mail letters automatically carry the date. They don't require salutations.*

Chapter 13 • Punctuation: End Marks and Commas

Correcting Run-on Sentences and Sentence Fragments

To correct a **run-on sentence**, use the following strategies.

◖ Add end punctuation and a capital letter to break up the run-on sentence.

RUN-ON   About four thousand years ago, Stonehenge was a center of worship, it was the Bronze Age.

CORRECTED   About four thousand years ago, Stonehenge was a center of worship. It was the Bronze Age.

◖ Change the run-on into a compound sentence.

RUN-ON   Most people in the ancient world lived in humble houses, the Minoan palace at Knossos had bathrooms.

CORRECTED   Most people in the ancient world lived in humble houses**, but** the Minoan palace at Knossos had bathrooms.

CORRECTED   Most people in the ancient world lived in humble houses**;** **however**, the Minoan palace at Knossos had bathrooms.

◖ Change one of the sentences into a subordinate clause.

CORRECTED   **Although most people in the ancient world lived in humble houses,** the Minoan palace at Knossos had bathrooms.

To correct a **sentence fragment**, use these strategies.

◖ Add the missing subject, verb, or both.

FRAGMENT   Spread from the Mediterranean through Europe.

CORRECTED   Trade routes spread from the Mediterranean through Europe.

◖ Attach the fragment to a complete sentence before or after it.

FRAGMENT   Cleopatra's Needle, an obelisk from ancient Egypt, still stands. In New York's Central Park.

CORRECTED   Cleopatra's Needle, an obelisk from ancient Egypt, still stands in New York's Central Park.

◖ Drop a subordinating conjunction.

FRAGMENT   Because percussion instruments were added to Egyptian orchestral music nearly four thousand years ago.

CORRECTED   Percussion instruments were added to Egyptian orchestral music nearly four thousand years ago.

Writing Hint

To avoid paragraphs that sound monotonous, aim for variety when you correct fragments or run-ons. Read your revised sentences in your head or quietly aloud. Listen to how they sound.

Enriching Your Vocabulary

The French words *em,* or "in," and *barca,* meaning "ship," form the roots of the word *embark,* which means "to go on board a ship or vehicle." As on page 306, it can also mean "to undertake an enterprise." You may *embark* on a career after high school.

Editing a Paragraph

Review the following paragraphs to correct run-on sentences and sentence fragments. Read your revision aloud to see that the sentences sound smooth together. Students' revisions will vary. Sample revisions are given.

¹In about 2000 B.C., the Achaeans invaded. ²~~Invaded~~ the Greek peninsula.
They
³P̌ushed farther south, conquering new territory throughout Greece. ⁴The

Achaean kings ruled walled cities,̤through trading and looting, they built

palaces and filled them with treasures. ⁵Outside the fortresses lived farmers,
They
artisans, merchants, and traders. ⁶P̌aid tribute to the king.

⁷The Achaeans built on the achievements of the earlier Minoan civilization,̣

their artisans reproduced Minoan designs on pottery̗ ~~and~~ jewelry.̗ ⁸A̗nd ~~on their~~

tools. ⁹From the Minoans, the Achaeans also learned writing,̤they adapted

symbols from the Minoan alphabet.

¹⁰In about 1300 or 1250 B.C., Achaean kings banded together, ~~they~~ embarked
and
on a war against the rival commercial power, Troy. ¹¹~~Troy.~~ which controlled key

trade routes between the Aegean Sea and the Black Sea. ¹²The Achaeans emerged

as the victors after a bloody war. ¹³The story of the fall of Troy and the

aftermath is told in the *Iliad* and the *Odyssey*, two epic poems attributed to the
who   Homer
poet Homer, ~~he~~ probably lived about five hundred years later. ¹⁴Čomposed these

poems based on oral stories that had been passed along over many generations.

¹⁵Until nineteenth-century excavations proved the existence of Troy,

historians had treated Homer's poems as fictions,̤now, although scholars do not

look upon the *Iliad* and the *Odyssey* as pure history, they realize that the poems

provide insights into the lives and values of ancient Greeks.

Exercise 13 **Creating and Checking an Exercise**

From a newspaper or magazine, copy a paragraph or two, removing all capital letters, end punctuation, and commas. Give the lowercased, unpunctuated text to a classmate, who will try to put in the missing capital letters and the punctuation. Then review your classmate's work against the original to see how the two are the same and how they are different. Answers will vary.

Editing and Proofreading Worksheet 1

Correct sentence fragments and run-ons in the following paragraphs, and make any other changes you think will improve the passage. Carefully check for the correct use of commas, periods, and other end punctuation marks. Watch spelling. Work with a partner or small group. Write your revised paragraphs on a separate piece of paper, and compare your revisions with those made by other groups. Students' revisions will vary. Sample revisions given.

¹Three ancient civilizations arose in the fertile valleys of the Nile River, the Tigris River, the Euphrates River and the Indus River. ²A fourth civilization developed along the Yellow River in northern China. ³Then between 5000 and 3000 B.C., ⁴People in China began to form permanent villages and discovered effective ways to produce food. ⁵By about 1600 B.C., the Shang civilization arose. ⁶Lasting about five hundred years. *and lasted*

⁷Archaeologists unearthed more than 130 Shang sites. ⁸Which reveal a great deal about the Shang civilization. ⁹Like the Sumerians and the Egyptians, the Shang developed a system of writing with pictographs! ¹⁰As time passed, they introduced ideograms, symbols that express ideas rather than objects. ¹¹They had ideograms for ideas such as unity or wisdom, all together the Shang *Altogether,* written language contained more than three thousand characters.

¹²Within Shang society, there was a strict class system, although most of the people were poor peasants. ¹³The king, his nobles, and the priests assumed all political and religious responsibilities. ¹⁴In contrast to the lavish homes of the wealthy, the farmers lived in simple, small, partially underground houses. ¹⁵These peasants, as you might expect, were called upon to serve as soldiers, they also had to give a portion of their harvest to the king or to one of his local representatives.

Editing and Proofreading Worksheet 2

Correct sentence fragments and run-ons in the following paragraphs, and make any other changes you think will improve the passage. Carefully check for the correct use of commas, periods, and other end punctuation marks. Watch spelling. Work with a partner or small group. Write your revised paragraphs on a separate piece of paper, and compare your revisions with those made by other groups. Students' revisions will vary. Sample revisions shown.

[1]King Arthur's Camelot has captured the imagination of one generation after the next; in fact, tales of Arthur and his Knights of the Round Table have been enchanting people for more than a thousand years. [2]In dozens of languages and in many storytelling genres, ranging from medieval epics to modern musicals, movies, and cartoons. [3]The legend's plot alone! [4]Which makes the story irresistible.

[5]According to the legend, Arthur, an ordinary boy, pulls a sword, which is named Excalibur, from a stone. [6]Based on that deed, Arthur becomes the king of England. [7]Subsequently, he marries the beautiful Guinevere, forms a brotherhood of chivalrous knights, and undertakes a quest for the Holy Grail. [8]His realm is ultimately destroyed by passion, evil, and treachery. [9]With the end of Arthur's realm, comes the loss of loyalty and righteousness throughout the land. [10]Indeed, there arises a civil war in which brother fights against brother.

[11]Did Arthur's court really exist, and if it did exist, where was it. [12]One site often cited is Cadbury Castle on a hill in Somerset, England, near the town of Cadbury, which is in the southwestern part of the country. [13]Cadbury Castle was first identified as Camelot in 1542. [14]Excavations in the 1960s unearthed ruins from fifteen hundred years ago. [15]Archaeologists found evidence of a fortified gate tower and even a wood building, that might have been a great hall. [16]Do these ruins mean King Arthur and Camelot existed. [17]Could these ruins be proof, not just a coincidence.

Exercise A Using Commas and End Marks Correctly

In the following sentences, insert all missing commas, periods for abbreviations, and other end punctuation marks. Correct run-on sentences.

1. Did you know that musical theater existed before Greek tragedy, Roman comedy, satire, and mime?

2. Stone Age people used instruments they crafted from their surroundings to celebrate harvests, births, and successful hunts.

3. A Stone Age painting dating from about 10,000 B.C. portrays a man wearing a buffalo mask, dancing exuberantly, and playing a stringed instrument.

4. Although hardly a Broadway poster, that cave painting from Ariege, France, is the oldest document of musical theater.

5. What do you think of that?

6. Musical theater continued with the Greeks, whose earliest dramas featured some music sung by a chorus.

7. After Athens, Greece, fell in about 400 B.C., dramatists began theater groups that included professional musicians.

8. The role of music in theater grew with Greek mime.

9. By the sixth century A.D., the Christian church had suppressed theater, which it thought sinful.

10. But by the seventh and eighth centuries, a new form of musical theater developed, and that form, in turn, led to the mystery and miracle plays of the Middle Ages.

11. In the sixteenth century, music and dance were prominent in Florence, Italy, and in Paris, France.

12. By the middle of the following century, dance and singing theater split: dance became ballet, and singing theater became opera.

13. The nineteenth century gave us Sir W. S. Gilbert and Sir A. Sullivan and the light opera.

14. Then the light opera evolved into what has become America's unique contribution to theater, the musical comedy.

15. Yes, the heyday of American musical comedy was from the 1930s through the 1960s, wasn't it?

Exercise B ## Revising Paragraphs

Revise the paragraphs below by inserting commas and end punctuation. Correct all run-on sentences and sentence fragments. Be sure to begin each sentence with a capital letter. Students' revisions will vary. A sample revision is given.

¹You know what a hula hoop is, don't you? ²Have you ever tried one? ³A hula hoop craze first swept the United States in 1958. ⁴As soon as the hoops arrived in stores, the stores ran out of them. ⁵Within six months, Americans bought twenty million plastic hoops. ⁶Then there followed significant back injuries, neck injuries, and even heart failure. ⁷However, the hula hoop idea was not a new one, nor were the related medical problems new. ⁸In ancient Egypt, Greece, and Rome, kids made hoops from dried grape vines. They rolled these toys, tossed them, and swung them around their waists. ⁹In ancient England, the center of the rolling toy formed a target for darts. ¹⁰In some South American countries, ¹¹kids used sugarcane plants to make hoops.

¹²Indeed, children's hoop games have been around for a while. ¹³In the fourteenth century, England had another hoop craze. ¹⁴The hoops, made of wood this time, gave doctors fits. ¹⁵The attachment of the word *hula* to *hoop* dates to the eighteenth century. The movements of the hips needed to rotate the toy hoop match the movements in the beautiful, traditional Hawaiian dance.

Exercise C ## Writing Rules of Thumb

Rules of thumb are easy-to-remember recipes for how to do everyday things—such as how to buy a computer or how to fend off a pushy sales clerk. Work with a group or a partner to come up with ten rules of thumb. Refer to your own experiences or to what parents or others have told you. When you've finished, check your sentences for the correct use of commas, periods for abbreviations, and end punctuation marks.

EXAMPLE   When taking a multiple-choice test, never change your first guess when you're not sure of your answer; your first guess is usually correct. Students' rules of thumb will vary; check for the correct use of commas, periods for abbreviations, and end punctuation.

Punctuation: All the Other Marks

Direct students to
chapter-specific
portfolio projects
on Sadlier-Oxford's
web site.

STUDENT WRITING
Movie Review

Godzilla
by Andrew Young
high school student, Yonkers, New York

Godzilla hit theaters with a seemingly weak punch. The movie had an enormous budget but came up short in the box office, which is why I didn't spend eight dollars to see it. I talked to people who saw it, and most reviews were extremely poor. It recently hit the stores, so I decided to pick it up. The movie is amazing. The special effects top those of *Jurassic Park* and *Independence Day*. The story line is a little weak, but still enjoyable. Matthew Broderick is funny and was an excellent choice.

The special effects seem so real that you will believe a giant monster is actually rampaging through Manhattan. Look for landmarks such as the Brooklyn Bridge and Madison Square Garden. The action scenes are well done, mixed with suspense and excitement. Just when you think the excitement has ended, it keeps going. This is true until the very end of the film. Watching this movie brings back memories of the old Japanese Godzilla movies. The thought of a man in a costume ravaging a homemade city makes me laugh when I see the computer-animated Godzilla of today.

I was extremely disappointed that I didn't see the movie in the theater. A thirty-five inch screen with plain stereo does not do it justice. Like the *Star Wars Trilogy*, *Independence Day*, and the *Jurassic Park* movies, *Godzilla* must be viewed in the theater to truly appreciate its stunning effects.

For those who saw this movie already, see it again. If you are one of the unfortunate people who didn't see it in the theaters, I strongly suggest you rent this movie. Pop the popcorn, crank up the volume, sit back, and enjoy.

Andrew Young's movie review includes details about the movie's special effects, the setting, the plot, and the acting. His comparison of the recent movie to the original version of *Godzilla* gives his review both depth and perspective.

Did you notice that all the movies Andrew mentions are in italics? In this chapter, you'll learn when to use italics for titles and when to use quotation marks around titles. Make sure you punctuate titles correctly as you write your own movie and book reviews.

Allow time for students to discuss the student writing. Suggest that they identify its strengths and propose possible improvements. Use the model to introduce the concepts in the chapter.

Colons

🖌 Use a **colon** before a list of items, especially after the words *the following* or *the following items*.

> Among the after-school jobs some seniors hold are the following: video store clerk, sneaker salesperson, food service worker, and cashier.

🖌 Use a colon before a formal statement or quotation and before a long quotation that is set off as a block (any quotation of more than three lines).

> One student, who works evenings at a family entertainment center, explains why her long hours don't bother her: "I don't sleep that much anyway. If I were home, I'd be watching TV or wasting time."

When a long quotation (more than three lines) is set off as a block, indent the quotation, and don't use quotation marks.

> Research shows that most often students work not to save money for college or to help support their families but to have spending money. Here is one student's view:
>
> > I'm not any good at saving. I earn about $700 a month, and each month I spend it all. My salary this month has paid for a cellular telephone, clothes, and an ear piercing. Whatever is left goes toward my prom.

🖌 Use a colon between two independent clauses when the second restates or explains the first. Use a capital letter after the colon if what follows is a complete sentence.

> Some states restrict the number of hours that kids who are sixteen or seventeen can work per week during the school year: In New York, the limit is twenty-eight hours; Washington State's limit is twenty.

🖌 Use a colon to set off a word or phrase you want to emphasize.

> Because she holds down an after-school job, Iris no longer has to do her two least favorite household chores: washing dishes and walking the dog.

🖌 Use a colon in these situations: (1) between the hour and minutes, (2) between the chapter and verse in references to the Bible, (3) after the greeting of a business letter, (4) between a book's title and subtitle, and (5) in a bibliography, between the city and publisher.

> 9:42 P.M.   Luke 10:24–28   Dear Sir or Madam:
> Jobbs, Maya. *Kids at Work: Does it Pay?* New York: Carmel, 2000.

Don't use a colon between a verb and a subject complement or between a verb and a direct object (unless that object is a direct quotation). Don't use a colon between a preposition and its objects.

COMPLEMENT
Hannah's jobs were **salesperson and lifeguard**.

DIRECT OBJECT
Hannah threw **a ball and a frisbee**.

PREPOSITION
Hannah ran **to** the bridge, the track, and the school.

Don't use a colon after *such as, including,* and *especially*.

Adding Colons to Sentences

Insert colons where they are needed in the following sentences. **Hint:** Not every sentence requires a colon. Write *C* if the sentence is correct without a colon.

1. The top two reasons teens give for working are to have spending money and to buy something expensive. C

2. Of the many jobs Jake held, he enjoyed all but the following: shoe salesperson, porter, busboy.

3. Jimea had to be at her job by 5:15 every day.

4. Youth employment boomed in the 1990s: roughly one out of every four high school students had a job at any given time. Accept a semicolon in lieu of the colon.

5. This trend has been fueled by the following conditions: a plentiful supply of jobs in the service industry, a demand for teen workers, and the teens' desires for expensive clothes and other costly items.

6. Students are reading *After School Is Out: Earn, Earn, Earn.*

7. Lia held four jobs in one two-year period: video-rental worker, cashier, sneaker sales clerk, and dog walker.

8. The rise in student workers is a concern among safety experts, legislators, and educators. C

9. These professionals cite the following as concerns: health and safety risks and negative effects on schoolwork.

10. Studies have shown the following effects of working more than twenty hours each week: doing less homework, getting lower grades, and skipping more classes.

11. Some observers think part-time work helps teens. C

12. In fact, the president of one retailers' association claims that students learn valuable skills at work: interpersonal communication and fluency with math.

13. Many educators strongly disagree: they assert that the jobs lack challenge, impose time pressures, and create extra stress. Accept a semicolon in lieu of the colon.

Exercise 2
Answers will vary. Give students full credit if they have stated an opinion and attempted to support their opinions. Look for grammatically complete sentences that begin with a capital letter and end with an appropriate end punctuation mark.

Exercise 2 **Write What You Think**

Decide whether you agree or disagree with the following statement:

Federal law should continue to put strict limitations on the numbers of hours teens can work each week during the school year.

■ **Refer to Composition, Lesson 3.3 to find strategies for writing persuasively.**

To respond to this issue, consider the advantages and disadvantages of after-school work as well as the financial needs students may have. Then state your opinion and support it with anecdotal evidence. Work at least two properly placed colons into your response.

Semicolons

A **semicolon** can show that two or more ideas are closely related.

● Use a semicolon to join independent clauses in a compound sentence *without* a coordinating conjunction.

> Claude McKay was a great poet and essayist of the Harlem Renaissance; McKay did not write much after 1930. [Semicolon alone joins two independent clauses.]
>
> Claude McKay had few equals as a poet; **however**, his novels were not as well crafted. [Semicolon (before conjunctive adverb) joins two independent clauses.]
>
> Claude McKay had few equals as a poet; **as a result**, his poems still appear in textbooks. [Semicolon (before transitional expression) joins two independent clauses.]
>
> Claude McKay was a great poet and essayist of the Harlem Renaissance, **but** he did not write much after 1930. [With a coordinating conjunction, a comma joins two independent clauses.]

You may use a semicolon between independent clauses joined by coordinating conjunctions if either clause contains a comma. But you don't have to.

> She was the last one to read; but when she recited her poems, we were glad we'd stayed.

● Use a semicolon to separate items in a series when one or more of the items contain a comma.

> McKay was born in Upper Clarendon Parish, Jamaica; Langston Hughes was born in Joplin, Missouri, but grew up in Lawrence, Kansas; and Countee Cullen, born in Louisville, Kentucky, and adopted by a Methodist minister, grew up in New York City.

Common Conjunctive Adverbs

accordingly	meanwhile
also	moreover
besides	nevertheless
consequently	otherwise
furthermore	still
however	then
indeed	therefore

Common Transitional Expressions

as a result	in fact
for example	in other
for instance	words
from that	on the other
point on	hand
in addition	that is

Editing Tip

Do not use a semicolon between an independent clause and a dependent clause or phrase.

We read poems by Langston Hughes who is probably the best known of the Harlem Renaissance poets.

Exercise 3 ## Using Semicolons and Colons

Some of the following sentences need a semicolon; others require colons. Review the rules for colons in Lesson 14.1, and then add the proper punctuation marks below. If a sentence is correct, write *C*.

1. Khalilia says that the following are her favorite Harlem Renaissance poets Langston Hughes, Arna Bontemps, and Countee Cullen.

2. Jean Toomer wrote the groundbreaking novel *Cane* (1923) however, his later work never matched it.

3. Early in his writing life, Toomer wrote about African American themes on the other hand, his later work departed from those themes.

4. Toomer developed an interest in a Russian mystic from that point on, his production and fame dropped off considerably.

5. Toomer defined himself not as an African American but as an American.

6. Bontemps and Hughes collected folklore, and they also wrote original works. C

7. Zora Neale Hurston was also a folklorist she collected folktales, spirituals, sermons, blues, work songs, and children's games. Accept colon in lieu of semicolon.

8. In her search for art from the Deep South, Hurston traveled through the following states Florida, Alabama, and Mississippi.

9. Her years of research led to the publication of *Mules and Men* it was the first volume of African American folklore by an African American.

10. Her most famous novel is *Their Eyes Were Watching God*, but some prefer *Dust Tracks on a Road.* C

Exercise 4 Combining Sentences into Compound Sentences

On a separate piece of paper, combine each set of independent clauses into a compound sentence. Do *not* use coordinating conjunctions. You may introduce conjunctive adverbs and transitional expressions. Check your combined sentences for proper punctuation. Answers will vary. Sample answers given.

1. Zora Neale Hurston believed that folklore was priceless. It constitutes the art of the people, who never recognized it as art.
   > constituted

2. Hurston was a self-styled literary anthropologist. She used literary techniques to shape oral narratives.
   > that is, she

3. She created a new literary language. The language reflected the poetry in the oral culture of rural blacks in the South.
   > it

4. Hurston wrote four novels, a memoir, and more than fifty shorter works. She was more prolific than any black woman writer had been before.
   > indeed, she

5. Hurston grew up in Eatonville, Florida. Eatonville was the first incorporated black community in the United States.
   > it

6. Hurston's mother was a teacher in Eatonville. Hurston's father served three terms as mayor there.
   > moreover, her

7. Hurston worked while in high school and college. She worked as a maid, waitress, and manicurist.
   > in fact, she

8. As an English major at Howard University, Hurston began writing short stories and poems. She joined the literary club there.
   > as a result, she

Underlining (Italics)

Italic type is the slanted type that looks like this. When you write by hand, use **underlining** to represent **italics**.

🖐 Use underlining (or italics) for the following kinds of titles and names:

BOOKS	*Wuthering Heights* (novel) *Songs of Jamaica* (book of poems) *The Republic* by Plato
MAGAZINES	*The Nation* *TV Guide* *Smithsonian*
NEWSPAPERS	*The New York Times* *Denver Post*
PLAYS	*Hamlet* *Waiting for Godot* *A Streetcar Named Desire*
MOVIES	*Chariots of Fire* *It's a Wonderful Life* *Titanic*
TV/RADIO SERIES	*48 Hours* *The Lucy Show*
PAINTINGS, SCULPTURES	*Mona Lisa* *Three Musicians*
ALBUMS AND LONG PIECES OF MUSIC	the Beatles' *Abbey Road* Brahms's *German Requiem*
SHIPS, PLANES, SPACECRAFT	*SS United States* *The Spirit of '76* *Challenger*

🖐 Use italics for words and expressions from other languages and for words, letters, numbers, and symbols referred to as such.

OTHER LANGUAGES	*Ad infinitum* means "without end or limit."
WORDS AS WORDS	Is *effect* or *affect* the correct word here?
LETTERS	How many *n*'s and *t*'s are there in *Cincinnati*?
NUMBERS, SYMBOLS	The @ sign is above the *2*.

Exercise 5   Underlining (Adding Italics)

Read the following anecdote. Add underlining to indicate italics.

[1]Last Tuesday afternoon, I went as usual to my teacher's house for my weekly piano lesson. [2]When I arrived, I learned that she'd been called away by an emergency involving her boat, Calypso. [3]I found myself with time on my hands, but it was beginning to rain.

[4]I had no umbrella but was carrying my music book, The Virtuoso Pianist in 60 Exercises, and a copy of the Tulsa Daily Journal. [5]To protect the book and me, I held the Journal over my head. [6]A block away, a theater was advertising two films, Godzilla and Godzilla Meets Titanic.

⁷I ducked under its awning to wait out the storm. ⁸I stood there for a while, humming the title tune from Gene Kelly's movie <u>Singin' in the Rain</u>. ⁹On the

accept without underlining

rains came, <u>ad nauseam</u>. ¹⁰Across the street was a bookstore with a small café. ¹¹I made a beeline for it.

¹²In the magazine section, I found a copy of <u>SportsWeek</u>, my favorite. ¹³I took it and <u>Pop Music World</u> with me to the café. ¹⁴There, under a copy of Grant Wood's painting <u>American Gothic</u>, I ordered a lemonade and sat down to read. ¹⁵Soon, the rain stopped, but I didn't. ¹⁶I was so thoroughly enjoying myself that when I finished my magazines, I read an article in <u>Scientific Teens</u>, which someone had left there, as well as the sports pages of <u>America Today</u>, which someone else had just finished. ¹⁷Sitting there in that bookstore, reading and also listening to Gershwin's opera <u>Porgy and Bess</u> playing in the background, I totally lost track of time. ¹⁸By the time I got home, dinner was cold, and <u>The

accept no underlining for with Jim Lehrer

NewsHour with Jim Lehrer</u> was on TV.

Exercise 6 Writing Brief Reviews

■ **You may wish to refer to the strategies for writing about literature in Composition, Lesson 3.7.**

Imagine that you are the culture critic for your school paper. On a separate piece of paper, write a brief review of (1) a magazine article you've read, (2) an album you've listened to, (3) a movie you've seen, or (4) a concert you've attended. Be brief, but be honest. Explain why you give the work or performance a thumbs-up or thumbs-down. Then swap papers with another class critic. Check each other's work for the correct use of italics (underlining).

Reviews will vary. Check for the correct use of underlining (italics).
You might use this opportunity to have students present their reviews to the rest of the class. Emphasize correct speaking skills before students begin. See teacher pages for assessment rubrics.

Quotation Marks

Lesson 14.3 shows italics (underlining) for certain works of art. This lesson tells when to use quotation marks for shorter works and for other purposes as well.

● Use **quotation marks** for titles of short works.

POEMS	"Ode to a Grecian Urn" "The Lake Isle of Innisfree"
SHORT STORIES	"Araby" "The Fall of the House of Usher"
ARTICLES	"Going Out of Our Gourds Over Pumpkins"
SONGS	"The Star-Spangled Banner" "Penny Lane"
SINGLE TV PROGRAMS	"Rescue at Sea" (an episode of *American Experience*)
PARTS OF BOOKS	Part I, "Essays and Memoirs"

● Use quotation marks at the beginning and end of a direct quotation, but not with an indirect quotation.

Introduce a short, one-sentence quotation with a comma or a colon; introduce a quotation that is a long sentence or more than one sentence with a colon.

> Of T. S. Eliot, critics wrote**,** "Eliot was better equipped than any other poet to bring free verse into the twentieth century."

When only a word or two is quoted, use a lowercase letter if the quoted words do not begin the sentence.

> T. S. Eliot referred to W. B. Yeats as "the greatest poet."
> [no capital letter in quotation]

Editing Tip

Don't use two question marks with a single quotation mark.

Do you know the line after "Where have all the flowers gone?"?

Don't use quotation marks for nicknames or slang.

His nickname is "Spike"; he's a "yuppie."

● Use single quotation marks for titles or quotes within a quotation.

> Brenda asked, "Have you read T. S. Eliot's poem 'Gerontion'?"

● The following rules apply to quotation marks with other marks.

Commas and periods These marks go inside a closing quotation mark.

> "Dinner is ready**,**" he announced.   The title of the story is "Araby**.**"

Semicolons and colons These marks go outside a closing quotation mark.

> Here are three reasons I like "Araby"**:** its characters, its plot, its poetry.

Question marks and exclamation points These go inside closing quotation marks if the quotation is a question or an exclamation; they go outside if the whole sentence is a question or an exclamation.

> "Did everyone read the poem**?**" she asked.
> Was she surprised when you said, "No"**?**

Check the punctuation in the following sentences, and add or change punctuation marks or italics as needed. Some sentences may have more than one problem. If a sentence is punctuated correctly, write *C*.

1. Matthew Arnold's poem "Dover Beach" begins with "The sea is calm tonight."

2. Virginia Woolf wrote the short work "The Lady in the Looking Glass."   C

3. In her introduction to her novel <u>Frankenstein</u>, Mary Shelley refers to "Childe Harold's Pilgrimage," a poem by Lord Byron.

4. The Swedish Academy granted Derek Walcott the 1992 Nobel Prize for Literature and said, "West Indian culture has found its great poet."

5. James Berry, another leading Caribbean poet, wrote the poem "Thoughts on My Mother."

6. In his short story, "The Rocking-Horse Winner," D. H. Lawrence explores the upper middle class.

7. E. M. Forster wrote many novels, including <u>A Passage to India</u> and <u>A Room with a View</u>.

8. Elizabeth Barrett Browning wrote, "How do I love thee? Let me count the ways."

9. Browning's poem also contains these words: "I shall love thee better after death."

10. Eavan Boland dedicated her 1967 book of poems, "New Territory," to her mother.

Exercise 8 Write Your Own Exercise

On a separate piece of paper, write one or more complete sentences for each item below. Mention actual titles wherever possible, but leave out all punctuation marks. Then exchange papers with a classmate. See if you agree on how to punctuate each sentence.   Students' sentences will vary.

1. Your thoughts about an episode of a TV program you watched recently (Make up a name for the episode if you don't remember it.)

2. A song that you've heard recently

3. A direct quotation (actual or made up) at the beginning of a sentence

4. A quotation within a quotation

5. A short story or magazine article you've read and your thoughts about it

6. A poem you've read and your thoughts about it

7. A title of a chapter of a book you are reading and a summary of that chapter

More on Quotation Marks

Dialogue is the conversation between characters in a story or script. The best dialogue is natural sounding—the way real people actually talk. The part of the sentence that identifies the speaker is called the **dialogue tag**. Follow these accepted rules for punctuating dialogue when you write fiction or nonfiction.

- Begin a new paragraph every time the speaker changes.
  "Carl, let me hear your part from the beginning," Ms. Cronin said.
  "OK, here I go," Carl responded.

Note: The following rules also apply to punctuating other kinds of direct quotations, not only dialogue.

- When a direct quotation comes at the beginning of a sentence, use only one punctuation mark—a comma, question mark, or exclamation point (but *not* a period)—to separate it from the dialogue tag that follows.
  "Carl, try that line one more time and with feeling**,**" Ms. Cronin said.
  "Show us that you are angry and upset**!**" Mr. Tandy added emphatically.
  "How do I show that**?**" Carl ventured.

- When a dialogue tag interrupts a quoted sentence, begin the second part of the quotation with a lowercase letter.
  "I'll try again, Ms. Cronin," Carl replied, "**a**nd you'll see that I can do it better."

- Do not use a comma (or colon) and generally do not use a capital letter before a quotation that you introduce with the word *that*.
  The proverb says, "**A**ll good things must come to an end."
  The proverb says **that** "**a**ll good things must come to an end."

Exercise 9 **Punctuating Dialogue**

Add all the appropriate punctuation marks to the passage with dialogue below. Insert a paragraph symbol (¶) to show where a new paragraph should begin.   See Answer Key.

[1]It's Friday, and Zoe and Joseph are having lunch in the school cafeteria. [2]The new British group Ear Plugs is going to give a concert at the Imperial Theater next week Zoe tells Joseph. [3]When do tickets go on

sale? ⁴Joseph asks. ⁵They're on sale starting tomorrow Zoe replies. ⁶Well, why don't you go over there and get us a pair? ⁷I can't Zoe answers because tomorrow's a busy day for me. ⁸My cousins are in town, and I have to show them around all day. ⁹Why don't you go? ¹⁰I can't do it either says Joseph. ¹¹The two stare at each other across their food trays for what seems like hours. ¹²Are you talking to Nell again, Zoe? ¹³Joseph asks. ¹⁴Sort of she replies. ¹⁵Well, can you 'sort of' sit through a concert with her? he wonders aloud. ¹⁶I guess Zoe answers. ¹⁷Are you thinking what I think you're thinking? ¹⁸He nods. ¹⁹OK, she says. ²⁰I'll invite Nell to join us, and I'll ask her to go and pick up the tickets. ²¹Joseph beams. ²²Good thinking he says.

Exercise 10 ## Writing a Dialogue

Work with a partner or small group to create a passage with dialogue. Write the passage on a separate piece of paper, following the conventions for punctuating dialogue. When you write, try to make the dialogue as natural sounding as you can. You may use one of the following suggestions or an idea of your own.

1. Write a humorous conversation between two lions (or other animals) in a zoo.

2. Write a dialogue in which people are in conflict. The people can be friends, teammates, boyfriend and girlfriend, brother and sister, student and teacher, and so on.

Dialogues will vary. Check for correct punctuation, looking in particular for the proper use of quotation marks, end punctuation marks, and capitalization when a tag interrupts a quoted sentence. Suggest that students read the dialogue aloud to make sure it sounds natural.

Apostrophes

● Use an **apostrophe** to show where letters or numbers have been omitted.

I've   we're   they've   we've   doesn't   Class of '02   o'clock

● To show possession, add an apostrophe and -s ('s) to singular nouns. Add an apostrophe and -s ('s) to plural nouns that do not end in -s.

our cousin's house   a day's wait   Cass's skirt   Dickens's novels
bus's windshield   women's clothes   deer's trail   sheep's wool

● To show possession, add only an apostrophe (') to a plural noun that ends in -s.

students' addresses   five cents' worth   the Flores' pool

Use an apostrophe and -s ('s) to show the possessive form of indefinite pronouns.

everybody's favorite   anyone's guess   anyone else's father

● Add only an apostrophe to certain expressions that end in -s or have the sound of /s/.

for goodness' sake   for conscience' sake

● A few compound nouns have two correct possessive forms.

spider web *or* spider's web   rabbit foot *or* rabbit's foot

● To signal individual possession by two or more, make each noun possessive.

Erin's and Jenny's coats   Jess's and Talia's jobs

● To signal joint possession, make only the final noun possessive.

Lulu and Meg's dance class   Lewis and Clark's trip

● Use an apostrophe and an -s ('s) to form the plurals of letters, numbers, symbols, and words referred to as such.

The word *television* has two *e*'s and two *i*'s.
Her social security number has three *0*'s and two *4*'s.
Don't use &'s in your report.
The dialogue has too many *very*'s and *like*'s.

When you write about decades, both **1990s** and **1990's** are acceptable.

Writing Hint

Some proper nouns made up of plural nouns do not take an apostrophe.

Teachers College of Columbia University

Writers Workshop at Iowa

Boys and Girls High School

Exception:
To make pronunciation easier, add only an apostrophe after ancient classical names of more than one syllable and after the names *Moses* and *Jesus*.

Sophocles' writings
Moses' sister
Jesus' life

Editing Tip

Don't use an apostrophe to form the plural of a common or proper noun.
pianos
Those piano's belong to the school.

Never put an apostrophe in a possessive personal pronoun; it already shows possession.
hers
Don't touch that; it's ~~her's~~.

Exercise 11 Using Apostrophes

Write the contraction or possessive for these words or expressions.

1. is not it _____ isn't it _____   6. everybody _____ everybody's _____

2. he would _____ he'd _____   7. everybody else _____ everybody else's _____

3. they have _____ they've _____   8. another _____ another's _____

4. we are _____ we're _____   9. each other _____ each other's _____

5. will not _____ won't _____   10. one another _____ one another's _____

Exercise 12 Correcting Apostrophes

Correct all errors in the use of apostrophes in the following sentences. If a sentence is punctuated correctly, write *C*.

1. Sophie said she couldn't get to the dance recital on time.

2. Should there be +'s in that equation?   C

3. How many y's are in *mystery*?

4. If the 1970s was the "Me Decade," what were the 1980s, the "More Me Decade"?
   accept 1970's   accept 1980's

5. Simone's and Michel's tickets are being held at the booth.

6. Chris's choreography was too difficult for the young dancers.

7. Here's how to learn: study.

8. It's only five minutes' work.

9. First we went to the women's tournament, then the men's.

10. Hannah's parents' new kitchen is a chef's kitchen.
    accept parent's

11. Jacob applied to Teachers College of Columbia University.   C

12. I think the license plate had three 6's.

13. After a day's rest, Carmine went back to work.   C

14. Did you read about Hercules' labors?   C

15. At the poetry reading, we heard several poets' works.

Hyphens, Dashes, Parentheses, Brackets, and Ellipsis Points

● Use a **hyphen** (-) in some compound nouns, in compound adjectives before a noun, and in fractions and numbers from twenty-one to ninety-nine.

In this text, ethnic American nouns and adjectives are not hyphenated (African American, Native American etc.).

president-elect   ice-cold soda
two-ton truck   two-thirds

P.S. Is it *teenager* or *teen-ager*? Dictionaries show which compound nouns take hyphens.

● Use a **dash** (—) or a pair of dashes to highlight material; to show an abrupt break in thought or an interruption; or to mean "namely," "in other words," or "that is."

A World Series ring—a prized possession—was his goal.

TOM   Yesterday, you confiscated my books. You had the nerve to—
AMANDA   I did. I took that horrible novel back to the library—that awful book by that **dissident**, Mr. Lawrence.

● Use **parentheses**—( )—to enclose material of less importance.
The finals (a five-set series) starts today.
The finals start today. (They can go for five matches.)
The finals (they can go for five sets) start today.

● Use **brackets**—[ ]—to enclose parenthetical material that is itself in parentheses and to enclose words that you insert as a comment or explanation into a quotation.

He retired from Harvard in 1999 (he did occasionally lecture at Boston University [BU]) and took up gardening.

Scott Turow said, "Michael Jordan [who retired in 1999] plays basketball better than anyone else in the world does anything else."

● Use three **ellipsis points** (. . .) to indicate omissions from quoted material. Use ellipsis points and a period at the end of quoted material.

I pledge allegiance to the flag . . . and to the Republic for which it stands. . . .

Enriching Your Vocabulary

The Latin roots of *dissident* are *dis-*, meaning "apart," and *sidere*, meaning "sit." As someone who opposes the norm, a *dissident* might disagree with social standards.

Punctuating Sentences

Check the punctuation in the following sentences, and add or change punctuation marks as needed. If a sentence is punctuated correctly, write *C*.

1. Edith Houghton was the first woman scout [1946] (1946) for a major baseball team.

2. Not many women, I can't think of any, scout for the major leagues today.
Accept parentheses in lieu of dashes.

3. Mary H. Donlon was the first woman editor in chief of a law review.   C
Accept *editor-in-chief*.

4. Donlon was also the first woman from New York to become a federal judge.
See (see article on Genevieve Cline).   Accept: judge (see article on Genevieve Cline).

5. Cline was the first woman to be appointed as a federal judge (1928).
Accept substitution of parentheses for dashes.

6. Jacqueline Cochran set a new altitude record for flying—55,253 feet—in 1961.   C

7. Bessie Coleman, the first licensed African American woman pilot, learned French (she was not allowed to take flying lessons in the United States) so that she could take flying lessons in Europe.   Accept dashes in lieu of parentheses; also accept parentheses or dashes in lieu of commas around appositive.

8. In Germany, Coleman flew a plane powered by a 220-horsepower engine.

9. Dorothy Fields was the first woman to win an Oscar for songwriting (1937).

10. Fields wrote song lyrics for forty-one years.

Using Ellipsis Points

Read the familiar passage from the Gettysburg Address by Abraham Lincoln below. Then copy over the passage with the three omissions specified below the passage. Use ellipsis points (three or four) to mark each omission you make.

[1]Now we are engaged in a great civil war, testing whether that nation, or any nation so conceived and so dedicated, can long endure. [2]We are met on a great battlefield of that war. [3]We have come to dedicate a portion of that field, as a final resting place for those who here gave their lives that that nation might live. [4]It is altogether fitting and proper that we should do this.

1. In sentence 1, delete the words *or any nation so conceived and so dedicated* and the commas around those words.

2. In sentence 3, delete the comma and the rest of the sentence.

3. In sentence 4, delete the words *altogether fitting and.*
[1]Now we are engaged in a great civil war, testing whether that nation . . . can long endure. [2]We are met on a great battlefield of that war. [3]We have come to dedicate a portion of that field. . . . [4]It is . . . proper that we should do this.

Editing and Proofreading Worksheet 1

Add punctuation marks to the following paragraphs. Correct all run-on sentences and sentence fragments, and make whatever other changes you think will improve the paragraphs. **Hint:** Look for errors in verb usage.
See Answer Key.

[1]What do writers John Updike and Robert Penn Warren have in common. [2]Well: among other things each has written a poem about baseball. [3]John Updike who has wrote other sports:related literature wrote the poem Tao in the Yankee Stadium Bleachers and Robert Penn Warren wrote the poem *He Was Formidable*. [4]Both of these poems appear in the book "Hummers, Knucklers, and Slow Curves, Contemporary Baseball Poems" [University of Illinois Press; Urbana and Chicago, 1991.] an anthology. [5]The books' editor is Don Johnson.

[6]For people who thought that baseball and poetry were mutually exclusive, this is the book. [7]To change their minds. [8]Baseball poetry, they'll see, goes beyond the ballad Casey at the Bat, this volume including eighty four poems written by fifty seven poets in the 1950s through the 1980's. [9]Some of them first appeared in the baseball literary magazine, Spitfire. [10]The poems Johnson has included here are as "varied, evocative, and enigmatic as the game itself", he claims. [11]They are odes not to famous or legendary players but to the game. [12]From the major leagues to the minor leagues high school games Little League contests and pickup games in neighborhood fields or on the streets.

[13]The collection of poems in this book gets at the essence of the game of baseball. [14]For example: one poem, The Base Stealer, begins by describing the potential base thief as follows "taut like a tightrope walker." [15]Another, entitled Pitcher, begins with the sentence His art is eccentricity.

[16]In his foreward to the poems in the book, Johnson writes the following Baseball is poetry. [17]Baseball is ballet. [18]Baseball is chess. [19]Baseball is mystery.

Editing and Proofreading Worksheet 2

Add punctuation marks to the following draft of a story beginning. Correct all run-on sentences and sentences fragments, and make whatever other changes you think will improve the passage. Add paragraph symbols (¶) to show where each paragraph should begin. **Hint:** Change some of the *said*'s.   See Answer Key.

¹The new department store that had opened in the mall was hiring. ²Reggie and several of his classmates lined up: to fill out job applications in the hopes of getting an interview. ³I certainly need this job Reggie said. ⁴Not as much as I need it said Irene. ⁵But I need it more than either of you since I'm only $500 short on the car I have my eye on said Ben. ⁶Irene laughed and said. ⁷Ben, you'll never save $500? ⁸Not by the time youre twenty one. ⁹Not by the time your ninety nine! ¹⁰You'll spend everything they pay you. ¹¹Now Reggie laughed and said Hey, none of us even has the job yet and there are fifty kids in line here for ten jobs. ¹²What skills and qualities do you think they-ll be looking for said Ben will they be impressed that I worked as a sales clerk. ¹³Did you say a sales clerk? Irene asked. ¹⁴You mean the time you worked at your uncle's bowling alley and handed out shoes? she continued. ¹⁵Oh, I pointed out where the balls were, too and answered all the questions I was asked he replied. ¹⁶Just as Ben was beginning to embellish his explanation, they came to the head of the line. ¹⁷Reggie was the first to be spoken to. ¹⁸Do you speak French fluently? ¹⁹How about Russian? ²⁰Are you familiar with blinis, fois gras, and caviar. ²¹We are looking for experienced sales help in the gourmet department. ²²Oh said Reggie. ²³Oh said Irene. ²⁴Bon jour answered Ben.

Chapter Review

Exercise A Using Colons and Semicolons

Insert colons and semicolons where they belong in the following sentences.
Hint: One sentence needs more than one punctuation mark.

1. The following appeared for the first time in the early 1950s: the telephone-answering machine, 3-D film, and Mr. Potato Head.

2. The Russians launched *Sputnik* in 1957; consequently, the space race was off and running.

3. In 1958, the Brooklyn Dodgers moved to Los Angeles; the Giants moved from New York to San Francisco that same year.

4. In 1960, the first fiber-tipped pens appeared; it was also the year that halogen lamps first made their appearance.

5. Key historical events of the 1960s include three assassinations: JFK's in Dallas, Texas; RFK's in Los Angeles, California; and Martin Luther King, Jr.'s, in Memphis, Tennessee.

Exercise B Using Italics and Quotation Marks

Insert underlining (to represent italics) and quotation marks as required in each of the following sentences. Make sure you place quotation marks in the right position in relation to other punctuation marks. If a sentence is correct as given, write *C*.

1. Joseph Conrad wrote the novel <u>Lord Jim</u> in 1900.

2. In that same year, Puccini's new opera <u>Tosca</u> was performed in Rome.

3. In 1900, the <u>Daily Express</u> first appeared on newsstands in London.

4. In 1899, John Dewey wrote the influential book <u>School and Society</u>.

5. The first trial flight of a *zeppelin* (a rigid airship) took place in 1900. C

6. In 1897, Edwin Arlington Robinson composed the Realist poem "Richard Cory."

7. In line 3, the character Richard Cory is described as "a gentleman from sole to crown."

8. William Dean Howells, who espoused Realism, said: "Let fiction cease to lie about life; let it portray men and women as they are."

9. In 1899, Scott Joplin, the composer and pianist, released the tune titled "Maple Leaf Rag."

10. Sigmund Freud's book <u>The Interpretation of Dreams</u> appeared in 1900.

Exercise C Adding Punctuation to Dialogue

Rewrite the following dialogue on a separate piece of paper. Use quotation marks and other punctuation marks correctly. See Answer Key.

¹Their senior year has just ended, and Maya and Dan are talking about their summers. ²The college I got into has asked me to read several books during the next two months Maya complained, but I'll be traveling and then so busy working that I don't know when I'll find the time. ³How many books are we talking about? Dan asked. ⁴Eight! ⁵Really? ⁶Eight? ⁷Dan responded. ⁸My school wants me to read four novels, but I've already read two of them. ⁹Which ones Maya asked. ¹⁰Oh I read Ragtime by E. L. Doctorow and also Doris Lessing's The Golden Notebook, Dan replied. ¹¹Ragtime is on my list, too, Dan. ¹²Maybe I'll just see the play or rent the video. ¹³Don't do that, Dan answered. ¹⁴The book is far better than either one; you'll really like it. ¹⁵Well, Maya wondered aloud, what about the other seven on my list?

On a separate piece of paper, continue the dialogue between Maya and Dan for at least four more sentences. Avoid the use of *said* as much as possible.

Exercise D Using Other Punctuation Marks

Revise or add punctuation in the following sentences. Decide whether to use apostrophes, hyphens, dashes, parentheses, brackets, quotation marks, or ellipsis points. **Hint:** Some sentences need more than one punctuation mark.

1. Hamlin Garland wrote in the late 1800s and early 1900s; his most famous story is "Under the Lion's Paw." Accept 1800's and 1900's.
2. The Wright brothers' first successful flight occurred in 1903.
3. In 1904, Chicago (an American League team) beat Chicago (a National League team) to win the World Series. Accept commas in lieu of the parentheses.
4. France established the ten-hour workday in 1904.
5. In 1906, the 12.5-mile Simplon Tunnel opened between Switzerland and Italy.
6. In 1906, African American poet Paul Laurence Dunbar died; he was thirty-four. Accept commas in lieu of the parentheses.
7. Jack London (1876–1916) published the story "To Build a Fire" in 1908.
8. The U.S. population in 1910—92 million—was less than half of what it is today. Accept commas or parentheses in lieu of dashes.

Capitalization

Direct students to chapter-specific portfolio projects on Sadlier-Oxford's web site.

STUDENT WRITING
Research Paper

Woodrow Wilson's "Peace Without Victory" Address, January 22, 1917
A Continuity of Thought
by Uthara Srinivasan
high school student, Flossmoor, Illinois

On January 22, 1917 [as European crises threatened to draw the United States into World War I], President Woodrow Wilson delivered a speech to the Senate titled "Peace Without Victory," in which he claimed America had "no concern with the 'causes or objects' of the war."[1] He did not reiterate this theme in his address on April 2. Rather, he asked Congress to recognize the state of war with Germany, and he urged the American people to give their "blood and treasure"[2] for democracy's sake. This dramatic shift from neutrality to belligerence has been presented as proof of Wilson's deceptiveness and his mastery of words. Former President Theodore Roosevelt charged that Wilson was part of a "nauseous hypocrisy."[3]

Yet, if one carefully scrutinizes a few lines of the "Peace Without Victory" speech, one detects a strong resemblance to the Fourteen Points and other [of President Wilson's] wartime speeches. This suggests that despite the metamorphosis of America's policies, there was a goal that remained constant. This goal that drove Wilson tirelessly from one means to another was the hope for a liberal post war order. Regardless of what Wilson's critics allege, there is a powerful degree of continuity in his wartime speeches. An analysis of his "Peace Without Victory" speech and its striking similarities to previous and following speeches proves this point.

[1]"Peace Without Victory," in Henry Steele Commager, ed., *Documents of American History, Volume II: Since 1898,* 9th ed. (Englewood Cliffs, NJ: Prentice Hall, Inc., 1973), p. 125.

[2]Arthur S. Link, *Woodrow Wilson: A Brief Biography* (Cleveland: The World Publishing Company, 1963), p. 113.

[3]Patrick Devlin, *Too Proud to Fight: Woodrow Wilson's Neutrality* (New York: Oxford University Press, 1975), p. 684.

Uthara Srinivasan's paragraphs make an effective introduction to her full research paper. In the first paragraph, the author introduces the problem that the paper will deal with and then states her thesis in the second paragraph. The final sentence of the second paragraph tells the reader what to expect in the body of the paper.

As you reread the introduction, notice the many different uses for capital letters. You'll review the rules for capital letters in the lessons and exercises in this chapter.

Allow time for students to discuss the student writing. Suggest that they identify its strengths and propose possible improvements. Use the model to introduce the concepts in the chapter.

Proper Nouns and Proper Adjectives

Both **proper nouns**, which name particular places, persons, things, or ideas, and **proper adjectives**, which derive from proper nouns, begin with a capital letter.

◖ Capitalize the names of people.

Emily Dickinson   Richard the Lion-Hearted   Martin Luther King, Jr.

Some last names have more than one part. Find out whether the name is spelled with only one or with more than one capital letter; customs vary.

MacNeill   O'Conner   Martin Van Buren
Ludwig van Beethoven   Leonardo da Vinci   Miguel de la Torre y Díaz

◖ Capitalize geographic names.

PLANETS, CONSTELLATIONS	Mars the Milky Way the constellation Orion
CONTINENTS, DIVISIONS	Asia Africa Arctic Circle Tropic of Cancer
ISLANDS	Cuba Trinidad Staten Island Majorca
COUNTRIES	Egypt China Great Britain the Netherlands
STATES	Texas Utah Delaware South Dakota
CITIES	Detroit Salt Lake City Miami Dar es Salaam
BODIES OF WATER,	Aegean Sea the Great Lakes Hudson River
MOUNTAINS	Mount Everest Appalachian Mountains
LOCALITIES, REGIONS	Cape of Good Hope the Dustbowl
STREETS, HIGHWAYS	Broadway River Road Thirty-fourth Street
BUILDINGS, MONUMENTS	the Chrysler Building Buckingham Palace
PARKS, FORESTS	Yosemite St. Mary's Park Muir Woods

> ### Editing Tip
> In these examples, articles and short prepositions that are part of a name are *not* capitalized, for example *of* in *Tropic of Cancer*. Also, do not capitalize common nouns. Write *East River* but the *river*.

Do not capitalize compass directions. Capitalize directional words only when they refer to a region of the world or of a country.

Drive east on Interstate 70.
Gold was discovered in the American Southwest.

◖ Capitalize some nouns, verbs, and adjectives that derive from proper nouns.

Persian rug   Elizabethan England   Stalinize   Stalinism

Some words that owe their existence to a proper noun have become so popular in English that they no longer take a capital letter. Again, use a dictionary to check when to capitalize and when not to.

SOURCE OF WORD	COMMON TERM
Louis Pasteur, microbiologist	pasteurize
John Montague, Earl of Sandwich	sandwich
James Watt, inventor	watt

> ### Writing Hint
> Whenever you're not sure about whether to capitalize an adjective, check a dictionary, which sometimes gives two spellings, the preferred spelling first.
>
> french fry *or* French fry *but* French horn
>
> india rubber *or* India rubber *but* Indian pudding

Exercise 1 Proofreading Sentences

Insert capital letters where they belong in the following sentences. To indicate a capital letter, write in the proofreading symbol of three underscores beneath the letter: (t). Use a dictionary or atlas for help if necessary.

1. Last night, we were able to see the constellation capricorn.

2. The potomac river forms the border between virginia and maryland.

3. Is captiva the name of an island off florida's west coast?

4. Did you know that monument valley is a tribal park in southern utah?

5. Gold was discovered on john augustus sutter's property in california.

6. Our hike up long's peak took us above the timber line.

7. Along seventy-fourth street, you'll see a series of townhouses.

8. The vietnam war memorial is a must for visitors to our nation's capital.

Exercise 2 Writing a Report

Work with a partner or small group to write a report based on the following notes. First, capitalize all the words on the note card that should be capitalized. Then, write your report on a separate piece of paper. Proofread it carefully to make sure you've written complete sentences and capitalized all the words that need to be capitalized   Students' reports will vary. See teacher pages for assessment rubrics.

---

windsor castle—the patriarch of palaces

castle located on cliff along thames river, 25 miles from london, england

founded by william the conqueror in about 1070 as stronghold

became royal residence in 1110; replaced an ancient saxon palace

english kings and queens in residence at windsor castle for centuries

rooms remodeled in turn by edward III, charles II, george IV

george III liked it; wife (queen charlotte) had her private rooms moved to part called southeast tower

tower officially named queen's tower after coronation of elizabeth II

today Queen elizabeth: private weekends there

Titles

● Capitalize titles and abbreviations of titles when they are used before names but not when they appear without a name. Also capitalize abbreviations of academic degrees after a name.

Senator Charles Schumer	a United States **s**enator
Queen Christina	several **k**ings and **q**ueens
Enid Lopez, **D.D.S.**	the **d**entist's office

Exceptions: A few important titles may get capital letters even without a person's name: *the President of the United States; the Pope; the Chief Justice of the Supreme Court.* Sometimes, in internal communications, organizations capitalize the titles of their officers.

The **Chairman** will address stockholders.

Usually, the word *the* before a title is *not* capitalized.

the **Prime Minister**.

● Capitalize a word that shows a family relationship only when it is used before a name but without a possessive pronoun.

Uncle Dan   Grandma Alice   my cousin Rosalie   her step-brother

● Capitalize all the important words in the salutation of a business or friendly letter but only the first word of the closing.

Dear Sir or Madam: Dear Li,   Yours truly,   Your friend,

● Capitalize the first and last word and all important words in the titles and subtitles of works.

Note: Unless they are the first word in a title, do not capitalize the following small words: articles (*the, a, an*), coordinating conjunctions (such as *and, but*), and prepositions with fewer than five letters (such as *into, with, to*).

BOOKS	*Of Mice and Men* *Uncle Tom's Cabin*
PERIODICALS	*The New York Times* *Smithsonian* magazine
STORIES, ESSAYS,	"A Mild Attack of Locusts" "The Night the Bed Fell"
HISTORICAL DOCUMENTS	the Gettysburg Address
POEMS	"Song of Myself" "The Raven"
PLAYS	*Pygmalion* *The Sound of Music* *A View from the Bridge*
TV SERIES	*Law and Order* *Cheers* *Live from Lincoln Center*
WORKS OF ART	Homer's *Breezing Up* Rodin's *The Thinker*
MUSICAL WORKS	Beethoven's *Fifth Symphony* "Singin' in the Rain"
MOVIES	*The Wizard of Oz* *The Graduate*
TRAINS, SHIPS, PLANES	the *Orient Express* the *Titanic* the *Enola Gay*
SPACECRAFT	*Apollo 11*

Exercise 3 · Proofreading Sentences

Insert capital letters where they belong in the following sentences. To indicate a capital letter, use the proofreading symbol of three underscores beneath the letter: (n̲). If a sentence is correct, write *C*.

1. Graham Greene is my uncle John's favorite author.

2. Indeed, uncle John likes Greene's short story "across the bridge."

3. His favorite novel is Greene's *our man in havana*.

4. Marissa's favorite TV show is a soap opera, *the days of our lives*.

5. Ed wanted to watch both *monday night football* and *live from the met*.

Exercise 4 · Proofreading a Letter

Work with a partner to insert capital letters where they belong in the letter of recommendation that follows. Use the proofreading symbol of three underscores beneath a letter to indicate that it should be capitalized: (f̲).

---

¹Dear professor Smith:

²I recommend my student Henry Harper for a part-time position at manassas national battlefield park. ³He is well read and self-motivated.

⁴While doing research for his term paper, "the immediate aftermath of the civil war," Henry developed a passion for that American tragedy. ⁵He began his study of the conflict by reading two general history books, *a people and a nation* and *the reader's companion to american history*. ⁶For a closer look at the mid-nineteenth century in america, he obtained James McPherson's book *battle cry of freedom*. ⁷For information on the causes of the war, he picked up Freehling's *the road to disunion*. ⁸He also obtained several books about military figures, including Freeman's biography of general Lee and Henry's own distant cousin pvt. James Harper's 1865 diary.

⁹I think you will find mr. Harper an impressive addition to your staff at the park.

¹⁰sincerely,

Pauline Esserman
Pauline Esserman, ph.d.

To practice using capital letters, you may wish to have students write a review for a local newspaper that compares two new movies. Have students exchange papers and check other's work for correct capitalization.

First Words, Organizations, Religions, School Subjects

Capitalize the first word in a direct quotation when the quotation either was originally a complete sentence or, as quoted, makes a complete sentence. But do not capitalize the first word in an indirect quotation, and do not capitalize a quotation if you precede it with *that*.

DIRECT	Julie said, "Your last move was sloppy. Do it again."
INDIRECT	Julie said that our move was sloppy.
DIRECT	The Declaration of Independence states, "All men are created equal." [Here, the *a* in *All* is capitalized even though it is not capitalized in the original.]
THAT + DIRECT	The document states that "all men are created equal."

If a quoted sentence is interrupted, begin the second part with a lowercase letter.

"Now," she said firmly, "let's try it again."

Editing Tip

Capitalize a parenthetical sentence that stands on its own.

The test is on verbs. (Review irregular verbs.)

In general, do not capitalize a parenthetical sentence within another sentence.

The test is on verbs (review irregular verbs) and French culture.

🔹 Use a capital letter after a colon if what follows is more than one sentence or if it is a formal statement or a quotation.

The dean issued the following statement: No smoking.
The new rule did not appeal to everyone: It bothered some faculty members who smoke as well as local tobacco shops.
It didn't appeal to everyone: "We protest," said some faculty members.

🔹 Capitalize the names of languages, nationalities, peoples, races, and religions.

The national language of Iran is Farsi, and most Iranians are Muslim.
The Seminoles were part of the Muskogee Confederacy.

🔹 Generally, capitalize the names of groups, teams, businesses, institutions, government agencies, and organizations.

American Library Association	the U.S. Senate	William H. Sadlier, Inc.
Binghamton University	Greenpeace	Toronto Blue Jays

Watch out! Some companies use capital letters unconventionally.

WordPerfect	PaineWebber	eWorld	aquaCorps

🔹 Capitalize the names of school subjects that are followed by a number. Also capitalize the names of all languages and proper adjectives.

Jonathan is taking French, Algebra 1, chemistry, and American history.

The terms *Black* and *White* may be capitalized or lowercased when referring to people. Whichever style students choose should be used consistently.

Exercise 5 **Proofreading Sentences**

Insert capital letters where they belong. To indicate a capital letter, use the proofreading symbol of three underscores beneath the letter: (s).

1. do you know who it was who described Washington as "first in war, first in peace, and first in the hearts of his countrymen"?

2. She explained, "the baseball teams that play their preseason games in Arizona are part of the cactus league."

3. horses came to north america thanks to europeans.

4. spanish explorers were the first europeans ever seen by the aztecs.

5. after he graduated from brown university, my uncle joined the organization called volunteers in service to america.

6. baseball teams recruit players from latin american countries. (currently, cuba is off-limits.)

7. he played in the national league and then coached for the orioles in the american league.

8. charles had to take algebra 2 in summer school.

9. he was the first jewish member of the house of representatives.

10. while he was there, the democratic party was in power.

Exercise 6 **Create Your Own Exercise**

On a separate piece of paper, write one or more complete sentences in response to each numbered item. When you've finished writing, exchange papers with a classmate. Check each other's sentences for the correct use of capital letters.
Students' sentences will vary.

1. Tell what subjects you are taking this term.

2. Write a sentence in which you quote a writer, songwriter, or speaker.

3. Name two organizations you'd like to join in order to do volunteer work. Explain your choices.

4. Name two of your favorite sports teams, and compare their recent efforts.

5. Write a sentence about a religious holiday and how it is celebrated.

6. Name a country you'd like to visit and what you'd do once you got there.

7. Think of a quotation that has some meaning for you, and rewrite it in the form of an indirect quotation.

8. Name a company for which you'd never work. Give your reasons.

9. Name a club you'd consider joining and tell why.

10. Write a question that you think high schools should ask graduating seniors.

I and *O*; Historical Events, Documents and Periods; Calendar Items; Brand Names; Awards

🖌 Capitalize the words *I* and *O*.

Always capitalize the first-person pronoun *I* and the rare interjection *O*. Capitalize the modern interjection *oh* only when it is the first word in a sentence.

> I used to want to be a firefighter; now I want to be a poet.
>
> She was running, oh, about five miles a day.
>
> "O **valiant** cousin! Worthy gentleman!"—*Macbeth*, Act I

P.S. You may quote a writer's use of *O*, but chances are, you won't be putting *O*'s into your own poetry or prose.

🖌 Capitalize the names of historical and special events, documents, and periods.

HISTORICAL EVENTS	World War I Battle of Waterloo
SPECIAL EVENTS	Kentucky Derby the Special Olympics March Madness
DOCUMENTS	Declaration of Independence the Magna Carta Treaty of Paris
PERIODS	the Dark Ages the Industrial Revolution the Cenozoic Era

🖌 Capitalize calendar items but not seasons.

CALENDAR ITEMS	Passover Palm Sunday Monday, June 4
SEASONS	autumn colors a hot summer fall semester

Do not use capital letters to refer to a century.

> twenty-first century   seventeenth-century painting

🖌 Capitalize brand names for manufactured products.

> Microsoft Word for Windows   Honda Civic   Boeing 727

Do not capitalize the common noun that follows a brand name.

> Freshmouth mouthwash   Grovestand olives

🖌 Capitalize the names of awards and prizes.

> the Pulitzer Prize   an Academy Award   the Newberry Medal

Writing Hint

In general writing, you may spell a word in all capitals for emphasis.

STOP!

Avoid this practice in e-mail, where all capitals are interpreted as rude screaming. Instead, for emphasis in e-mail, use asterisks before and after a word or group of words.

You *must* meet me at 3 P.M.

You will also see the word **prize** or **award** lowercased as in "Pulitzer prize."

Exercise 7 **Proofreading Sentences**

Proofread the following sentences for the correct use of capital letters. Use the proofreading symbols of a slash to indicate lowercase and three underscores to indicate a capital.

$\cancel{S}$ummer = lowercase letter   the o̲lympics = capital letter

1. Barbara Tuchman's book, *A Distant Mirror*, is set in the $\cancel{F}$ourteenth $\cancel{C}$entury.

2. When I was a kid, I loved $\cancel{C}$hocolate $\cancel{C}$hip $\cancel{C}$ookies by Chunky.

3. My uncle drives a b̲uick c̲entury.

4. Early every $\cancel{S}$pring, Wallace takes out his baseball glove to oil it.

5. Pat prefers club soda to p̲epsi or s̲prite, two popular brands of flavored soda.

6. Sophie wrote, "When i̲ read the g̲ettysburg a̲ddress, i̲ was truly moved."

7. During the dig, the archaeologists discovered tools from the b̲ronze a̲ge.

8. The w̲ars of the r̲oses were fought in the $\cancel{F}$ifteenth century between two English royal families.

9. She won an e̲mmy for her performance on the sitcom.

10. In New Orleans, participants prepare year-round for m̲ardi g̲ras.

Students' paragraphs will vary. See teacher pages for assessment rubrics.

Exercise 8 **Writing a Paragraph**

Write one or more paragraphs based on the information in the table below. Mention names and figures from the table as well as other information you know about those movies or other successful ones. Include your opinions about the movies and their popularity. Check your paragraphs for the correct use of capital letters. Share your writing with classmates.

All-Time Top 20 American Movies Through 1996			
RANK/TITLE/DATE	GROSS[1] (millions)	RANK/TITLE/DATE	GROSS[1] (millions)
1. E.T.: The Extra-Terrestrial (1982)	$399.8	11. Raiders of the Lost Ark (1981)	$242.4
2. Jurassic Park (1993)	357.1	12. Twister (1996)	241.7
3. Forrest Gump (1994)	329.7	13. Ghostbusters (1984)	238.6
4. Star Wars (1977)	322.7	14. Beverly Hills Cop (1984)	234.8
5. The Lion King (1993)	312.9	15. Toy Story (1995)	228.1
6. Independence Day (1996)	306.2	16. The Empire Strikes Back (1980)	222.7
7. Home Alone (1990)	285.8	17. Mrs. Doubtfire (1993)	219.2
8. Return of the Jedi (1983)	263.7	18. Ghost (1990)	217.6
9. Jaws (1975)	260.0	19. Aladdin (1992)	217.4
10. Batman (1989)	251.2	20. Back to the Future (1985)	208.2

(1) Gross is in absolute dollars based on box office sales in the U.S. and Canada. Ticket prices favor recent films, but older films have the advantage of reissues. Source: *Variety* magazine.

Revise and proofread these paragraphs. Correct sentence fragments and run-on sentences, eliminate wordiness, and make any other changes you think will improve the paragraphs. Write your revised report on a separate piece of paper. **Hint:** Watch out for spelling mistakes, too, although all place names are spelled correctly.   Answers will vary. A sample revision is given.

¹Jane Austen, who was born near the town of basingstoke in the late Eighteenth Century and lived into the Nineteenth, was an english writer whose treatment of ordinary people gave the Novel its modern flavor. ²Although her Formal Education was brief, she grew up within a loving network of family and friends, who provided a stimulating environment for her writing. ³(she would later populate her writing with these country people; in fact, austen once said, "three or four families in a country village is the very thing to work on.")

⁴Austin's first serious work, which she wrote in 1793–1794. ⁵Was a short novel entitled *lady susan*. ⁶In 1801, when Jane was twenty-six, the family moved West to the city of bath. ⁷After that, they moved around lots, going *the family*   *a great deal*

to London, clifton, warwickshire, and southampton. ⁸In 1809, Austen moved with her Mother and Sister to a cottage in clawton. ⁹It was a small village. *the small village of*

¹⁰Their she wrote *sense and sensibility* and *pride And prejudice*. ¹¹These were published in 1811 and 1813, respectively. ¹²*Pride and prejudice* begins with the famous statement that "A single man in possession of a good fortune must be in want of a wife." ¹³austen wrote all her books anonymously; it was only after her death in 1817 that her brother Henry made publick her authorship. *There*   *which*

¹⁴austen's focus on character and personality and on the tensions between her heroines and society makes her writing seem more like Modern Writing than that of the Eighteenth or early Nineteenth Centuries. ¹⁵This modern feel, along with an abundance of wit and realism, makes Austen's novels appealing to readers today.

Editing and Proofreading Worksheet 2

Work with a partner or a small group to proofread and revise these paragraphs. Correct sentence fragments and run-on sentences, eliminate wordiness, and make any other changes you think will improve the paragraphs. Write your revised report on a separate piece of paper. Compare your response with those made by other pairs or groups of classmates. **Hints:** The word *sun* does not take a capital. Watch out for spelling mistakes, too.

Revisions may vary. A sample revision is given.

¹I knew that earth was the planet between venus and mars and the only one known too be inhabited by carbon-based Life Forms. ²But i didn't know much more about my home planet;·in fact,·my understanding belonged in the middle [since] ages, so I did a ~~tad~~ [bit] of research. ³I learned ~~millions of~~ [many] things.

⁴First of all, I learned about the Theory that a gas cloud began to form about 10 to 15 billion years ago. ⁵~~Cool.~~ [Later, it cooled.] ⁶About 5 or 6 billion years ago, shock waves caused the collection of dust and gases to collapse and spin. ⁷The spinning cloud flattened, and all its material started to drop toward its center. ⁸This falling action was the beginning of today's sun.

⁹~~Now, listen up.~~ ¹⁰Turbulence at the outer edge of the cloud caused particles to clump together and form planetoids. ¹¹~~These planetoids~~ [which] began acting like gravity collectors, ~~sweeping~~ [that swept] through space and ~~gathering~~ [gathered] mass. ¹²~~Like~~ [As] they say, "a rolling stone gathers no mass; just planetoids do." ¹³Meanwhile, the real action was at the center of the collapsing cloud; ~~their~~ [there] it was getting hotter, and pressure was increasing. ¹⁴Eventually, thermonuclear reactions ignited the sun. ¹⁵Then the planets evolved. ¹⁶~~And~~ there you have it; Now you know what I know. ¹⁷(for more information on Astronomy, ~~check out,~~ [read] ~~like~~ [as] i did, the essay "a short history of the solar system" in our Science textbook.)

Chapter Review

Exercise A Proofreading Sentences

Insert capital letters where they belong in the following sentences. To indicate a capital letter, use the proofreading symbol of three underscores beneath the letter: (d).

or Best Actor

1. who won the academy award for best actor in 1990?
2. Is seneca lake (near ithaca, new york) one of the finger lakes?
3. Robert e. lee lived in arlington, across the potomac river from washington, d.c.
4. humphreys peak (no apostrophe), home of the snow bowl, is the tallest mountain in arizona and one of the highest in the southwest.
5. Terry applied to universities in Georgia and alabama; her interest is archaeology.
6. Miguel moved to his aunt martha's apartment on twenty-sixth street in the neighborhood called chelsea.
7. Thanks to the invention by John McAdam, an engineer, we followed a macadamized road to hagerstown.
8. The board of directors of the continental oil company met with queen Elinor.
9. The mountains southeast of the sierras aren't nearly as high.
10. The gettysburg address is stored in the institution known as the library of congress.

Exercise B Proofreading Paragraphs

Proofread the following sentences for the correct use of capital letters. Use the proofreading symbol of three underscores to indicate a capital letter; use the proofreading symbol of a slash to indicate a lowercase letter. **Hint:** Names of chemical elements, such as zinc and plutonium, do not require capitals.

¹marie Sklodowska and pierre curie met at the university of paris in the late Nineteenth Century. ²they married in 1895 and were among the pioneers of a new field of study: The field of radioactivity.

³While the curies were at the University, a professor there, dr. henri becquerel, discovered that the element uranium had unusual properties: It gave off something that darkened a photographic plate. ⁴becquerel had

Chapter 15 • Capitalization **343**

discovered radioactivity. [5]After this discovery, marie curie, who was his student, began studying pitchblende, the mineral that contains uranium. [6]she concluded that there were other radioactive substances in pitchblende.

[7]Pierre put aside his own research and worked with his wife to study the pitchblende. [8]The work was tedious, difficult, smelly, and physically taxing. [9](they had to stir, for hours at a stretch, the boiling matter in a smelting basin.) [10]in 1898, their efforts resulted in a key finding.

[11]the curies discovered that in addition to the uranium, the pitchblende contained two other radioactive elements: Polonium and Radium. [12]polonium was chosen as a name because marie was polish. [13]Radium, they found, was a hundred times more radioactive than uranium. [14]In 1903, the world recognized the efforts of becquerel and the curies: they

or Physics

were awarded the nobel prize in physics. [15]Marie Curie won another nobel prize in 1911, this time in chemistry, for her study of the chemical properties of radium.

[16]it wasn't until world war I that the disastrous effects of radioactive poisoning became known to the Public. [17]A number of workers who used a radioactive substance to illuminate dials had been wetting the points of their brushes on their lips. [18]in so doing, these workers had been accumulating significant amounts of radium internally. [19]Twenty-Four of them died of cancer within two Decades. [20]When marie curie died in 1934, she left her only property of value, a gram of pure radium, to her Daughter.

Spelling

STUDENT WRITING
Persuasive Essay

Student Parking Lot a Wild and Crazy Place
by Adam Andress
high school student, Clearwater, Florida

It's 2:40 P.M. at CCC. The crows are chirping, and the squirrels are happily looking for leftover lunch food in the trash cans. So far it has been a nice and quiet day. As the announcements come on, students hover near the classroom doors and get into position. The tension rises. The bell rings, aannd . . . "They're Off!!"

Students sprint to the parking lot with a speed only matched by the velocity they will achieve in their cars as they race to get out of school the fastest. Seniors usually get there first due to many advantages. They are closer to Haines Bayshore, and the juniors and sophomores have to swim to their cars after a rainy day.

"There is a drainage problem in the junior parking lot," said junior John Boni. "We have Lake Marauder in the parking lot, and my car is right in the center."

For lingering students on their way to their cars, it is now time to cross the road of death. If you have ever played the game Frogger, you know what it is like to cross the parking lot. As you wait to cross, the wind from the 50-mph cars blows your hair and slaps at your face. You then see a hole and run like you have never run before. You cross one lane in the parking lot successfully, but then a car pulling out of another lane almost gets you.

You jump into your car, but you drop your bag. Like Indiana Jones, you reach your hand out and grab it just in time to recoil before a car flies by and almost takes your hand with it. It is now time to pull out. Either there is a car heading in your direction at Mach 3, or the slowest-walking person is behind you. After about five minutes, you eventually succeed in pulling out on Haines Bayshore.

Wait a minute! Is that the sound of thunder? It's beginning to get louder. El Ninō? Nope, it's the $3,000 stereo system installed in a car worth about half that. The volume is cranked up so that every single person on the campus can hear it. Who in his or her right mind can drive with such bass, one that makes the windows in your car rattle?

Some students might think that there needs to be more regulation during dismissal, but what faculty member would go on a suicide mission like that? We need to just take our time and not rush, especially on Friday, or someone may get hurt.

We have made many requests to drive more safely, but the student body has not listened to a word of advice. So don't forget to buckle up, and please try to keep it under 20 mph.

Adam Andress wrote this persuasive essay for an audience of his peers. His word choice is informal and friendly; he uses exaggeration and humor to make his point. In spite of his friendly style, however, he offers specific details and examples for his opinion.

Can you find any misspelled words in Adam's essay? Look again. Adam's essay is effective partly because it is error free. In this chapter, you'll go over rules and advice to help you spell words correctly whenever you write.

Allow time for students to discuss the student writing. Suggest that they identify its strengths and propose possible improvements. Use the model to introduce the concepts in the chapter.

Using a Dictionary

◖ If you're in doubt about how to spell a word, use a dictionary.

In addition to verifying the spelling of an entry word, a dictionary helps with several other spelling issues related to the entry word. The call-outs on the entries below show the following information: how to spell an irregular plural of a noun; the comparative and superlative forms of an adjective; the past, past participle, and present participle of a verb; and words related to the entry word.

Entry word with syllable breaks · Past and present participle forms of verb

ac·cu·mu·late \ə-'kyü-m(y)ə-,lāt\ *vb* **-lat·ed; -lat·ing** [L *accumulatus*, pp. of *accumulare*, fr. *ad-* + *cumulare* to heap up — more at CUMULATE] *vt* (15c): to gather or pile up esp. little by little: AMASS <~ a fortune> ~ *vi:* to increase gradually in quantity or number.

Pronunciation · Part of speech · Etymology, or word history

ac·cu·rate \'a-kyə-rət\ *adj.* [L *accuratus*, fr. pp. of *accurare* to take care of, fr. *ad-* + *cura* care] (1596) **1 :** free from error esp. as the result of care <an ~ diagnosis> **2 :** conforming exactly to truth or to a standard: EXACT <providing ~ color> **3 :** able to give an accurate result <an ~ gauge> *syn* see CORRECT *adv* — **ac·cu·rate·ly** *n* — **ac·cu·rate·ness** · Related words

Irregular plural of noun

ac·cused *n. pl* **accused** (1593) : one charged with criminal offense; *esp*: the defendant in a criminal case · Comparative and superlative forms of adjective

achy \āk' ē\ *adj.* **ach·i·er; ach·i·est** (1875) : afflicted with aches — **ach·i·ness** *n*

—from *Merriam Webster's Collegiate Dictionary*, Tenth Edition

In doing the following exercises, use a college dictionary to find or check your answers.

Exercise 1 Using a Dictionary to Check Spelling

Write the letter of the correct spelling in the blank. If you're not sure of the correct spelling of a word, look up the item in a dictionary to check the correct spelling.

1. __b__ (a) anilize (b) analyze (c) analize (d) annalyze

2. __c__ (a) compatant (b) competant (c) competent (d) compitent

3. __d__ (a) cirkit (b) cuircit (c) cercuit (d) circuit

> ### Writing Hint
> If you can't find a word in a dictionary after trying a few possible spellings, ask someone for help, or use a computer spell checker. The spell checker may "guess" the word you're looking for.

4. __c__ (a) contious   (b) consious   (c) conscious   (d) conscius

5. __a__ (a) attendance   (b) attendence   (c) atendance   (d) atendence

6. __c__ (a) elligible   (b) elegible   (c) eligible   (d) elidgible

7. __b__ (a) hipocrisy   (b) hypocrisy   (c) hippocrisy   (d) hypacrisy

8. __d__ (a) gratious   (b) gracius   (c) grashus   (d) gracious

9. __c__ (a) morgige   (b) morgage   (c) mortgage   (d) moregage

10. __a__ (a) intelligence   (b) inteligence   (c) intellagence   (d) intellegence

Exercise 2   Using a Dictionary

Answer the following spelling-related questions. Use a college dictionary, as necessary, to answer the questions. Answers are based on *Merriam Webster Collegiate Dictionary*, Tenth Edition.

1. What are two plurals for the noun *index*? __indexes, indices__

2. What are all the points at which you can place a hyphen to hyphenate the word *possibility* at the end of a line? __pos si bil i ty__

3. How do you spell the past tense and present participle of the verb *regret*? __regretted, regretting__

4. What is an acceptable three-letter abbreviation for *phenylthiocarbamide*? _____PTC_____

5. What is an adjective form of the noun *phlegm*? _____phlegmy_____

6. What is an alternate spelling for *jujitsu*? __jujutsu, jiujitsu, jiujutsu__

7. How do you spell the verb that means "to get off to a speedy start"?
a. jump start   b. jumpstart   c. jump-start _____c_____

8. What does your dictionary say about capitalizing (or not) geologic eras? Should you write *Precambrian* or *precambrian*? __Precambrian__

9. How do you spell the word for the symbol for the medical profession? The word begins with the letters *cadu-*. _____caduceus_____

10. What choices, if any, does your dictionary give you for spelling the past tense of the verb *program*? __programmed, programed__

Exercise 3   Create Your Own Exercise

Work with a partner to write two paragraphs. Your paragraphs can be the beginning of a personal anecdote, story, autobiographical incident, or letter to an editor at a newspaper or magazine. Purposely misspell some of the words you use. Then exchange papers with another pair of classmates to find and correct all misspellings. Answers will vary.

Spelling Rules

In spite of the many irregularities in English spelling, there are some rules—there are also exceptions to the rules.

● Write *i* before *e* except after *c*.

Note that the words in the first line below have a long /e/ sound. But *i* also comes before *e* in *friend* and *mischief*, which do not have a long /e/ sound.

FOLLOW RULE	retrieve	relieve	niece	siege	
AFTER *C*	perceive	ceiling	conceit	receipt	deceive
EXCEPTIONS	seize	(n)either	leisure	weird	caffeine

P.S. If these rules and exceptions don't help, remember that you can always rely on your dictionary.

● Write *ei* when these letters are not pronounced with a long /e/ sound, especially when the sound is a long /a/, as in *neighbor* and *weigh*.

	height	their	foreign	forfeit		
SOUNDS LIKE *AY*	eight	freight	sleigh	reign	vein	veil

● Watch out for words with more than one syllable that end with the sound /seed/; only one word is spelled with *–sede*. Three words end in *–ceed*. All other words end in *–cede*.

-SEDE	supersede			
-CEED	exceed	proceed	succeed	
-CEDE	concede	intercede	precede	recede	secede

● Spell out numbers that can be expressed in one or two words. Rephrase a sentence so that you don't begin with a numeral.

The pool was twenty-five feet long.
The conference attendance was 9,782 students and 652 advisors.

250 people registered late. [rephrase sentence]
There were 250 late-registration attendees.

Some writers prefer not to mix numerals and spelled-out numbers in the same sentence. They'd recommend the following:

He began swimming only 25 meters at a time but worked up to 125.

Remember to use a hyphen when spelling out numbers from *twenty-one* to *ninety-nine*.

Exercise 4 Spelling Words with *ie* and *ei*

Fill in the blank in each of the following items with *ie* or *ei* to spell an English word correctly. Use a dictionary as necessary.

1. b_ei_ge
2. conc_ei_vable
3. financ_ie_r
4. gr_ie_f
5. p_ie_ce

6. s_ie_ve
7. s_ie_ge
8. c_ei_ling
9. misch_ie_vous
10. pr_ie_st

11. ch_ie_f
12. for_ei_gn
13. p_ie_r
14. retr_ie_ver
15. br_ie_f

16. sl_ei_gh
17. counterf_ei_t
18. sh_ie_ld
19. r_ei_gn
20. r_ei_n

Exercise 5 Spelling Words with the Sound /seed/

Fill in the blank in each of the following items with four letters to correctly spell an English word ending with the sound /*seed*/. Use a dictionary as necessary.

1. pro_ceed_
2. ac_cede_
3. con_cede_
4. pre_cede_
5. ex_ceed_

6. suc_ceed_
7. re_cede_
8. super_sede_
9. se_cede_
10. inter_cede_

Exercise 6 Spelling and Placing Numbers

Decide if you should use numerals or spelled-out numbers in the following sentences, and, on a separate piece of paper, rewrite the sentences as necessary. Rearrange words or add words to a sentence as necessary to avoid starting with a numeral. Write *C* if a given sentence is correct.   Answers may vary.

1. In 2090, where do you think the United States will be? C

   The year
2. ₳2090 will probably hold some surprises.

3. Thinking one hundred years ahead is a challenge. C

   ninety-nine
4. Thnking 99 years ahead is a challenge, too.

   sixteen
5. The guests ranged in age from twelve to 16.

6. Forty‑Four of the invited guests showed up.

   Fifty-two
7. 52 invitations had gone out.

   122
8. The banquet room can hold up to one hundred twenty-two guests.

9. 122, in other words, is the maximum allowed for safety.

10. A gross of something is equal to twelve dozen things. C

Prefixes and Suffixes

Prefixes and suffixes are groups of letters that change a word's meaning. A **prefix** (such as *de-*, *in-*, *mis-*, and *un-*) is added to the beginning of a word; a **suffix** (such as *-er*, *-ly*, *-ment*, and *-ness*) is added to the end.

◖ Adding a prefix does not change the spelling of the original word.

   deformed   **il**legal   **mis**spell   **un**necessary

◖ If a word ends in *-y* preceded by a consonant, change the *y* to *i* before adding any suffix except *-ing*.

	business	funnier	happiness
	loneliest	hurrying	
EXCEPTIONS	shyly	shyness	dryness

◖ If a word ends in *-y* preceded by a vowel, keep the *-y*.

	joyous	buoyant	enjoyment	played
EXCEPTIONS	daily	said		

◖ Drop a word's final silent *-e* before a suffix that begins with a vowel.

   caring   likable   loving   creative   subtly

Note: American dictionaries give *likable, lovable, movable,* and *sizable* as preferred spellings but also include *likeable, loveable, moveable,* and *sizeable*.

◖ Keep the final silent *-e* if the word ends in *-ge* or *-ce* and the suffix begins with *a* or *o*.

   manageable   courageous   noticeable   outrageous   replaceable

◖ Keep the final silent *-e* before a suffix that begins with a consonant.

	useful	boredom	resourceful	definitiveness	
EXCEPTIONS	argument	awful	ninth	truly	wisdom

Note: American dictionaries give *judgment* and *acknowledgment* as the preferred spellings; *judgement* and *acknowledgement* are British spellings.

◖ Double the final consonant in some one-syllable words when the suffix begins with a vowel.

Doubling occurs when the word ends in a consonant preceded by a single vowel.

   grabbing   dropped   hottest   hitter

Writing Hint

Sometimes, a word keeps the silent *-e* to distinguish it from another word that would otherwise be spelled the same. Examples include *dyeing* and *dying*, and *singeing* and *singing*.

Some Prefixes and Their Meanings

Prefix	Meaning
circum-	around
dis-, un-	the opposite
il-, im-, in-, ir-	} not
post-	after
pre-	before
re-	again
sub-	below
super-	above, beyond

Some Suffixes and Their Meanings

Suffix	Meaning
-able	capable of being
-ate, -en -fy	} become, make
-dom, -hood	} state of being
-er, -or	a person who
-less	without
-ment	state or condition of
-ous, -ful	full of

● Double the final consonant in some words of more than one syllable when the suffix begins with a vowel.

Doubling occurs if the root word ends in a single consonant preceded by a single vowel and the new word is accented on the next-to-last syllable. Do not double the final consonant when the new word is not accented on the next-to-last syllable.

| DOUBLE CONSONANT | referred | submitted | occurrence | rerunning |
| SINGLE CONSONANT | reference | preference | preferable | |

Note: Some words have two options for what happens when *-ed* and *-ing* suffixes are added. Dictionaries usually give the preferred option first. Examples include *traveled* and *travelled*, *canceled* and *cancelled*, and *programmed* and *programed*.

Exercise 7 Adding Prefixes and Suffixes

Write the word that results when the following prefixes or suffixes are added.

1. achieve + -able ___achievable___
2. argue + -ment ___argument___
3. dis- + appearance ___disappearance___
4. in- + consistency ___inconsistency___
5. un- + conscious ___unconscious___
6. definite + -ly ___definitely___
7. fatal + -ity ___fatality___
8. excessive + -ness ___excessiveness___
9. conceive + -able ___conceivable___
10. in- + frequent ___infrequent___
11. grab + -ed ___grabbed___
12. notice + -able ___noticeable___
13. insure + -ance ___insurance___
14. natural + -ly ___naturally___
15. happy + -ness ___happiness___
16. un- + naturally ___unnaturally___
17. dis- + possess ___dispossess___
18. in- + sensibility ___insensibility___
19. use + -ful ___useful___
20. sophomore + -ic ___sophomoric___
21. dis- + similar ___dissimilar___
22. tremendous + -ly ___tremendously___
23. un- + specific ___unspecific___
24. acknowledge + -ment ___acknowledgment___
25. prefer + -able ___preferable___

Exercise 8 Writing New Words

Hold a competition. In a preestablished period of time (say, ten minutes), write as many words as you can that contain a given prefix or suffix (or both). Then get together with a group to compare lists. See if you can define all of the words you've listed. **Hint:** Use a dictionary throughout the competition.
Students' words will vary; check for the correct use of prefixes and suffixes.

Noun Plurals

For any noun, start with the singular form, and follow the directions below to form the plural.

Making Nouns Plural		
KINDS OF NOUNS	**WHAT TO DO**	**EXAMPLES**
Most nouns	Add -s to the singular.	amateur**s**, circuit**s**, benefit**s**
Nouns that end in -s, -x, -z, -ch, -sh	Add -es to the singular.	flourish**es**, box**es**, waltz**es**, kiss**es**, hunch**es**
Family names	Follow the two preceding rules.	the Lincoln**s**, the Koch**es**, the Lomax**es**, the Rabinowitz**es**
Nouns that end in -y preceded by a consonant	Change the -y to i, and add -es.	flur**ries**, vacan**cies** possibilit**ies**, personalit**ies**
Nouns that end in -y preceded by a vowel	Add -s.	survey**s**, delay**s**, buoy**s**, chimney**s**
Family names that end in -y	Add -s.	Kennedy**s**, Kolody**s**, May**s**, Carney**s**
Most nouns that end in -f	Add -s.	chief**s**, tariff**s**, sheriff**s**, belief**s**
A few nouns that end in -f or -fe	Change the f to v and add -s or -es.	kni**ves**, shel**ves**, lea**ves**, cal**ves**, li**ves**
Nouns ending in -o preceded by a vowel	Add -s.	kazoo**s**, patio**s**
Most nouns ending in -o preceded by a consonant	Add -es.	veto**es**, hero**es**, potato**es**, tornado**es**
Most musical terms ending in -o	Add -s.	alto**s**, soprano**s**, solo**s**, piano**s**, cello**s**
Compound nouns	Make the most important word plural.	surgeon**s** general, mother**s**-in-law, passersby, **men** of straw, spoonful**s** or spoon**s**ful
Letters, numbers, and words referred to as words	Use an apostrophe (') + -s.	B**'s**, 5**'s**, &**'s** no if**'s**, and**'s**, or but**'s**
Irregular plurals, foreign plurals, and words that stay the same for both singular and plural	No rules apply! Memorize these forms.	children, mice, women, men, feet, teeth, data, geese, series, moose, oxen, trout, sheep, deer, species

Editing Tip

Watch out for words that look misspelled but aren't. For example, sometimes *fishes* is the correct plural for *fish*.

A few nouns have two acceptable forms: hoo**fs** or hoo**ves**, scar**fs** or scar**ves**, dwar**fs** or dwar**ves**.

Exceptions: *memos, silos*

A few nouns have two acceptable forms: volcano**s** or volcano**es**, mosquito**s** or mosquito**es**, flamingo**s** or flamingo**es**.

Forming Noun Plurals

Write the plural form of each noun. If you're unsure of the correct form, check a dictionary to see if it lists irregular plurals or alternate plural forms. If no plural form is listed, follow the rule in the preceding chart.

1. secretary-general secretaries-general

2. deer deer

3. Jones Joneses

4. focus foci *or* focuses

5. Tuesday Tuesdays

6. acquaintance aquaintances

7. chief chiefs

8. committee committees

9. debtor debtors

10. fraternity fraternities

11. glimpse glimpses

12. waltz waltzes

13. medium mediums *or* media

14. sister-in-law sisters-in-law

15. Berry (proper noun) Berrys

16. Martinez Martinezes

17. grouse grouse *or* grouses

18. judgment judgments

19. piccolo piccolos

20. obstacle obstacles

21. woman women

22. picnic picnics

23. policy policies

24. square meter square meters

25. cupful cupfuls *or* cupsful

26. stadium stadia

Exercise 10 **Writing with Noun Plurals**

Imagine that there is a mission to another solar system and that you are in charge. You must bring two or more of everything. Write two or more paragraphs in which you tell what and whom you have decided to take. Be specific. When you've finished writing, check to see that all noun plurals are correctly spelled. Exchange papers with a classmate, and check for properly spelled noun plurals.

Students' paragraphs will vary; check to see that all noun plurals are correctly spelled. See teacher pages for assessment rubrics.

Editing and Proofreading Worksheet 1

Read the following paragraphs. Correct all spelling errors, sentence fragments, and run-on sentences. Feel free to make any other changes that you think will improve the paragraphs. Write your revised paragraphs on a separate piece of paper. Answers will vary. A sample revision is given.

[1]A sandwich is ~~too~~ *two* or more ~~slice~~ *slices* of bread with a filling in between. [2]~~It's~~ *Its* origin is interesting. [3]The first sandwich may have been the tidbit that the Jewish ~~scolar~~ *scholar* Hillel ate about two thousand ~~yeares~~ *years* ago and that is now a fixture at the Passover meal. [4]It consisted of bitter herbs and a flat bread. [5]The Romans also ate a form of sandwich which they called *offula*. [6]But the sandwich as we experience it today is a more recent invention.

[7]According to one ~~vershion~~ *version* of the story, early in the morning of August 6, 1762, John Montagu, the fourth earl of Sandwich, was ~~hungary~~ *hungry*. [8](Yes, there had been three ~~earl~~ *Earls* of sandwiches before him.) [9]The problem was that he was busy ~~gambleing~~ *gambling* away in one of his all-night ~~sessiones~~ *sessions* of playing cards. [10]He didn't want to leave the table. [11]So he ~~concieved~~ *conceived* of a solution by ~~orderring~~ *ordering* his servant to toast two slices of bread and to bring them to him along with a couple of ~~chunkes~~ *chunks* of roast beef. [12]When the man reappeared with the food, [13]The earl ~~grabed~~ *grabbed* the meat and stuck it between the toast and found it ~~noticably~~ *noticeably* ~~tastyer~~ *tastier* than anything else he had ~~eatten~~ *eaten*. [14]The first of ~~moren~~ *modern* quick ~~lunchs~~ *lunches* had been created. [15]Within ~~eighth~~ *eight* years, the word *sandwich* was coined.

[16]In his life of ~~liesure~~ *leisure*, Lord Sandwich ~~acheived~~ *achieved* little else that was useful. [17]He had ~~recieved~~ *received* a fine education at Eton and Cambridge. [18]He acquired at one point a high post in the navy, *but* [19]He was accused of ~~mismanagment~~ *mismanagement*. [20]Then sandwich gave up on public service and ~~proceded~~ *proceeded* to devote himself to a life of ~~gambleing~~ *gambling*. [21]But he had the ~~approvel~~ *approval* of at least one of his acquaintances: Captain James Cook, the explorer whose ~~journies~~ *journeys* Sandwich had ~~outfited~~ *outfitted*. [22]~~Cheifly~~ *Chiefly* to thank the earl for his ~~finantial~~ *financial* backing, Cook named the ~~gorgous~~ *gorgeous* Sandwich Islands in the Pacific for him.

Editing and Proofreading Worksheet 2

Read the following paragraphs. Correct all spelling errors, sentence fragments, and run-on sentences. Feel free to make any other changes that you think will improve the paragraphs. Work with a partner or small group. Write your revised paragraphs on a separate piece of paper, and compare your revisions with those made by other pairs or groups.   Answers will vary. A sample revision is given.

[1]Paul Laurence Dunbar (1872–1906) was a poet and fiction ~~writter~~ *writer*. [2]He ~~atended~~ *attended* public schools in Dayton, Ohio. [3]His mother taught him to read, and his father taught him to tell ~~storys~~ *stories*.

[4]Dunbar was the only black student in his high school. [5]~~Their~~ *There* he was not only one of the outstanding ~~editor~~ *editors* in ~~cheifs~~ *chief* of the school newspaper but also class poet and president of the ~~literery~~ *literary* ~~soceity~~ *society*. [6]After ~~succeding~~ *succeeding* in high school and ~~graduateing~~ *graduating*, Dunbar worked as an elevator operator in a Dayton hotel. [7]He continued ~~writting~~ *writing* and ~~finely~~ *finally* was discovered. [8]He ~~recieved~~ *received* the ~~privalege~~ *privilege* of reading his poems at the 1892 meeting of the Western Association of Writers.

[9]Dunbar published his first volume of poetry in 1893. [10]He received ~~encouragment~~ *encouragement* from influential African Americans at that time. [11]Soon, however, he began ~~sufferring~~ *suffering* from tuberculosis and ~~dyed~~ *died* very young. [12]Still, he managed to write many essays and eleven volumes of poetry before he had to ~~conceed~~ *concede* to the illness. [13]~~33~~ *He* was ~~his age~~ *thirty-three* when he ~~past~~ *passed* away.

[14]Dunbar's parents were former slaves. [15]Dunbar ~~hisself~~ *himself* ~~acheived~~ *achieved* widespread recognition in his ~~breif~~ *brief* lifetime. [16]The journey from slavery to cultural ~~hieghts~~ *heights* seems great, but it was not without ~~difficultys~~ *difficulties* that ~~embitterred~~ *embittered* Dunbar. [17]The poet's major ~~unhappyness~~ *unhappiness* had to do with language. [18]He wrote some poems in dialect and some in ~~gloryous~~ *glorious* and grand language. [19]He ~~regreted~~ *regretted* that many people in his audience ~~prefered~~ *preferred* the dialect poems. [20]Today, fortunately, both kinds of Dunbar's poems ~~usualy~~ *usually* appear in poetry ~~anthologys~~ *anthologies*.

Chapter Review

Exercise A Spelling with Prefixes and Suffixes

On a separate piece of paper, create as many words as you can from the
following lists of prefixes, suffixes, and words. See Answer Key.

PREFIXES		WORDS		SUFFIXES	
dis-	re-	announce	copy	-ed	-ly
un-	in-	read	imagine	-ment	-able
mis-	pre-	appoint	taste	-ful	-ing

Exercise B Spelling Noun Plurals

Write the plural form of each noun in the space provided.

1. bench _____ benches

2. monkey _____ monkeys

3. dormitory _____ dormitories

4. "at" sign (@) _____ @'s

5. dolly _____ dollies

6. doily _____ doilies

7. dogcatcher _____ dogcatchers

8. dog day _____ dog days

9. emergency _____ emergencies

10. radio _____ radios

11. mortgage _____ mortgages

12. Lipschultz _____ Lipschultzes

13. Kenney _____ Kenneys

14. father-in-law _____ fathers-in-law

15. flamingo _____ flamingos or flamingoes

16. silo _____ silos

17. percentage _____ percentages

18. survey _____ surveys

19. index _____ indexes or indices

20. crisis _____ crises

Exercise C Choosing the Correct Spelling

Look carefully at each choice and then choose the correct spelling of each
word. Write the letter of the correct spelling in the blank.

___c___ 1. (a) alotment (b) allottment (c) allotment (d) alottment

___d___ 2. (a) refering (b) reffering (c) refferring (d) referring

___c___ 3. (a) misquito (b) misquotoe (c) mosquito (d) mosquitoe

___b___ 4. (a) disengenuous (b) disingenuous
         (c) disingenous (d) disinjenuous

___b___ 5. (a) persperation (b) perspiration
         (c) pirspiration (d) perspirasion

<u>a</u> 6. (a) tendency   (b) tendancy   (c) tendincy   (d) tendencey

<u>b</u> 7. (a) shepard   (b) shepherd   (c) shephard   (d) sheperd

<u>d</u> 8. (a) sherrif   (b) sherif   (c) sherriff   (d) sheriff

<u>a</u> 9. (a) similar   (b) similer   (c) simmilar   (d) similiar

<u>a</u> 10. (a) rhythm   (b) rythem   (c) rhythum   (d) rhythem

Exercise D **Proofreading Paragraphs**

Proofread the following paragraphs to correct all spelling mistakes. **Hint:** All proper nouns are spelled correctly.

[1]Today, scuba divers need a certificate ~~verifieing~~ (verifying) their ~~competance~~ (competence). [2]But people have been diving for ~~centurys~~ (centuries), ~~allways~~ (always) ~~fasinated~~ (fascinated) by the idea of moving freely underwater. [3]In ~~medeival~~ (medieval) Europe, people enjoyed romances in which Alexander the Great ~~desended~~ (descended) to the ocean bottom in a glass diving bell. [4]Alexander's ~~acomplishment~~ (accomplishment) was complete fiction; the first real ~~evedence~~ (evidence) of the use of technical aids to explore beneath water comes from the writings of Alexander's ~~knowldgable~~ (knowledgeable) tutor, Aristotle. [5]In one of his ~~writen~~ (written) works, Aristotle mentions, in passing, that divers of his time used ~~breatheing~~ (breathing) tubes. [6]He ~~refered~~ (referred) to them as "instruments for respiration, through which they can draw air from above the water."

[7]Subsequent descriptions of breathing tubes and masks ~~occurr~~ (occur) in German ballads of the ~~twelth~~ (twelfth) century and, later, in Chinese accounts of pearl divers off the southern coast of the mainland. [8]But the most detailed of these early accounts are those of the eleventh-century ~~sientist~~ (scientist) al-Biruni. [9]He describes the ~~peculier~~ (peculiar) equipment worn by pearl divers in the Arabian gulf. [10]He writes that the divers wore leather hoods filled with air. [11]He explains that a long sealed tube attached to the hood was connected on ~~it's~~ (its) other end to a dish with a hole in its center, through which air passed. [12]The dish, in turn, rested on the surface of the water, kept afloat by one or more inflated bags. [13]The diver, according to al-Biruni, could ~~reasonabley~~ (reasonably) expect to stay underwater for days ~~useing~~ (using) this ~~efficent~~ (efficient) ~~devise~~ (device).

Cumulative Review

Exercise A Punctuation Marks

Correct or add commas, end marks, and other punctuation marks in the following sentences. Correct errors in capitalization. You may add or rearrange words.

1. <u>In the year</u> 1920 ~~was the year that~~ Eugene O'Neill wrote the play "Beyond the Horizon" for which he won the pulitzer prize.

2. In Paris France the organization called the League of nations came into being in 1920?

3. The movie *The Cabinet of Dr. Caligari* was made in 1920.

4. In 1920 new Universities opened in Honolulu Hawaii and in Rio de Janeiro brazil.

5. In 1920 the United States produced 645 million tons of coal, Great Britain produced 229 million tons.

6. That year, Novelist Edith Wharton won a Pulitzer for her novel "The Age of Innocence."

7. When a bomb exploded in 1920 on wall street in New York City, thirty-five people were killed.

8. In 1920 Mohandas K. Gandhi emerged as Indias leader in the struggle for independence from Great Britain.

9. In 1920 Harvard beat Oregon 7-6 in the Rose Bowl Sacco and Vanzetti were arrested and the Russian Civil War ended.

10. <u>In the year</u> 1920 ~~was the year of~~ the boston red sox *made a* great mistake, *or They* they sold Babe Ruth to the New York yankees?

Exercise B Capitalization

Add capital letters where they are needed in the following expressions. If an item is correct, write *C*.

1. the phoenix gazette newspaper

2. the declaration of independence

3. the james river

4. the italian ambassador

5. the world's largest lake C

6. the town of pine hill in the catskill Mountains

7. aunt mildred and uncle cal

8. the worst fast-food joint in town C

9. the united nations

10. last year's winter vacation C

11. the song "guys and dolls"

12. the nobel peace prize

13. renaissance art in italy

14. algebra 2 and physics
15. mike's submarines and soda shop
16. my favorite eatery C
17. a clothing store on main street

18. dr. alan goldstein
19. valentine's day
20. arthur miller's play *a view from the bridge*

Exercise C Spelling

On a separate piece of paper, rewrite each sentence, correcting the misspelled words.

1. ~~Niether~~ Jared nor I will be able to compete on the ~~paralel~~ bars.
   Neither ... *parallel*
2. The lonely ~~nieghbor~~ was ~~wierd~~.
   neighbor ... *weird*
3. The ~~commitee~~ was not ~~competant~~ or ~~consistant~~.
   committee ... *competent* ... *consistent*
4. The sign ~~mispelled~~ the word *procede*.
   misspelled ... *proceed*
5. The ~~liutenant~~ was criticized for ~~interceeding~~ for the ~~financeir~~.
   lieutenant ... *interceding* ... *financier*
6. The ~~forgoten~~ hero had been ~~couragous~~.
   forgotten ... *courageous*
7. There was ~~practicaly~~ no pressure on the ~~psycology~~ ~~profesor~~.
   practically ... *psychology professor*
8. When the ~~sargent~~ spoke officially, his ~~persperation~~ was particularly ~~noticable~~.
   sergeant ... *perspiration* ... *noticeable*
9. Sophomores are not known for the ~~qualitys~~ of ~~suabtlety~~ and ~~shareing~~.
   qualities ... *subtlety* ... *sharing*
10. The ~~judgemental~~ ~~cheif~~ surprised us when he ~~mispoke~~.
    judgmental chief ... *misspoke*

Exercise D Proofreading a Passage

A block of words looks like a puzzle if it has no capital letters or puntuation marks. As you can see below, it's very hard to read such a block of words. On a separate piece of paper, rewrite the passage, adding all of the missing punctuation marks and capital letters.   See Answer Key.

doriot anthony dwyer the great grandniece of susan b anthony achieved a distinction of her own she was the first woman to be appointed to a first chair in a major symphony orchestra dwyer who began playing the flute at the age of eight was trained at the eastman school of music in rochester new york after getting her BS in music in 1943 she joined the washington national symphony two years later she joined the los angeles philharmonic as the second flutist then in 1952 she joined the boston symphony as the first chair flutist in 1974 dwyer was named to the womens hall of fame of the seneca falls historical society in seneca falls new york

Mechanics Test

Exercise 1 Identifying Errors

Directions: Each of the numbered items is either correct or contains an error in one of its underlined parts. In the answer section to the right of each item, circle the letter of the underlined sentence part that contains the error. If the sentence is correct, circle E for NO ERROR.

EXAMPLE   The demands of <u>world war II</u> made <u>physicists and chemists</u>
          　　　　　　　　　　　A　　　　　　　　　　　　　　B

          <u>work together</u> with <u>technicians to develop</u> technologies to win
          　　　　　C　　　　　　　　　　　D

          the war.   <u>NO ERROR</u>
          　　　　　　　　　E

Ⓐ B C D E

1. Pure and applied science worked together to produce <u>important results.</u>
   　　　　　　　　　　　　　　　　　　　　　　　　　　　　　　　A

   For example, <u>in Great Britain a team</u> of scientists developed <u>radar, a device</u>
   　　　　　　　　　　B　　　　　　　　　　　　　　　　　　　　　C

   that uses radio waves to detect things. In the United States, a team worked

   to build the <u>world's</u> first atomic bomb.   <u>NO ERROR</u>
   　　　　　　　D　　　　　　　　　　　　　　E

1. A Ⓑ C D E

2. When the <u>war ended,</u> <u>scientists, technicians, and engineers</u> continued to
   　　　　　A　　　　　　B

   team up to solve challenging problems. The money for <u>research, billions of</u>
   　　　　　　　　　　　　　　　　　　　　　　　　　　　　　C

   <u>it,</u> came from <u>Governments and corporations.</u>   <u>NO ERROR</u>
   　　　　　　　　　　D　　　　　　　　　　　　　E

2. A B C Ⓓ E

3. <u>After the war, some</u> German scientists joined those in America and
   　　　A

   <u>Russia. They</u> worked to develop rocket and missile programs. <u>The result, by</u>
   　　B　　　　　　　　　　　　　　　　　　　　　　　　　　C

   the 1950s, both the United States and the Soviet Union had constructed

   rockets powerful enough to leave <u>Earth's</u> atmosphere.   <u>NO ERROR</u>
   　　　　　　　　　　　　　　　D　　　　　　　　　E

3. A B Ⓒ D E

4. The beginning of <u>the space race</u> began in 1957 <u>when, in October,</u> the
   　　　　　　　　A　　　　　　　　　　　　B

   Soviet Union launched <u>Sputnik I, the</u> first orbiting <u>satelite.</u>   <u>NO ERROR</u>
   　　　　　　　　　　　　C　　　　　　　　　　D　　　　　　　E

4. A B C Ⓓ E

5. Four years later, <u>Soviet cosmonaut Yuri Gagarin</u> was the first person
   　　　　　　　　A

   sent into orbit. Soon <u>thereafter,</u> the <u>astronaut, John Glenn,</u> orbited the
   　　　　　　　　B　　　　　　　C

   <u>planet</u>. He was the first American to do so.   <u>NO ERROR</u>
   　　　　　　　　　　　　　　　　　　　　E

5. A B Ⓒ D E

Exercise 2 **Correcting Errors**

Directions: In the following sentences, the underlined part may contain one or more errors. In the answer section to the right of each item, circle the letter of the choice that correctly expresses the idea in the underlined part of the sentence.

EXAMPLE   "Remember to leave <u>the windows open</u>".   Ⓐ B C D
           A. the windows open."   C. the windows open,"
           B. the windows open"!   D. NO ERROR

1. <u>Henry and Alex are coming and Erin</u> is coming later.   1. A Ⓑ C D
   A. Henry, and Alex, are coming and Erin
   B. Henry and Alex are coming, and Erin
   C. Henry and Alex, are coming, and Erin
   D. NO ERROR

2. He is a <u>creative thoughtful person</u>.   2. A Ⓑ C D
   A. creative, thoughtful, person   C. creative thoughtful, person
   B. creative, thoughtful person   D. NO ERROR

3. The teacher told us to bring the <u>following pad or notebook, pen,</u>   3. Ⓐ B C D
   <u>calculator and good shoes!</u>
   A. following: pad or notebook, pen, calculator, and good shoes.
   B. following pad: or notebook, pen, calculator, and good shoes.
   C. following, pad or notebook, pen, calculator, and good shoes.
   D. NO ERROR

4. The <u>Chrysler building is on third avenue</u> in New York.   4. A B Ⓒ D
   A. Chrysler building is on Third Avenue
   B. Chrysler Building is on third avenue
   C. Chrysler Building is on Third Avenue
   D. NO ERROR

5. "I asked him, and he <u>said, Don't worry, I'll fix it.</u>"   5. A Ⓑ C D
   A. said, "Don't worry, I'll fix it.""   C. said, 'don't worry, I'll fix it."
   B. said, 'Don't worry, I'll fix it.'"   D. NO ERROR

6. The theater is on <u>thirty-fourth street</u>.   6. Ⓐ B C D
   A. Thirty-fourth Street   C. Thirty-fourth street
   B. Thirty-Fourth Street   D. NO ERROR

7. On our trip, we saw <u>The queen of England.</u>   7. A Ⓑ C D
   A. The Queen of England.   C. the queen of England.
   B. the Queen of England.   D. NO ERROR

8. The <u>Kennedies</u> of Massachusetts have held a variety of political offices.   8. A B Ⓒ D
  A. Kennedyies   C. Kennedys
  B. Kennedes   D. NO ERROR

Exercise 3 Identifying Errors

Directions: In each numbered group of sentences, one or more of the items may contain mechanics errors. In the answer section to the right of each item, circle the letter of every sentence that contains an error. If you think all four sentences are correct, circle E for NO ERROR

EXAMPLE   A. Watch out for the banana peel?   Ⓐ B Ⓒ D
          B. She slipped on the banana peel.
          C. People slip on banana peels only in Cartoons.
          D. Banana peels aren't so slippery.
          E. NO ERROR

1. A. "turn at the next light," she directed. Turn   1. Ⓐ B Ⓒ D E
   B. The chef made pasta, pasta, and more pasta.
   C. The confused, frightened child stood stock still.
   D. "Look out for the cord!"
   E. NO ERROR

2. A. The Fairlawn market opens tomorrow. Market   2. Ⓐ B C D E
   B. The company's president spoke on Friday.
   C. The meeting went smoothly, but not much was accomplished.
   D. Mei, who practices every afternoon, has become an
      accomplished performer.
   E. NO ERROR

3. A. Mike is the only senior who applied for early admission.   3. A B Ⓒ D E
   B. The teacher, who counseled me, has become my friend and confidant.
   C. He subscribes to <u>Country</u>, a magazine about hiking. *Country*
   D. Dawn lives in Ogden, Utah.
   E. NO ERROR

4. A. Why, the whole idea sounds terrific!   4. A B Ⓒ Ⓓ E
   B. John Davis, Jr., was his name.
   C. The newspaper is delivered at 7,00 every morning. 7:00
   D. "I know," said Kendra, "That he's wrong." "that
   E. NO ERROR

5. A. The boys' team won its first game.
   B. Look at all the choices; don't select the first one that looks right.
   C. The winners were: Wilson, first place; Reilly, second place; and Rosen, third place.   winners were Wilson
   D. Her favorite magazine is *Soap Opera Digest.*
   E. NO ERROR

5. A B (C) D E

6. A. I spoke with superintendent Chen.   Superintendant
   B. No, senator Harrison, that's not my view on the subject.   Senator
   C. I took chemistry, Spanish, social studies, and Art 101.
   D. Her parents stayed at Broadway hotel.   Hotel
   E. NO ERROR

6. (A) (B) C (D) E

7. A. The World Series is in October.
   B. Eric's interest in marxism began today after Lunch.   Marxism, lunch
   C. First it was legal; now it is illegal.
   D. Her bitterness finally got to all of us.
   E. NO ERROR

7. A (B) C D E

8. A. I've seen that play all ready.   already
   B. He doesn't altogether understand it.
   C. There were no leftovers after the party.
   D. We caught several trouts on our fly-fishing trip.   trout
   E. NO ERROR

8. (A) B C (D) E

9. A. I checked in several appendices.
   B. There are two t's in *setting*.   *t*'s (italics)
   C. Men-of-war were fighting ships.
   D. The finds, not surprisingly, were pre-Colombian.
   E. NO ERROR

9. A (B) C D E

10. A. On July 20 1969, Apollo 11 reached the moon.   July 20, 1969,
    B. Margaret was thrilled to receive an invitation.
    C. The fire marshal said, "Walk, don't run to the exit."
    D. My favorite poem is "As Weary Pilgrim."
    E. NO ERROR

10. (A) B C D E

Exercise 4   Correcting Errors

Directions: Look back at each item in Exercise 3, and double-check your answers. Make sure you have identified all of the sentences with errors. On a separate piece of paper, rewrite correctly all of the incorrect sentences in each numbered item. Write the entire sentences.

Glossary

absolute adjective modifiers, such as *unique* or *flawless*, that do not take compartive or superlative forms.

absolute phrase a phrase that consists of a noun and either a participle or a participial phrase. It stands alone; it is neither the subject nor the verb.

abstract noun a noun that names ideas.

acronym a word, such as *laser*, formed from the first letters of several words ("*l*ight *a*mplification by *s*timulated *e*mission of *r*adiation").

active voice the form of a verb that shows the subject performing an action.

adjective a word that modifies (tells more about) a noun or pronoun.

adjective clause a subordinate clause that functions as an adjective and that modifies a noun or pronoun.

adjective phrase a prepositional phrase that modifies a noun or pronoun.

adverb a word that modifies (tells more about) a verb, an adjective, or another adverb.

adverb clause a subordinate clause that modifies a verb, an adjective, or another adverb. In an elliptical adverb clause, some words are omitted (or understood).

adverb of manner an adverb that ends with the suffix *-ly*.

adverb phrase a prepositional phrase that modifies a verb, an adjective, or another adverb.

agreement the correct relationship between subjects and verbs in number and person or between pronouns and antecedents in number and gender.

analyze to carefully consider each part or element of a subject. This is a key word to look for in an essay test question; it tells you how to approach the topic.

anecdote an incident that actually happened, often based on personal experience or observation. It is one type of evidence that may be used in persuasive writing (also called **incident**).

antecedent the word or words that a pronoun refers to.

appositive a noun or pronoun that identifies or explains the noun or pronoun that precedes it.

appositive phrase a phrase made up of an appositive and all of its modifiers.

articles three common adjectives. *A* and *an* are indefinite articles; *the* is the definite article.

audience the person or persons who will read a written work.

autobiographical incident a true story about something that happened to you.

body the part of an essay that explains the information introduced at the beginning of the essay.

brainstorming a step in the prewriting process; the method of generating ideas for writing by focusing on a single word and listing every related idea regardless of its quality.

call to action a statement or statements in a persuasive essay that tell the reader what to do.

cause a condition, situation, or event that makes something happen (the effect).

character a person who appears in a story; an element of all fiction.

chronological order the order in which events occurred; a method of organizing used by writers of fiction and nonfiction.

clause a group of words that contains a subject and a verb but that does not express a complete thought. There are several types of clauses: **independent**, **subordinate**, **essential**, **nonessential**, **adjective**, **adverb**, and **noun**.

clause fragment a subordinate clause incorrectly punctuated as a sentence. It does not express a complete thought.

clincher sentence a restatement or summary of the main idea of a paragraph that was expressed in the topic sentence. It ends the paragraph.

clustering a step in the prewriting process; the method of generating ideas for writing by creating a diagram to explore a topic, to break a large topic into smaller parts, or to gather details (also called mapping or webbing).

coherence the logical organization of ideas.

collective noun a noun that names a group of people or things.

comma splice a run-on sentence with only a comma separating the independent clauses.

common noun a noun that names a general, rather than a particular, person, place, thing, or idea.

compare to identify the way two or more topics are similar.

complement a word that completes the meaning of a sentence.

complete predicate in a sentence, the verb and all its modifiers (such as adverbs and prepositional phrases), objects, and complements.

complete subject the simple subject of a sentence and all its modifiers (such as adjectives and prepositional phrases).

complex sentence a sentence that has one independent clause and at least one subordinate clause.

compound-complex sentence a sentence that has two or more independent clauses and at least one subordinate clause.

compound noun a noun that consists of two or more words. It may be hyphenated, written as one word, or written as two words.

compound preposition a preposition that contains several words.

compound sentence a sentence that has two or more independent clauses joined by a conjuction and no subordinate clauses.

compound subject two or more subjects sharing the same verb.

compound verb two or more verbs sharing the same subject.

conclusion the part at the end of an essay that summarizes the main ideas.

concrete noun a noun that names an object you can see, hear, smell, taste, or touch.

conjunction a word that joins other words or groups of words. There are three kinds of conjunctions: **coordinating**, **correlative**, and **subordinating**.

conjctive adverb an adverb (such as *however*, *moreover*, and *therefore*) used to combine two simple sentences into a compound sentence.

connotation the emotional associations attached to a word.

contrast to identify the way two or more topics are different.

coordinating conjunction a conjunction (such as *and*, *but*, and *for*) that joins words or groups of words that are of equal importance.

correlative conjunctions a pair of conjunctions (such as *either . . . or* and *neither . . . nor*) that are always used together.

dangling modifier a modifier that does not describe or limit any word or group of words in a sentence.

declarative sentence a sentence that makes a statement and ends with a period.

degrees of comparison the forms of a modifier that indicate the extent of a quality. The three degrees are positive (used to describe one thing), comparative (used for two things), and superlative (used for three or more things).

demonstrative pronoun a pronoun (such as *this*, *that*, and *those*) that points to a specific thing or person.

denotation the meaning of a word given in a dictionary.

dependent clause a clause that has a subject and a verb but that does not express a complete thought (also called a **subordinate clause**).

descriptive paragraph a paragraph that uses sensory details and spatial order to give the reader an image of a person, place, object, or animal.

dialect a way of speaking in certain regions or among certain groups of people.

direct object a noun or pronoun that receives the action of an action verb. It answers the question *whom* or *what* following the verb.

discuss to write about a topic in any way you choose. This is a key word to look for in an essay test question; it tells you how to approach the topic.

double negative two negative words used together incorrectly to convey a negative meaning.

drafting in the writing process, the step of putting thoughts into sentences and paragraphs.

editing the process of correcting grammatical and usage errors in a piece of writing.

effect the result of a cause.

elaboration the process of adding details to support the main idea (also called development).

elements of fiction the basic components of a work of fiction. These components include **character**, **plot**, **point of view**, **setting**, and **theme**.

emphatic form a verb form that is made up of the verb *do* and another verb to provide emphasis.

essay a piece of writing on a limited topic. All essays have an **introduction**, a **body**, and a **conclusion**.

essential clause a clause that adds information necessary to understand the sentence. It is not set off by commas.

evaluation essay an essay that evaluates a work of literature according to established criteria, such as believability of plot.

evidence information supplied to support an opinion. Types of evidence include **anecdotes**, **incidents**, **examples**, **facts**, **quotations**, and **statistics**.

example a type of evidence used as an illustration to support an opinion.

exclamatory sentence a sentence that expresses strong feeling and ends with an exclamation point.

explain to help a reader understand something by giving reasons or information. This is a key word to look for in an essay test question; it tells you how to approach the topic.

expository paragraph a paragraph that explains or informs.

eyewitness report a firsthand account of an incident that focuses more on the significance of the incident to the community or the society than on the writer.

fact a statement that can be proven. It is a type of evidence used to support an opinion.

5W-HOW? questions the questions *Who? What? When? Where? Why?* and *How?* Asking these questions about a topic will help you narrow (or limit) your essay.

fragment a group of words that is not grammatically complete and is incorrectly punctuated as a sentence.

freewriting a step in the prewriting process; the method of generating ideas for writing by recording ideas for a specified time without stopping, while ignoring grammatical and mechanical rules.

fused sentence a run-on sentence with no punctuation separating its sentences.

gender   a quality of pronouns, which are either male (*he, his*), female (*she, her*), or neuter (*it, its*).

general-specific order   a method of organizing an essay in which the writer presents ideas by making a general statement first and then specific statements to back up the generalization.

gerund   a verb form that acts as a noun and always ends in *-ing*.

gerund phrase   a phrase made up of a gerund and all of its modifiers and complements. The entire phrase functions as a noun.

grammar   in any language, the rules that govern how words are arranged to form meaningful structures.

imperative mood   the imperative mood gives a direct command or makes a request.

imperative sentence   a sentence that commands or makes a request. It ends with either a period or (if the command shows strong feeling) an exclamation point.

incident   a ministry that has a plot, characters, and a setting. It is a type of evidence that can be used to support an opinion.

indefinite pronoun   a pronoun (such as *everyone, all,* and *none*) that refers to an unspecified person or thing or that expresses an amount.

independent clause   a clause that has a subject and a verb and expresses a complete thought (also called main clause).

indicative mood   the indicative mood states a fact, an opinion, or a question.

indirect object   a noun or pronoun that answers the questions *to whom, for whom, to what,* or *for what* following an action verb.

infinitive   a verb form that is almost always preceded by the word *to* (the *sign,* or *marker,* of the infinitive). In a sentence, an infinitive can act as a noun, adjective, or adverb.

infinitive phrase   a phrase made up of an infinitive and all of its modifiers and complements.

intensifier   an adverb that answers the question *to what extent.*

intensive pronoun   a pronoun that ends in *-self* or *-selves* and adds emphasis to a noun or pronoun.

interjection   a word that expresses mild or strong emotion. It has no grammatical connection to the rest of the sentence.

interpret   to support an idea about the meaning of a statement or event by using examples, facts, or quotations.

interrogative pronoun   a pronoun (such as *who, whom,* and *whose*) that begins a question.

interrogative sentence   a sentence that asks a question and ends with a question mark.

intervening clause   a clause that comes between the subject and the verb.

intervening phrase   a prepositional phrase that comes between a subject and a verb.

intransitive verb   an action verb that stands without a direct object.

introduction   the part of an essay that identifies the subject and lets the reader know what will be discussed. It is the first paragraph of the essay.

inverted sentence   a sentence in which the verb comes before the subject.

irregular verb   a verb that does not form its past and past participle by adding *-d* or *-ed* to the present tense.

I-search paper   the story of how and why you wrote your research paper and what you experienced in the process.

linking verb   a word that joins the subject of a sentence with a word that identifies or describes it.

literary analysis a discussion of one or more of the elements of a work of fiction (**character**, **plot**, **setting**, **point of view**, and **theme**).

loaded words words that carry positive or negative connotations that may sway emotions.

logical order a method of organizing an essay in which the writer presents ideas in a way that makes sense to the reader.

mechanics the correct use of capital letters, punctuation marks, and spelling rules.

misplaced modifier an adjective or adverb placed far from the word it modifies.

modifier a word that describes or limits another word or group of words. Adjectives and adverbs are modifiers.

mood the mood of a verb shows the speaker's intent. There are three moods: **indicative**, **imperative**, and **subjunctive**.

narrative paragraph a paragraph that tells a fictional or true story.

narrator a person who tells a story.

nonessential clause a clause containing information that is not necessary for the sense of the sentence. It is set off by commas.

noun a word that names a person, place, thing, or idea. Nouns that name ideas are **abstract nouns**. **Concrete nouns** name things that can be seen, heard, smelled, tasted, or touched. There are four types of nouns: **proper**, **common**, **collective**, and **compound**.

noun clause a subordinate clause that functions as a noun.

noun of direct address a proper noun that names the person being spoken to. It has no grammatical relation to the rest of the sentence.

noun phrase a noun and all of its modifiers.

number pronouns are either singular or plural.

object complement a noun, pronoun, or adjective that follows the direct object or indirect object and renames or describes it.

object pronoun a pronoun that functions as the direct object, the indirect object, or the object complement in a sentence, clause, or phrase.

opinion statement a clear expression of the writer's point of view.

order of importance a method of organizing an essay in which the writer presents ideas according to their increasing or decreasing order of importance.

outline the bare bones (or skeleton) of a piece of writing. It includes the most important points that will be discussed in the piece.

paragraph a block of text that includes a sentence stating the main idea and other sentences supporting that idea. There are four types of paragraphs: **descriptive**, **expository**, **narrative**, and **persuasive**.

paraphrase to restate in your own words every idea in the same order as in an original source.

participial phrase a phrase made up of a participle and all of its modifiers and complements. The whole phrase acts as an adjective.

participle a verb form that acts as an adjective (modifies a noun or a pronoun). Present participles always have an *-ing* ending. Past participles of regular verbs end in *-d* or *-ed*, but those of irregular verbs have different endings.

parts of speech the eight categories into which English words are classified according to their function in a sentence.

passive voice the form of a verb that shows a subject receiving an action.

person pronouns are either 1st person (*I, we*), 2nd person (*you*), or 3rd person (*he, she, it, they*).

personal pronoun a pronoun (such as *I*, *we*, *she*, *he*, and *you*) that refers to the speaker or to another person. The personal pronouns have **subject**, **object**, and **possessive** forms.

personal response essay a discussion in which you share the thoughts and emotions that strike you as you read a particular passage in a work.

persuade to try to make someone agree with your opinion or to take action.

persuasive paragraph a paragraph that aims to convince the reader that the writer's opinion is correct or to take action.

phrase a group of related words that has no subject or predicate. There are several types of phrases: **adjective**, **adverb**, **appositive**, **gerund**, **infinitive**, **noun**, **participial**, **prepositional,** and **verb**.

plagiarism using someone else's words or ideas without acknowledgement.

plot an element of fiction; the sequence of events in a fictional work.

point of view an element of fiction; the perspective of the person who tells the story.

possessive form a form of nouns or pronouns that indicates possession. Most nouns form the possessive case by adding an apostrophe and *-s* (*'s*).

predicate the part of the sentence that tells what the subject does, what it is, or what happens to it. A predicate may be **simple** or **complete**.

predicate adjective an adjective that follows a linking verb and modifies (or describes) the subject of a sentence.

predicate nominative a noun or pronoun that follows a linking verb and renames or identifies the subject.

prefix a meaningful group of letters added at the beginning of a word to form a new word.

preposition a word that connects another word in a sentence to a noun or pronoun (and its modifiers, if any) to form a prepositional phrase.

prepostitional phrase a phrase that begins with a preposition and ends with an object (a noun or pronoun). There are two types of prepositional phrases: **adjective** and **adverb**.

prewriting the step of the writing process that includes all of the thinking, planning, and organizing that is done before writing begins.

primary source an original text or document, such as a literary work, diary, letter, speech, interview, or historical document.

principal parts the four basic forms of a verb. They are the **present**, the **present participle**, the **past**, and the **past participle**.

pronoun a word that takes the place of a noun or another pronoun. There are eight kinds of pronouns: **personal**, **indefinite**, **demonstrative**, **interrogative**, **reflexive**, **intensive**, **relative**, and **reciprocal**.

proofreading a step in the writing process; reading a piece of writing to look for and correct mistakes in spelling, punctuation, and capitalization.

proper adjective an adjective formed from a proper noun. It begins with a capital letter.

proper noun the name of a particular person, place, thing, or idea.

publishing sharing or presenting what you've written.

purpose the reason for writing, such as to describe, to inform, to tell a story, to persuade, or a combination of these.

quotation exact spoken or written words. It is a type of evidence used to support an opinion.

reciprocal pronoun a pronoun that expresses mutual action or relation.

reflexive pronoun a pronoun that ends in *-self* or *-selves* and refers to an earlier noun or pronoun in the sentence.

regular verb a verb that forms its past and past participle by adding *-d* or *-ed* to the present.

relative adverb an adverb (such as *when* or *where*) that introduces an adverb clause.

relative pronoun a pronoun (such as *who, whom, whose, that,* and *which*) that introduces an adjective clause.

research paper a written work based on a thorough investigation of a limited topic.

résumé an organized list of your educational background, extracurricular activities, and work experience.

revising the process of improving the content, organization, and style of a piece of writing.

run-on sentence a sentence made up of two or more sentences that are incorrectly run together as a single sentence (also called stringy sentence).

secondary source a writer's comments on a primary source. Some types of secondary sources are reference books, biographies, works of literary criticism, and textbooks.

sentence a grammatically complete group of words that expresses a thought. A sentence may be **simple, compound, complex, compound-complex, declarative, exclamatory, imperative, interrogative,** or **run-on**.

sentence fragment a group of words that is not grammatically complete and is incorrectly punctuated as a sentence.

setting an element of fiction; the place and time of the events in a story.

simple predicate a verb or verb phrase that tells something about the subject of a sentence.

simple sentence a sentence that has one independent clause and no subordinate clauses.

simple subject the key word or words in the subject of a sentence.

spatial order a method of organizing a piece of writing in which the writer describes the physical placement of someone or something (for example, from left to right or from inside to outside).

statistics facts expressed in numbers. Statistics are a type of evidence that may be used in persuasive writing.

stereotyping overlooking individual differences among members of a group.

story map a graphic device that can be used for gathering details when you write a story or report on an autobiographical incident.

style the manner in which you express your thoughts.

subject the part of the sentence that names the person, place, thing, or idea that the sentence is about. A subject may be **simple** or **complete**.

subject complement a noun or pronoun (**predicate nominative**) or an adjective (**predicate adjective**) that follows a linking verb and is necessary to express a complete thought.

subject pronoun a pronoun that functions as the subject of a sentence or clause.

subjunctive mood the subjunctive mood states a wish, a requirement, or a condition contrary to fact.

subordinate clause a clause that has a subject and a verb but that does not express a complete thought (also called **dependent clause**).

subordinating conjunction a conjunction (such as *that, although, because,* and *unless*) that introduces an adjective or adverb clause.

suffix   a meaningful group of letters added at the end of a word to form a new word.

summarize   to give the most important ideas in your own words. This is a key strategy to use in writing a research paper.

synthesize   to put together to form a new whole.

theme   an element of fiction that conveys a message (for example, about people or life).

thesis statement   a summary of an essay's main or controlling idea (also called **opinion statement** or position statement). It belongs in the introduction and may be one or two sentences.

tone   refers to your word choice and attitude toward your topic.

topic sentence   a sentence that states the main idea of a paragraph. In an essay, it also ties the paragraph in which it appears to the preceding paragraph.

transitive verb   an action verb that is followed by a direct object.

unity   a paragraph has unity when all of its sentences focus on a single main idea.

usage   in any language, the customary rules governing the use of words and groups of words to communicate ideas.

Venn diagram   a useful prewriting graphic organizer for identifying similarities and differences.

verb   a word that expresses an action or a state of being. Some action verbs express an action that can be observed; others express an action that usually cannot be seen. **Linking verbs** join the subject of a sentence with a word that identifies or describes it. A **verb phrase** contains a main verb plus one or more helping (or auxiliary) verbs.

verbal   a verb form that functions as a different part of speech. There are three kinds of verbals: **participles**, **gerunds**, and **infinitives**.

verb phrase   a verb and all of its modifiers.

verb tense   a form of a verb that expresses the time an action is, was, or will be performed. The three simple tenses are present, past, and future. The three perfect tenses are present perfect, past perfect, and future perfect. Each tense also has a progressive form made up of a helping verb and the present participle (the *-ing* form).

voice   verbs have two forms of voice: the **active voice**, in which the subject of a sentence performs an action, and the **passive voice**, in which the subject receives an action.

Works Cited list   a list that provides information about each source you have used in a research paper.

writing process   the method of creating and finalizing any piece of writing. The steps in this process include **prewriting**, **drafting**, **revising**, **editing**, and **proofreading**.

***you* understood**   the understood subject of a command or request (an imperative sentence).

Index

emphasis
    colon to set off word or phrase for, 313
    showing in e-mail, 339
    transitional words and expressions showing, 28
emphatic form of verb, 207
English, standard, 201, 219, 259, 261
essays, 33–35
    body in, 34–35
    capitalizing titles of, 335
    cause-effect, 60–65
    compare and contrast, 53–59
    conclusion in, 35
    defined, 33
    evaluation, 71
    introduction in, 33–34
    personal response, 71
    persuasive, 49
    problem-solution, 66–70
    thesis statement in, 33
essential clauses, 171, 301
essential phrases, 151, 301
etc., and etc., 274
evaluation essay, 71, 77
evaluation paper, 77
everywheres, nowheres, somewheres, anywheres, 275
evidence in persuasive writing, 32
examples, 24
    in persuasive writing, 32, 50
    transitional words and expressions showing, 28
except, accept, 273
exclamation point
    after abbreviations, 295
    to end exclamatory sentences, 125, 295
    to end imperative sentence, 295
    with quotation marks, 319
    to separate quotation from dialogue tag, 321
    to set off interjections, 117
exclamatory sentences, 125
    punctuation with, 125, 295
experts
    quoting in persuasive essays, 49
explicit, implicit, 277
expository writing, 31
    and the block method, 56
    cause-effect essay in, 60–65
    and charts in, 56
    compare and contrast essay in, 53–59
    critical thinking in, 54, 61, 67
    drafting in, 58–59, 65, 69, 91

    literary analysis as, 71–76
    logical order in, 31
    main idea in, 31
    and the point-by-point method, 56
    prewriting in, 55–58, 61–63, 67–69, 84–90
    problem-solution essay in, 66–70
    proofreading in, 59, 65, 70, 92
    publishing in, 65, 70, 92
    research paper as, 77–92
    revising and editing in, 59, 65, 70, 91–92
    thesis statement in, 58
    and Venn diagrams in, 55
    writing strategies in, 55–57, 61–63, 67–68, 84–88
eyewitness report in narrative writing, 42–46

F

facts, 24, 58
    indicative mood to express, 211
    in persuasive writing, 32, 49
"The Fall of the Berlin Wall" by Andreas Ramos, 42–43
false analogies, avoiding in persuasive writing, 50
family relationship, capitalization of words that show, 335
farther, further, 277
fewer, less, 259, 277
first person, 219
first-person point of view, 39, 44
first words in sentences, capitalization of, 125
5W-How? questions, 40
foreign languages, italics for words and expressions from, 317
forests. *See* geographical terms
formal outline, 34
fractions, hyphens in, 325
fragments, sentence, 125
    correcting, 131, 305
freewriting, in prewriting, 10, 24
friendly letters. *See also* letters
    capitalization of salutation and closing of, 335
    commas following closing of, 303
    commas following greeting in, 303
full-block style in business letter, 93, 96
further, farther, 277
fused sentence, 137

future perfect tense, 207
future progressive tense, 207
future tense, 207

G

gender, pronoun agreement in, 247
general-specific order, 28
geographical terms
    capitalizing, 333
    commas to separate, 303
gerund(s), 157
gerund phrases, 157
glossary, usage, 273–82
good, well, 257, 277
government agencies, capitalization of names of, 337
greeting
    capitalization of words in, 335
    colon after, in business letter, 313
    comma after, in friendly letters, 303
groups, capitalization of names of, 337

H

had ought, hadn't ought, 277
helping verbs, 105, 199
    and passive voice, 209
highways, capitalization of names of, 333
historical documents, capitalizing titles of, 335
historical events, capitalization of names of, 339
historical periods, capitalization of names of, 339
hopefully, 278
human interest in narrative writing, 45
hyphen(s), 325
    in compound nouns and adjectives, 101, 325
    in compound numbers, 325, 349
    in fractions, 325

I

I, capitalization of, 339
-ie, spelling rules for, 349
if clauses, 211
illogical comparisons, 259
illusion, allusion, 274
imagery in literary analysis, 75
immigrate, emigrate, 277
imperative mood, 211
imperative sentences, 125
    finding subject in, 129
    punctuation with, 125, 295

implicit, explicit, 277
imply, infer, 278
importance, order of, 27, 32
    transitional words and
      expressions showing, 28
in, into, 278
incidents, 24
    brainstorming about, 44
incomplete construction, 245
indefinite articles, 107
indefinite pronouns, 103, 221, 247,
  323
    listing of, 103, 221
    plural, 221
    singular, 221, 247
    subject-verb agreement with,
      221, 225
independent clauses, 169
    colon to separate, 313
    commas between, 133, 137, 299
    in complex sentences, 181
    in compound-complex
      sentences, 181
    in compound sentences, 169,
      181, 315
    semicolons to join, in
      compound sentences, 315
    in series, 297
    in simple sentences, 169, 181
indicative mood, 211
indirect objects, 139, 141, 239, 241
indirect questions, 295
indirect quotations, 319, 337
infer, imply, 278
infinitive(s), 157, 159, 199
    avoiding split, 159
    sign or marker of, 159
infinitive phrases, 159
InfoTrac's General Reference
  Center, 86
institutions, capitalization of
  names of, 337
intensifiers, 109
intensive pronouns, 103, 245
    listing of, 103
interjection(s), 117
    capitalization of *O*, 339
    commas to set off, 303
Internet sources, 86
interrogative pronouns, 103
    listing of, 103
interrogative sentence(s), 125. *See*
  also question(s)
    finding subject in, 129
    punctuation with, 125, 295
interrupters, commas to set off, 301
intervening clauses, 219

intervening phrase, 219
into, in, 278
intransitive verb, 139
introduction in essay, 33–34
introductory adverb clause, comma
  after, 173, 299
introductory elements, commas
  with, 149, 299
introductory prepositional phrase,
  commas after, 141, 299
invent, discover, 277
inverted sentences, 129
irregardless, regardless, 277, 278
irregular comparisons, 257
irregular verbs, 201, 203
    principal parts of, 201, 203
I-search paper, 77, 91
islands. *See* geographical terms
italics, 317
items in series
    commas to separate, 297
    semicolons to separate, 315
it's, its, 278

L

languages
    capitalization of names of, 337
    italics for expressions from
      other, 317
lay, lie, 203, 279
lend, loan, borrow, 275
less, fewer, 259, 277
letters. *See also* business letters;
  friendly letters
    of application, 93
    cover, 93, 95, 96–97
    to the editor, 49
letters as letters
    forming plurals of, 323, 353
    italics for, 317
lie, lay, 203, 279
like, as, as if, as though, 279
"The Lincoln–Douglas Debates" by
  David Herbert Donald, 53–54
linking verbs, 105
    listing of, 141
    need for subject complement,
     141
lists
    colon to introduce, 313
    parallel structure in, 183
    in prewriting, 55
literary analysis, 71–76
    characters in, 74
    critical thinking in, 73
    drafting in, 75–76
    imagery in, 75
    plot in, 74

    plot summary in, 73
    point of view in, 74
    present tense in, 74
    prewriting in, 73–75
    proofreading in, 76
    publishing in, 76
    quotations in, 73, 74
    revising and editing in, 76
    setting in, 74
    sound in, 75
    speaker in, 75
    stage directions in, 75
    structure in, 75
    theme in, 74
    thesis statement in, 73
    tone in, 74
    and writing strategies, 73–74
literary works. *See also* books;
  periodicals
    capitalizing titles of, 335
    and subject-verb agreement,
     229
loaded words in persuasive writing,
  50
loan, borrow, lend, 275
localities. *See* geographical terms
logical order, 27
    in expository writing, 31
loose, lose, 279

M

magazines. *See* periodicals
main clauses, 169. *See also*
  independent clauses
main idea, 23
    in expository writing, 31
main impression, creating, 30
manner, adverbs of, 109
mapping in prewriting, 10–11
marker of the infinitive, 159
may, can, 276
media, 227
might of, 276
misplaced modifiers, 263
*MLA Handbook for Writers of
  Research Papers*, 88
MLA style, 88, 207
mnemonics, 349
modified-block style in business
  letters, 93
modifiers. *See also* adjective(s);
  adverb(s)
    dangling, 265
    inserting single-word, in
     combining sentences, 113
    irregular, 257
    misplaced, 263

parenthetical documentation, 88, 91

parenthetical expressions, commas to set off, 301

parenthetical material, brackets to enclose, 325

parenthetical sentence, capitalizing, 337

parks. *See* geographical terms

participial phrases, 153

participles, 153
 past, 153, 199, 201, 203
 present, 153, 199, 201, 203
 present perfect, 153

part of speech. *See also* adjective(s); adverb(s); conjunction(s); interjection(s); noun(s); preposition(s); pronoun(s); verb(s)
 determining for word, 119

passed, past, 279

passive voice, 209

past participles, 153, 199, 201, 203
 alternate forms of, 199

past, passed, 279

past perfect tense, 207

past progressive tense, 207

past tense, 199, 207
 alternate forms of, 199

peer editing, 17, 41

people, capitalizing names of, 333, 337

percent, percentage, 279

perfect tenses, 207

period(s)
 after abbreviations, 295
 capitalization of names of, 339
 to end declarative sentences, 125, 295
 to end imperative sentences, 125, 295
 to end indirect question, 295
 with quotation marks, 319

periodicals
 capitalizing titles of, 335
 italics for titles of, 317
 quotation marks for titles of articles in, 319

personalizing attacks in persuasive writing, 50

personal pronouns, 103, 141, 247
 listing of, 103
 possessive, 323

personal response essay, 71

persons, 219
 first, 219
 second, 219
 third, 219

persuade
 definition, 47

persuasive writing, 47–50
 anecdotes in, 32, 50
 call to action in, 32, 50
 and counterarguments, 50
 critical thinking in, 49
 definitions in, 49
 drafting in, 52
 evidence in, 32, 49
 examples in, 32, 50
 facts in, 32, 49
 false analogies in, 50
 loaded words in, 50
 opinions in, 32, 49
 opinion statement in, 32, 49
 order of importance in, 32
 overgeneralizing in, 50
 oversimplifying in, 50
 personalizing attacks in, 50
 prewriting in, 51
 proofreading in, 52
 publishing in, 52
 quotations in, 325
  quoting experts in, 49
 reasons in, 32, 49
 revising and editing in, 52
 statistics in, 32, 50
 thesis statement in, 49
 writing strategies in, 49–50

phrases
 absolute, 153
 adjective, 149
 adverb, 149
 appositive, 151, 161, 179
 colons to emphasize, 313
 in combining sentences, 161
 essential, 151, 301
 gerund, 157
 infinitive, 159
 intervening, 219
 nonessential, 151, 301
 noun, 101
 participial, 153
 prepositional, 115, 149
  introductory, 149, 299
 verb, 105, 199

place, transitional words and expressions showing, 28

plagiarism, 88

planes
 capitalizing names of, 335
 italics for names of, 317

planets, capitalizing names of, 333

play titles
 capitalizing, 335
 italics for, 317

plot
 in literary analysis, 74
 in narrative writing, 40

plot summary in literary analysis, 73

plural indefinite pronouns, 221

plural nouns, 101, 229, 259
 in showing possession, 323
 spelling, 353

poems
 capitalizing titles of, 335
 quotation marks for titles of, 319

point-by-point method in organizing compare and contrast essay, 56, 57

point of view
 first-person, 40, 44
 in literary analysis, 74
 third-person, 44

positive as degree of comparison, 257, 259

possessive nouns, 101
 apostrophes in, 323

possessive pronouns, 103, 323
 as adjectives, 107

precede, proceed, 279

predicate(s). *See also* verb(s)
 complete, 127
 compound, 133
 defined, 127
 simple, 127

predicate adjectives, 107, 141

predicate nominatives, 141, 237, 239, 241
 compound, 237

prefixes, 351

preposition(s)
 capitalization of, in names and titles, 333
 compound, 115
 defined, 115
 distinguishing between adverbs and, 115, 149
 list of common, 115
 object of, 149, 239, 241

prepositional phrases, 115, 149
 commas after introductory, 149, 299
 intervening, 219

present participles, 153, 199, 201, 203
 alternate forms of, 199

present perfect participle, 153

present perfect tense, 207

present progressive tense, 207

present tense, 207
 in literary analysis, 74